POLITICAL POLITICAL THEORY

Political Political Theory

Essays on Institutions

JEREMY WALDRON

 Harvard University Press

Cambridge, Massachusetts, & London, England | 2016

Copyright © 2016 by the President and Fellows of Harvard College
All rights reserved

Second printing

Library of Congress Cataloging-in-Publication Data
Waldron, Jeremy, author.
   Political political theory : essays on institutions / Jeremy Waldron.
      pages cm
   Includes bibliographical references and index.
   ISBN 978-0-674-74385-4 (alk. paper)
 1. Political science. 2. Constitutional law. 3. Political science—
Philosophy. 4. Constitutional law—Philosophy. I. Title.
   JA71.W243 2016
   320.01—dc23
                                             2015030858

For Carol, with my love and thanks.

CONTENTS

Preface ix

1 *Political* Political Theory 1

2 Constitutionalism: A Skeptical View 23

3 Separation of Powers and the Rule of Law 45

4 Bicameralism and the Separation of Powers 72

5 The Principle of Loyal Opposition 93

6 Representative Lawmaking 125

7 Principles of Legislation 145

8 Accountability and Insolence 167

9 The Core of the Case against Judicial Review 195

10 Five to Four: Why Do Bare Majorities Rule on Courts? 246

11 Isaiah Berlin's Neglect of Enlightenment Constitutionalism . . . 274

12 The Constitutional Politics of Hannah Arendt 290

Notes *309*

Index *385*

PREFACE

This book sprang from the conviction, expressed in the Inaugural Lecture I gave as Chichele Professor of Social and Political Theory at Oxford, a position I held from 2010 to 2014, that the theory of politics needs to devote more attention to structural, constitutional, and institutional issues in politics. That lecture appears as Chapter 1, the title track of this album. Chapters 2 through 10 are an attempt to *show* rather than say that this can be done—to show that institutional questions are amenable to the full discourse, all the techniques, and the whole vocabulary of normative political theory. They address issues such as constitutionalism, the separation of powers, bicameralism, loyal opposition, representation, and judicial review of legislation.

The final two chapters return to the importance of this approach in the subject matter of political theory. Its importance might be illustrated by reference to the work of almost any figure in the historical canon of the subject: Aristotle, Machiavelli, Hobbes, Locke, Rousseau, Madison, and Mill. Their writings are ample testimony to the fact that this business of political institutions was once privileged as the main agenda of our discipline. But I decided instead to engineer a sort of representative faceoff between two more modern enemies—Isaiah Berlin and Hannah Arendt—one of them disdainful, or at any rate neglectful, of this institutional focus, the other convinced that no responsible approach to politics could be undertaken without it.

I hope that the whole package will encourage young political theorists to understand that there is life beyond Rawls, life beyond the abstract understanding of liberty, justice, and egalitarianism—not that those issues are unimportant. But there is life in the old institutional questions still.

With three exceptions (Chapter 5, "Loyal Opposition"; Chapter 8, "Accountability and Insolence"; and Chapter 11, "Isaiah Berlin's Neglect of Enlightenment Constitutionalism"), these chapters have already been published in various journals and venues. Some modifications have been made. They are not listed chronologically, but in some cases writing the later chapters has caused me to modify some of what I wrote in the earlier ones. (This is true of the relation between Chapter 12 and the beginning of Chapter 2, for example.) The details of the earlier publications are as follows:

Chapter 1: "Political Political Theory," *Journal of Political Philosophy*, 21 (2013), 1–23;

Chapter 2: "Constitutionalism: A Skeptical View," in Thomas Christiano and John Christman (eds.), *Contemporary Debates in Political Philosophy* (Copyright © 2009 Blackwell Publishing Ltd), 267–82;

Chapter 3: "Separation of Powers in Thought and Practice?" *Boston College Law Review*, 54 (2013), 433–68;

Chapter 4: "Bicameralism and the Separation of Powers," *Current Legal Problems*, 65 (2012), 31–57;

Chapter 6: "Representative Lawmaking," *Boston University Law Review*, 89 (2009), 335–55;

Chapter 7: "Principles of Legislation," in Richard Bauman and Tsvi Kahana (eds.), *The Least Examined Branch: The Role of Legislatures in the Constitutional State* (Copyright © 2006 Cambridge University Press. Reprinted with permission.), 15–32;

Chapter 9: "The Core of the Case against Judicial Review," *Yale Law Journal*, 115 (2006), 1346–1406;

Chapter 10: "Five to Four: Why Do Bare Majorities Rule on Courts?" *Yale Law Journal*, 123 (2014), 1693–1730;

Chapter 12: "Arendt's Constitutional Politics," in Dana Villa (ed.), *The Cambridge Companion to Hannah Arendt* (Copyright © 2000 Cambridge University Press. Reprinted with permission.), 201–19.

I have incurred many debts in writing and revising these chapters. Many of them were presented first as lectures at various law schools and political science departments around the world. If I were to list all who helped with comments and suggestions, it would read like the telephone book. I am grateful to everyone who has listened critically to and commented on these pieces. Particular thanks are due to Larry Alexander, Ronald Dworkin, Richard Fallon, John Ferejohn, Barry Friedman, Moshe Halbertal, Bob Hargrave, Rick Hills, Christopher Hood, Michael Ignatieff, Sam Issacharoff, David Johnston, Tsvi Kahane, George Kateb, Aileen Kavanagh, Desmond King, Jeff King, Lewis Kornhauser, Sanford Levinson, Steven Lukes, John Manning, Frank Michelman, Liam Murphy, Bill Nelson, Pasquale Pasquino, Vlad Perju, Richard Pildes, Eric Posner, Peter Pulzer, Peter Raina, Nancy Rosenblum, Meg Russell, Adam Samaha, Carol Sanger, Sam Scheffler, Stephen Sedley, Marc Stears, Dennis Thompson, Nadia Urbinati, Adrian Vermuele, John Vickers, Patricia Williams, and two reviewers for Harvard University Press. Ian Malcolm of Harvard University Press has been an enthusiastic, supportive, and—not least—patient editor.

Many of these chapters were written while I was at the University of Oxford as Chichele Professor. I want to acknowledge the Warden and Fellows of All Souls College and also my colleagues in and around the Department of Politics and the Law Faculty at Oxford for their friendship and support during that time.

CHAPTER ONE

Political Political Theory

IT IS A question, said David Hume, "whether there be any essential difference between one form of government and another and, whether every form . . . may not become good or bad, according as it is well or ill administered,"[1] administered well by men of virtue—that is, people of good character, wisdom, and high principle—or administered badly by fools and knaves who know or care nothing for justice and the common good. "Were it once admitted," Hume continued, "that all governments are alike, and that the only difference consists in the character and conduct of the governors, most political disputes would be at an end, and all zeal for one constitution above another, must be esteemed mere bigotry and folly."[2] Hume imagined people who take that view adopting the maxim of Alexander Pope in the *Essay on Man:* "For forms of government let fools contest / Whate'er is best administer'd is best."[3]

Institutions or the character of those who inhabit them? Should students of politics make a study of the one or the other? Both, surely, would be the obvious answer. They should understand something of political virtue and the demands that the requirements of good government make on the character of those who take on responsibility for public affairs, even if it is no more than the ethic of responsibility that Max Weber recommended.[4] But maybe there is a special reason for studying institutions: to understand the ways in which institutional forms can be designed so as to outwit and outflank what Hume called "the casual humours and characters of particular men."[5]

> Political writers have established it as a maxim, that, in contriving any system of government, and fixing the several checks and controuls of the constitution,

> every man ought to be supposed a knave, and to have no other end, in all his actions, than private interest. By this interest we must govern him, and, by means of it, make him, notwithstanding his insatiable avarice and ambition, co-operate to public good. Without this . . . we shall in vain boast of the advantages of any constitution, and shall find, in the end, that we have no security for our liberties or possessions, except the good-will of our rulers; that is, we shall have no security at all.[6]

The idea that we can devise structures and processes to balance the self-interest of men against one another to promote the common good, even when that is not the prime aim of the individuals whose political habitat we are designing, is familiar to Americans from James Madison's discourse about the separation of powers in *The Federalist Papers*:

> Ambition must be made to counteract ambition. . . . It may be a reflection on human nature, that such devices should be necessary to control the abuses of government. But what is government itself, but the greatest of all reflections on human nature? If men were angels, no government would be necessary.[7]

It is anticipated precisely in the Humean essays I have been quoting from, written a generation earlier than Madison.

1. CHOICES FOR POLITICAL THEORY

One of the places in which Hume pursued the considerations I have mentioned is in an essay devoted to the question of whether politics may be reduced to a science. Hume seems to have believed that political science would be impossible if everything depended on individual character. There would be no political science, just bedside biographies. Fortunately for the scientist, however, "the force of laws, and of particular forms of government" is so great and has "so little dependence . . . on the humours and tempers of men, that consequences almost as general and certain may sometimes be deduced from them," such as those we can deduce in the natural and mathematical sciences.[8]

Hume was talking about political science, but similar choices have to be made in political theory. As theorists of politics, where should we direct our philosophical attention? Should we focus on institutions? Or should we focus on the virtues—looking, for example, to test Machiavelli's claim that politics demands a set of virtues quite different from those extolled in the Christian tradition,[9] or the claim of some political theorists that republican and democratic forms of government cannot survive without the prevalence of certain virtues of self-restraint among the politically active section of the population.[10] Is the republican claim correct? Or is there a version of the Hume/Madison thesis for subjects as well as their rulers? Can we design the institutions of our modern democracy in such a way that its constitution can survive the corruption of the people, their obsession with material wealth, and their revealed unwillingness to sacrifice anything for their country? What matters—structures or character, institutions or virtue?

2. THE DOMINANCE OF JUSTICE

Or is there a third choice? Maybe our main focus ought to be not on virtue, not on institutions, but on the aims and ideals that direct our politics. I mean ideals such as justice, equality, human rights, toleration, liberty, prosperity, wealth maximization, and the common good. Perhaps we need to replace Hume's dichotomy with a *tri*-chotomy, so that the question now is whether we should direct our theoretical energy to questions about (1) the individual virtues that good governance requires, (2) the political institutions that are needed in a good society composed of humans rather than angels, or (3) the ends and ideals that a good society should be seeking to promote.[11] I think it is fair to say that, for some time now, the main focus in political theory has been on (3), the ends and ideals that a good society should seek to promote.

Indeed, an enormous amount of energy has been devoted and is being devoted to normative argument and conceptual analysis about the ends of political action—beginning most prominently with John Rawls's detailed and articulate theory of justice, published in 1971. Rawls's work has inspired a whole industry comprising thinkers as diverse as Robert Nozick, Ronald Dworkin, Amartya Sen, Michael Walzer, and G. A. Cohen.[12] All of this is focused on topic (3), the aims and policies of a good society and the basic structure of its political economy; precious little attention is paid in the justice industry to questions about political process, political institutions, and political structures.

I want nothing I say here to be heard as denigrating the study of justice and equality. I have contributed to that project myself, including an article exploring and defending the idea of the primacy of justice among the values that may be explored in political philosophy.[13] But I worry nevertheless that this emphasis on justice as the key topic of political theory is a little one-sided.

3. ISAIAH BERLIN

Sometimes it seems that political theory is understood as just applied moral philosophy—as it seems to have been, for example, in Isaiah Berlin's understanding. Asked in a 1997 interview a few months before his death "What do you think are the tasks of political philosophy?" Berlin replied: "To examine the ends of life."[14] And he added that "[p]olitical philosophy is in essence moral philosophy applied to social situations."[15] True, he went on to say that the social situations to which moral philosophy is applied "of course include political organization, the relations of the individual to the community, the state, and the relations of communities and states to each other." But he gives no indication that these are worth study in their own right.[16]

> The business of political philosophy is to examine the validity of various claims made for various social goals, and the justification of the methods of specifying and attaining these. . . . It sets itself to evaluate the arguments for and against various ends pursued by human beings. . . . This is the business of political philosophy and has always been such. No true political philosopher has omitted to do this.[17]

In fact, Berlin himself undertook a rather larger agenda than this, looking not just at the ends of life but at broad zeitgeist issues such as the clash between romantic nationalism and human individualism,[18] and big-picture diagnosis of the pathologies of certain general currents of thought about man in society. Again, I don't want to convey the impression that any of this is unimportant. But I do think there are problems with Berlin's specification of this agenda for political philosophy.

To read almost any of Berlin's work is to read essays that are resolutely uninterested in the political institutions of liberal society. Beyond airy talk of freedom and openness, Berlin was simply unconcerned with the ways in which liberal or democratic political institutions might accommodate the pluralism he thought so important in human life.[19] Invited by his interviewer to consider "What possible support can your theory of pluralism give to the problem of democracy?," Berlin simply repeated the commonplace that "[d]emocracy need not be pluralistic,"[20] indicating, by an immediate focus on the prospect of the tyranny of the majority, how his understanding of political theory had inherited philosophy's ancient grudge against democracy nurtured since the trial and execution of Socrates.

4. REALISM VERSUS MORALISM

So is that it? Is political philosophy just a study of the ends of life? Very recently, we have begun to get glimpses of a different approach, in some of the essays that Bernard Williams wrote toward the end of *his* life. I have in mind Williams's critique of what he called "political moralism," of the alleged "priority of the moral over the political," the application of what is essentially moral philosophy to the resolution of social issues.[21]

But Williams's alternative was to turn away from moral ideals and to look for distinctively political ideals, such as *security*. He was interested in the relation between legitimacy and what he called "the 'first' political question," Hobbes's question about "the securing of order, protection, safety, trust, and the conditions of cooperation."[22] Williams was helping us cultivate or recall a sense of different and distinctive ends for politics—different from justice, for example.[23] Alas, his was not an attempt to locate the distinctive subject matter of political theory in the realm of political institutions.[24]

5. TOPICS AND PRINCIPLES

It is time to lay my own cards on the table. I think institutions are massively important. Exactly because we disagree in our ethical and political aims, we need to inquire into the structures that are to house and refine our disputes and the processes that are to regulate the way we resolve them. I mean the processes by which we (in our millions) resolve disagreements over disparate aims that we severally regard as fundamentally important—without degenerating into fighting driven either by self-interest or worse still by the militias of self-righteousness.[25]

First and foremost, we need to understand the foundations of democracy, but not just democracy in a crude, undifferentiated sense. As Nancy Rosenblum has taught us, we need to understand democratic representation and political parties.[26] We need to understand the different ways in which the institutions of a modern political system are democratic, theorizing the difference between a representative legislature, an administration headed by a directly or indirectly elected government, and courts in a democracy. We need to appreciate the differences between different sorts of elected officials: an elected president, elected lawmakers, and even, in some U.S. states, an elected judiciary.

But it is not only democracy. It is our responsibility as theorists of politics to reflect on a broader array of issues about constitutional structure. I mean traditional, even fuddy-duddy, topics that I worry we have lost sight of in British political theory:[27] federalism and devolution; the choice between a unicameral and a bicameral legislature; sovereignty; the separation of powers; checks and balances; the independence of the judiciary; the principle of loyal opposition; and the rule of law. Those are the big principles, and there are a bunch of lesser ones too, like civilian control of the military (think of S. E. Finer's great book *The Man on Horseback*),[28] the separation of church and state, constitutional monarchy, and the neutrality of the civil service.

All of this, I believe, is important for us as political theorists to study and write about. Even if our main preoccupation remains with justice, liberty, security, and equality, we still need to complement that work with an understanding of the mechanisms through which these ideals—these ends of life—will be pursued. This is what I mean by *political* political theory—theory addressing itself to politics and to the way our political institutions house and frame our disagreements about social ideals and orchestrate what is done about whatever aims we can settle on.

I do not argue this on the sort of grounds that Hume invoked to argue for the primacy of institutions over virtue: the Hume/Madison argument that we can set up institutional structures to produce good results whatever the state of individual virtue in the polity. I have no version of that argument for the choice between a theoretical emphasis on institutions and a theoretical emphasis on justice. In jurisprudence, Lon Fuller toyed with something like this on the rule of law: he thought that if you do things the right way—follow the right formal, procedural, and institutional pathways that he called the inner morality of law—you are more likely to end up doing the right thing. If you do things explicitly, coherently, transparently, and with due process, you are less likely to find yourself administering injustice. Bad things happen mainly in the dark, in Fuller's account, and unjust aims do not have the same coherence as good ones.[29] It is an intriguing hypothesis, but the consensus in legal philosophy has been that it cannot be pushed very far.[30]

Nor is my emphasis on institutions as opposed to ultimate aims born of any doubts concerning the ends of political life, or any skepticism about justice and right answers. The fact is that whether these values are objective or not, we have disagreements about them; people who are thoroughly committed to their objectivity disagree about them. This means that our philosophy departments have to accommodate theoretical disagreement—with John Rawls and Robert Nozick working away in the same corridor in Emerson Hall at Harvard University—and philosophers have to also frame their disagreements in the way they organize conference panels and published debates.[31] And if that is true of our professional life in the academy, how much more urgent is it in politics itself to structure an institutional environment to house and accommodate those with rival views, all of whom are convinced that they are right—some of them wrongly, no doubt, but which ones (for the purpose of this structuring)? We need institutions to frame the hard choices and decision-making that our disagreements give rise to. And we need to find ways of respecting one another in our politics in the environment that those institutions provide.

Institutions matter, and in a moment I am going to talk about the variety of ways in which they matter. In legal systems and in nation-building (whether we are overhauling our own constitution or trying to establish a new one in Iraq or Afghanistan), it matters what processes we set up. Institutions make a difference, not just to the political game but, through the inclusiveness of the order they establish, to the security, prosperity, and openness of the societies in which they are established. A recent book entitled *Why Nations Fail: The Origins of Power, Prosperity, and Poverty* is just the latest in a long line of persuasive arguments to this effect.[32]

6. THE VALUE OF INSTITUTIONS

Very well, you may say, but isn't the study of institutions and political processes a matter for empirical political science? Isn't it a matter for the Gladstone Professor of Government, not the Chichele Professor of Political Theory? Well, yes and no. Certainly it is a task for political science. The study of how politics actually works within the institutions we have established is the immense and challenging agenda of political science, one that I greatly respect and that political theorists should take much more notice of and dovetail their work with.

But that does not preclude the reflective interest of political theory. Institutions are theoretical matters too. And not just for what is sometimes called *"positive"* political theory.[33] The study that I am envisaging is emphatically normative, for we have *choices* to make about our institutions and processes. Look at the agenda for political and constitutional reform in the United Kingdom right now: the recent referendum about independence for Scotland; the continuing debate about reform of the House of Lords; and issues that arise concerning Britain's relation to the European Union and also to the European Court of Human Rights. We bring to these choices reasons of various kinds, and the reasons in turn implicate values and principles that are also the basis for our assessment of existing institutions—parliament, the monarchy, the courts, the administration, the political parties, the country's division into nations with devolved legislatures, and the international laws and institutions in which we participate.

Moreover—and this is very important—not all of the values that are at stake in our understanding of institutions and institutional choices are the straightforward pragmatic or consequentialist values that our realist colleagues in positive political theory or empirical political science are comfortable talking about. There are many layers of additional value to be considered. Certainly the consequentialist assessment of institutions is important. And it is complicated: on the one hand, there is our assessment of the output of a given institution (compared with the different output that a different institution or a different system of institutions might have yielded). Assessing this means mapping values such as justice, equality, liberty, and aggregate prosperity onto the laws or the effects of administering the laws, and onto our policies and the social results of implementing our policies. As Rawls put it in *A Theory of Justice,* "The fundamental criterion for judging any procedure is the justice of its likely results."³⁴ Second, there are the side effects of the operation of our institutions on people—often good side effects, such as the educational impact that John Stuart Mill or, in twentieth-century political theory, Carole Pateman expected from participatory democracy,³⁵ but sometimes also bad side effects such as political corruption and pandering.

Third, and still in the realm of consequences, there is analysis of the cost of operating a given institution—salaries, buildings, and so on. I mean efficiency. Recently there has been discussion in Britain of how much more an elected House of Lords would cost the taxpayer than the present unelected version.³⁶ Why will it cost more? Well, we need to understand this in a way that perhaps the budget people from Treasury do not. It is not because an elected chamber is more profligate. It is because people may want to elect individuals who have to give up their jobs to become legislators, people who can't just make do on an allowance. This has always been a problem with candidates for office who are not independently wealthy. In general, we have to be very careful with any sort of cold-eyed budgetary approach, applying a ruthless value-added test for each step or phase in our institutional politics. In my home country, New Zealand, it was budgetary considerations that explained the abolition of the upper house, the Legislative Council, in 1950,³⁷ and in recent years a similarly ruthless efficiency-based approach has led to the elimination of a parliamentary quorum in the House of Representatives, not to mention the elimination of any requirement that members have to be personally present in the chamber in order to vote (what a waste of their time, it is said, when it could be spent more efficiently somewhere else); the Whips just call out their nominal party strength whenever there is a division. And, in general, the efficiency approach to political institutions has engendered in New Zealand the growth of a bullying mentality that insists that, since the government is almost always bound to get its way in the House of Representatives, there can be no real objection to the truncation of formal parliamentary debate by repeated use of urgency and closure motions. It is a sorry spectacle.³⁸

So these are some layers of consequentialist analysis. But then we have to reflect as well—and this is subtler and more difficult—on certain elements of *non*-consequential assessment: values of truth, transparency, and fidelity. We must reflect also on the deeper layers of dignitarian value, for example, that explain why certain processes such as democratic decision-making are important quite apart from their output and quite apart from their efficiency.

We have to consider the ways in which institutional alternatives embody various kinds of respect for the persons on whom and in whose name our laws and policies are administered—respect for them as persons, as centers of intelligence, and for their dignity as individuals.

In a courtroom, to take one illustration, we justify the rigid procedural safeguards that are imposed, not only because (consequentially) they make accurate verdicts more likely but also because of the tribute they pay to the dignity of the individual on trial. Deciding what to do about a suspected offender is not like deciding what to do about a rabid dog or a dilapidated house. This is a *person* who is on trial. He will have a case of his own to make, his own version of the facts, or his own legal argument to present, and room has to be made for respecting all of this whether we think it promotes truth-finding or not.[39]

The same is true in our elective institutions. In his great book *Considerations on Representative Government,* John Stuart Mill pondered the arguments about outcomes, but he also insisted that

> [i]ndependently of . . . these considerations, it is a personal injustice to withhold from any one . . . the ordinary privilege of having his voice reckoned in the disposal of affairs in which he has the same interest as other people. If he is compelled to pay, if he may be compelled to fight, if he is required implicitly to obey, he should be legally entitled to be told what for; to have his consent asked, and his opinion counted at its worth. . . . Every one is degraded . . . when other people . . . take upon themselves unlimited power to regulate his destiny. . . . Every one has a right to feel insulted by being made a nobody, and stamped as of no account.[40]

Dignity, respect; these are not just abstract philosophical theses about Kantian imperatives.[41] The respect and dignity that are embodied in some political systems, and the indignity, humiliation, and dismissiveness that are embodied in others, are among the most important values that there are—not least because they entangle themselves with and intensify what people fear from, or hope for, so far as their political institutions are concerned.

If I may use a literary example, Mrs. Gaskell in her 1848 novel *Mary Barton* tells of a time when desperate and impoverished mill workers all over England resolved to take their case to Parliament:

[T]he starving multitudes had heard that the very existence of their distress had been denied in Parliament; and though they felt this strange and inexplicable, yet the idea that their misery had still to be revealed in all its depths, and that then some remedy would be found, soothed their aching hearts, and kept down their rising fury. So a petition was framed, and signed by thousands in the bright spring days of 1839, imploring Parliament to hear witnesses who could testify to the unparalleled destitution of the manufacturing districts. Nottingham, Sheffield, Glasgow, Manchester, and many other towns, were busy appointing delegates to convey this petition, who might speak, not merely of what they had seen, and had heard, but from what they had borne and suffered. Life-worn, gaunt, anxious, hunger-stamped men, were those delegates.[42]

And she writes of the initial pride of Mary Barton's father, John, at being selected as one of those delegates—"the . . . gladness of heart arising from the idea that he was one of those chosen to be instruments in making known the distresses of the people."[43]

But, then, as Mrs. Gaskell says, though the delegation went down to London, "Parliament . . . refused to listen to the working-men, when they petitioned, with all the force of their rough, untutored words, to be heard concerning the distress which was riding, like the Conqueror on his Pale Horse, among the people."[44] And John Barton returned to Manchester crushed and in silent despair: "Tell us what happened when you got to th' Parliament House," said a friend of the family. After a little pause, John answered,

"If you please, neighbour, I'd rather say nought about that. It's not to be forgotten, or forgiven either. . . . As long as I live, our rejection that day will bide in my heart; and as long as I live I shall curse them as so cruelly refused to hear us; but I'll not speak of it no more."[45]

Except to say to his daughter when they were alone: "Mary, we mun speak to our God to hear us, for man will not hearken; no, not now, when we weep tears o' blood."[46]

An institution is not just a sociological construct; it is a human entity that confronts human pleas, human claims, human proposals, and human petitions. And in that confrontation there is room for respect and dignity and for degradation and insult; and neither of these may be ignored in our theoretical assessment of the institutions we have.

There is room for indignity too, in the relation between institutions. In a remarkable book called *Law and the Shaping of the American Labor Movement*, William Forbath, who teaches legal history in Texas, has gathered some observations voiced by labor organizers and labor legislators in America in the 1890s and the early years of the twentieth century, when statute after statute regulating working hours and working conditions was falling victim to judicial review.[47] "It has been preached to the men that legislation was the only proper means to secure relief. They were led to believe they could win at the ballot box, and they believe they did win," but the courts struck down their enacted laws as unconstitutional. "[W]e have tried different laws," said another labor organizer, "and we have tried framing the laws in different ways . . . and it appears we have always been defeated by the Courts."[48] Imagine the frustration. "I would kill them all and see if that would be considered unconstitutional," said one despairing Colorado mine worker (according to a company spy).[49] These are *insiders* in a legislative institution confronting a dismissive and high-handed rebuff by another institution, the judiciary. And again, we need to reflect on all this not just in terms of the value or justice of the laws that were struck down but also the bitter indignity of the treatment meted out to these working men and labor politicians in the political life of the communities to which they belonged.

Somebody in our discipline must have the job of reflecting in these terms on our institutions and our choices among institutional alternatives. The public lawyers do some of it, especially in the United States, and if I had my way there would be a much closer connection between political theory and law (even if it came at the expense of the connection between political theory and philosophy). But really, we need both. We certainly do need a sophisticated philosophical understanding of the layers of value that are implicated in the assessment of political institutions. Somebody has to make sure that we do not lose sight of the dignitarian and deontological elements. Someone has to consider how these questions of honor and dignity, truth and loyalty, political justice and respect, stand alongside the criteria we use (such as Rawlsian justice) for evaluating the output of our politics. They don't fit easily together—that much we can accept from the value-pluralism of Isaiah Berlin. But they are not to be neglected.

7. EVEN BEYOND VALUE: PRESENCE

There are also other layers in the evaluation of political institutions. I mean the importance of history, of political aesthetics and the symbolic, ceremonial, maybe even sacramental, aspects of the processes we use for assembling and deliberating about the common good.[50] There are questions of stability and longevity,[51] about the importance of constitutional reformers being able to look on their work, as Hannah Arendt put it, with the eyes of generations to come.[52]

And if we want to go even deeper, there are layers of reflection about the ontology of political institutions—the ordering presence that they have among us in what might otherwise be a crushing scramble for individual advantage, the roar of millions of blind mouths, shouting slogans and threats at one another, bellowing to get out of each other's way—each convinced that we can forget about processes, that it is only the interest or the justice of the outcome that matters.

Here I draw very heavily on the work of Hannah Arendt. (I know Isaiah Berlin never had any time for the person he called "the egregious Hannah Arendt": "I do not greatly respect the lady's ideas," he said, and though Berlin himself was neither the most rigorous nor most consecutive thinker, his verdict was that "[s]he produces no arguments, no evidence of serious philosophical . . . thought. It is all a stream of metaphysical free association."[53] This is one of many disagreements I have with Berlin. I have been entranced by Arendt's work since the days of the great Hannah Arendt Reading Group in Edinburgh in the 1980s. That politics needs housing and that building such accommodation can be equated with the framing of a constitution is an image that recurs throughout Arendt's writings. Sometimes it is less a metaphor of bricks and mortar than of the furniture that enables us to sit facing one another in politics, separated but brought into relation with one another in just the right way. "The public realm [that] . . . gathers us together and yet prevents our falling over each other, so to speak."[54] Sometimes this is quite literal, whether in the design of legislative chambers or the shape of the table at the Paris peace talks during the Vietnam War.[55]

Let's go back to what we want from our political institutions. We want there to be (in John Stuart Mill's words)

[a] place where every interest and shade of opinion in the country can have its cause even passionately pleaded, in the face of the government and of all other interests and opinions, can compel them to listen, and either comply, or state clearly why they do not.[56]

We want there to be a place for talk as well as decision, particularly when, as Mill puts it, "the subject of talk is the great public interests of the country, and every sentence of it represents the opinion either of some important body of persons in the nation, or of an individual in whom some such body have reposed their confidence."[57] But we cannot have this without procedural rules and processes that enable deliberation among people who have been assembled precisely on account of their diversity and disagreement. Rules of order are needed precisely because we are not transparent to one another and we disagree radically with one another, yet nevertheless we want to be able to listen and respond to each representative's difference from and disagreement with what various others have to say.[58]

Those of you who know the HBO TV series *The Wire* may remember the episode at the beginning of the third series in which the drug lord Stringer Bell introduces parliamentary procedure, Robert's Rules of Order, to try to make meetings of his lieutenants and his drug dealers more orderly and more productive—yielding a wonderful array of quotations like "Motherfucka's got the floor" and "Chair ain't recognize yo' ass."[59] It's not exactly John Stuart Mill; it is exactly what I'm talking about.

Max Weber spoke of an ethic of responsibility in politics.[60] Part of that is the duty of respect for the structures and procedures that frame the political enterprise and that make deliberation and action with others possible. Since the invention of politics, some politicians have thrived on institutional irresponsibility. In a remarkable biography published originally in 1982, German historian Christian Meier wrote this about Julius Caesar:

> Caesar was insensitive to political institutions and the complex ways in which they operate.... Since his year as consul, if not before, Caesar had been unable to see Rome's institutions as autonomous entities.... He could see them only as instruments in the interplay of forces. His cold gaze passed through everything that Roman society still believed in, lived by, valued and defended. He had no feeling for the power of institutions..., but only for what he found useful or troublesome about them.... In Caesar's eye's no one existed

but himself and his opponents. It was all an interpersonal game. . . . The scene was cleared of any suprapersonal elements. Or if any were left, they were merely props behind which one could take cover or with which one could fight.[61]

Meier's judgment of Caesar is complicated by his understanding that other participants in Roman politics had the opposite vice. They failed to grasp that the decrepit institutions of the Republic did need to be seen and maybe even "seen through" in a way that would permit the question of their restructuring to be raised.[62]

But the point I want to make is that there is something reckless, even pathological, about a mode of political action in which the walls and structures intended to house actions of that kind become suddenly invisible, transparent, even contemptible, to the actor. Such drastically unmediated proximity—"Now there is just you, and me, and the issue of my greatness" or "Now there is just you and me and our interest in justice"—is alarmingly like the press of millions of bodies against each other that Arendt associates with the destruction of thought and deliberation in mass society.[63]

8. POLITICAL THEORY TEACHING

This chapter began life as an Inaugural Lecture in Oxford, and some readers may be interested in what my analysis entails for the way we teach the theory of politics in Oxford, one of two compulsory politics papers in *Philosophy, Politics, and Economics* (PPE).

It is partly a matter of orientation. I am conscious that for most of this lecture I have run the terms "political theory" and "political philosophy" together. My suggestion has been that even if there is a difference between them, both need to be more political—in the sense of focusing on issues of institutions as well as the ends, aims, and ideals of politics, such as justice. But what I am suggesting may involve a slight redirection of interdisciplinary energy. Political philosophy is surely a branch of philosophy, and, inasmuch as our teaching in the theoretical side of PPE presents itself as political philosophy, we naturally orient ourselves toward the Philosophy Department. My predecessors G. A. Cohen and Charles Taylor were comfortable, I think, with that orientation. I am more happy with an orientation toward law, and also with an approach that looks for political theory to dovetail its concerns with those of empirical political science.

At present, when we give undergraduate lectures and tutorials in this subject, we are careful to ensure that our students understand contemporary arguments about equality, rights, liberty, and justice (including recent arguments about global justice—the expansion of justice from the domestic to the international realm). We would normally expect six out of eight tutorials to be devoted to these topics, with the remaining two devoted to questions that are slightly more institutional in character, but only *slightly:* our students read up on the obligation to obey the law and the philosophical foundations of democracy. As things stand, we have not devoted any substantial time in this curriculum to institutional principles such as constitutionalism, the separation of powers, the nature of sovereignty, the rule of law, the legal process, the role of the courts in modern governance, or the case for or against bicameralism. We are lucky if there is time for anything more than a few minutes on representation.

Of course, the first set of issues is important. Our students do need to be fluent in arguments about justice, liberty, and equality, particularly if that can be brought to bear on the work they are doing on political economy. This is especially so for those who are looking to go on to graduate work and perhaps enter the academic profession. At the same time, one wonders whether the vast majority of our PPE students, who will not become lecturers but will take up positions in business and industry, in journalism or think tanks, in the arts or in government, are being given the preparation that they need in the theory of politics.

I mentioned earlier that the United Kingdom faces unprecedented issues of constitutional reform and institutional design. There is the possible secession of Scotland: What are the theoretical dimensions of the debate about the scope, timing, and possible repetition of a referendum? There is the establishment of a UK Supreme Court and the perceived increase in judicial activism associated with it, under the auspices of the Human Rights Act, or the great debate about the influence of the European Court of Human Rights in our political decision-making. There are now proposals to revise or repeal the Human Rights Act and replace it with a "British Bill of Rights," not justiciable in the Strasbourg court. Political theory students in America are prepared as a matter of course for a debate about judicial review and the challenge to democracy that it gives rise to. But are *our* students in Oxford prepared to debate the British equivalent of these issues, on questions such as prisoner voting, for example?[64]

Last, there is the question of further reform of the House of Lords: the expulsion of most of the hereditary peers; the precipitation out of the judges; the retention of the bishops; and the debate about whether we want a mostly elected upper house, an appointed one, or some combination of the two. My impression is that students of the theory of politics emerge from their tutorials and lectures untouched by and unfamiliar with any of the detailed theoretical arguments that are relevant to Lords reform—arguments by Mill and Bentham on the topic of bicameralism, for example.[65] They will know the crude terms in which these issues are debated in the newspapers, but they will have nothing distinctive from their training in the theory of politics to contribute to the debate.

For example, why exactly was it important to move the judges out of the House of Lords? Separation of powers, you will say. Alright, then: Are there any other issues of the separation of powers that are relevant to Lords reform? For example, do we want to reproduce in a second chamber the same executive dominance that we see in the lower house? In Britain, the cabinet dominates the House of Commons, more or less by constitutional definition. Is that why certain people want to maintain the ascendancy of Commons? Because it is the one chamber that the executive can continue to dominate? Is it possible that our upper house could be a genuinely independent legislative assembly, like the U.S. Senate, for example? Or are we wary of setting up such an entity in the midst of our Westminster system?

What would it be like to have the genuinely independent legislature that is promised by the ideal of the separation of powers? That is, what would it be like to have an institutional setting where assembled representatives of the people could consider and debate, in a resolutely general way, carefully and through formalized deliberation, the laws that we want to be governed by, without worrying all the time about their prospects for cabinet office? It is hard, under the best of circumstances, to maintain the focus at this general level. But that is what legislatures are for, at least in our *theory* of governance, and the separation of powers is supposed to facilitate that by making it harder for those whose focus is more on the day-to-day issues of administration to insinuate their executive and political agendas.[66] Should any of this be relevant to House of Lords reform? Or have we given up on the separation of powers, preferring a more compressed, undifferentiated, unarticulated exercise of political power and political accountability?[67] On the other hand, if we *do* want to pay some tribute to the separation of powers, can we really look forward to an *independent* second chamber in our parliament if its members are not elected but appointed as a result of cronyism, rewards for favors, and government patronage?

For now, these are questions, not answers. I believe the citizens of the United Kingdom ought to be thinking along these lines—as should our theorists and our students. We need to deepen everyone's sense of what is at stake here, and we cannot do that without examining all the layers of value that, as I said, are relevant to institutional assessment.

9. BEYOND OXFORD

My concerns in this chapter, however parochial they were in their inception, actually take us far beyond Oxford: they have to do with the orientation of political theory generally. My main home is in the academic world of the United States, and I must say that there is greater receptivity in America to institutional political theory—what I am calling *political* political theory—than there is in Great Britain.

Partly it is because the distinction between political theory and political philosophy is more pronounced in the United States, though some of the best work on democratic structures in recent years has emerged from American philosophy departments. I have in mind David Estlund's work on the epistemic dimension of our attachment to democracy and Tom Christiano's writing on the relation between democracy and political equality.[68] Detailed work on the justification and the normative dimensions of democratic institutions occupies a large part of the space that I have in mind when I talk about *political* political theory, and theoretical reflection on it is no doubt sponsored and sustained in the United States by a keen awareness of the arguably counter-majoritarian aspect of constitutional review, which plays such an important role in political life. Even those of us who are inclined to impugn the democratic credentials of judicial review are convinced that it is not a simple matter, and theoretical attempts to grapple with this have led to a deepening and an enrichment of our contestation about the true nature of democracy.[69]

I should also mention the role American law schools and legal scholars have in bringing these issues into unrelenting focus. Questions about constitutional structure and the theory of democracy are written about in law reviews and taught in law school classes by an array of impressive scholars, such as John Ferejohn, Stephen Holmes, Sam Issacharoff, Sanford Levinson, Rick Pildes, and Adrian Vermuele, along with hundreds of others.[70] In many ways, the huge amount of detailed normative work on constitutionalism and democracy done by legal scholars is one of the most striking differences between political theory in the United States and political theory in the United Kingdom. The debate is deepened also by the work of political theorists such as Charles Beitz, writing about political equality and the extent to which it can and cannot underpin a purely procedural account of democracy, and Dennis Thompson, bringing to vivid life theoretical issues about electoral justice (as opposed to justice generally) in the American polity.[71]

Beyond democracy and its structures, we also need much better theoretical understanding of the role of adjacent institutions and practices. I have already mentioned Nancy Rosenblum's admirable work on political parties, breaking through a whole reef of theoretical indifference to that subject, which illuminates not only democratic competition but ideas about loyal opposition in American politics as well. Some of this work might be described as a crossover from empirical political science to political theory, but I prefer to see Thompson's work, for example, and Rosenblum's as an attempt to reunite the study of politics under theoretical auspices that lose nothing in their ethical sensitivity and their philosophical ambition by being applied to real-world institutional questions.

And that, it seems to me, is worth emphasizing, on both sides of the Atlantic. Political theory loses nothing if it is taught from start to finish in a way that focuses on questions about institutions, structures, and processes. It loses nothing by being made intelligible to our empirical colleagues and open to their input and interests; we political theorists lose nothing when we insist that our particular concerns and the values and principles that we particularly emphasize are concerns in the first instance about elections, parties, legislatures, courts, states, regimes, and agencies. We are political theorists, not poets, and though the values embodied in our reflections go well beyond the calculation of consequences, they are nevertheless political values, not the ends and virtues of ethical life.

10. POLITICAL THEORY AND THE CANON

None of what I have said is new; in some ways, it is quite old-fashioned. Certainly the issues I have raised, about the study of political institutions, are issues that dominate the canonical writings of the philosophers we study in the history-of-ideas side of our discipline.

I have mentioned John Stuart Mill a few times, particularly his *Considerations on Representative Government*—still the most important book on democracy in our tradition. But the study of political institutions has been the focus of the theory of politics since Aristotle. In the early modern tradition, we have Hobbes on the structure of sovereignty and the absolutist challenge to the rule of law. There is John Locke with his paradoxical combination of legislative supremacy and legislative constraint and his views on separation of powers. We have Jean-Jacques Rousseau on the difference between democratic lawmaking and democratic government, and his repudiation of representation at least so far as the first of these functions is concerned. And, opposed to Rousseau, we have James Madison, of course, on the ways in which a popular republic can establish itself over a country of wide extent without becoming trapped in the pitfalls of direct democracy.

Of course, there is a case for studying these issues directly, not just as ventriloquists for dead white males from the seventeenth and eighteenth centuries. There is a case for having a modern paper on theory of politics that encourages our students to approach it in their own twenty-first–century voices. But at present that is not what we do. Instead, we study different topics—Rawls's theory, the fifty-seven different varieties of luck-egalitarianism, and global justice—neglecting the issues of structure, process, sovereignty, and constitution set out in *Leviathan, The Social Contract, The Federalist Papers,* or the *Two Treatises of Government*. In this regard, by the way, it is quite remarkable that in all his great essays on the history of ideas, Isaiah Berlin managed to avoid precisely those thinkers who were interested in political institutions, or, in the case of Mill and Montesquieu, whom he did write about, he seems to have chosen deliberately to focus on precisely those aspects of Mill's output that had the least to do with representative government and precisely those aspects of *The Spirit of the Laws* that were furthest from Montesquieu's concerns about the structures and processes of government.[72] I know that Berlin had distinct work of his own to do in the history of ideas, but in retrospect, the balance seems a little one-sided.

11. MONTESQUIEU AND, ONCE MORE, DAVID HUME

Montesquieu had a theory about all this. He believed that a lack of interest in forms, processes, and structures was typical of a society en route to a despotic form of government.[73] And, he said that, notwithstanding most people's love of liberty, most nations are subject to despotic government.

> This is easily accounted for. To form a moderate government, it is necessary to combine the several powers; to regulate, temper, and set them in motion; to give, as it were, ballast to one, in order to enable it to counterpoise the other. This is a masterpiece of legislation; rarely produced by hazard, and seldom attained by prudence. On the contrary, a despotic government offers itself, as it were, at first sight; it is uniform throughout; and as passions only [like fear and terror] are requisite to establish it, this is what every capacity may reach.[74]

Despotism is not quite a default position. But it is the one that is least characterized by institutional complexity and makes the least demands on our institutional imagination.

David Hume, who admired Montesquieu (in a letter, he predicted that Montesquieu's work would in due course be regarded as "the wonder of all centuries"[75]), was inclined to agree. He believed, as we have seen, that forms and processes were important in public life as in private life. Even in the ordinary conduct of business,

> [i]n the smallest court or office, the stated forms and methods, by which business must be conducted, are found to be a considerable check on the natural depravity of mankind. Why should not the case be the same in public affairs?[76]

But in politics, nevertheless, "it may be proper to make a distinction." In an absolute government, said Hume, everything depends very much on the personal quality of the ruler, because there are no intermediate structures and no checks and balances to constrain him; just the acclamation of a leader whose qualities and policies happen to appeal to the people.[77]

The deliberative and deliberate processes of a free society slow things down; their articulated and articulate structures stretch things out; they cost money for salaries, furniture, and buildings; they provide an irritating place for the raising of inconvenient questions; and at their best they respect the dignity of the poorest he or the poorest she that is in England by providing a place for their petitions to be heard. The political institutions of a free society sometimes even require the government to retire from the field defeated when its victory in some courtroom or legislative battle was supposed by political insiders to be a foregone conclusion. I think *all of this* is to be valued and cherished. Some colleagues and some politicians disagree; they celebrate the decline of parliamentarism and the rise of a more decisive executive politics that eschews the laborious channels of an inconvenient constitutionalism.[78] I am not laying odds on who is right. But I am saying that we should reasonably expect the theory of politics, as it is taught in our universities, to make a contribution to this debate, the political politics of which confront us now at every turn.

CHAPTER TWO

Constitutionalism: A Skeptical View

THE TERM "CONSTITUTIONALISM" means many things, and I would not have written this book if I were not in favor of some of them. But, in this chapter, I am going to sound a note of skepticism about a very common conception of constitutionalism. The conception I want to criticize equates *constitutionalism* with *limited government.* I will argue that it is a mistake to put all the emphasis on limitation and little or nothing on the affirmative tasks of empowerment that constitutions also have to perform. I have my doubts about other common conceptions of constitutionalism, too—particularly those that associate it with the authority of judges. But that will have to wait until Chapter 9. Mostly, what I want to do is to deprecate the "limited government" account and separate it from other more helpful meanings of the term.

1. THE WEAKEST MEANINGS OF CONSTITUTIONALISM

We are all supposed to be in favor of constitutionalism now, and so we should be. But anything so universally applauded has a tendency to drift into the realm of the banal. There is a danger that faith of this kind in any ideal may become (in the words of John Stuart Mill) a dead dogma rather than a living truth, a prejudice clinging accidentally to a form of words that once conveyed something interesting and controversial.[1]

The potential for "constitutionalism" to degenerate into an empty slogan is exacerbated by the fact that the word is sometimes used in a way that conveys no theoretical content at all. Sometimes it seems to mean just the thoughtful and systematic study of constitutions and various constitutional provisions. People talk about Canadian constitutionalism and contrast it with U.S. constitutionalism; all they mean is the study and comparison of the constitutions of Canada and the United States. There is a book called *The Constitutionalism of American States* that is just a study of state constitutions.[2] When Akhil Amar writes about "unwritten American constitutionalism,"[3] he means nothing more than that there are parts of U.S. constitutional law that are not codified in the written document. There is nothing wrong with this usage but nothing very illuminating either. But it is accepted by the *Oxford English Dictionary*.[4]

Sometimes the term is used as a label for referring to a constitutional doctrine—*any* constitutional doctrine. We contrast "living constitutionalism" with "originalist constitutionalism," and we talk about "comparative constitutionalism" (referring not to the comparative study of constitutions but to the doctrine that says courts engaged in constitutional adjudication in one country have the right to invoke principles, doctrines, and precedents that are used in other countries).[5] There is nothing wrong with these usages either, but again they are not freighted with anything interesting or controversial so far as the meaning of "constitutionalism" is concerned. (Of course, each of these doctrines is freighted with intense interest and controversy in its own right, such as controversies about originalism and about the use of foreign law.)

2. CONSTITUTIONALISM AS A THEORY

The last two syllables of "constitutionalism"—the "-ism" suffix—should alert us to the possibility of *additional* meanings that involve a theory or a set of normative claims. Constitutional*ism* is like liberal*ism,* social*ism,* or scient*ism.* It is worth asking what that theory is and whether the normative claims it comprises are true or valid.[6]

I mentioned a moment ago the dictionary definition of the term. In the second meaning it gives for "constitutionalism," the *Oxford English Dictionary* refers to an attitude or disposition—"[a]dherence to constitutional principles."[7] A constitutionalist is one who takes constitutions very seriously and who is not disposed to allow deviations from them even when other important values are involved. "Constitutional*ism*" refers apparently to the sort of ideology that makes that attitude seem sensible. So constitutionalism the theory includes the claim that a society's constitution matters, that it is not just decoration, and that it has an importance that may justify making sacrifices of other important values for its sake. These are important and interesting claims.

3. GENERAL AND PARTICULAR CONSTITUTIONALISM

Different countries have different constitutions, and the claim that constitutions matter might be the view that the principles of a particular constitution are important, or it might be the more general view that constitutions *as such* are important.

If it is the first, then "constitutionalism" means different things in different settings. In the 1950s, it might have referred both to an Englishman's affection for parliamentary sovereignty and to an American's affection for judicially enforced limitations on legislative authority.[8] On the more general approach, we would try and look at what various constitutionalisms have in common, even when they chauvinistically celebrate differently shaped arrangements. Roger Scruton's definition of the term in his *Dictionary of Political Thought* is helpful as an example. He defines "constitutionalism" as the advocacy of constitutional government, of "government channeled through and limited by a constitution."[9] In this view, a constitutionalist is one who thinks it important for government—any government—to be organized through and constrained by a set of constitutional rules. Such a person will be opposed, for example, to various forms of absolutism (in the technical sense of "absolutism")[10] because that seems to involve repudiating the idea of rules constraining government at the highest level.

So, despite the differences between (say) Canadian and Australian constitutionalism, we might say that constitutionalists in both countries celebrate and advocate the same abstract thing: forms of political structuring that constrain the power of government. Some of these forms are similar (such as federalism); some of them are different (such as the more extensive provision for judicial review of legislation in the United States). But the idea of using formally articulated structure to constrain government is held in common by the two sets of constitutionalists, and it may be contrasted, on the one hand, with the older English view that governments are best constrained by an unarticulated ethos of moderation—"Not cricket, old boy"—and, on the other hand, with the absolutist conviction that it may not be appropriate to try to constrain the activities of government at all.

4. EXPLICIT AND IMPLICIT CONSTITUTIONS

But maybe these are false contrasts. They are if we say that every stable system of government has a constitution, meaning by "a constitution" a set of fundamental rules establishing the way governmental powers are exercised, who exercises them, what their jurisdiction is, how laws are made and changed, and so on.[11] So the British, the Israelis, and the New Zealanders have a constitution just as much as the Americans and the Australians; the rules just exist in a different form. In this account, even a dictatorship has a constitution. Its constitution may differ radically from that of a system of parliamentary sovereignty or from a republican system of checks and balances, but it is still a constitution. It is still *an ordering* of the institutions of government.

According to this line of thought, if government were imaginable without a constitution, it would have to be as the adventitious persistence of traditional ways of doing things without any consciousness of them as rules. But even then, some theorists will say that these ways of doing things can be identified as constitutional norms at least by outsiders, even if it doesn't occur to participants to think about them in those terms. When Alexander Hamilton remarked at the very beginning of *The Federalist Papers* that

> it seems to have been reserved to the people of this country, . . . to decide . . . whether societies of men are really capable or not of establishing good government from reflection and choice, or whether they are forever destined to depend for their political constitutions on accident and force[12]

he seemed to be assuming that countries whose systems of governance are not established by "reflection and choice" do still have constitutions.

Still, even if that is right, I think constitutionalism—the general ideology—might be difficult to apply to such societies. Their customs may be so implicit and so opaque to those whose political life they govern that adherence to them never rises to the level of an "-ism."¹³ So let us say that, as a theory or ideology, constitutionalism is a product of thought directed at the significance of rules and practices in political life, and it is unlikely to take hold in circumstances where political arrangements are not themselves the products of reflection and choice.¹⁴

5. CONSTITUTIONALISM AND WRITTEN CONSTITUTIONS

Is constitutionalism the celebration of *written* constitutions? It depends a bit what you mean by "written." Is it writtenness as such, as opposed (say) to the customary character of the relevant norms? Or is it about the concentration of all or most constitutional norms in one single canonical document? The British constitution is to a large extent written in the former sense, if you count the Bill of Rights of 1689, the Act of Union of 1707, the European Communities Act of 1971, the Human Rights Act of 1998, and the various Parliament Acts and Representation of the People Acts from 1918 to 2000. It is not codified in a single document, but I am not sure why a constitutionalist should think this matters.

It is sometimes said that the main advantage of putting one's constitution into writing is that it establishes its authority as higher law, making it enforceable by the judiciary. This is what Justice Marshall said in *Marbury v. Madison:*

> [A]ll those who have framed written constitutions contemplate them as forming the fundamental and paramount law of the nation, and consequently the theory of every such government must be, that an act of the legislature repugnant to the constitution is void. This theory is essentially attached to a written constitution.¹⁵

However, on its face, this is an implausible argument. The writtenness of a constitutional provision is perfectly compatible with its being treated as ordinary legislation, like the New Zealand Constitution Act of 1986. Or it is compatible with its being treated merely as a piece of paper with little legal effect, like the Soviet Constitution of 1936. On the other hand, judicial review of legislation can be thought legitimate even where the relevant provision of higher law is unwritten; or at least that was the position of Sir

Edward Coke in *Dr. Bonham's case*,[16] which many American constitutionalists take seriously even if most English lawyers have never heard of it.

One often hears it said—by Americans, for example—that rights and rules restraining government are insecure unless they are laid down in the terms of a written constitution. One is reminded of Walton Hamilton's ironic riposte: "Constitutionalism is the name given to the trust which men repose in the power of words engrossed on parchment to keep a government in order."[17] One would think Americans might have taken on board the caustic observations of James Madison and Alexander Hamilton on "parchment barriers" as a "greatly overrated" form of security.[18] But no; we persist with our faith that bullets cannot pass through paper.

Anyway, security is not the only virtue that may be claimed for writtenness. Other claims are more plausible. One is that writtenness allows the constitution to have a palpable presence in the polity. Hannah Arendt said that in America it was important that the Constitution be "a tangible worldly entity," "an endurable objective thing, which, to be sure, one could approach from many different angles and upon which one could impose many different interpretations . . . but which nevertheless was never [just] a subjective state of mind."[19]

This may be particularly important when constitutional arrangements are being considered and debated. A set of implicit rules is very hard to reflect upon in any coherent way among a large number of people. That has always been the frustrating thing about the unwritten elements of the U.K. constitution, those that consist of custom, convention, or understandings as opposed to statute law. The subject matter is constantly shifting under one's gaze, and the line between a normative provision of the constitution in this sense and a normative view about what the provisions of the constitution ought to be is the subject of constant equivocation.[20] Deliberation can seem futile unless it is focused on a text that can serve as a focal point (even an imperfect focal point) for debate—a written text, by which issues are separated, and on which amendments may be registered.[21]

I do not want to quarrel with this aspect of constitutionalism, but I would enter two caveats. First, what is important is that writtenness should facilitate reflection, not stymie it with a sort of fetishism of either the written text itself or its interpretation. Once a text starts to be venerated, the words and the phrasing take on a life of their own, becoming a sort of obsessive catchphrase for expressing certain underlying substantive concerns in a way that makes it difficult to focus on what is really at stake. (For example, in assessing American social and economic legislation in the early years of the twentieth century, was it really worth spending so much energy discussing whether "due process" can be substantive?) Also, with a written constitution as their battlefield, lawyers and judges are likely to be heavily distracted in their discussions by side arguments about interpretive theory, and these abstract interpretive debates can sometimes crowd out serious arguments focused on the merits of the question under discussion, whether it is abortion, affirmative action, or campaign finance reform.

Second, what is important is not just that there should be some form of conscious and explicit reflection on constitutional arrangements but that this should be the work of *the people whose society is to be governed by these arrangements*. Notice how the two caveats go together. For many self-styled constitutionalists, especially in America, reflection and choice is a matter of history, often quite distant history—a matter for "the Framers" not for current politics. Our interpretations are driven by their debates. From this perspective, the value of the written text lies in the way the venerable calligraphy of the eighteenth century endues the rules with an aura of ancestral authority. That seems to me to count against writtenness. The frustration I referred to earlier of having an unwritten constitution in (say) the United Kingdom is present frustration, not ancestral frustration. When I said that in a country without a written constitution the ground is constantly shifting and it is hard to focus the debate about the fundamental structuring of governance, I meant the debate that is going on now concerning our political institutions, not the debate that took place between the Federalists and the anti-Federalists or between Locke and Bolingbroke. And the difficulty with the American model of textual fetishism is that it makes little contribution to normative debate about our governance arrangements here and now. I don't mean that Americans lack such a debate; I mean only that the reverence for the Framers' written text is not a good way of facilitating it.

6. CONSTITUTIONALISM AND CONSTRAINT

I turn now to a more substantive aspect of constitutionalist ideology. Unlike, say, the rule of law, constitutionalism seems to be not just a normative theory about the *forms* and *procedures* of governance.[22] It is a theory about the importance of controlling, limiting, and restraining the power of the state in a substantive way. Numerous books on constitutionalism make this theme clear in their titles. Scott Gordon has written a book called *Controlling the State: Constitutionalism from Ancient Athens to Today*, and András Sajó entitles his book *Limiting Government: An Introduction to Constitutionalism*.[23] In a foreword to Sajó's book, Stephen Holmes writes that "[c]onstitutions are giant restraining orders . . . . They are inevitably propelled by the desire to escape specific dangerous and unpleasant political outcomes."[24] There are some more nuanced views. Cass Sunstein insists that limited government is just one of many principles associated with constitutionalism.[25] But this goes against the general trend. "In all its successive phases," according to C. H. McIlwain, "constitutionalism has one essential quality: it is a legal limitation on government."[26]

So, the assumption seems to be that the power of the state needs to be restrained, limited, or controlled, lest it get out of hand. Constitutionalism (the ideology) is part of what Judith Shklar called "the liberalism of fear."[27] The concentration of power in the state leads to its abuse, people think, and this is why the power-dispersing, the power-slowing, and the power-checking elements of constitutional structure are thought to be important.

How seriously should we take this language of constraint? I wonder. Maybe we should examine it more closely than casual users of the term "constitutionalism" are wont to do. Consider the terms that are used for this connection between constitutions and various forms of constraint. The most commonly used phrase is "limited government," but there is also talk of a connection between constitutionalism and "restraints" on power and of constitutionalism as a doctrine of "control" (as in Scott Gordon's title *Controlling the State*). Now, considered analytically, these phrases—"limited government," "restrained government," and "controlled government"—are not synonymous. They mean different things, and they have different connotations in the theory of politics.

I'll begin with "control." The idea of *controlling* the state is not necessarily a negative or constraining idea. If I control a vehicle, I determine not only where it doesn't go but also where it does go. Often, constitutional structures involve this sort of control. For example, we subordinate the executive to the legislature so far as the implementation of ordinary legislation is concerned, so that the sort of control envisaged in legislation is conveyed to those responsible for executing the law. This control means that if the legislature says that something is to be done, the executive must see that it *is* done. Is this the sort of control that constitutionalists have in mind? I don't think so.

Someone may respond that what I have just said is about *intra*-governmental control, whereas those who talk of controlling the state have in mind control of the whole edifice, of the legislature, for example, as well as the executive. But even in this context, we need not take the view that control equals constraint. In a democracy, we say it is important for the government as a whole to be controlled *by the people,* and again we may understand this control not as something purely negative but as a matter of affirmative response to the people's will. If the people want their government to ameliorate poverty, for example, it is the task of the constitution to provide institutions that can be controlled by this desire.

Restraint, by contrast, is definitely a negative idea: it is the idea of preventing the government from doing certain things. A "restraint" view proceeds on the basis that we can identify certain abuses that we want to avoid and we specifically prohibit them, building these prohibitions into the very document that constitutes governmental authority. Such prohibitions often take the form of rights—a right not to be tortured, a right to be free from interference with religious practice, and so on. The idea is that whatever the government affirmatively does, it must not do *these* things. In some cases, the prohibition is absolute—as in most constitutions, it is in the case of torture. In other instances, the prohibition works as a specification of the conditions under which things may be done that might otherwise be oppressive: no detention without trial, no trial without the assistance of counsel, and so on. Many rights provisions are like this, and much of the popularity of modern constitutionalism is due to the fact that it seems to connect with human rights in this way. But it is interesting that few constitutionalists are willing to rest their theory on these restraints alone. Not content with specific, piecemeal constraints, they also say that an important function of constitutions is to impose broader limitations on the sorts of projects that governments can take on.

Constitutionalists talk of *limited* government, and in their mouths "limited government" means not just the avoidance of particular abuses but a broader sense that many of the aspirations that governments—particularly democratic governments—have sometimes had are per se illegitimate. No doubt, there is some continuity between the two ideas. One might say, as a matter of restraint, that government may not interfere with religious freedom.

Or one may say, as a matter of limits, that it is not the government's function to establish any public form of worship. These amount to roughly the same thing. For other cases, however, the overlap between restraint and limit is deceptive. One might say, as the U.S. Constitution says, that the government is restrained from passing "any . . . law impairing the obligation of contracts."[28] But it would be a further step—quite a drastic step—to say, as a matter of limits, that it is not the function of the government to interfere in the market economy.

If, however, one treats limited government as the core principle of constitutionalism, as the title of Sajó's book does, then one is in a position to move more directly to the idea that many of the aspirations of government—particularly democratic government—are per se illegitimate. Those who set up a democracy may be hoping for government regulation to ameliorate poverty, promote public health, and protect the environment. They know they are likely to face opposition from opponents who claim that this is none of the government's business. But now it seems that these opponents can phrase their opposition not just as a political position; they can take on the mantle of constitutionalism, and add to their case against intervention the claim that the interventionists do not take the constitutional dimension of governance seriously. They will say that interventionists are not constitutionalist enough. With this sense of limitation, constitutionalism forfeits any claim to political neutrality; it is associated instead with conservative criticism of "big government." People talk of "*laissez-faire* constitutionalism," not just as one extreme form of constitutionalist ideology but in connection with a positioning of constitutionalism *as such* in favor of market provision, rather than state provision, of many important goods and services.[29]

Am I being too pedantic in this explication of the differences between control, limitation, and restraint? Surely all that is meant, when these terms are used loosely as synonyms of one another, is that a constitution consists of rules that regulate the actions and practices they apply to. But actually, no: I think a great many self-styled constitutionalists are happiest with a situation in which no one looks too closely at the content of their position, so that they are free to capitalize on a certain looseness in the rhetoric, using the equivocations made possible by the juxtaposition of "control," "restraint," and "limit" to leverage the moderation of a person who believes that the government shouldn't be allowed to do just anything into an acceptance of the doctrine that it is unwise to allow the government to do a lot.

I see similar moves being made in discussions about *the rule of law*. People say the rule of law is about legal control of government, which it is; but some of them infer from this that therefore the rule of law is a doctrine of limited government, which it is not. Legal control of government, subjection of government decisions to the constraint of overarching law, can either limit or expand what government is doing. Consider for example section 26 of the Constitution of South Africa, which requires the state to take reasonable legislative and other measures to achieve progressive realization of the right to adequate housing. If the government escapes legal control, it might neglect this priority and devote its resources to a more limited agenda. A government under law, however, is required to expand its agenda to include housing among its high priorities, and that is what the South African constitutional court decided in the *Grootboom* case.[30] Yet I have heard people say that the rule of law is not interested in the enforcement of social and economic rights (such as section 26), that the enforcement of that provision or its legislative equivalents does not count as the rule of law because the rule of law is about legal control of government, which means *limited* government, not advocacy lawyering designed to expand the governmental agenda. And this feeds into a conservative strategy of appropriating the rule of law as an ideal for something like an IMF/World Bank agenda, which sees its aim as that of securing property rights and external investment against legislative encroachment. I have argued elsewhere that a respectable jurisprudence should have nothing to do with that conception of the rule of law,[31] and I believe we should also give no credit to the equivocating toggle between control of government and limited government that facilitates it.

Constitutionalists sometimes say ingenuously that their creed is simply that "there is a proper and improper use of state authority" and that it is the job of a constitution to "confine" the exercise of state authority to proper uses.[32] Proper and improper: that's two options. But normative logic is *trivalent*, not bivalent: actions are prohibited, permitted, *or required*. Neglecting the third category—what is required, as opposed to permitted—can distort our analysis. Suppose we say, then—more accurately—that there are proper, improper, and required uses of state authority; then we will have to say that the job of the constitution is as much to ensure that the state does what it is required to do as to ensure that it is restrained from doing what is prohibited. The U.S. Constitution does not have much in the way of affirmative requirements, and constitutional courts have made a virtue of this in cases such as *Jackson v. City of Joliet,* where Richard Posner observed that "[t]he men who wrote the Bill of Rights were not concerned that government might do too little for the people but that it might do too much to them."[33] Judge Posner may be right about our constitutional tradition, but we should not have much patience with an ideology that tries to foist this on everyone else in the world on the grounds that this is what is required by constitutionalism as such.

7. EMPOWERMENT AND AUTHORITY

What do constitutions do that constitutionalists (the ideologists of constitutionalism) downplay? First and foremost, constitutions empower: they establish institutions that allow people to cooperate and coordinate to pursue projects that they cannot achieve on their own.[34]

To take a simple but obvious example, we need an agency to act decisively in large-scale natural emergencies for which individual or voluntary efforts will be inadequate; a constitution provides the institutional auspices under which such an agency can be created and empowered. The need may be for people to act in concert in large numbers (perhaps hundreds of thousands, even millions), and they cannot do that without the sort of articulated power that public norms provide.

Constitutions also invest institutions like this with public authority. By this I mean that they not only provide the institutions with powers of coercion but also ensure that they can act credibly in the name of the whole society, and they see to it that this amounts to not just a label but a substantial source of legitimacy. Governmental institutions have to have standing in the community as a focus of loyalty and as a point of orientation for the millions of people in the society who are figuring out how their concerns, actions, and resources are to be related to those that the institution commands.

All sorts of institutions need to be established in this spirit. We need an institution in which representatives of the community can assemble to debate and enact various measures to stand over and among us as laws. That is, we need legislatures, manned (peopled) in a certain way and invested with public authority so that they can deliberate credibly in the name of us all. A constitution has to set up courts to administer and interpret its laws and resolve disputes in the name of the whole society; it has to establish armed organizations to keep the peace in a society; it has to set up standing organizations of operatives to carry out the work that its legislation requires; and it has to empower institutions and personnel to deal with other governments, similarly established in other countries, for purposes of peace, trade, and war. The manner in which a constitution performs these affirmative constitutive tasks, the modes of operation it establishes for these institutions, and the way it relates them to one another are all crucial components of the establishment of public authority.

What I have just said is platitudinous, and you may think that constitutionalists can be forgiven for brushing past these obvious points and cutting straight to the question of how the institutions set up for these purposes are to be limited and restrained. They may accept that constitutions are necessary in an affirmative way to constitute the power of the state, but their constitutional*ism* is something extra. In Sajó's words, "[c]onstitutions are about power; [but] a constitution impregnated with the ideas of constitutionalism is about *limited* power."[35] But even putting the matter like that still leads to a distortion in our thinking. It indicates that the establishing of political power does not need the sort of attention that constitutionalism devotes to the subset of provisions concerned with restraint and limitation.

Besides actually establishing centers of public power, constitutions lay down procedures for their operation, often quite formalistic procedures limiting not so much what can be done but *how* it is done. A constitutionalized politics is an articulate politics that moves deliberately and deliberatively from stage to stage and forum to forum, taking seriously the integrity of each part of (say) the lawmaking process or of other processes of political decision.[36] I have in mind things like bicameral legislation, the requirement of executive consent, and the articulate relation between the legislature on the one hand and, on the other hand, the courts and the agents of the executive who administer, interpret, and enforce the laws. From a constitutionalist perspective, there is a tendency to think simplistically of devices like these: they are conceived just as *brakes* on the lawmaking process, ways of slowing things down, points of possible resistance against oppressive legislation. Equally, there is a tendency to think of the formal separation of powers between (say) legislature, executive, and judiciary simply as a way of diluting power and making it harder for it to be exercised. Everything is seen through the lens of restraint and limitation.

But constitutional structure need not be seen in that light. Articulate process can be seen as a way of structuring deliberation, allowing a multiplicity of voices to be heard, and securing multiple points of access for citizen input. Bicameral arrangements can be seen as ways of empowering different voices in the community or voices in the community sampled for the purposes of representation in different ways.[37] And the separation of powers can be seen—as Dicey saw it—as a way of taking seriously the integrity of what comes into existence as the result of a genuine legislative exercise.[38]

In general, we need to understand the importance of the way in which a constitution provides *housing* for the political activity of a society, establishing an in-between of furniture and formality so that public deliberation becomes a structured enterprise, allowing the views of one person to be brought articulately into relation with the views of others and facilitating the formation of well-thought-through, responsible, and politically effective opinions. This is not primarily a matter of constraint;[39] it is a matter of what a constitution affirmatively makes possible out of what would otherwise be the loose, lurching, and dangerous politics of the street.[40]

8. DEMOCRACY: CONSTRAINT OR EMPOWERMENT?

Many of the points I have made apply most vividly to democracy, and the skeptical notes that I am sounding about constitutionalism as an ideology are intended to be democratic notes.

When a constitutionalist thinks of democracy, his first thought is: How can we prevent it from degenerating into the tyranny of the majority? What devices are available, what moves can be made, to restrain the tyrannical excesses to which democracies are endemically liable?

But of course there are prior questions that need to be attended to as well, questions of affirmative empowerment. How is the democracy to be constituted? What is to be the system of representation? What are to be the different democratic requirements for different kinds of political office (the election of a head of the executive, for example, versus the election of a legislator or maybe even the election of judges)? What are the qualifications of voters? How is the integrity of the electoral process to be guaranteed? And, above all, dominating all of these questions: How is the central principle of *political equality,* which is the foundation of democracy, to be upheld and enforced?

I actually think there is an important contrast here between the constitution of power in democratic societies and the constitution of power in nondemocratic societies. In *non*democratic systems of government, it is usually the task of the constitution to formalize and ratify the authority of those to whom, as it were, power comes naturally or who, as it happens, have been vested historically with power over a given society. The constitution of a democracy, by contrast, involves empowering *those who would otherwise be powerless,* the ordinary people who in most polities are the subjects, not the agents, of political power. The man whom Colonel Rainsborough referred to as "the poorest he that is in England" is the hardest man to empower, because if things are left to themselves he will have no political power at all.[41] If his empowerment is secured, it is the affirmative achievement of a democratic constitution that has had to go out of its way to ensure that he has as much formal political authority as "the greatest he."

Also, it is not enough to *give* people equal political power; one has to *maintain* them in that status, because this equality is endemically liable to subversion from all sorts of directions. When one is dealing with millions of people, the maintenance of political equality requires considerable attention. It is something a political system has to work at, for there is a standing tendency to dilute, compromise, or (if possible) bypass the enfranchisement or effective representation of the common people. Maintaining a democratic constitution means paying attention to the surrounding phenomena of politics such as the influence of wealth and other forms of social and economic power to ensure that the political equality definitive of democracy remains a reality for all members of the society and not just an ideological decoration.

If, on the other hand, we preoccupy ourselves—as constitutionalists do—with checking, restraining, and limiting political power in the hands of those to whom it is formally assigned, then there is a danger that this constant necessary attention to political equality will fall by the wayside. Constitutionalism is a doctrine about where attention is properly directed so far as a society's basic legal and political arrangements are concerned; by being directed constantly toward constraint, attention is distracted from those constitutional arrangements whose function it is to keep faith with the enfranchisement of ordinary people.

9. CONSTITUTIONALISM VERSUS DEMOCRACY

If anything, matters are in even worse shape than this. The problem is not just that constitutionalism neglects the task of democratic empowerment; constitutionalism takes democracy and the power assigned to ordinary people through elective and representative procedures as its natural enemy. One would think that a theory of politics devoted to imposing constraints on the abuse of power would have in its sights all forms of tyranny, all forms of oppression. But again and again in the constitutionalist literature, one reads that it is the tyranny *of the majority* that constitutionalism is concerned with checking, not tyranny in general. So, for example, we hear scholars talking of "constitutionalism's fundamental commitment to protect certain decisions from current majoritarian impulses"[42] and describing constitutionalism as "at base, protection against the consequences of majoritarian power."[43] It is possible, I suppose, that this emphasis on *majoritarian* oppression (as opposed to oppression by powerful families or firms) and the dangers of democratic rule (as opposed to the dangers of oligarchy) is born of a sense that we can take the ascendancy of democracy for granted, and that it is only its abuses that we have to worry about.[44] But then that returns us to the concerns of the previous section. Democracy in its fullest sense—the genuine empowerment of ordinary people under the auspices of political equality—is not a secure or resilient achievement. It requires continual constitutional attention.

I don't want to be painting too Manichean a picture from either perspective—democracy as constitutionalism's nemesis or constitutionalism as the constant object of a democrat's fear and suspicion. One way in which the opposition might be blurred is through the *redefinition* of "democracy" to associate it more closely with the constitutionalist ideal. Ronald Dworkin took this approach. He maintained that true democracy does not exist unless the members of a political community treat one another as their equals in a sense that goes far beyond formal political equality: they must also evince equal concern for one another and equal respect for one another's autonomy. Without this, he says, any version of democracy that requires "deference to temporary majorities on matters of individual right is . . . brutal and alien, and . . . nations with firm democratic traditions now reject it as fake."[45] So he concludes that a true democracy will contain in its ruling structures provisions that ensure this more extensive form of equal concern and respect, even at the cost of disempowering a majority. How far we should take this is a matter of debate.[46]

10. POPULAR SOVEREIGNTY

One area where we find that constitutionalists *are* prepared to flirt with democratic ideas is in their conception of the proper authorship of a constitution. A constitution may be conceived as a set of constraints, but it is important—for various purposes—that these constraints be understood as constraints that in some sense we have imposed on ourselves rather than had imposed on us from the outside. So, for example, in the United States, we say that the Constitution is a product of popular sovereignty—"We the People . . . do ordain and establish this Constitution"—and its constraining power depends on that. The U.S. Supreme Court in *Marbury v. Madison* began from the premise that "the people have an original right to establish, for their future government, such principles as, in their opinion, shall most conduce to their own happiness" and argued that a judicial power to strike down unconstitutional legislation was necessary to give effect to the "original and supreme will" of the people.[47]

If constitutionalism is committed to popular sovereignty in this way, then what becomes of what I have described as its inherent hostility to democracy? The two elements are not inconsistent. Popular sovereignty and democracy share obvious common elements, but the idea that the people have the right to establish their own form of government is in theory compatible with their establishment of a nondemocratic constitution or a heavily compromised or truncated form of democracy.[48] Popular sovereignty can be the source of nondemocratic government.

In any case, popular sovereignty is not always a stable position, even as an account of constitutional origins. In America, a great many constitutionalists are as comfortable talking about "the Framers" and their extraordinary virtue—which is a decidedly *non*populist conception—as they are talking about popular sovereignty. They will scramble back to the rhetoric of popular sovereignty whenever they feel the need to give constitutional limits and restraints credentials that can stand up to those of the legislative enactments they are supposed to strike down. But their true view of constitutional origins reveals itself as a decidedly aristocratic conception.[49]

And even when the popular-sovereignty origins of constitutional constraints *are* emphasized, their current application tends to be radically dislocated from popular politics. Most such restrictions were phrased by their authors in very vague and general terms, leaving open major choices about how they are to be applied. A genuine commitment to the popular origins of these restrictions might lead one to suppose that these open questions should also be answered by the people—the people *now* if necessary. But constitutionalists abhor this implication. Their view of these restrictions as constitutional in character leads—in the constitutional*ist* model—to a conviction that at all costs questions about their interpretation must not be answered by a current majority. If they are to be answered at all (in the ordinary life of the polity), they are to be answered by a nonmajoritarian branch of government, such as the judiciary, who are (somehow) empowered to speak for the popular sovereign whose work gave rise to these questions in the first place.

The other important difficulty has to do with the perceived distance in time between the decisions of the popular sovereign (if that is what constitutional constraints represent) and the popular majority that it is supposed to be presently constraining. Larry Alexander has argued that constitutionalism represents the power of past majorities over present and future majorities.[50] But obviously there is a legitimacy problem depending on how distant in the past the constraining majority is perceived to be. We may revere the Framers of the Constitution, but ancestor worship by itself is a poor competitor to the sort of legitimacy that a measure enacted by a current democratic majority can claim. If we want to present the constraint on the current majority as a precommitment of the sovereign people themselves, then we must find a way to connect the people who supposedly made that precommitment six generations ago to the people who now seem to be subject to its constraint.[51] Maybe we can say that if the people have not bothered to amend the constitution, then that signifies their present consent. But this is almost always an unconvincing argument, resting everything as it does on a tenuous and contestable extrapolation from mere acquiescence, in order to oppose a measure that has the real (as opposed to notional) imprimatur of the people and their representatives granted through a democratic process working actually and explicitly right now.

In the end, modern constitutionalists tend to scuttle back to an argument about the moral necessity of the constraints they are defending, an argument that bypasses popular sovereignty as well as democracy altogether. And this is where the real issue is joined. Evidently, there is disagreement about the moral necessity of the constraints; otherwise the legislation in question would not have been enacted. The legislators' best moral judgment seems to have been that the constitutional norm is wrong or outdated or that it should be interpreted and applied in a different way; that is why they voted for the present measure. They may be wrong about that, but then the constitutionalist's position begs the question of how these rival claims of right and wrong are to be sorted out in a constitutional context.

11. JUDICIAL REVIEW OF LEGISLATION

This brings us, finally, to the question of judicial power in a constitutional system. If a constitution is not to be merely a set of paper rules, there must be some way in which the force of its provisions is brought to bear on current political activity. Various methods are possible. One is to nurture an ethos of respect for the constitution among members of the polity, particularly among active players in the political system, so that a sense of constitutional obligation becomes a shared point of reference in all their decisions. Another is to design institutions so that the way in which they accommodate the dynamics of power and ambition yields constitutional outcomes by a sort of invisible hand, even when few or none of the participants takes constitutional obligation seriously for its own sake.[52] Few modern constitutionalists are satisfied with options like these. They tend to be interested in formal mechanisms of enforcement, among the most popular of which is the use of judicial power in the constitutional system to patrol breaches of constitutional constraints by other branches of government. If constitutional rules are seen as constitutional law, then it seems appropriate to entrust their enforcement to courts in the way that the enforcement of other legal rules is entrusted. And if, as constitutionalists believe, the point of the most important provisions of a modern constitution is to restrain or limit the exercise of legislative authority, then it makes sense to see these not just as law but as higher law, enforceable by the courts against ordinary statutes. Support for judicial review therefore seems to be part and parcel of what is meant by modern constitutionalism.

Elsewhere, I have criticized the practice of strong judicial review as undemocratic.[53] That critique of course is question begging in the present context since, as we have seen, most constitutionalists think (openly or secretly) that being undemocratic is part of the point of constitutional arrangements. Remember, constitutionalism (the ideology) and democracy are natural antagonists. But there are a couple of further difficulties.

Treating judicial authority as the main basis for constitutional enforcement leaves the constitutionality of judicial power itself effectively unchecked. Connected with this is the danger that judicial review might too easily become a form of constitutional lawmaking by the judiciary. Many of the provisions found in modern constitutions are left deliberately vague or abstract, usually as the cost of securing the sort of popular acceptance of them (at the time of their framing) that would justify their imposition as constitutional constraints. As a result, major features of the country's political arrangements, the limits on government, or the restraints imposed on governmental power are left undefined. (American experience has shown that these issues are not always marginal or borderline issues; often they are major watershed issues about the shape and nature of the polity and of individual and minority rights.) This can lead to the following difficulty. When a legislative measure is challenged in court for violating one of these provisions, it is likely that the court will try to settle the constitutional issue by pinning down the meaning of the provision in question more precisely. From the court's point of view, this may seem no more than fulfilling its duty to interpret the provisions it is required to apply. But from a point of view that pays attention to the real sources of constitutional change, it will seem as though a major decision about the shape and character of the society's constitution is now being made by a body that has no greater right than the elective branches to take on the mantle of popular sovereignty.

Some constitutionalists may be happy to say that the courts are entitled to speak for the popular sovereign when the people cannot (or will not) actually assemble in a constitutional convention to settle some point of uncertainty or dispute. Others are simply resigned to the prospect, reckoning that any other method of settling disputed points would have the effect of disempowering the courts, even in cases where judicial review does not run into this difficulty, and that it would also have the effect of empowering the very majorities that constitutional provisions are supposed to disable.

Still, unless the commitment to popular sovereignty is nothing but lip service, one cannot avoid the thought that current deliberations by the elective branches of government on constitutional matters have at least as much claim to be identified with popular sovereignty as the deliberations of unelected judges. It is probably a mistake for *any* branch of government to assume the mantle of popular sovereign.[54] But if there is a major unresolved issue in the constitution and if the matter needs to be settled right now, one would think that whoever finds themselves stuck with the decision ought to be as sensitive as possible to the views of all elements in the polity, and not just insist that their one branch—let alone the least representative branch—be the one to make the decision.

One way or another, we are left with the conclusion that any commitment to popular sovereignty on the part of modern constitutionalists is really rather thin. Constitutionalists will use the language of popular sovereignty when it is useful to legitimatize the constraints they propose to place on current majorities. But they will quickly retreat from its logic as soon as it threatens the authority of nonpopulist institutions such as courts, whom they trust with the task of restraining and limiting the popular will.

12. CONCLUSION

I have tried in this chapter to present a view of constitutions that differs somewhat from the picture usually put forward in the name of constitutionalism. Constitutions are not just about restraining and limiting power; they are about the empowerment of ordinary people in a democracy and allowing them to control the sources of law and harness the apparatus of government to their legitimate aspirations. That is the democratic view of constitutions, but it is not the constitutionalist view. Accordingly, I have emphasized the opposition between constitutionalism and democracy and, through constitutionalism's embrace of the idea of limited government, the ideological antipathy between constitutionalism and many of democracy's characteristic aims.

Of course, it is always possible to present an alternative to constitutionalism as an alternative form *of* constitutionalism: some scholars talk of "popular constitutionalism" or "democratic constitutionalism."[55] I have nothing against such usages, though I have tried to sharpen the issues under discussion by avoiding them. No doubt, this has led to some exaggeration. No doubt, a more moderate constitutionalism can be envisaged. (And, no doubt, all sorts of equivocations are imaginable by which the issues discussed in this chapter can be fudged.) But I thought it was worth using this chapter to set out a stark version of the antipathy between constitutionalism and democratic self-government, if only because that will help us to measure more clearly the extent to which a new and mature theory of constitutional law takes proper account of the burden of ensuring that the people are not disenfranchised by the very document that is supposed to give them their power.

CHAPTER THREE

Separation of Powers and the Rule of Law

MY TOPIC FOR this chapter is the separation of powers, conceived as a political principle for evaluating the legal and constitutional arrangements of a modern state. What is this principle, and why is it important? The question takes us in interesting directions if we distinguish the separation of powers from a couple of other important constitutional ideas that are commonly associated with it. The first of these is the principle of the dispersal of power—a principle that counsels us to avoid excessive concentrations of political power in the hands of any one person, group, or agency. The second is the principle of checks and balances—a principle that holds that the exercise of power by any one power-holder needs to be balanced and checked by the exercise of power by other power-holders. Does the principle of the separation of powers have any meaning over and above these two principles? I think it does, and in this chapter I want to explore aspects of the separation of powers that are independent of what we value in these two other principles.

The separation of powers counsels a qualitative separation of the different functions of government—for example, legislation, adjudication, and executive administration. But the justification for this separation is not made clear in the canonical literature of seventeenth- and eighteenth-century political theory: Montesquieu's "justifications," for example, were mostly tautologies.[1] And in the spirit of those tautologies, modern constitutionalism has, until recently, taken the separation of powers for granted. I mean it takes for granted that the separation of powers is necessary to avoid tyranny, but it does not explain why. I think a qualitative separation *is* necessary; this is not a debunking paper. The point of the chapter is to find out something about its distinctiveness and its justification.

By contrast, much recent work on the separation of powers has had a critical edge. Eric Posner and Adrian Vermeule are skeptical about its value in relation to the exigencies of modern government,[2] and John Manning has expressed doubts about the legal/constitutional status of the principle.[3] The former critique provides an occasion for us to identify specific justificatory considerations that Posner and Vermeule may be in danger of pushing too brusquely aside, whereas Manning's critique opens up space for us to conceive of this principle in political-theory terms, uncontaminated by particular judicial formulations.

Let me anticipate briefly the argument of this chapter. My question is: What, specifically, is the point of the separation of powers? The answer I give is twofold. I look first to the integrity of each of the distinguished powers or functions—the dignity of legislation, the independence of the courts, and the authority of the executive, each understood as having its own role to play in the practices of the state. And second, I look to the value of articulated, as opposed to undifferentiated, modes of governance. The idea is that instead of just an undifferentiated political decision *to do something about person X,* there is an insistence that anything we do to X or about X must be preceded by an exercise of legislative power that lays down a general rule applying to everyone and not just X, a judicial proceeding that makes a determination that X's conduct in particular falls within the ambit of that rule, and so on. As well as the integrity of each of these phases, there is a sense that power is better exercised, or exercised more respectfully so far as its subjects are concerned, when it proceeds in this orderly sequence. These are preliminary thoughts. In what follows, I will try to make them clearer.

1. IS THE SEPARATION OF POWERS A LEGAL PRINCIPLE?

John Manning has made a good case for the proposition that the separation of powers is not a principle of the U.S. Constitution. The Constitution, says Manning, "adopts *no freestanding principle of separation of powers.* The idea of separated powers unmistakably lies behind the Constitution, but it was not adopted wholesale."[4] (The contrast here may be between the federal constitution, which, as Manning points out, contains no Separation of Powers Clause, and some of the state constitutions, which, at least textually, do.)[5]

I think Manning has made a reasonable case, though I would have liked to have seen his argument related more explicitly to Dworkinian methodology: whatever it says in the Constitution, does the best interpretation of the Constitution's provisions require us to embrace this as a background legal principle?[6] I guess Manning thinks that this is the view held by those he calls "functionalists," and he judges their interpretive exercise unsuccessful.[7]

Assuming Manning is right about the legal and constitutional situation, the separation of powers may remain an important principle of our *political* theory—indeed an important principle of the body of theory we call constitutionalism.[8] Not everything that a constitutionalist political theory commits us to is found in our constitution—a proposition that is self-evident in the case of a country such as the United Kingdom, which lacks a codified constitution, but is true also, I think, of the United States.

Think of a couple of analogies. There is no principle of *democracy* in the U.S. Constitution. (True, we can infer the importance of certain democratic considerations from Article I, 2.1, and also from the Fifteenth, Nineteenth, Twenty-Fourth, and Twenty-Sixth Amendments, but the principle of democracy itself cannot be regarded as legally enshrined.) Nevertheless, democracy is an indispensable part of our best theory of governance, and it would be wrong to forego any interest in it simply on account of its lacking explicit legal status in the text of the Constitution. The same is true of *the rule of law*. Although the framing of the U.S. Constitution was permeated by the spirit of the rule of law, still the rule of law is not presented in the Constitution as a free-standing principle and cannot be judicially enforced as such.[9] These examples suggest that even when a principle lacks specific legal status, it may still be an indispensable touchstone for evaluating the operation of, and any change in, our constitutional arrangements.

I take it that Professor Manning would have no difficulty with this analysis: the separation of powers, like democracy and the rule of law, may be an indispensable part of our theory of politics (in America) or our American constitutional*ism,* even if it is not, in the legalistic sense, a free-standing principle of our constitution. So we are not excused by Manning's argument from considering the meaning of this principle. On the contrary, that consideration can take its course more easily now, because we can focus steadily on what is conceptually distinctive about the principle without being distracted by the various uses that judges found for it when they treated it—wrongly in Manning's view—as one of the principles that it was their sworn duty to uphold.

By saying we should treat the separation of powers as an important political principle albeit a nonlegal one, I do not mean to suggest that it has merely "moral" force, as though it were just something a particular theorist dreamed up and now wants the rest of us to apply. The principle of the separation of powers has a powerful place in the tradition of political thought long accepted as canonical among us. Think of the way it was present to the minds of the founding generation, Federalists and anti-Federalists alike. Its presence was positive, not just normative, but its positive presence was not a matter of legal positivity. It was already accepted among the founding generation as an established touchstone of constitutional legitimacy. We see this in the way James Madison introduced the topic in *Federalist* Number 47, where he said of "the political maxim, that the legislative, executive, and judiciary departments ought to be separate and distinct,"

> No political truth is certainly of greater intrinsic value, or is stamped with the authority of more enlightened patrons of liberty, than that on which the objection [about the separation of powers] is founded. The accumulation of all powers, legislative, executive, and judiciary, in the same hands, whether of one, a few, or many, and whether hereditary, self-appointed, or elective, may justly be pronounced the very definition of tyranny. Were the federal Constitution, therefore, really chargeable with the accumulation of power, or with a mixture of powers, having a dangerous tendency to such an accumulation, no further arguments would be necessary to inspire a universal reprobation of the system.[10]

It is not that Madison is uncritical of the heritage of, say, "the celebrated Montesquieu," the "oracle who is always consulted and cited on this subject."[11] He was perfectly capable of excoriating Montesquieu and other "enlightened patrons of liberty" when he thought they had things wrong.[12] It is just that he did not regard it as an open possibility to simply repudiate this maxim. And this was not only because his opponents had made an issue of it, though they had. Sometimes standards of political evaluation are compelling for us even when the compulsion is not legal.

2. DISPERSAL OF POWER AND CHECKS AND BALANCES

Understood in this way, the separation of powers does not operate alone as a canonical principle of our constitutionalism. It is one of a close-knit set of principles that work both separately and together as touchstones of political legitimacy. The principles I have in mind are the following:

1. The principle of the separation of powers (i.e., of the functions of government) from one another.
2. The principle of dispersal of power, which counsels against the concentration of too much political power in the hands of any one person, group, or agency.
3. The principle of checks and balances, which requires the ordinary concurrence of one governmental entity in the actions of another (and thus permits the first entity to veto the actions of another).
4. The principle of bicameralism, requiring two coordinate legislative assemblies.
5. The principle of federalism, distinguishing between powers assigned to the federal government and powers reserved to the states.

Principle 2—which I call the principle of the dispersal of power—has, I think, the same sort of status as Principle 1, the separation of powers. It is not a legal principle, not an enforceable principle of the legal constitution. (True, the Constitution does divide power, but Principle 2 embodies a particular theory about why this is important that the Constitution does not necessarily embrace.) Principles 4 and 5, by contrast, are evidently principles of the U.S. Constitution, and Principle 3 is an umbrella term for a number of principles such as the presidential veto, the Senate's "advise-and-consent role" in a number of areas, and the principle of judicial review of legislation.[13]

It is common in essays of this kind to go on to excoriate judges and colleagues for "confusing" Principles 1 through 5 with one another and for using the language of separation of powers loosely and inaccurately. No doubt, Professor Vile is right to say that the separation of powers "represents an area of political thought in which there has been an extraordinary confusion in the definition and use of terms."[14] But it is futile for the analytic philosopher to go on pedantically in those tones. People use a phrase as they use it. All I want to say is that Principle 1 (the separation of executive, judicial, and legislative powers from one another) has some importance in our constitutional theory even apart from—or over and above—the importance of the four other principles I mentioned. What matters to me is that we isolate and understand that importance. We can then choose to use the *phrase* "separation of powers" as we like, maybe as though it represented a conglomeration of the considerations that pertain to Principles 1, 2, and 3 on my list, and perhaps 4 and 5 as well. But at least we will now have some grasp on a particular set of considerations that really can't be identified with any one of the other principles except Principle 1.

Also, I don't at all mean to deny the importance of the other principles, particularly (in this context) Principles 2 and 3. According to Rick Pildes and Daryl Levinson, "the great problem to be solved" at the time of the Founding "was to design governance institutions that would afford 'practical security' against 'excessive concentrations of political power.'"[15] That was important for a number of reasons:

(a) It was important perhaps just to reduce the amount of power in anyone's hands and thus the amount of damage to liberty or other interests that any fallible or corrupt official might be able to do.
(b) Or, maybe competition between dispersed centers of power might have been thought healthy and productive: Pildes and Levinson talk of "vigorous, self-sustaining political competition between the legislative and executive branches."[16]
(c) We may divide power because we want there to be multiple centers of recourse—many places to which citizens can appeal when they are not receiving satisfaction from other centers of government.
(d) Or its value might be purely symbolic (and no less important for that): it was crucial, I think, to republican thought in America to avoid the institution, internally, of any sovereign power within the Constitution comparable (for example) to the "sovereignty" of the British Parliament.[17]

From this point of view, the separation of powers might be thought of as a means to the division of power. Since we want to divide power in order to disperse it, what better than to begin by dividing the power of a judge from that of a legislator and from that of an executive official?

But that cannot be the whole story about the separation of powers. For one thing, Principle 2 might require a much finer-grained division than Principle 1 can supply: it might look for bicameral division within the legislature, for example, or it might look to reject any theory of the unified executive. Moreover, certain justifications for the dispersal of power, such as justification (b), might make no sense so far as the functional separation is concerned: in what sense are we to imagine "self-sustaining competition" between, say, courts and legislatures, particularly if courts are thought of, as they usually are in the separation-of-powers tradition, as performing straightforward adjudicative functions (deciding cases) rather than reviewing legislation. In what sense can we speak of "healthy competition" between deciding cases and making law?

On the other hand, the separation of powers may have features that are unpalatable from the perspective of Principle 2. The functional separation of powers may be associated with something like a principle of legislative supremacy, at least in the sense that it envisions the legislature as having an initiating place on the assembly line of lawmaking and law enforcement. That is what John Locke thought, and I believe M. J. C. Vile is wrong to say that "the main objection to seeing Locke as a proponent of the doctrine [of the separation of powers], even in a modified form, is his emphatic assertion of legislative supremacy."[18] Since Locke is emphatically not suggesting that legislative supremacy entitles legislators to perform adjudicative and executive functions, Vile's complaint against Locke must be premised on something like Principle 2 or Principle 3, not on Principle 1 in and of itself.

I have less space to devote to it, but I think something similar can be said about the relation between Principle 1 and Principle 3. We did not invent a distinction among legislative, executive, and adjudicative powers in order to establish the existence of entities that could check and balance one another. The Framers may have had a "vision that power should be divided and balanced creatively to prevent misuse,"[19] but that was not the only vision in play and not the vision specific to Principle 1. The distinction of powers under Principle 1—if it makes sense at all—is given to us by a theory of articulated governance that distinguishes these functions for what they are, not what they can do to hold one another in check. Ordinary adjudication is different from legislating, and the difference is important—important, as I will say, for the rule of law—and it would remain important on that ground whether or not judicial power was also conceived as a way of limiting legislatures.

In a recent article, Adrian Vermeule considers various constitutional and other legal devices for ensuring that no one person or agency can act without the concurrence of another.[20] This makes sense under the auspices of Principle 3, and it may be an advantage of what is envisaged by Principle 2 that it makes available separate entities for performing this task. But I cannot really see why Vermeule identifies this function with the separation of powers, among other principles.[21] Or rather I can sort of see it: using his example, the fact that there is a legislature that is distinct from the presidency means that we can set things up so the president cannot declare war on his own initiative; there is this other entity that we can say has to concur as well. But the idea that this could be one of the reasons why we have a separation between legislative and executive powers seems strange. At best, it is a side benefit of a separation set up on intrinsic grounds of differentiation of function.

I have said that the importance of Principles 2 and 3, great though it is, does not account for all of the importance of Principle 1, the separation of powers. The importance of Principle 1 is predicated on the vital distinction between various functions of governance—legislative, adjudicative, and executive functions—considered in and of themselves, and the vitality of *that* distinction may be of little inherent interest from the point of view of Principles 2 and 3. All that Principle 2 cares about is that power be dispersed; it doesn't care particularly what the dispersed powers are. And all that Principle 3 cares about is that power check power or be required to concur in another power's exercise; again, what the powers are that counterpoise each other in this manner is of incidental interest.

We can put the same point the other way around. People worry about whether the functional separation envisaged in Principle 1 is archaic; they worry about the difficulty of applying it to modern administrative agencies, for example, which seem to perform both rulemaking and quasi-adjudicative functions. Professor Vile speaks of a "realization that the functional concepts of the doctrine of the separation of powers were inadequate to describe and explain the operations of government" in the modern world. He says "we have seen the emergence of terms such as "quasi-judicial," "delegated legislation," or "administrative justice," representing attempts to adapt the older categories to new problems.[22] I do not think Vile actually accepts the obsolescence of the doctrine, but he sees the problem as important. But it is not important, and cannot be made important, from the point of view of Principle 2 or Principle 3. A quasi-judicial body is just as good a place to disperse power into or to use as a check against other exercises of power as a judicial body: what matters is the dispersal or the checking, not the taxonomy. But for the separation of powers, considered separately as Principle 1, the taxonomy is all-important. And now we have to begin our discussion of why.

3. FOR THE MAINTENANCE OF LIBERTY?

At the beginning of *Constitutionalism and the Separation of Powers,* M. J. C. Vile goes to considerable trouble to produce a pure definition of the separation of powers, distinguished from adjacent principles. He says "[a] 'pure doctrine' of the separation of powers might be formulated in the following way":

> It is essential for the establishment and maintenance of political liberty that the government be divided into three branches or departments, the legislature, the executive, and the judiciary. To each of these three branches there is a corresponding identifiable function of government, legislative, executive, or judicial. Each branch of the government must be confined to the exercise of its own function and not allowed to encroach upon the functions of the other branches. Furthermore, the persons who compose these three agencies of government must be kept separate and distinct, no individual being allowed to be at the same time a member of more than one branch.

It is a fine definition, as is the meditation on the difficulties of "pure" theory that accompanies it.[23]

It is interesting though that Vile chose to incorporate into his "pure" definition a reference to the value consideration that he thought made the separation of powers important: "It is essential for the establishment and maintenance of political liberty . . ." Are we to be committed by definition to that account of the principle's importance? I am not sure. On the one hand, Vile could say that the positive presence of the principle in our canonical political theory is as a principle crucial for liberty. That is how Madison described it, and Montesquieu, too. Others, however, might be mindful of the possibility of explicating the value of the principle in other terms: Jeremy Bentham complained that Montesquieu's discussion of the separation of powers was "destitute of all reference to the greatest happiness of the greatest number."[24]

I do not want to pander to Bentham, but I think we should keep an open mind on this. Maybe the separation of powers matters most for liberty. Maybe it matters also for other values such as the rule of law. (Of course, the rule of law may in turn be thought to matter mainly for liberty's sake, but that is not necessarily so; many people relate the rule of law to values such as dignity rather than or as well as liberty.)[25] I want to keep this possibility open, for I think the rule of law may possibly offer a refreshing account of why the separation of powers is important. And the first canonical account of the importance of the separation of powers that I want to look at does invoke what we would call rule-of-law considerations, though, as I said, it is arguable that those considerations in turn point us to liberty.

4. THE LOCKEAN JUSTIFICATION

One of the earliest and most interesting arguments specifically about the separation of powers is found in John Locke's *Second Treatise of Government*.[26]

Early on in his discussion of political or civil society, Locke makes a pitch for investing legislative power in a large representative assembly. Legislative authority should be placed, he says,

> in collective Bodies of Men, call them Senate, Parliament, or what you please. By which means every single person became subject, equally with other the meanest Men, to those Laws, which he himself, as part of the Legislative had established: nor could any one, by his own Authority, avoid the force of the Law, when once made, nor by any pretence of Superiority, plead exemption, thereby to License his own, or the Miscarriages of any of his Dependents.[27]

The idea here is that oppressive laws are less likely if the lawmakers are ordinary citizens and have to bear the burden of the laws they make themselves:

> [T]he legislative power is put into the hands of divers persons who, duly assembled, have . . . a power to make laws, which when they have done, being separated again, they are themselves subject to the laws they have made; which is a new and near tie upon them to take care that they make them for the public good.[28]

It is a well-known argument, and it continues to be invoked in modern political theory.[29] It is not perfect, of course: a fanatical legislator may be prepared to have the burdens of his oppressive law fall on him or his family, or the generality of laws may be mitigated by the use of predicates such as race or gender, which make it less likely that the legislator in particular will suffer under its auspices. It is an imperfect prophylactic against oppression, but an important one nonetheless.

But the point is that it definitely will not work if the lawmakers can control the application of the law (i.e., if the lawmakers can make prosecutorial decisions or participate in adjudication), for then they will have the power to direct the burden of the laws that they make away from themselves. As Locke puts it,

> [I]t may be too great temptation to human frailty . . . for the same persons who have the power of making laws to have also in their hands the power to execute them, whereby they may exempt themselves from obedience to the laws they make, and suit the law, both in its making and execution, to their own private advantage.[30]

So as a necessary condition for this prophylactic against oppression to work, we must separate the function of lawmaking from the other functions of executive and adjudication. Necessary, I emphasize, not sufficient. As Pildes and Levinson indicate, party cahoots between legislators and executive officials may have the effect of undermining the separation, even if the powers themselves are put in different hands.[31]

Locke's argument is not the most sophisticated argument in the world, but it is an interesting one. And it has the advantage of pointing specifically to functional separation. It is not a theory about the dispersal of power as such, or about checks and balances. It is a theory oriented specifically toward Principle 1.

5. SEPARATION IN THOUGHT

I also want to mention one other argument Locke makes, though I am afraid this is an argument *against* separation of powers. Well, sort of.

It begins from his realization that the tripartite division of functions envisaged in the traditional formulas may not be satisfactory. Locke envisages a fourth power, the federative power: "the power of war and peace, leagues and alliances, and all the transactions with all persons and communities without the commonwealth."[32] We can't go into the details here, but Locke makes a pretty good case for saying that this power should be united with, not separated from, the executive power. Or at least it should be united in the same hands, the same agency, even if it is understood to be separate in principle.[33]

And that's a point I want to stress. Even while he accepts that the same person will have to exercise both powers, Locke maintains that it is important for everyone to understand that the powers in question are in principle separate. Listen to how he puts the point:

> Though, as I said, the executive and federative power of every community be really distinct in themselves, yet they are hardly to be separated, and placed at the same time, in the hands of distinct persons: for both of them requiring the force of the society for their exercise, it is almost impracticable to place the force of the common-wealth in distinct, and not subordinate hands; or that the executive and federative power should be placed in persons, that might act separately, whereby the force of the public would be under different commands: which would be apt some time or other to cause disorder and ruin.[34]

The distinction may not seem to matter much, but compare it to what the U.S. Constitution does in Article II. It simply assumes in the juxtaposition of clauses 1 and 2 of the article that domestic enforcement of the laws and direction of foreign policy are the same—both executive functions. I have heard esteemed colleagues say that is what Locke thought also, but it is not. He thought that the federative and the executive were quite different powers—not least because the federative power "is much less capable to be directed by antecedent, standing, positive laws, than the executive."[35] So even if the powers are placed in the same hands, it is going to be very important for people to be extra clear in some other way about the distinction, lest the inherent lawlessness of the federative power infect the emphatically law-governed nature of the ordinary (as opposed to the prerogative) actions of the domestic executive.

The importance of this kind of separation *at least in thought* is usually neglected in the separation of powers tradition. And probably for good reason; by itself, it is hardly enough to satisfy the requirements of constitutionalism. But think about it for a moment anyway.

Consider, for example, judges in "Diplock courts" in Northern Ireland, where, during the troubles, criminal cases were often tried without juries. Though the same individual combined in himself the functions of judge and jury, he did not fail to separate them in thought and to a certain extent in action. A judge hearing a case would scrupulously differentiate the functions, for example, by laboriously issuing end-of-trial directions to himself and then taking the time to make distinct findings of fact, and only then proceeding, if there was a guilty verdict, to sentence the defendant. It is not a perfect example, because it involves an intrajudicial separation. But I think it is possible to grasp the difference between a Diplock judge insisting on the articulation of these different roles and a Diplock judge merely blurring them.

Or, for a second example, consider the political theory of Thomas Hobbes. We know that Hobbes was an adamant opponent of the separation of powers. The various powers of government are, he says, "indivisible," "incommunicable and inseparable."[36] But there is all the difference in the world between (i) a Hobbesian ruler exercising the united powers of sovereignty in a crude, undifferentiated way and (ii) his exercising those powers as separable incidents of his authority, even though they are united in one set of hands. And Hobbes's sovereign is mostly a ruler of type (ii). He does not rule in an undifferentiated way. He thinks it is important, for example, that there be legislation enacted and promulgated prior to the exercise of sovereign power against any person, so that people know where they stand and so there is no misunderstanding.[37] And he envisages courts—which are of course the sovereign's courts—to deal with the application of the laws.

I think this distinction is important between (i) a sovereign who just blurs the distinction between the powers he has because, in crude and simple terms, they are all *his,* and (ii) a sovereign who unites all power in his person but nevertheless articulates the powers in his exercise of them. For a type (i) absolutist, power is just exercised in a lashing-out kind of way. Not only is the one person judge, jury, and executioner, but he barely discerns the difference between adjudicating, fact-finding, and punishment.

It may be hard, though, for a type (ii) absolutist to resist falling back into type (i) undifferentiated authority. We find Hobbes backsliding on a number of occasions, as in this passage from *De Cive,* in effect denying the distinction between execution and judgment:

> [B]ecause the right of the Sword is nothing else but to have power by right to use the sword at his own will, it followes, that the judgement of its right use pertaines to the same party: for if the Power of judging were in one, and the power of executing in another, nothing would be done.[38]

He came close again to blurring the line when he suggested that one reason the sovereign cannot be bound by the general laws he enacts is that he can change them whenever he likes:

> The sovereign of a Commonwealth ... is not subject to the civil laws. For having power to make and repeal laws, he may, when he pleaseth, free himself from that subjection by repealing those laws that trouble him, and making of new; and consequently he was free before. For he is free that can be free when he will: ... and therefore he that is bound to himself only is not bound.[39]

All of this goes to show that this distinction may not matter very much in and of itself, and that our tradition of separation of powers has been wise to insist on separation of institution, office, and personnel, not just on an abstract identification and mental awareness of differentiated functions.

But the fact that this distinction is insufficient in itself does not mean that it may not be important in the context of a more full-blooded principle. It may still be the case that part of what we deplore about violations of the separation of powers is that they often fail to distinguish even between the various phases of power or the various functions that one and the same person or institution is exercising.

6. WHAT MONTESQUIEU MIGHT HAVE MEANT

I suspect this is part of what worried Montesquieu about concentration of powers—not just that they would be in one set of hands but that in those hands even the conceptual distinctions between legislating and judging, and between judging and enforcement, would be erased.

One of Montesquieu's images, indeed a very common image in mid- and late eighteenth-century political thought, is the image of "Turkish" justice—a judge in a despotic state who simply comes on someone doing something and lashes out at him, beating him, killing him, or taking his property, without anything remotely like an account of what the victim is supposed to have done,[40] let alone any sort of hearing. "Among the Turks, where the three powers are united in the person of the Sultan, an atrocious despotism reigns."[41] That is from the famous chapter in *The Spirit of the Laws* on the constitution of England.

A little earlier in the book, Montesquieu tells us something odd. He observes, "It is constantly said that justice should be rendered everywhere as it is in Turkey."[42] Really? Constantly said by whom? The answer, it turns out, is that this is constantly said by people who are irritated by the elaborate technicality and legalism of French law, where there are innumerable rules, privileges, and jurisdictions, and interminable procedures for securing any sort of relief. Each claim is broken down into its detailed parts and assessed against the relevant standards and the repository of judicial decisions. And many good-hearted people apparently protested against this elaborate legalism, imagining that it would be better to be ruled by a sort of Solomonic cadi figure, able to cut through all the legalism and see through to the moral essentials of the matter.[43] And Montesquieu could hardly believe his ears: articulate legal structures, he says, are all that stand between monarchy and despotism.[44] You don't get wise King Solomon if you take the Turkish option; you get lazy, unthinking, undifferentiated exercises of power:

> In Turkey, where one pays very little attention to the fortune, life, or honor of the subjects, all disputes are speedily concluded in one way or another. The manner of ending them is not important, provided they are ended. The pasha is no sooner informed than he has the pleaders bastinadoed according to his fancy and sends them back home.[45]

What's important, I think, about this image of the failure of the separation of powers is not just that the powers are all in one set of hands; it is that the person who holds them has not even thought to distinguish them.

7. WHERE ARE THE REST OF THE EIGHTEENTH-CENTURY ARGUMENTS?

Admittedly, this is a bit of a reach as far as Montesquieu is concerned. But everything is a bit of a reach as far as Montesquieu is concerned. Montesquieu actually provides next to nothing in the way of a tissue of argument for the separation of powers in the most famous passages devoted to the subject.

Vile asks, "What does Montesquieu have to say about the separation of powers?" and replies, "A remarkable degree of disagreement exists about what Montesquieu actually did say."[46] In fact, Montesquieu said very little. He announced several times that unless the different powers of government are separated, tyranny would result, but he never really explained why. Much of what he said consists of simple assertions: "When legislative power is united with executive power in a single person or in a single body of the magistracy, there is no liberty." Why not? "Because one can fear that the same monarch or senate that makes tyrannical laws will execute them tyrannically."[47] Tyrannical execution of the laws is always, no doubt, a fearsome possibility, but why is it more likely when the laws have been enacted by the same person as the person applying them? The argument is not spelled out.[48] I guess Montesquieu might be endorsing the argument spelled out by Locke about ways of avoiding oppressive laws, so that "tyrannical execution of the laws" refers to their execution in such a way as to exempt the lawmakers. But one has to do an awful lot of construction to reach that interpretation.

Often Montesquieu offers little more than tautologies:

> Nor is there liberty if the power of judging is not separate from the legislative power and from executive power. If it were joined to legislative power, the power over the life and liberty of the citizens would be arbitrary, for the judge would be the legislator.[49]

In other words, the failure to separate powers leads to arbitrariness because it involves . . . a failure to separate the powers. There is the same tautology in this passage:

> If . . . the executive power were entrusted to a certain number of persons drawn from the legislative body, there would no longer be liberty, because the two powers would be united, the same persons belonging and always able to belong to both.[50]

It is time we acknowledged Montesquieu's failure to provide us with arguments explaining in detail why the separation of powers is necessary for liberty. It is not unusual. Among serious students of Montesquieu, it is widely recognized that linear argument is not his forte.[51] (I can say that; I am a devotee of *The Spirit of the Laws,* but I learn from what is hinted at rather than articulated in its assertions.)

I fear that Montesquieu's failure to spell out the arguments infected James Madison as well. When Madison was trying to establish that Montesquieu argued for a limited rather than a complete separation of powers, he referred to Montesquieu's reasons for the principle:

> The reasons on which Montesquieu grounds his maxim are a further demonstration of his meaning. "When the legislative and executive powers are united in the same person or body" says he, "there can be no liberty, because apprehensions may arise lest the same monarch or senate should enact tyrannical laws, to execute them in a tyrannical manner." Again "Were the power of judging joined with the legislative, the life and liberty of the subject would be exposed to arbitrary controul, for the judge would then be the legislator. Were it joined to the executive power, the judge might behave with all the violence of an oppressor." Some of these reasons are more fully explained in other passages; but briefly stated as they are here, they sufficiently establish the meaning which we have put on this celebrated maxim of this celebrated author.[52]

Madison doesn't tell us, however, where these other passages are (where Montesquieu's reasons are supposed to have been spelled out more explicitly) or what they say. And Madison himself just falls in with Montesquieu's practice of abbreviated argumentation, with the bare assertion that

> The accumulation of all powers, legislative, executive, and judiciary, in the same hands, whether of one, a few, or many, and whether hereditary, self-appointed, or elective, may justly be pronounced the very definition of tyranny.[53]

He adds that "it will be proper to investigate the sense in which the preservation of liberty requires that the three great departments of power should be separate and distinct," but that turns out to be just an investigation of the extent of desirable separation, not an account of the connection with liberty.

I suspect, too, that this is why we tend to blur the distinction between the various principles I described in Section 3 of this chapter—particularly the distinction between separation of powers, on the one hand, and the principle of the division of power and the principle of checks and balances on the other. We quickly switch over to the latter two when we are pressed for an argument about the importance of the separation of powers, because we understand *their* justifications but we have not been bequeathed any good arguments specific to the separation of powers by our heritage of political thought.

I don't mean the tone of these comments to be skeptical. I am just lamenting the lack of argument in the canonical sources. When Donald Elliot sought to explain why our separation of powers jurisprudence was so abysmal, he might have acknowledged that we came by it honestly. The political theory was abysmal even in its pre-jurisprudential form, and we haven't done nearly enough since the time of Montesquieu and Madison to acknowledge that and to try and fill it out.

8. ARTICULATED GOVERNANCE

So we have to do a lot of the work on our own. We get a little bit of help from John Locke in the seventeenth century; we do not get much help from the eighteenth-century theorists, even the ones nearest and dearest to us (i.e., James Madison), though there are things we figure out for ourselves that we can read back into their work.

Fortunately, the terms in which the principle presents itself offer us good clues to its importance. The principle takes the basic process of governance and divides it conceptually into three main functions: enacting a law, adjudicating disputes on the basis of a law, and administering a legal decision. That conceptualization suggests two things. It suggests first that it is a mistake to think of the exercise of political power as something simple—as a straightforward use of coercive force by public authority, for example. And second, it suggests that each of the phases into which the principle divides the exercise of power is important in itself and raises issues of distinct institutional concern.

I alluded to the first argument in Sections 6 and 7, suggesting (in Section 6) that even if one has a Hobbesian sovereign who will not cede power to any coordinate entity, it is still a good thing for the sovereign to be aware of political power as something articulated rather than simple.

The point is not so much about the oppressiveness of the exercise. It may be: A. V. Dicey illustrates his account of the importance of the rule of law with a story about Voltaire, who "was lured off from the table of a Duke, and thrashed by lackeys in the presence of their noble master . . . and because [he] complained of this outrage, [he] paid a visit to the Bastille."[54] Our outrage about Voltaire's treatment fuels our anger about any lack of process in the matter and about the absence of legal recourse. But even if it were a deserved thrashing, we would still want the exercise to be preceded (by a considerable length of time) by the enactment of a statute prohibiting whatever it was that Voltaire was supposed to have done and threatening corporal punishment; we would want it also to be preceded by a judicial hearing at which Voltaire could state his side of the matter; and by a solemn executive determination that the sentence of the court was to be carried out in such-and-such a fashion, and at such-and-such a time (after opportunities for appeal, etc.) We would want the thing to be slowed down in this way and an orderly succession of phases to succeed one another in due form.

Notice, therefore, that this is not necessarily a way of *limiting* government, in the sense of curbing its action, though I guess it could be described as a way of making action more difficult because more is involved.[55] But the idea is to channel it, not restrict it, and, through the channeling, to open up the decision-making for access by Voltaire or anyone else at various points.

As the Diceyan context of our illustration reveals, these concerns are in large part concerns associated with the rule of law.[56] The rule of law is not just the requirement that where there *is* law, it must be complied with; it is the requirement that government action must, by and large, be conducted under the auspices of law, which means that, unless there is very good reason to the contrary, law should be created in advance to authorize the actions that government is going to have to perform. This usually means an articulated process of the sort we have been talking about, so that the various aspects of lawmaking and legally authorized action are not just run together in a single gestalt.

We begin with an action or type of action that it is envisaged the state may want to perform, and that would affect one or some of its citizens. We propose and deliberate on the contours of that as a matter of general policy. The representatives of the people settle, deliberatively, on a clear set of formulations and they vote. Those formulated and authorized norms are then communicated to the people and to the agencies that will be responsible for their administration.⁵⁷ The people have time to take the norms on board, internalize them, and begin to organize the conduct of their lives accordingly, while the agencies begin the process of weaving these norms into the broader fabric of their supervision of various aspects of social life and begin developing strategies for (as it might be) inspection and enforcement. In these ways, the norms embodying the original policy have time to "settle in" and become a basis on which people can order their expectations. At that time, disputes or allegations about violations of the norms may arise. The agencies responsible for the norms may initiate an action—a prosecution or something of the sort. If the matter is not resolved, it will go before a court, where the issue of compliance will be argued out, not just factually but in terms of how the norms that were communicated to the people are to be understood and how they are to be related to the rest of the law. After a hearing, there will be a determination, and if necessary further enforcement of, or supervision of compliance with, whatever order the court makes.

This, by my count, is a ten-part process. But the numbers don't matter. What matters is that the governmental action has become articulated and many of the stages in that articulation correspond to rule-of-law requirements, such as the principles of clarity, promulgation, the integrity of expectations, due process, and so on. Each of those elements embodies the concerns about liberty, dignity, and respect that the rule of law represents. They offer multiple points of access to norms and multiple modes of internalization. Severally and together, they represent the stepwise incorporation of new norms into the lives and agency of those who are to be subject to them. There is a serious failure of the rule of law when any of these various steps is omitted, or when any two or more of them are blurred and treated as undivided. And that, I think, is where we find the overlap between respect for the rule of law and respect for the principle of the separation of powers.

I am not saying that the separation of powers and the rule of law are one and the same. The rule of law has some aspects that have nothing to do with the separation of powers. Some would say that this picture doesn't do justice to the full tenor or force of rule-of-law concerns. That is probably right; it is not meant to. But the two principles engage similar or overlapping concerns. To insist on being ruled by law is, among other things, to insist on being ruled by a process that answers to the institutional articulation required by separation of powers: there must be lawmaking before there is adjudication or administration, and there must be adjudication and the due process that that entails before there is the enforcement of any order (or of other preexisting settled standing laws). To insist, as Dicey does, that "no man is punishable or can be lawfully made to suffer in body or goods except for a distinct breach of law" is to insist that his punishing or suffering must be preceded by a process as elaborate as this.[58] It may not be an extempore or off-the-cuff use of political authority.

For these purposes, it does not matter whether the authority in question is legitimate in itself, for example on account of its democratic credentials. It does not matter that it has been, in some overall sense, authorized by the people. Even if the exercise of power has been legitimated democratically—in the sense that someone has been chosen as a political leader in free and fair elections and now he wants to put the policies that he ran on into force—*still,* what he proposes and regards himself as authorized to do must be broken down into these component parts. It must be housed in and channeled through these procedural and institutional forms, successively one after the other. That is what the rule of law requires, and I believe that is what is mandated also by the separation of powers. The legislature, the judiciary, and the executive must each have its separate say before power impacts on the individual.

9. THE INTEGRITY OF THE THREE PARTICULAR INSTITUTIONS

That last formulation—"the legislature, the judiciary and the executive; each must have its separate say before power impacts on the individual"—sounds like a version of checks and balances, a requirement of separate concurrences in the proposed exercise of power from three institutions or agencies. But that really doesn't get at what the separation of powers requires.

The separation of powers requires not just that the legislature, judiciary, and executive concur in the use of power against some particular person, X. Instead it requires that the legislature should do its kind of work—*legislative* work—in this matter, which really means not addressing X's particular situation at all; it requires that the judiciary should do its kind of adjudicative work in regard to X and X's relation to the law that the legislature has enacted; and it requires that the executive should do its work of administration, not only the prosecution of X and the enforcement of any order made against him but also the development of broad strategies of implementation for the law that the legislature has enacted.

The principle holds that each of these respective tasks has an integrity of its own, which is contaminated when executive or judicial considerations affect the way in which legislation is carried out, when legislative and executive considerations affect the way the judicial function is performed, and when the tasks specific to the executive are tangled up with the tasks of lawmaking and adjudication.

Some kinds of such contamination are familiar to us. Madison and others were concerned that state legislatures in the immediate post-Revolutionary period were enacting resolutions aimed at the situations of particular individuals: putting them out of business, for example, or confiscating their estates.[59] We see the concern against this referred to in the bills of attainder clause of Article I of the U.S. Constitution, but it also reflects concerns about the rule of law, in the sense discussed in Section 8, and overlapping concerns about the separation of powers. The idea is that it is not appropriate for a legislature to proceed in that way. Not only does it run together what ought to be distinct functions of government, but it means that society does not get the benefit of the legislature's doing the distinctive and important work it is set up to do for matters of this kind (if anybody, like X, is to be put out of business or their estates confiscated). We want there to be a place where that sort of thing is deliberated, not with reference to X in particular but in general. That is, we want there to be an institutional setting where the assembled representatives of the people can consider and discuss, in a general way (i.e., at the level of normative generalization and general justificatory considerations), laws that could conceivably authorize this sort of thing. It is hard, under the best of circumstances, to maintain the focus at this general level. But that is what legislatures are for, in our scheme of governance, and the separation of powers tries to facilitate that by making it harder for those whose focus is more on individual cases (either in an executive way or in an adjudicative way) to bring their specific mentality into play to affect or undermine the legislative mentality.

I mention the possibility of executive-minded people or judicially minded people coming into the legislature as a sort of distraction from its quintessentially legislative task. Equally, the legislature can be distracted from the inside, by its own failure to focus deliberations in the way and at the level of abstraction that the legislative function requires. For example, if, as in a Westminster-style constitution, the executive is a committee of the ruling party in the legislature, then there is a danger that the legislature will gravitate naturally toward the administration's agenda. That is not necessarily a bad thing, so long as members of the cabinet, say, are able to distinguish genuinely legislative agenda-setting—proposing that this general policy be embodied in a statute or this bill enacted—from an agenda that is executive-minded in its character. (That again is a way in which the considerations discussed earlier about separating powers at least in thought matters for our discussion.)[60] But if the legislature is dominated and overborne by the executive's need just to "get things done"—*whatever it takes* to be able to act against X, for example—then that is a problem from the point of view of this principle.

We are also familiar with concerns about the contamination of the adjudicative function with executive functions, ranging from the Soviet practice of "telephone justice"[61] to the famous dissent of Lord Atkin in the wartime British case of *Liversidge v. Anderson* [1942] AC 206, 244: "I view with apprehension the attitude of judges who on a mere question of construction when face to face with claims involving the liberty of the subject show themselves more executive minded than the executive."[62] This is not to say that it is inappropriate for judges to apprehend and even sympathize with the needs and exigencies of executive government, particularly in wartime or a state of emergency; but their job is to balance executive claims and concerns against those of liberty, for example, *according to law,* not simply to swat away irritating challenges to executive authority. The role of a court is to settle disputes according to law and to conduct highly formalized hearings on any question about whether action should be taken against an individual, an agency, or a firm for a failure to comply with applicable law.

What about judicial lawmaking? We all know that judges make law as well as discover it; through their collective power to establish a line of precedent, they in effect create and promulgate new norms for the community as well as putting authoritative new glosses through their powers of interpretation on norms created by other institutions. There is much to be said about this familiar topic, and most of it we cannot pursue here. Suffice to say that our familiarity with judicial lawmaking, especially in a common law system, should not blind us to the difficulties it poses from a separation-of-powers point of view. It certainly poses difficulties from the point of view of the particular parties before the lawmaking court, who find in effect that their rights are being determined by new law imposed on them retroactively. And we see, in cases such as *Teague v. Lane* and its progeny, the heroic and convoluted efforts that have to be made to prevent this retroactivity from reaching further into the legal system.[63] Maybe the difficulties are neither avoidable nor insuperable, but they are the kinds of difficulties that arise when the logic of one kind of governance function is contaminated with another. The separation of powers endorses and upholds the distinct character of each of the three functions of government, and what we see in the case of adjudication is that it can impose on legal governance.

It is a little harder to see the threats that the executive faces in this regard—the threats to the authority or purity of its essential function. This is partly because the executive usually seems to be the aggressor in separation-of-powers issues: it is always the executive threatening the independence of the judiciary or the executive undermining the integrity of the legislative process. When this happens, the executive is usually conceived to be powerful enough that the damage, if there is any, is always done to the other power in the equation. So it is hard to think of cases where the integrity of the executive's distinct function in government is corrupted by the encroachment of the other powers.

Still, the sort of thing that might be at stake here can be illustrated by a couple of examples, neither of them perfect. Forgetting for the moment John Locke's distinction between the executive and the federative powers, we may want to say that control of military action and the conduct of war is a quintessential military function. Both generals and executive officials often complain about the encroachment of the judiciary on the conduct of armed operations. They say, "You cannot hold hearings on the battlefield." This is a sort of illustration of apprehensions about damage done to the performance of executive functions as such by the encroachments of other branches.

Similarly, in all executive operations, there may be complaints that processes of deliberation, more appropriate to the legislature, are being imposed on the executive, hobbling and limiting its agility and decisiveness of action, which are defining features of its modus operandi as an executive. The executive, it may be said, is not supposed to be a talking shop; or, the kind of talk executive officials have to engage in is much more a matter of strategizing and planning public administration than debating the general merits of policy. Its shape is appropriately managerial rather than dialectical and, however much we believe in deliberative democracy, we should be wary of trying to transform executive deliberation into a mode of discussion more appropriate for one of the other branches. Lon Fuller's arguments about the inappropriateness of adjudicative procedures in allocative economic decision-making in a mixed economy are also relevant here.[64]

What, finally, should we say about administrative rulemaking, which seems to represent an assumption of legislative responsibility by agencies within the executive branch? One advantage of treating the separation of powers as a distinct political principle, disentangled from the legal details of the U.S. constitutional scheme, is that we can deal with this issue more sensitively than those who are concerned with nondelegation doctrines and so forth. Let us assume—what seems more or less right—that agency rulemaking is a sort of legislative function. Then, the first thing the separation of powers commands is that, as far as possible, the processes and perhaps even the personnel devoted to this sort of lawmaking should be separate from the processes and perhaps the personnel involved in the administration of the rules and in the adjudication of cases arising under them. It is important that these functions be conceived as distinct and that they be distinguished in institutional space—even if the whole thing is happening under the auspices of the branch of government labeled "executive."

The Constitution, as framed, sets up a branch called "the legislative," establishes it as an elective institution, and assigns important legislative functions to it. Indeed, Article I of the Constitution begins by saying that *"All legislative Powers herein granted shall be vested in a Congress of the United States, which shall consist of a Senate and House of Representatives"* (emphasis added). But the principle of the separation of powers, conceived (as it must be, if John Manning is right) as a political principle rather than a legal principle does not require that. What it requires is that legislative powers, wherever located, should be separated in conception and, as far as possible, institutionally from executive and judicial powers. Even if Article I (1) amounts to a nondelegation rule, such a rule is not necessarily endorsed by the principle of the separation of powers.[65] The latter principle is indifferent to delegation, provided that the institution to which lawmaking is delegated remains distinctively legislative in character and, as I said, provided it is distinguished clearly in conception and, as far as possible, institutionally, from judicial and enforcement functions wherever they, in turn, are located. What is important, from the separation-of-powers point of view, is that there be a legislative stage to the enforcement of administration policy, and that the integrity of that stage be protected against encroachment both as a matter of process and as a matter of mentality by other stages of governance.

In this section, I have argued that the principle of the separation of powers commands us to respect the character and distinctiveness of each of the three main functions of government. But I do not mean that we should regard the separation-of-powers principle as a conglomerate of three separate principles: one commanding respect for the legislature, one commanding respect for the courts, and a third commanding respect for the executive. There are aspects of what the separation of powers requires that can be seen in this light—for instance, people commonly talk about the independence of the judiciary as a distinct principle of modern constitutionalism. And I have tried to encourage similar solicitude for the dignity of legislation.[66] But it would be unfortunate if each of these were conceived entirely independently of the others. Commanding respect for the integrity of each of these three operations of government is important precisely because they have to fit together into the general articulated scheme of governance on which I placed so much emphasis inthis section. We want these three things, each in its distinctive integrity, to be slotted into a common scheme of government that enables people to confront political power in a differentiated way.

10. A FORLORN AND OBSOLETE PRINCIPLE?

In their book *The Executive Unbound*, Eric Posner and Adrian Vermeule talk of the separation of powers as suffering these days "through an enfeebled old age."[67] Their understanding of the separation principle is probably too closely tied to Madisonian checking and balancing to be of much use in our analysis.[68] But I suspect they would say also that the particular meaning I have assigned to the principle of the separation of powers is also one that is obsolescent in modern circumstances. They may be right.

If they are, does this mean that the effort undertaken in this chapter to understand the distinctive character and justification of the principle of the separation of powers is forlorn and useless? No. Even if the principle is dying a sclerotic death, even if it misconceives the character of modern political institutions, it still points to something that was once deemed valuable—namely, *articulated government through successive phases of governance, each of which maintains its own integrity*—and it may still be valuable even though we can't have the benefit of it anymore. It is always useful to have a sense of what we have lost, and often—regrettably—we only see something clearly as it falls away from our grasp. The principle of the separation of powers—as distinguished from the principle of checks and balances and as distinguished from the general principle commanding the dispersal of power—had something distinctive to offer in our constitutionalist thinking. Let others be ruthless and dismissive of the dying; I say we need to know, even if only elegiacally, what it is a pity we have lost.

Conversely, in my account, the separation of powers raises a genuine set of concerns and warns against a certain oversimplification of governance—concerns and a warning that are not given under the auspices of any other principle (though perhaps the rule of law comes close). The concerns do not evaporate even as the principle is made to seem impracticable. Posner and Vermeule insist strongly on "ought implies can."[69] They say we should not shed tears for something we can no longer have. Okay. But as we dry our eyes and look clear-headedly to the future, we will see the concerns about undifferentiated governance (endorsed by an undifferentiated process of elective acclamation) still standing there, concerns we wouldn't have recognized but for our thinking through this forlorn principle. Grinning or grimacing, we need to be aware of what these concerns are that we now say cannot be answered, what dangers (previously warned against) we now seem willing to court or embrace.

CHAPTER FOUR

Bicameralism and the Separation of Powers

MY TOPIC FOR this chapter is bicameralism. I want to explore the virtues of a second legislative chamber, the basis of election to a second chamber, the functions that may be served by debating and voting on legislation in two chambers rather than one, and the relationship of all of this to the principle of the separation of powers, which we discussed in Chapter 3. Our discussion in this chapter will also help open up some other institutional topics in the theory of politics. I want to ask: What is the relation between bicameralism, on the one hand, and the theory of representation, the theory of legislative due process, and, as my title suggests, the separation of powers?

1. THE DEBATE IN THE UNITED KINGDOM

Let us focus for a moment on the U.K. House of Lords, which has been much reformed—though incompletely—in recent years. It has moved away from being a plenary assembly of hereditary peers;[1] the hereditary element is now represented rather than assembled and hereditary peers can also stand now for seats in the House of Commons. The judges have been moved out.[2] The bishops are still there,[3] but they and the representative rump of earls, dukes, and viscounts are now seen as an anomaly in what is really an appointed assembly, although the appointments basis has operated over the past fifty years as much as a system of public honors (a step or two above a knighthood) as a system of senatorial selection.[4] Until recently, people were appointed as life peers for their service in the past, with not much thought to the prospect of their legislative service in the future.

Everything I say in this chapter will be *relevant* in some way or other to the debate that has taken place in Britain about the future of the House of Lords. But the particularities of that debate will not be my focus, for there is a world out there that wrestles with issues about bicameralism that have nothing to do with what Bentham called Britain's particular "aristocracy-ridden" and "blind-custom-begotten" arrangements.[5] Some of these issues are particular to other countries, like the creaky and decrepit appointments-based system for the Senate of Canada[6] and the demographically disproportionate basis of representation in the U.S. Senate compounded by the peculiar supermajoritarian arrangements that chamber has adopted,[7] not to mention the disgraceful abandonment of legislative due process in what has been since 1950 the unicameral Parliament of New Zealand.[8]

There are also broader issues in political and legal theory such as the relation between bicameralism and judicial review (can they be, in effect, substitutes for one another?) or the relation between bicameralism and supermajoritarianism within a parliamentary assembly (again, is this an either-or choice?),[9] and the relation between bicameralism and other second-look or two-heads-are-better-than-one doctrines in constitutional theory—I mean, for example, principles in the U.S. Constitution that do not allow the president to act in certain matters (such as judicial appointments or treaty-making) without "the advice and consent of the Senate."[10]

I want to allow some of these broader themes to emerge without worrying too much about how they might be embodied in the British context or how their realization in Britain could possibly be brought about. We are going to have to talk a little bit about the U.K., because one of my main themes addresses the possibility that a second chamber might help establish the legislature of that country as an institution genuinely independent of the executive in a way that is not true of the House of Commons or indeed of elected legislatures in any Westminster-style system. When people in Britain say how important it is for the House of Commons to retain its ascendancy in the constitution, I sometimes wonder whether it is really the ascendancy of an elected chamber that they want or whether what they really want to preserve is the guaranteed ascendancy of the Crown and its ministers acting through their whip-based domination of the Commons.

2. BENTHAM AND THE ISSUE OF DIFFERENCE

The key to bicameralism is difference. If a second chamber offers nothing different from the first, then as an aging Bentham wrote in 1830 (after the July Revolution) in a letter to the only slightly younger General Lafayette—*Jeremy Bentham to his Fellow-Citizens of France, on Houses of Peers and Senates*—then it is redundant, every cost incurred in its establishment and maintenance is wasted, and every legislative delay incurred as a result of its separate proceedings is "so much net loss in the account of profit and loss."[11]

Now Bentham's letter is often quoted, but I think seldom read. One commentator writing in 1928 called Bentham's letter "succinct."[12] It is not. It runs to about forty-five repetitive pages, much of it ranting, but a form of breathless, batty, and garrulous[13] ranting that is distinctively Benthamite.[14]

There are one or two lovely touches. Bentham often refers to his fellow citizens of France—Bentham was made an honorary French citizen in 1792—as "my children" (*mes enfants*); he was, after all, eighty-four.[15] And he referred to the United States, when he wanted to talk about the Senate, as "the Anglo-American Union" (not exactly a title that has caught on).[16] Also, at eighty-four, Bentham hadn't lost the power to sting.[17] He thought that American enthusiasm for an upper house—their "quasi-Lords"[18]—resulted from their excessive veneration of Blackstone, whose "servility" and "anility," Bentham said, were well known.[19] Nor have Bentham's stinging critiques lost their power to stop us in our tracks, as for example in his denunciation of the endemically corrupting effect on British public life of the whole system of placeholding and honors—the peerage.[20] He was even prepared to toy with antimonarchism:

> Well then, my fellow-citizens of France! Well then, my fellow-citizens of England! My fellow-citizens of the civilized world! My fellow-citizens of future ages! . . . If no use can be found for a house of peers, why should I not say so? If no use can be found for any second chamber, or any sovereign governing body, other than a set of men chosen and commissioned by the people at large—why should I not say so? If no use can be found for any such functionary as a . . . as a . . . king—(there—the word is written, and the world is not yet come to an end)—why should I not say so? If king and second chamber are—both of them—worse than useless—why should I not say so?[21]

Having said that, it is only fair to acknowledge that Bentham's apprehensions about the delays and abuses of a second chamber were motivated by something more serious than antiaristocracy, antimonarchism, or even anticorruption. What mattered for him above all was legislation,[22] and to the extent that it held up legislation, the downside of bicameralism consisted of "all the evils which . . . the community is suffering, for want of such remedies as it may be in the power of legislation to supply."[23]

3. IMPERFECTABILITY OF REPRESENTATION

We know that Bentham was utterly hostile to second chambers such as the House of Lords. But Bentham was also opposed to the prospect of an *elected* second chamber, though he wrote much less about it. There were few if any models, for even the Senate of the "Anglo-American" Congress was not elected in Bentham's day. Bentham's objection to an elective second chamber was the same as the objection attributed to Emmanuel Sieyès a generation earlier: "[I]f a second chamber dissents from the first, it is mischievous; if it agrees it is superfluous."[24] Bentham's strategy was to say that if there were features of a second house that were thought important for serious and responsible legislating—like the particular aptitude of the members of the second chamber, their longer parliamentary terms, or the gravity of consideration given to legislative measures in the second chamber—then that should be treated as an argument for changing the character of the first chamber, not for instituting a second.

> No need of a second chamber. . . . For, to the first [chamber] belongs the power of giving to the measure whatsoever length of consideration is, in the opinion of that same first chamber, best adapted to it: and the correspondent quantity of deliberation and time being bestowed upon it, any further quantity must, according to that same opinion, be useless.[25]

Or again

> [W]ill it be said that to the second chamber belongs more appropriate aptitude . . . than to the first? . . . [T]his cannot be said: if to this same second

chamber more such appropriate aptitude belongs than to the first, [then] not second ought it to be, but first, or rather . . . the only chamber.²⁶

Or, as Adrian Vermeule has put it, "if the upper house supplies the sober second thought, why have a politically intemperate lower house in the first place?"²⁷

What Bentham did not consider, however (though Vermeule did), was what we may call the Tristram Shandy principle. In his great comic novel *The Life and Opinions of Tristram Shandy, Gentleman,* published in the middle of the eighteenth century, Laurence Sterne reports an observation by Herodotus about the ancient Goths of Germany.²⁸ Apparently, the ancient Goths of Germany, when they had to decide anything important, like going to war, moving their settlements, or entering into a treaty, would debate it not once but twice. The first time, they would debate the issue drunk, and the second time they would debate the issue sober: drunk to give a bit of vigor and spirit to their deliberations, but also sober to add a dimension of prudence and discretion.²⁹ Well, similarly, it is possible that when we want to improve legislative deliberation, we don't just want to introduce sobriety (or whatever virtue) into the legislature; we might actually *want* our measures to be debated *both* ways—to be debated soberly and also to be debated drunkenly. Tacitus, who also reports this custom of the ancient Goths of Germany, tells us that the Germanic tribes believed that drunken consideration produced honesty and enthusiasm:

> At no other time, they think, is the heart so open to frank thoughts or so warm towards noble sentiments. . . . [I]n the freedom of such [deliberation] their inmost feelings are still expressed. . . . On the next day the subject is discussed again, and account is taken of both occasions. They debate while they are incapable of deceit and take the decision when they cannot make a mistake.³⁰

The example is a bit silly, but the principle is not, particularly if we direct it to the idea of representation. Forget drunk and sober. There may be some virtue in arranging different bases of legislative representation in *two* assemblies or two separate occasions of assembly rather than putting all one's eggs in one basket, so to speak, and trying to perfect a single scheme of legislative representation. That—abstracted from Sterne's novel—is what I call the Tristram Shandy principle.

The Bentham line of argument assumes that anything we want in the way of election to and representation in a second chamber can be melded with what we already have or what we already want in the first chamber, to produce both a more complicated and a more perfected unicameral scheme. But the argument can be turned on its head. No matter how good we make the scheme of representation in a given chamber, no matter how many of our good thoughts about election, representation, and deliberation we have already taken on board, the Tristram Shandy principle might suggest that it is also possible to improve things by complementing that scheme of representation with another.

It is a kind of antiperfection thesis. Bagehot observed that "[w]ith a perfect lower House, . . . if we had an ideal House of Commons perfectly representing the nation . . . it is certain that we should not need a higher chamber."[31] I suppose that is a tautology, except that there is no such thing as perfect representation of the people. I am inclined to say there is no such thing as the people.[32] There is just a large array of individual persons, millions of them, related to one another in various ways, with various interests, desires, and views. And there are innumerable ways of mapping onto that array another array, namely the five or six hundred seats that there are in a given legislative assembly. We call these various ways of mapping the one array onto the other relations of representation. They involve things like elections (their nature and frequency), the separation of the country into constituencies on various bases, and functions such as "mixed-member proportional representation," which enable territorial representation to be cut with party affiliation to make possible outcomes that are in various ways "proportional." There are all sorts of ways of doing this, and of course intense controversy along all these dimensions. As always, the fact of disagreement does not mean that some views are not better than others. But my theorem is that even the best of the contesting views should acknowledge the possibility of enrichment by still other modes of representation, which cannot necessarily be incorporated into the best view while keeping it practicable in and of itself.

Perhaps Bentham's perfecting maneuver would work if there were no constraints of manageability and practicability as far as schemes of representation were concerned. Perhaps an ideal scheme could be infinitely complex, taking on board successively every good feature that is said to distinguish the scheme of representation in a putative second house from the scheme of representation in the first. I actually doubt whether even this is true, except for the limit case of a direct democracy, where the whole array of persons is represented literally by itself. It is evidently untrue for manageable and politically practicable schemes of representation.

As Nicholas Aroney has pointed out, the assumption of the Sieyès/Bentham approach is that each political society "can be conceived of as being composed of a unitary 'people' which can be represented unproblematically in a single institution—the lower house—based on a particular electoral process."[33] But this is a wrong assumption. Because there is no such unitary thing as "the people," there can be no single canonical way of representing it. There are *people* to be represented—persons, not the people—and they are diverse along many more thousands of axes than can possibly be incorporated into a single electoral scheme. So there are many—perhaps infinitely many—ways of representing them.[34] I don't mean to infer that electoral reform for the lower house is futile. Of course it is not. But even if it succeeds, there will still be other possible schemes of representation with which to complement it. One very powerful argument for bicameralism, then, is the possibility of enriching the ways in which the people are represented in the legislature. This may be valued in and of itself, as a participatory matter, or it may be valued inasmuch as the additional layer of representation affords a qualitatively distinct basis for legislative scrutiny and accountability.

4. MILL'S PRINCIPLE OF SEPARATE CONCURRENCE

A second point to make against the Benthamite approach challenges the preoccupation with qualitative difference. Even if the new layer of representation does not differ strikingly from the basis of representation in the other chamber, it may still be a valuable addition. In the English debate, people make a big deal about there having to be "distinct logics of representation"—Meg Russell's phrase.[35] Vernon Bogdanor asks: "How can the same electorate be represented in two different ways in two different chambers?"[36] Bogdanor is particularly exercised by the prospect of the most recently established system of representation coming to convey an implicit reproach against the system of representation in the other place—a diminution of its legitimacy. I guess some people will seize the opportunity of an elected second chamber to experiment with proportional representation or forms of quasi-federal representation, which are intended eventually to transform the first chamber as well. But other differences are imaginable that would not raise questions about the legitimacy of the system of representation in the first chamber. The second chamber might be elected on a different schedule rather than under a radically different system; and another concern of Bogdanor's—his concern about one house being able to claim that its mandate was more recent than the other's[37]—could be solved by having an American-style system of rolling elections, with one-third of the senators facing election (for a six-year term) every two years. There is, as I said, a world out there, and some of these problems have been faced and dealt with in other countries.

"Distinct logics of representation" might still be important. But even without them, bicameralism would ensure that each given bill or legislative measure would have to get by two different sets of representatives, sampling the spirit of the country in two different ways—once by an assembly of representatives of the nation elected according to one schedule and then a second time by a structurally similar assembly of representatives elected according to a second schedule.

So, in principle, in order to answer Bentham's challenge, the lines of difference need not be particularly great.[38] The quality yield from relatively small differences may be quite considerable. Even if the two houses are elected on exactly the same scheme of representation, they may still exhibit what Chief Justice Warren called "differing complexions and collective attitudes" by virtue of the different personalities that inhabit them and the interactions among them. "Every large assembly," said Bagehot, "is . . . a fluctuating body. . . . It is one knot of men tonight and another tomorrow night."[39] Not only that, but the mere fact that the examination of a bill in the first house may precede its examination in the second will mean that there are different things to think about and talk about in the other place. Among these different things will be the reactions of the electorate at large to what has been said in the first house, for we should always understand formal deliberation in the legislature as something connected to, helping to focus, and being affected by informal deliberation in civil society. Our thinking about bicameralism should be informed by that also.

John Stuart Mill, whose *Considerations on Representative Government* is still the best book on democracy in the canon of political thought, is sometimes cited as a fellow traveler of Bentham's on this matter of bicameralism and sometimes as an opponent. He began his chapter "Of a Second Chamber" by touching all the Benthamite bases: two chambers of similar composition will both "obey the same influences," and if there is a case for more deliberation, we can modify "the established forms of business" in the primary chamber.[40] But then Mill went on to say this:

> The consideration which tells most . . . in favour of two Chambers . . . is the evil effect produced upon the mind of any holder of power, whether an individual or an assembly, by the consciousness of having only themselves to consult. It is important that no set of persons should, in great affairs, be able, even temporarily, to make their *sic volo* prevail without asking any one else for his consent. A majority in a single assembly . . . when composed of the same persons habitually acting together, and always assured of victory in their own House—easily becomes despotic and overweening, if released from the necessity of considering whether its acts will be concurred in by another constituted authority.[41]

This, I think, is very important indeed. It need not matter much whether the second authority is constituted differently from the first, so long as it is not under the control of the first, so long as it is genuinely another constituted authority. Of course, the Principle of Separate Concurrence, as I will call this principle of Mill's, will have its salutary effect most strikingly when the second authority is constituted on a quite different basis than the first, and this was what Mill argued for in the second half of his chapter: an unelected Senate consisting of veterans of high office in the existing system. But, for the purposes of the Principle of Separate Concurrence, we should not underestimate the sheer power of separateness, quite apart from qualitative difference in the mode of selection. In this matter, we should not be bullied by Leibniz's identity of indiscernibles. Even people who are similar to one another talk about things in different places in different combinations with one another in different ways. And their different talk would be enough to open up substantial disagreement or allow it to express itself in different ways. That difference by itself might be enough to satisfy the Principle of Separate Concurrence, requiring as it would (and I am adapting some language from Mill) a willingness to concede something to opponents, when the opposing views are presented afresh or in different ways: "[O]f this salutary habit, the mutual give and take between two Houses is a perpetual school."[42]

5. INDEPENDENCE OF THE EXECUTIVE

What is crucial, I have said, is that the two chambers, however similar, should be independent of one another. The membership of the one should not be subject to the leadership of the other, nor should the two of them be subject to a single political leadership. That is the crucial thing if Bentham's accusation of costly redundancy is to be avoided and if Mill's Principle of Separate Concurrence is to be satisfied.

This brings me to the point that I want to emphasize in this chapter. The most important difference that can possibly be established between the two chambers of a bicameral legislature in a Westminster-style system—more important than aristocracy, more important than federal representation, more important than proportional representation—is a different relation to the executive.

We all know that what distinguishes a Westminster-style system is that the body that exercises the executive powers of the Crown is a committee of one of the houses of Parliament and dominates that house of Parliament through the party system and the system of whips. This committee—I mean the prime minister and the cabinet—not only exercises the highest executive powers, the royal prerogative, and (as Locke would call them) federative powers (i.e., foreign policy)[43] but also sets and dominates the legislative agenda. The very thing that entitles this body to exercise executive authority also, in the nature of things, gives it the power to determine what bills will be considered and what bills will be enacted. In both cases, the power stems from its ability to command from within a majority in what we fondly call the "lower" house.

This is a fundamental principle of the constitution in a Westminster-style system. The celebrated Montesquieu may have regarded the constitution of England as the matchless epitome of the separation of powers, but there—at the very core of the constitution—is a repudiation of the principle that requires each separate power (in this case legislature and executive) to have "a will of its own" and to be, in Madison's words, "so constituted that the members of each should have as little agency as possible in the appointment of the members of the others."[44] Now, Madison argued that even Montesquieu would have to accept that his idealization of England should be modified to reflect the involvement of the monarch in legislation through the

Royal Assent.[45] The British legislature is the Queen-in-Parliament. But that is not what I mean. Royalty is the least of the problems. I mean cabinet domination of Parliament, arising from the subordination of the Crown in all its functions to the advice of ministers, who arise out of the lower house and who in turn dominate it in the interest of the government's authority.

This is not the place to evaluate or denounce this feature of Westminster systems; Bagehot regarded "the nearly complete fusion of the executive and the legislature" as "the efficient secret" and the "characteristic merit" of the English constitution.[46] Others think of it as a constitutional abomination, transforming representative legislatures into instruments of elective dictatorship. For us, it is enough to say that this is a defining feature of a Westminster-style constitution, and it is not going away anytime soon. But we can take the opportunity in the reform of the second chamber to limit its scope, to limit the compromise or setback that this arrangement requires us to accept so far as the separation of powers is concerned.

We could do this by insisting that, no matter how the second house is constituted, it should be separated from the authority of the executive in a way that—as things stand—the first house is not. If that is not granted, then all else is lost. Effective extension of executive authority into the upper house not only compounds this inherent breach of the principle of the separation of powers but undercuts almost everything that can be said in favor of bicameralism. Extension of executive power into the second chamber would amount to a surrender to Bentham and a repudiation of Mill's Principle of Separate Concurrence. Why pay for two houses rather than one, when they are both effectively under the control of the prime minister? What is the good of requiring separate concurrence in a second chamber when it is bound to be forthcoming at the say-so of the body responsible in effect for eliciting the concurrence of the first?

It may seem difficult to do this, especially if—as I am assuming—the second chamber is elected. If it is elected, there will be politics; if there is politics, there will be party politics; and parties would naturally do what they could to ensure that their members in the second chamber were brought under the same discipline as their members in the first. There is probably no way of ruling that out. As Professor Bogdanor has wisely observed, "the dominance of party politics in modern democracies" means that "the practice of bicameralism bears very little relation to the theory."[47] Still, some prophylactic measures can be envisaged.

Some of the power that the executive has in a first, elected chamber has to do with the hopes and prospects of office for its more able and ambitious Members of Parliament. Members know that voting in defiance of party whips is a way of radically diminishing the chance that one will be tapped for ministerial office (or shadow ministerial office). So we might introduce a rule that members of the cabinet (or, more radically, ministers of the Crown) may not sit in the second chamber.[48] There are to be no hopes or prospects of executive office in the elected second chamber. In Britain, as things stand, the prime minister and (I believe) the chancellor of the exchequer may not sit in the House of Lords; they must be members of the Commons. The same was thought to be true of the foreign secretary, but the appointments of Lord Home in 1960 and Lord Carrington in 1979 revealed this to be a practice rather than a convention—assuming you accept the rather infuriating English distinction between the two. Extending this to cabinet or ministerial rank generally would, at a stroke, diminish the authority of the prime minister in the second house and already define that chamber in a quite different relation to the executive.

Apart from anything else, this would also cut off at the pass something that has threatened to creep in as an abuse. In 2008, Peter Mandelson, who did not at that time hold a seat in Parliament, was made eligible for membership in Gordon Brown's cabinet precisely by being made a life peer. This amounted to a surreptitious hijacking of the Westminster principles that govern cabinet office in the direction of something like the American arrangement, whereby individuals can be appointed to the cabinet whether they are members of Congress or not. The Mandelson appointment was effectively of this kind—facilitated by the prime minister's power over the system of peerage—with the difference (a characteristic one where British imitation of American arrangements is concerned) that there is no *safeguard* provision in the United Kingdom for the advice or consent of any other body to the appointment as there is under Article II of the U.S. Constitution. There, cabinet officers may be appointed by the president from private life but only with the advice and consent of the Senate.

I know it is quite a radical change I am envisaging—freeing a part, a half, of the bicameral legislature from executive domination. It is not a complete departure from the Westminster system, but it is one step toward some degree of legislative independence. In many legislatures in the world, both chambers are independent of the executive. And it is not as though the evils of executive domination have never occurred to anyone. James Madison made a famous observation in *The Federalist Papers* about the danger of legislators' neglecting their obligations to the people and pursuing some ulterior purpose:

> In this point of view, a senate, as a second branch of the legislative assembly, distinct from, and dividing the power with, a first, must be in all cases a salutary check on the government. It doubles the security to the people, by requiring the concurrence of two distinct bodies in schemes of usurpation or perfidy, where the ambition or corruption of one would otherwise be sufficient.[49]

(This is like Mill's Principle of Separate Concurrence again, but with a more radical tilt.) And it is worth remembering Walter Bagehot's gloss on this in chapter 5 of *The English Constitution*. Bagehot, who was by no means a fanatical enthusiast of bicameralism, conceded the danger of "sinister interest" in the lower chamber and acknowledged that it was "therefore of great use to have a second chamber of an opposite sort, differently composed, in which that interest in all likelihood will not rule." Do you know what he gave as his example of such a sinister interest? "The most dangerous of all sinister interests is that of the executive government,"[50] the cabinet, with the power that it has in the Commons.

There has not been nearly enough attention to this issue in the debate about constitutional reform in the United Kingdom: Nicholas Aroney is an honorable exception.[51] I hope that if I can drive one point home, it is that although we want a second chamber that is different from the first, to avoid Bentham's objection of redundancy, what we most want is a second chamber that is independent of the government so that it can perform functions of genuinely legislative debate, which is not just acclamation of the executive's agenda.

Probably for just this reason, it is not going to happen. Professor Anthony King's cynicism knows no bounds, but even he outdoes himself, calling it "highly unlikely that any government . . . based on the House of Commons, would wittingly create a second chamber with sufficient power and prestige to mount a serious challenge to its own authority. Pigs will fly; flies will turn into pigs."[52] Nevertheless, it is delicious to entertain the possibility of a genuinely independent legislature, is it not? Or half of one. We hope for genuine realization of the old principle that before it becomes law a bill should be debated and scrutinized in a representative body that is quite independent of, and has nothing to hope for or fear from, the agency that is going to be charged with its administration. Delicious but forlorn. Still, I emphasize these principles so at least we know what we are missing.[53] As Locke put it in another context, "You will say, then, the [government] being the stronger will have [its] will. . . . Without doubt; but the question is not here concerning the doubtfulness of the event, but the rule of right."[54]

6. SEPARATION OF JUDICIAL FUNCTIONS

We talk freely enough about the separation of powers. And most of us would accept, as the English say "in theory," that there is something inherently inappropriate about institutional entanglements that place all the functions of government—judicial, executive, legislative, prerogative, and federative—in one body (with the possible result that these functions will be accumulated in one set of hands). There has not been much trouble taking on board the idea that the judges who are charged with the administration of a statute should have no part in enacting it. It only took us a few centuries to get to the point where the ultimate power of appeal in matters judicial was removed from the upper house of Parliament and vested in an independent Supreme Court, thus ending the anomaly whereby Her Majesty's Lords of Appeal participated also in legislative debate, not to mention the problem that it was only by informal convention that Lords Spiritual and Temporal were precluded from voting on the outcome of legal cases.[55]

Bentham, oddly enough, thought he had to spend time refuting the proposition that one of the advantages of an upper house was that it could combine legislative and judicial functions. He made short work of that (to the extent that he made short work of anything in the letter [*T*]*o his Fellow-Citizens of France, on Houses of Peers and Senates*), substituting for it a rather batty proposal that the final power of judicial appeal should be vested in one judge electively accountable to the members of the lower house and punishable by it for "criminal misdecision"—something that might appeal perhaps to our present political leaders but that to the rest of us should cast doubt on Bentham's overall defense of unicameralism under the rubric of "the thirteenth chime of a crazy clock."[56]

Some readers will know about my opposition to the practice of strong judicial review of legislation, on the American model—a practice whereby legislation once enacted may be struck down by a court because a majority of judges reckon that it is at odds with a bill of rights.[57] I have said elsewhere that it is hard to sustain this opposition against a unicameral Westminster-style parliament (in New Zealand, for example), and certainly it is hard to sustain what I have called "the dignity of legislation" as a premise of this opposition when the legislative process is entirely dominated by the executive.[58]

The point of the debate about judicial review is not, as we sometimes put it, about a clash between elective and nonelective institutions, and majority rule and rule by some nonmajoritarian entity. The specific issue is about the constitutional standing of an elected representative assembly devoted specifically to legislative functions. That standing can come under attack in a variety of ways. Strong judicial review is one, but so is executive ascendancy, and the attack is still an attack even when the executive has independent elective credentials, as the presidency has for example in the United States, or even when the executive's elective credentials are partly those of the legislative assembly, as they are in the United Kingdom. To put it the other way around, executive ascendancy in, through, and over Parliament is not what opponents of judicial review should be seeking to vindicate. Opponents of judicial review are committed by their position to showing that the legislature itself—not the cabinet, not even the plebiscites of the people, but the institutions and processes of representative legislation—is the appropriate place for the community to air and resolve its fundamental disagreements about what the law should be on matters of rights, justice, and the common good. And that requires the legislative process to be robust and satisfactory on its own terms, not just satisfactory to its masters in Whitehall.

Whether the work of a properly constituted upper house could be conceived as an adequate substitute for judicial review is another matter. Many advanced democracies have both, and many supporters of judicial review defend the practice even for systems that have a powerful and independent senate. Meg Russell and a colleague authored a paper back in 1999 on "Second Chambers as Constitutional Guardians and Protectors of Human Rights" and, if I understand the authors' position correctly, it would be conceived as a supplement to rather than a substitute for the judicial protections that were envisaged at that time under the Human Rights Act.[59]

Probably what we say here depends a little on how far support for judicial review is based on suspicion of democratic procedures as such, even in their most responsible legislative manifestations. And it depends also on how far opposition to judicial review is based on the appointive rather than elective character of the institution doing the reviewing. My own view is that constitutional review by an appointed second chamber would be the worst of both worlds. Dawn Oliver is right to ask whether "attitudes to reform of the House of Lords [would] be changed if it were re-named 'The Council of State'?"[60] But I am inclined to agree with Professor Bogdanor that "[i]f one is looking for an upper house with the authority to fulfil the function of constitutional protection . . . the conclusion seems inescapable that it must be an elected body."[61]

7. THE ASCENDANCY OF THE LOWER HOUSE

I mentioned at the beginning of the this chapter the sentiment often expressed in Britain that it is important, in the course of second chamber reform, not to undermine the authority of the House of Commons.[62]

The concern is often expressed that the establishment of an elective second chamber might do just that. Certainly, the justification of the present ascendancy of the House of Commons defined by the Parliament Acts and the Salisbury Convention would find little justification in a fully elective bicameral arrangement. We must remember that the original Parliament Act—whose passage, in Anthony King's provocative formulation, led to Britain's legislature "abruptly becoming, in effect, unicameral"[63]—was passed explicitly as a stopgap: "[W]hereas it is intended to substitute for the House of Lords as it at present exists a Second Chamber constituted on a popular instead of hereditary basis, but such substitution cannot be immediately brought into operation."[64] Or at least that is the way it was phrased; Bogdanor says it was disingenuous.[65]

I am sure there are sentimental reasons for wanting to preserve the ascendancy of the House of Commons, but I wonder how much the real motive in the minds of our cold-eyed masters has to do with preserving executive hegemony via the ascendancy of the House of Commons rather than preserving the ascendancy of the latter institution for its own sake. Dawn Oliver may be right in her formulation, in *The Changing Constitution,* that this is more a matter of the relation between the second chamber and the government than of the relation between the second chamber and the first.[66] In any case, the arrangement I am envisaging is not necessarily incompatible with some sort of primacy for the Commons, at least in assigning to one of them the characteristic role of proposing and initiating legislation that the government is committed to and the other the characteristic role of scrutinizing and amending it.

Political theorists in the seventeenth and eighteenth centuries used to envisage a relation of this kind between the two houses in a bicameral system. Montesquieu, who was a proponent of bicameralism as much as the separation of powers, imagined that the assembly of nobles should take part in legislation only through its power of rejecting legislation, not through any faculty of ordaining or initiating the ordaining of law by its own authority.[67] And a century earlier, the republican theorist James Harrington drew an analogy between a bicameral legislature and the admirable practice of what he called "two silly girls" who have figured out how to divide a cake among themselves. "'Divide', says one unto the other, 'and I will choose; or let me divide, and you shall choose.'"[68] It is, he says, an indictment of unicameralism that it cannot offer this diversity:

> in a commonwealth consisting of a single council, there is no other to choose than that which divided; whence it is, that such a council faileth not to scramble, that is to be factious, there being no other dividing of the cake in that case but among themselves.[69]

But in a diversified system of governance, these functions—"dividing and choosing, [or] in the language of a commonwealth . . . debating and resolving" are assigned to different legislative bodies: "the wisdom of the commonwealth . . . in the aristocracy" and "the interest of the commonwealth . . . in the whole body of the people" or in a representative council "so constituted as can never contract any other interest than that of the whole people."[70] This, says Harrington, is

> the whole mystery of a commonwealth, which lies only in dividing and choosing; nor hath God . . . left so much unto mankind to dispute upon as who shall divide and who choose, but distributed them for ever into two or-

ders, whereof the one hath the natural right of dividing, and the other of choosing.⁷¹

I do not want to try your patience too much with this antiquarianism. The fact that something has been mentioned by a figure like Harrington or Montesquieu is no guarantee that it is sensible. Look at David Hume with his daft constitutional ideas: a Court of Competitors, for example, composed of those who are runners-up in senatorial elections and the idea, which Hume thinks is of Roman origin, of having two independent coequal legislatures, each capable of enacting laws on its own motion.⁷²

In particular, we are unlikely to accept the association that Harrington and Montesquieu make between the second chamber and aristocracy, a hereditary elite in the case of Montesquieu. (In Harrington, it is a little different, and I will come back to that in a moment.) A mixed regime in the classic sense—king, nobles, and commons—is no longer an option for us. However, we do not have to accept that in order to see the value of this sort of separation of function inside a bicameral legislature. There can still be a distinction between certain actions and tasks in relation to lawmaking. And maintaining the legislative initiative in the chamber where the executive is the more dominant is a way of keeping faith with some of our Westminster heritage without surrendering the whole of the legislative process to its domination. Equally, defining a role for the second chamber that does not include control over the legislative agenda can highlight the importance of deliberative functions within Parliament, understood independently of the urgent tasks of government.

8. ARISTOCRACY

Let me come back finally to this issue of aristocracy: houses of peers. In all of this, I have assumed an elected second chamber. There is considerable support in Britain for an appointed chamber, particularly (and—is this unfair?—predictably)⁷³ among those who already have seats by appointment in the House of Lords. I would have thought the Canadian experience would give us pause, but it is barely mentioned in the British debate. Anyway, it seems to me that if we want a second chamber over which the power of the prime minister and the cabinet is diminished, then it probably is not a good idea to fill it with people who one way or another have recommended themselves to the powers that be for appointment. Just as we do not want the business of the second chamber to be distorted by its members' hopes of ministerial office, we do not want it to be skewed by their sense of beholdenness to those who dominate the other house.[74]

James Harrington, the seventeenth-century republican I mentioned a moment ago, suggested that a senate might be aristocratic by election rather than inbreeding. He had a touching faith in the ability of the common people to recognize their betters, "a natural aristocracy diffused by God throughout the whole body of mankind."[75] Beginning with Harrington—actually beginning in a way with Aristotle—there is a constant theme in the canon of Western political theory that it may be a mistake to oppose elective and aristocratic forms too sharply. Election may be conceived as a way of identifying the best person; certainly it seems to be quite different from selection by lot, which the Athenians regarded as more democratic. I wonder whether this thought is something we can make use of.

In a book called *The Principles of Representative Government*, Bernard Manin has pursued this suggestion. Like the Athenians, he argues that the principle of election is that the best person is chosen and that this is so not only from the logic of the elector's choice—he or she is voting for whom they take to be the best person—but often also from the design point of view in regard to the electoral system itself. I actually think this is a mistaken view so far as voters' choice is concerned, because although voters may indeed be striving to identify the best person, the idea of the best leaves open the question—the best *what?* "The best legislator" is one possible answer and that might be a vaguely aristocratic idea; but "the best spokesman for my interests" or "the person best able to convey to others what it is like to be someone like me" are other possible answers, quite plausible in the context of class representation—and those are not aristocratic at all.

This is a difficulty for Manin's account but it represents an opportunity for ours. For although Manin is wrong that all election is necessarily aristocratic, he need not be wrong in the claim that election is sometimes aristocratic, and that there are ways in which an electorate can orient itself to electoral choice that brings into play elements that are appropriate to some of the work that the idea of aristocracy has sometimes done for bicameralism.

Some of the structural features I have mentioned may be important here. (i) I am voting for, choosing, a representative to help determine the political complexion of the government, the best representative for that purpose: that is one sort of electoral choice. Those are the auspices of electoral choice for the first or primary chamber. (ii) I am voting for, choosing, the best person (of the candidates presented to me) to hold office for a longer period and scrutinize and deliberate about legislation: that is a different sort of choice, more appropriate to a senate or a second chamber. In each case, choosing the best means something different. Idea (ii) might pick up on some of the attributes that make Manin's thesis plausible. It might pick up on some aspects of aristocracy, in Harrington's literal sense, that have nothing to do with class or breeding. Or anyway, aristocratic or not, the idea of choice with an eye to the specific functions performed by the members of a second chamber—a decision oriented to the choice of those who are best at *that,* uncontaminated by these questions of choosing a government, might help nourish the sense of the two chambers having somewhat different work to do. And it might do this—in a way that an appointed second chamber on the Canadian model could not—without sacrificing democratic legitimacy.[76]

9. AN ANATOMY LESSON

Bicameralism is an attractive topic for someone interested in the complexity of our legislative institutions. By conceiving of the legislature as a "them" rather than an "it"[77]—by focusing on Parliament as something composed of two separate parts (each, in addition, comprising an assembly of hundreds of members), it offers the political theorist something of an anatomy lesson.

Under the ancient regime of mixed government, the anatomy of the legislature mirrored the anatomy of the society at large in its different estates. But even in the modern era, dissection is instructive. With the two halves of Parliament opened up, we can look at systems of representation and election, each as just one possibility among others, each as possibly complemented by another in a still imperfect but now twofold sampling of the people. With the two halves opened up, we can easily think of legislation itself as a complexity of tasks—agenda-setting, particular proposal, principled deliberation, focused debate on particular parts or sections, constitutional scrutiny, and eventual resolution—an articulated sequence of functions mapped onto different institutions and processes. Finally, with the two halves of this branch of the state opened up, it is easier to grasp the various modes of connection and disconnection with other branches of government and to imagine new and different possibilities of respecting the principle of the separation of powers even in a Westminster system.

If I may be allowed one last digression, what we have been doing here is comparable to the way in which dissecting the executive (along Lockean lines) into its constitutive functions—its enforcement and administrative functions, its federative role, its prerogative powers, and its high-level representation of the state—opens up for clearer view its relations to other branches of government. In Lockean theory, this dissection of the executive opens up for clearer view its relations to other branches of government, and it enables us to see through the equivocations that sometimes cover up abuse.[78] And indeed the theorist's dissection of the executive actually works best when it is brought into relation with exactly the exercise in bicameral anatomy that we have been performing. (I have in mind here—as an exemplar—James Madison's insistence against Alexander Hamilton and George Washington in *The Pacificus-Helvidius Debates* of 1793 that the Senate must be allowed to play its part in the process of determining whether and how to honor the United States's treaty obligation to France, not only because the Senate advises and consents on foreign policy appointments but also because it participates in the ratification of treaties, which according to Article VI of the Constitution are part of the supreme law of the land.)[79]

These lessons in theoretical anatomy may excite impatience in political commentators—particularly in Britain—who prefer at best a blurred glimpse of institutional articulation in their rush to see who is winning in the bottom line of party politics. But there is an alternative perspective, even in the real world—we call it constitutionalism—that does take time to take structure and structural design seriously. And it is refreshing in this case study to see structure made prominent in the constitutional view, not (as so often) for limiting the legislative function but in order to constitute and actually vindicate the independence of this power against the other branches of government.

CHAPTER FIVE

The Principle of Loyal Opposition

1. POLITICAL COMPETITION

Democracy is a sort of competition with winners and losers. Joseph Schumpeter famously defined it as "an institutional arrangement for arriving at political decisions in which individuals acquire the power to decide by means of a competitive struggle for the people's vote."[1]

Why do we compete in democratic life? Well, every society has to choose its public policy positions from an array of alternatives, some of them starkly opposed to one another. And every alternative in that array is supported by some of the people in the society. There are many of us, and there is politics, as Hannah Arendt insisted, because not one man but men inhabit the world; not one person (with a social conscience just like mine) but people.[2] And we the people disagree with one another, though we all belong to one society.

There are all sorts of explanations for the existence of political dissensus. In a low-minded view, conflicts of opinion are generated by conflicts of interest—personal interest or class interest, interest in power pure and simple, or interests in material wealth. People struggle for power or for the opportunity to plunder the economic system, and they manufacture views on various issues that will aid them in this struggle, or they dress up various options that will redound to their benefit as policies intended to benefit the whole society. There is a lot of that, no doubt.

But the main reason people disagree is because the questions we face are difficult, and even with the best will in the world, with our thinking focused resolutely and honestly on the common good, the different perspectives and experiences that we bring to politics take us to different positions on every single question of what we should do together. These are what John Rawls called the burdens of judgment.

> Different conceptions of the world can reasonably be elaborated from different standpoints and diversity arises in part from our distinct perspectives. It is unrealistic . . . to suppose that all our differences are rooted solely in ignorance and perversity, or else in the rivalries for power, status, or economic gain.[3]

And so he concludes, quite rightly, that many of our most important judgments are made under conditions where it is not to be expected that conscientious persons with full powers of reason, even after free discussion, will arrive at the same conclusion.

Unfortunately, Rawls and his followers squandered this insight by maintaining that it applied only with regard to religion, ethics, and comprehensive conceptions of the good, not to issues of justice and social policy, on which clearly some consensus is necessary. But the need for consensus in these areas does not make the burdens of judgment go away. We disagree about justice and social policy, too, and for the same sorts of reasons. No doubt, each politician or political activist has confidence in her own principles and her own proposals; she thinks they are supported not just by her will or interests but by the objective balance of reasons. But that does not preclude disagreement: every political activist thinks of their convictions in this way (in this "objective" mode) and *still* they are opposed to one another. And the best explanation of that disagreement is once again the difficulty of the issues and the variety of the perspectives we bring to them. This is the premise of everything I am going to say in this chapter and a lot that I have written elsewhere.[4]

Political competition goes through phases. It has a periodicity to it, driven in modern democracies by the regular rhythm of elections.[5] (Indeed, democratic politics is arguably more properly described as competitive than what we call economic competition, because in politics there are well-defined contests and clear-cut criteria for winning—for counting as *the winner* for a certain period—that mostly do not exist in the economic realm. In political competition, some people are legally identifiable winners and others are legally defined as losers.)

So, groups of people in the society struggle to have the positions that they favor implemented as policy and legislation rather than the positions that other people favor. And when they lose, the losers have to live with policies they do not support, and those policies will be implemented among and in the presence of many people who oppose them. Or even if people are just struggling for power itself, without much interest in the positions they have manufactured to cover the cynicism of their class interest, once again the losers have to put up with a situation in which they turn out to be subjects, not rulers, and in which—gallingly—others, whom they reckon are no better than themselves, are reaping the spoils that they coveted. There are always losers, full of resentment. Losing in politics is a massive loss of recognition. And it is worth asking whether a political system can do anything to honor or empower those who have no choice but to be regarded as the unfortunate opponents of our rulers for the time being.

2. THE ROLE OF THE LOSERS: JUST WAITING THEIR TURN?

One obvious possibility is that the losers may hang around and hope for better luck next time. They can temper their resentment and their ambition, waiting patiently for vindication in the next election, when the winner's policies, which they knew all along were flawed, turn out to have been disastrous or unpopular in their implementation. But while they wait, are the losers anything more than pure subjects, subjugated by the victory of their opponents?

Rousseau complained that the English people prided themselves on being free because they elected their rulers. But they were not free at all, said Rousseau: "[A]s soon as the Members [of Parliament] are elected, the people is enslaved," presumably the losers in the election especially, along with everyone else.[6] They have to wait in resentful servitude for another Election Day, another opportunity to cast off their chains.

Maybe that is unkind. Alexis de Tocqueville put it more cheerfully when he said of another representative democracy that losers actually value the empowerment of the winners,

> for as the minority may shortly rally the majority to its principles, it is interested in professing that respect for the decrees of the legislator which it may soon have occasion to claim for its own.[7]

In general, we may say, there is nothing ignoble about taking one's turn. A citizen, says Aristotle, "is . . . one who has a share both in ruling and being ruled."[8] Citizens claim the right "to take it in turns to exercise authority."[9] They have to be good "at both ruling and obeying," which is why people who cannot stand being ruled—who cannot stand being losers in the sense that I have defined—may have to be ostracized and exiled in Aristotle's account.[10]

Still, is that all there is? Waiting to take one's turn, hoping that the electoral tables are eventually turned and that the loser turns out to be a winner in the next phase of competition?

3. RIGHTS GUARANTEES

One obvious further point is that our political system offers certain guarantees to everyone that, no matter whether they are winners or losers in the political process, there are certain interests and liberties they will not have to abandon. They will not have to give up their religion; they will not be interned without trial and will not be tortured; they will not be expropriated or killed, nor will the members of their families. The familiarity of these guarantees should not blind us to the fact that they protect losers in our politics from things that losers in other types of political system typically endure.

In this regard, it is particularly important that the losers, like other citizens, retain the right to persevere in vociferous dissent during the period of their opponents' ascendancy. We assume that the losers will continue agitating against their opponent's policies, looking for opportunities to discredit the faction that has won. It is not their responsibility to remain quiet or just congratulate the winners, like good sports at the end of a football game. For one thing, they have to prepare for the next round of competition: quite early in the term of an elected president in the United States, for example, we see politicians from other parties jockeying for position among potential presidential candidates. And indeed we hope this is not just preparation; we hope their competing oppositional attitudes will keep the current administration honest and establish a basis of accountability.

We take this for granted. But in many societies it is not easy to establish even this as a privilege of the losers; there have been periods in our society, too, when we have been tempted, in the words of Edmund Burke, to "confound the unhappiness of civil dissension with the crime of treason."[11] After all, the rulers have won the right to have their policies implemented in the name of the whole nation. Just as it would be wrong for civil servants to oppose the implementation of policies with which they happen to disagree, so can I imagine someone saying that it is wrong for political losers to try to stir up opposition to policies they opposed at the election, given that they have lost—wrong for them to try to make the implementation of these policies more difficult. After all, was that not the point of the competition—to see who would be allowed to implement their policies? And since the competition was conducted for the sake of the whole political community, is there not something almost treasonous in vociferously attempting to undermine the implementation of the winner's policies during the defined period of their victory?

It is remarkable that, despite the plausibility of such sentiments, most modern democracies pride themselves on preserving a right of robust dissent and on tolerating as a matter of routine political normality the free and vociferous expression of oppositional views.

Of course, opponents of the victorious regime may not find this right of dissident free speech in itself particularly satisfying. Sure it is better than the alternative. For most of us, though, it is hard to avoid the impression that rights of free expression are just freedoms to let our words go out into the wind, where by and large and for most of us they dissipate without any discernible effect on the government that is being conducted by others in our name and with our lives and livelihood. People sometimes talk about the waste or meaninglessness of an individual vote: What does one vote mean among so many? But at least each vote is counted. The expression of an opinion, anyone's opinion, is not even formally registered. Nobody really takes note.

We mitigate this frustration in various ways. To help make dissent and political activity meaningful, we organize. We associate our opinions with those of others in various ways—gathering together to hammer out and express opinions that can stand not as my view or yours but the view of an organization that comprises you, me, and thousands of others. We value freedom of speech, but effective and meaningful freedom of speech presupposes freedom of association. An organization can have an effective presence in a political system that an individual cannot.[12]

4. PARTIES

In an important book titled *On the Side of the Angels: An Appreciation of Parties and Partisanship,* Nancy Rosenblum has spoken out about the lack of interest in political parties in modern political theory. She identifies a major strand in the canon of political theory, associated with thinkers such as Rousseau, for whom the aim is the sustenance or restoration of some social whole—the people taken as a unity, the general will—and to whom the emergence of political parties is anathema.[13] Parties create division, Rosenblum says, and they sponsor a sense among the people of how important differences of political opinion are. In so doing, they elevate a line of division into general political awareness and make it a permanent feature of the social landscape.[14] From Rosenblum's own point of view, this is one of the most important things parties do: they reinforce "the assumption that the nation is not *une et indivisible.*"[15] But, of course, from the point of view of a philosopher preoccupied with the integrity of his own vision of social justice, the permanence of opinionated faction is a nightmare. It raises before him the horror that his own righteous vision may have to be compromised with other less worthy programs in the sordid mess of partisan politics.

That is a matter of political theory. From the more practical viewpoint of winners and losers, parties offer different advantages and disadvantages.

Losers can regard parties in the solace of solidarity. They are not alone in their galling defeat. By associating ourselves with a party, we enter political competition not just as individuals, with aspirations whose futility and insignificance have been revealed by the reality of political defeat, but also as large and permanent organizations, with experience of the rhythms and residual opportunities of politics. Defeat is no longer something hopeless; this organization to which we belong has been out of power before and regained office then. It is likely in due course to regain office now and to nourish its power as a collective by the prospect of that turnabout.

The ruling group, whom I have called the winners, may take a more jaundiced view. For their part, the existence of opposition in the form of an organized party might exacerbate the temptation to regard dissent as treason, for if the losers organize themselves into a party, they may develop an apparatus that mimics and rivals the rulers' own organization in scale and articulation. The losers' party may have branches throughout the country, and separate subentities that elaborate programs opposed to those that the government is pursuing. They will have spokesmen who play the role for the losers that ministers of state play for the winners. It may be hard not to see all this as a vast conspiracy to usurp the government or at least make the winners' task of governing much more difficult.

So, just as the toleration of dissident speech requires a considerable effort, so too the toleration of organized opposition—organized in the form of a party that seeks to match the government in scope and structure, if not in scale and resources—is a considerable achievement. And Rosenblum is right that the normalization of party competition—the understanding that faction is not a temporary or aberrant phenomenon but a settled part of the political landscape—is indispensable in this regard. The key move, she said, was to distinguish party opposition from sedition, treason, and a prelude to civil war. And, for that, several things were necessary: first, something like the accidental experience of rotation in office—that once upon a time the Whigs had power, and then the Tories did, and then the Whigs again—and no one happened to be hanged in the process; second, people started to regard this as business-as-usual; and third, it became more or less institutionalized. That was an achievement of the spirit of party; in Rosenblum's words, "[o]nly parties bring opposition into the frame of government, regularize it, eventually legalize it, and make it politically mundane." By going public, parties begin to act as responsible institutions and cease to be regarded "as secretive societies, or seditious cabals, nurseries of rebellion."[16]

5. HER MAJESTY'S LOYAL OPPOSITION

My theme is loyal opposition, and we are approaching an understanding of it through various stages: political competition; rhythm and turn-taking; the right of chronic dissent even during the period of the victors' ascendancy; and the toleration of the losers' ability to organize themselves into powerful political entities reproaching and challenging the government at every turn. All of this is a matter of liberty, and it is of the utmost importance. But the ideal of loyal opposition goes well beyond liberty. It is a matter of constitutional empowerment.

I want to begin with the best-known example of the sort of empowerment I mean, and then (in conjunction with other examples) I will move to a more abstract consideration of loyal opposition as a principle of politics. I start with Britain because, as Nevil Johnson has put it, "[t]he notion of opposition as an inherent feature of the political system itself is more sharply defined in Britain than anywhere else, and has been for a far longer time."[17]

In Britain (indeed in parliamentary systems throughout the English-speaking world)[18] they do something quite interesting for the losers in electoral competition. They do not just tolerate organized political opposition; they *institutionalize* it in the structure of the constitution. One party or one coalition wins an election, but the largest group of losers in Parliament (those who won their individual parliamentary seats but are not in the majority party in the House of Commons) are designated as Her Majesty's Loyal Opposition. Their leader, the Leader of the Opposition—defined by statute since 1937 as "that member of the House of Commons who is for the time being the Leader in that House of the party in opposition to His Majesty's Government having the greatest numerical strength in that House"[19]—holds a paid government office, with the salary equivalent of a cabinet minister, and an official car, staff, and so on.[20] When this arrangement was instituted, there was some opposition to it.[21] But the majority in the debate recognized that the Leader of the Opposition had "a definite and distinct part to play in constitutional government"[22] and that he would not always have independent wealth to eke out his salary as an ordinary MP for the taxing demands of this extraordinary office. As Sir Ivor Jennings put it: "It may seem strange that the Government should by taxation raise £2000 a year in order to enable its principal opponent to criticise it; but in truth opposition is an essential part of democratic government."[23]

Actually, Dean McHenry points out that the Leadership of the Opposition was already established as a salaried office in Canada and Australia before it was established in Britain. "In 1905 a resolution was introduced in the House of Commons at Ottawa, providing that the member occupying the recognized position of House opposition leader should be paid a sessional allowance of not exceeding $7,000, in addition to his stipend as M.P."[24] Wherever it began, this practice—"the institutionalization within the workings of everyday politics of a standing alternative to the government of the day"—has been described as "the greatest contribution of the nineteenth century to the art of government."[25]

Apart from the salary, the powers, privileges, and duties of the office and of the opposition party generally are defined mainly by practice.[26] The Leader of the Opposition, as a sort of alternative prime minister, has a ceremonial presence at events of state; he will normally meet with foreign dignitaries, and so on. He will be entitled to confidential briefings on foreign affairs and (some) security issues by the prime minister and he will cooperate with the prime minister or the latter's nominated Leader of the House of Commons and the whips in organizing the agenda in the legislature.[27]

Also, the Leader of the Opposition now appoints spokesmen in the various areas in which the ruling party has appointed cabinet ministers.[28] This is called the shadow cabinet, and there is the shadow foreign secretary, the shadow minister of justice, the shadow minister of education, and so on. As shadow ministers, they are subject to something like the discipline of the principle of collective responsibility that applies to the ruling cabinet.[29]

What is the point of all this? The opposition and its leaders have an officially designated role in the system of government, but what is that role? Primarily, it is to make the legislature work as a forum for genuine critical debate. If Bagehot is right that the principle of party is "inherent" in the House of Commons, then Jennings may also be right that "perhaps the most important part of Parliament is the Opposition in the House of Commons."[30] There is the organizational task I mentioned—the Opposition must work with the government to organize the agenda for parliamentary debate (a function that we shouldn't underestimate, for imagine how legislative and other business would be conducted without it)[31] and to ensure that sufficient time is allocated for criticism, explanation, and accountability.[32] The Leader of the Opposition also has, as Clement Atlee observed, a special responsibility to defend the rights and privileges of ordinary MPs considered simply as members of the legislative body, apart from their party affiliation, particularly the right of every Member to express his opinion freely on all matters of public policy."[33]

Beyond those matters of institutional responsibility, of course, the important thing is for the opposition party to oppose, to scrutinize the government, to hold them accountable for their decisions,[34] "to limit the extremity of the Government's action, to arouse public criticism of any dangerous policy, and to make the Government behave reasonably."[35] In short, it is the duty of the opposition to serve in Edmund Burke's words as a "vigilant watchman over those in power."[36] The point of this is not necessarily to defeat the governing party in a confidence vote in the Commons—though that has been known to happen.[37] It is to familiarize the winners and the country at large with the point that criticism is okay and that policies are to be presented and defended in an explicitly and officially sanctioned adversarial environment. Maybe this leads to an "exaggeration of adversarial relationships in the public sphere,"[38] though it is mitigated somewhat by the relation between this function of criticizing the government and holding it accountable and the next function I want to talk about—which is, if anything, even more important.

It has been said that the main role of the official opposition is to prepare for government.[39] "Our Constitution," wrote Sir Ivor Jennings, "assumes that at any moment, if the Government resigns, or is defeated, or breaks up, an alternative can be formed from the Opposition."[40] And he added: "Her Majesty's Opposition is Her Majesty's alternative Government. The leader of the Opposition is almost Her Majesty's alternative Prime Minister."[41] Obviously, this duty—to provide a government-in-waiting—affects the way in which the duty to criticize is performed. The early development of the doctrine of parliamentary opposition, at the hands of Burke and others, included promotion of a consistent program to be advocated in opposition and realized in office.[42] This imposes a certain discipline of responsibility (a degree of shared responsibility for the public world, born of the constant possibility that one might have to take office at the next election or after the next confidence vote in the House).[43] As Campion put it, the Opposition must have a positive policy of its own and not merely oppose destructively.[44] Even from a strategic point of view, the opposition party must take care that criticisms do not suggest the endorsement of extreme policies. It must identify its constituency with some very broad proportion of the mass of the people that it may be called on at any time to govern.[45] As Jennings puts it:

> Irresponsible opposition is not part of democratic government, though many democratic States have never learned that lesson. The Opposition is giving a hostage to fortune whenever it takes a decision. It may be called upon—it hopes that it will be called upon—to assume in a short time the burdens of government.[46]

And he concluded, perhaps chauvinistically: "Our system alone can produce a responsible Opposition, one with a consistent policy known to the country in broad outline, one which is not anxious to win at the expense of ruining the game."[47] This is, in Rosenblum's phrase, "*regulated* rivalry"[48]—regulated not by any particular constraints or focus of loyalty (I will say much more about that in a moment)—but just by this prospect, which the Opposition entertains and which it embodies symbolically for the nation. The nation knows it can be governed by different people with different policies: *there they are,* designated as such, present and recognized within the legislative institutions.

So, that is the practice of loyal opposition in the land where it is best known and institutionally most clearly identified. The term "His or Her Majesty's Loyal Opposition" is said to have come from an MP, a Mr. Cam Hobhouse, in a debate in 1826 in the House of Commons.[49] Obviously, it works well in a two-party system (Whigs and Tories, Labor and Conservative, maybe Democrat and Republican), perhaps less well in a multiparty system. Neville Johnson has observed that it involves "a certain kind of brutal disregard for those parties which are not players in the big league."[50] Shortly I will say something about how it works in relation to coalition government of the type we see in Britain at the moment.

We do not have the institution of Leader of the Opposition in the United States, though there is something like recognized opposition in the roles and privileges of minority parties and minority leaders in the legislature. The phrase is not heard as often in American politics as it is in British politics, though it was "The Word" on *The Colbert Report* on February 10, 2009—riffing on Pete Sessions's suggestion that to fight the Obama administration, "insurgency may be required."[51] Institutionally, it would have to be different anyway, because as we all know the United States has a quite differently shaped political system. As George Anastaplo put it,

> The preponderance of governmental powers in Great Britain is exercised or regulated, directly or indirectly, by Parliament. It is, therefore, clearer in that country than in the United States precisely where the Loyal Opposition is, for the most part, located. . . . It is the House of Commons which, in principle, authorizes and empowers the government of the day, with the Loyal Opposition prepared to provide an alternative government whenever the House of Commons is prepared to support it.[52]

I will say more about the U.S. situation shortly—I believe there are important parallels as well as important differences between the British and American practices—but first I want to see what we can extrapolate from the British constitutional position by way of a general principle.

6. THE VERY IDEA OF LOYAL OPPOSITION

Obviously, the idea of loyal opposition is something we can abstract from the British institution. Indeed, the idea can be abstracted from formal politics and used in any setting; one might talk—people often do talk—about loyal opposition within a corporation, church, or academic department. These uses often do not go very far beyond the idea of, on the one hand, the tolerance of continuing dissent and, on the other hand, the willingness to restrain one's consent so as not to bring down the structure that houses it. Both are important, but often the settings to which this talk is applied cannot capture the specific mode of empowerment that characterizes the institutionalized British practice. That opposition need not be construed as disloyalty is one part of the loyal opposition idea. But that opposition figures should actually be empowered and their oppositional practice sponsored and facilitated by the system that defines them for the time being as losers is more challenging. In nonpolitical settings, this is likely to be more a matter of the personal whims and preferences of the powerful than a settled affirmative feature of the constitution of any of the groups in question. So I will mostly pass by these other uses of the term.

There is a second regard in which we might choose not to focus only on specifically political arrangements. In a society such as Britain, Canada, or Australia, where there are formalized arrangements for loyal opposition, we may think that they are likely to work institutionally only when they are backed up by a suitable ethos in society at large. Within Parliament, for example, the role of the Opposition and its relations to the Government require a certain level of civility—Burke sometimes used the phrase "the civil opposition"[53]—and it may be difficult to sustain that civility unless it is nourished by broader civility at the level of society as a whole. People sometimes worry, for example, about the extreme antagonism that has in recent years entered informal American politics and that tends to contaminate and undermine the civil transaction of business in the House of Representatives. Neither the serious suggestion, on the one hand, that prominent members of the Bush administration should face investigation and trial after the Democratic victory of 2008 nor the suggestion by right-wing commentators that their liberal opponents are not just wrong but demonically so[54] bodes well for the civility on which traditions of loyal opposition depend. I will not say any more about this except that it is surely an important issue.[55]

But we should remember that formalized practices of loyal opposition probably make as much of a contribution to practices of civility and tolerance in the community as the other way around. As Russell Muirhead and Nancy Rosenblum put it, the formalized practices embody, highlight, proclaim, and assume that political opponents are to be regarded as "reasonable rivals not enemies to be destroyed."[56] Or, as Rosenblum puts it in her book, formalized oppositional practice gets people used to what she calls "the legitimacy of ongoing, managed, institutionalized conflict."[57]

I am concentrating, then, on loyal opposition as a constitutional principle. I believe it is one of the leading principles of the British constitution. It might seem ironic that the most advanced development of this constitutional idea is in a country that does not have a codified constitution either to embody this principle or to serve as the residual focus of loyalty in opposition—again, more on that in a moment. But British writers since Albert Venn Dicey have talked usefully of the principles of the constitution nonetheless. For Dicey, there were two of them: the sovereignty of Parliament and the rule of law.[58] I would add a few others, such as limited monarchy, the devolution principle, universal suffrage, the independence of the judiciary, respect for human rights, and—I now want to say—loyal opposition.

It is not a principle that gets much attention from English constitutional writers. Bagehot and Jennings wrote extensively about it, as we have seen. But more recently, Vernon Bogdanor simply ignored it in his book *The New British Constitution*—perhaps because it is such an entrenched feature of Parliament and party that he thinks it can be taken for granted.[59] I worry about this because now that there are some tentative moves to begin codifying British constitutional arrangements, it would be a pity to see this left out of the picture simply because it was too familiar, or crowded out of explicit consideration by other more sexy topics of constitutional concern.

We talk about free speech and a tolerant political culture—but again I want to emphasize that the principle of loyal opposition goes far beyond that. It is not just the negative idea of not treating one's opponents as though they were enemies of society; it is not just the idea of legitimizing dissent or "freedom of speech and the right to publicly and legitimately oppose the policies and actions of the government of the day."[60] It is not just the idea that one can oppose actively and, in an organization devoted to such opposition, continually criticize and proclaim alternatives to government policies. It is not just the idea of legitimizing vehement organized opposition, opposition seeking to discredit ministers and officials, and actively seeking to supplant the government that won the election, without being labeled a subversive or a traitor. All of that is important, but the principle of loyal opposition is also the idea of positive empowerment by the creation and sponsoring of an official recognized role for oppositional practice within the constitutional fabric, making "the propriety of opposition as integral a part of the constitutional structure . . . as the authority of government."[61]

7. A PREREQUISITE FOR DEMOCRACY?

The practice and acceptance of the principle of loyal opposition is, I think, an important prerequisite for democracy.[62] Maybe it is not a necessary or indispensable prerequisite,[63] but I mean to say that if a country does not have substantial experience of it, does not have this in the repertoire of its political culture, it is less likely to be successful in setting up a democracy; that is, a system that rotates rival factions in and out of office on the basis of periodic popular votes.

You may ask, "How can loyal opposition be a prerequisite? How can it predate democracy? How can there be any way of identifying an opposition party or an opposition leader except in a democracy? What else but a system of democratic elections could provide the medium in which parties alternate in and out of office?" One obvious answer is that the practice of loyal opposition may become familiar to a polity in a proto-democratic stage—Britain before the Reform Acts, or apartheid South Africa, for example—where there is voting and there are winners and losers in elections, but where the franchise is not fully extended to all.

Or political competition could take place in some other medium, and winners may be separated from losers in some currency other than ballots. There might be competition for royal favor, or the vicissitudes of the principle of heredity or the monarch's mortality (or, in the case of Henry VIII, the monarch's marriages) might provide a basis on which groups of politicians alternate in and out of power. Beyond that, we might imagine political competition and the rotation of winners and losers in terms of the waxing and waning of charismatic power, the fickle support of Praetorian guards, the whim of the gods revealed through auspices, or just the vicissitudes of manifest success and failure of policy revealed in famines, military defeats, fiscal crises, and so on.

In environments of these kinds, political practice might be such that people become used to the recognized presence of a defeated politician hanging around in some public role, not just tolerated but empowered as an oppositional presence, entitled to carp and criticize in the hearing of anyone at court who will listen, and waiting for the wheel of fortune to turn again. Getting used to this even in a nondemocratic environment makes it possible for people to approach both the powers of victory and the gall of defeat in democratic elections more responsibly.

I mention this because I think it is important for a democracy, early in its life, not to think of electoral victory and defeat in any sort of analogy with military victory and defeat. Military victory aims at the destruction of the enemy's force, even though it is often necessary for battles to be waged successively over a period of time in order to accomplish that. But elections don't aim at the permanent eradication of a losing party. They aim at its relegation to a loser's role for the time being. Yet political theorists persist, irresponsibly in my view, with this analogy. Adam Przeworski suggests that "voting constitutes 'flexing muscles': a reading of chances in the eventual war. If all men are equally strong (or armed) then the distribution of votes is a proxy for the outcome of war."[64] The idea is that the losers submit to the winner's rule because they are informed by the voting of how likely it is that they would be destroyed in a fight. All too often, powerful parties in new democracies face their first elections in this spirit, understanding that the point of the election is to settle once and for all, by some surrogate for fighting, which party is to prevail in the polity and which party is doomed to permanent exile from political life. That, as I say, is a bad model; much better to have had experience of rotation in and out of office and the empowerment of opposition in some nondemocratically competitive environment than to understand the environment of democratic competition in this militaristic spirit.

8. THE AMERICAN VERSION

With these reflections in mind, I want to turn now to a political system with which we are much more familiar but whose democratic environment honors the principle of loyal opposition in a rather different way.

In the United States, there is no equivalent of the role of Leader of the Opposition—though we came close to it in the old understanding of the vice-presidency (before the addition of the Twelfth Amendment in 1804), whereby John Adams's vice president in 1797 was his opponent, Thomas Jefferson. Nor is there any constitutional designation of a party in the legislature as the Loyal Opposition—the Constitution says nothing at all about political parties—though both houses have evolved the recognized office of "minority leader" and accorded it some modicum of standing.

But the principle of loyal opposition—though seldom labeled in that way—is still respected and has been since the time of the anti-Federalists.[65] George Anastaplo emphasizes that those who win the presidency by defeating an incumbent have usually been oppositionally active in national politics for several years in the period immediately preceding their election, either in the legislature or in a statehouse; and often they have had experience as an adviser, cabinet member, or other high appointee of a previous administration.[66] So we have the rotation idea.

More broadly, American politics remains intensely adversarial, and we expect parties to be engaged in organized, well-funded, root-and-branch opposition to the powers that be (sometimes opposition to the president, sometimes against the majority party in the legislature), not only without being designated as traitors to our society but also in terms of the recognition of multitudes of oppositional figures as prominent *players* in the political system. The United Kingdom focuses its acceptance of the principle in the specific office of the Leader of the Opposition, whereas in the United States loyal opposition is much more ubiquitous in character. Polsby remarks that

> [t]his is so much the case that it probably makes less sense to talk of opposition than to speak in the American context of political disagreement or conflict or checks and balances or oppositions (plural) and therefore to describe ways in which the varied forms of opposition are embodied in [various] institutions.[67]

Because there are diverse centers of power, separated from one another, there are diverse opportunities for oppositional politics and oppositional presence in various institutions. As Polsby puts it, "The fact that there is no consolidated, well-institutionalized, unified, system-wide opposition connects with the fact that government is spread among constitutional branches and levels and entities and is itself by design not consolidated or unified."[68] What this means is that it is possible for a party and its leaders to be powerholders in one institution (say, the House or the Senate) even while a different party and its leader are powerholders in the executive. (Something similar often happens between the two chambers of the federal legislature.) This is not preordained—the same party can be in power in the legislature and in the White House.[69] But it happens often enough that we can say the American system is capable of giving greater power than the British system gives to politicians whom we can regard (from one or another point of view) as opposition leaders. Constitutional theory, under the heading of checks and balances, legitimizes active opposition and resistance to the plans of those who dominate one branch by those who dominate another. We value that clash of branches and parties. And it also sets things up so that it is very difficult—not impossible—for a party to push through its program simply on the basis of its own political resources. The constitutional structure—bicameralism, the president's veto, advice-and-consent, and perhaps also judicial review—means that any party "in power" has to coordinate and usually compromise with leaders of other persuasions.[70]

Add to all of this the federal structure of the Constitution, with separate administrations in fifty states, and we have a whole additional layer of potential and piecemeal opposition, complicated, in turn, in a sort of fractal fashion by the way in which the constitutional structure of each state recognizes separation of powers, bicameralism (except in Nebraska), and the principle of checks and balances in the structure of its governance. State constitutions empower loyal opposition to state administration at various points, and state office and state institutions can also be centers of opposition in national politics. We can see all of this coming together, for example, in the diverse centers of opposition to "Obamacare"—the health care legislation enacted in 2009. The House of Representatives would repeal it if it could, but (at the time of writing) there is probably still a majority to sustain it (or sustain a presidential veto aiming to protect it) in the Senate. And there is ferocious opposition in the states. Note also that the situation is fluid because the presidency, the two chambers of Congress, and the states sometimes work on different electoral schedules, so that things reshuffle and rearrange themselves. The majority party in the House of Representatives was not oppositional to the Obama administration when the health care legislation was passed, but now it is. As we will see, this matter of different schedules of election (and appointment) is quite important for the way in which practices of loyal opposition play out in American politics.

Nor do I exclude the judiciary from this account. The courts can be a focus of opposition to the program of a powerful president or a powerful faction in Congress. They can strike down legislation that has been enacted by the elective branches, and—as we all know—whether they do so often depends on the interplay between the judges' own political predilections and their view of the often vague and ambiguous terms of the Constitution.[71] It is not just the Supreme Court. There is a hugely complicated picture here. Obamacare has been assailed by some district courts around the country (usually at the behest of state administrations) and supported by others. It has been upheld by some circuit Courts of Appeals and assailed by others. And, at the appellate level, we see that each court empowers a diversity of judges, with varying politics and allegiances.

All of this is enhanced by the point that, in American political life, people are appointed and empowered on different schedules. A judge may be appointed by a Democratic administration, confirmed grudgingly by a Republican-dominated Senate, and then has to take her seat among Republican appointees as well, some of whom may have been nominated when the Republican Party was a somewhat different creature than it is now. Different schedules of appointment, and no provision for regular reappointment or accountability, mean that our judiciary empowers judges of all political shades in a sort of layered representation of the country's political history. (There are justices who can be described as opposition leaders in the Supreme Court.) And the same is true of office-holding in the other branches of government and in the states as well.

Nelson Polsby uses a revealing phrase in his description of the way the American system accommodates opposition. He talks of "forms of opposition" being "embedded in the routines of American government as a natural consequence of the constitutional necessity for checks and balances."[72] I think what he has in mind or, whether Polsby had it in mind or not, what is the case is the following. The U. S. Constitution separates and disperses power, partly on federalist principles, partly simply to reduce the amount of power in the hands of any one person or agency, and partly on the basis of rule-of-law ideas that require the function of legislation to be sharply separated from the judicial and executive functions, lest legislators make oppressive laws in the confidence of being able to ensure that the laws are not applied to them or their

THE PRINCIPLE OF LOYAL OPPOSITION

family and friends.[73] This can often mean that separated powers are in the hands of people who are politically opposed to one another. Now, so far that is not an empowerment of opposition. The functional separation of powers requires the executive and the judiciary to faithfully interpret and execute the statutes that the legislature has enacted according to their terms, and it requires the executive to faithfully carry out judicial orders according to their terms. Functional separation requires a sort of assembly-line fidelity.

But in America we *also* associate the separation of powers with the doctrine of checks and balances; and the point of checks and balances is to empower the branches sometimes to act in opposition to one another. This empowerment is partly formal, as in procedures of judicial review or presidential veto, and it is partly informal, empowering—indeed taking for granted—that it is constitutionally legitimate for the president sometimes to square off against the legislature or vice versa.

There is the same combination of constitutional distinction and constitutional empowerment mutatis mutandis in the case of the states and their relation to the centers of national governmental authority. On the one hand, the authority of the states is sharply distinguished by the Constitution from the authority of the federal government, but we also accept as part of the informal constitution that state officials—state governors or state legislators, for example—should feel empowered from time to time to engage in oppositional politics vis-à-vis various elements at the federal level, and vice versa.

So that is the basis—the very loose and dispersed basis—on which America respects the principle of loyal opposition.

9. LOYAL OPPOSITION AND PARTICIPATION IN GOVERNMENT

The matter is complicated in an interesting way by the interaction of the principle of loyal opposition with another related practice—the actual mitigation of political defeat by the assignment of losers to actual political offices and the insistence that in various regards winners must share power with losers.[74] This business of opposition participation in government is partly what is going on with separation of powers, of course, and federalism. Even with its "spoils system," the United States does not operate on a winner-takes-all basis. Opposition figures work with government figures in various areas of policy, and leading opposition politicians are taken into the confidence of the current administration in various ways. (This is particularly true in respect to foreign policy, intelligence, and national security matters.) Something similar happens in the United Kingdom, sometimes under the auspices of Her Majesty's Privy Council, which counts opposition statesmen among its membership.

Obviously, the structure of modern legislatures ensures that this "opposition participation in government" happens or has the potential to happen to a very considerable extent. An individual or a party may be a loser, so far as majorities and minorities are concerned, but that makes sense only on the assumption that the members concerned do actually have a vote in the legislature. And that vote is sometimes used affirmatively in governance, not just oppositionally. Sometimes if a policy that the administration wants to enact is unpopular with some members of its own party, the administration will rely on opposition votes to get it through.

A further respect in which we see this "opposition participation in government" has to do with the rhythms of election and appointment. Different chambers in a bicameral legislature may be on different election schedules, and this may produce disparities between the two chambers that make it difficult—it is a healthy difficulty—to say who is government and who is opposition. And then there are appointed offices, whose empowerment often outstrips the administration that appointed them. As already indicated, this is obviously true as far as the judiciary is concerned. Life-tenure judges may be empowered governmentally even though they are political opponents of the current administration or the current legislature.

Finally, we need to remember that law itself operates in this way. No democracy adopts a year-zero mentality to the law in every change of administration. Law at any moment operates as a sort of archaeological midden, representing the residue of legislative and adjudicative activity of previous generations of judges and lawmakers, many of them in parties or with convictions opposed to the current generation of rulers. Rotation of various parties and judges of various political flavors in and out of power over a century or two produces a challenging patchwork of laws. Time does not permit me to explore here what legal theorists—most notably Ronald Dworkin—have made of this challenge in their attempt to treat such a patchwork as a coherent whole, with some unifying integrity, for the purposes of bringing the whole law to bear on any particular case.[75]

THE PRINCIPLE OF LOYAL OPPOSITION 113

The principle of opposition participation in government is evidently closely connected to the principle of loyal opposition. They work together, most notably in the American system; they work necessarily together to the extent that the locus of opposition is in a parliament that affirmatively empowers each of its members with a legislative vote.

But they are distinct principles. We can see this, I think, in some of the things that have been said in the British context about the distinction between the practice of loyal opposition, on the one hand, and the formation of coalitions—which obviously is a sort of opposition participation in government, with minority parties acquiring cabinet office, and so on. During the Second World War, in Great Britain, a "National Government" was formed, with members from all major parties. The country was engaged for five or six years in a desperate struggle for national survival, and it was felt that this required something other than adversarial politics as usual. (It is noteworthy, however, that even in these circumstances, parliamentary practice required that there be a Leader of the Opposition to carry out certain parliamentary functions, and one was created artificially, precipitated [so to speak] out of the National Government coalition.)[76]

After the war, it was suggested that this coalition be continued, because the country still faced national crises well into the 1950s. The proposal met with vehement opposition. Some said "that those who talk of a national Government misunderstand the whole nature of the present political situation. They forget especially that this country invented the concept of the loyal Opposition."[77] And even during the war, Sir Arthur Baxter said this in the House of Commons:

> When in 1940 the country was placed in a great crisis it seemed a wise and spontaneous act for a Coalition Government to be formed. That crisis in its intensity has passed. Now victory is reasonably within sight, and the problems of post-war development are closer and more urgent all the time. Therefore the real reason for maintaining this Parliament another year is to maintain the Coalition Government. I wonder whether we think enough of the effect of this upon the country. For decades upon decades the government of this country was carried on by the principle of the Government and His Majesty's loyal Opposition. It worked through great crises, it brought and developed human liberty to its present state here, and was an inspiration in the outside world. Then we said, "Here is a crisis; a war which cannot be handled on

that basis. We do not want His Majesty's loyal Opposition, we do not want an Opposition at all, save by a band of guerrillas who have got in here as Independents." That to my mind is a denial of the very strength of our Parliamentary system.[78]

I do not want to judge the case against coalition government. And anyhow, usually it does not have the totalizing effects of an all-party coalition, which is what Britain had during the war. Usually, it is more like the present situation in Britain (as I write in April 2014), with a coalition between one large party (the Conservatives) and a small party (the Liberal Democrats), but still with a large and active party (the Labour Party)—not much smaller than the ruling party and with very extensive experience in government—on the opposition benches.

Though the principles are closely related, then, the key difference is that the principle of opposition participation in government empowers losing parties with respect to affirmative governmental functions, while the principle of loyal opposition empowers losing parties specifically with the function of criticizing and preparing to supplant the party currently in office.

10. CO-OPTION?

Finally, I want to edge toward a discussion of this concept of *loyalty*. It is embedded, I think, in both the principle of opposition participation and the principle of loyal opposition, but explicitly of course in the principle of loyal opposition. George Anastaplo has said that "[a]t the heart . . . of a . . . spirit of Loyal Opposition is the settled opinion in the community that there are things more important than . . . the interests of one's party." Loyal opposition, he said, involves "a dedication to established common objectives that reminds political opponents that what unites them should be considered far more significant, and more enduring, than what happens to divide them for the moment."[79] I think we need to be very careful about this.

When I was at school, it was the enlightened practice of the principal to appoint as prefects some of the dissident and smart-ass elements in the school, flattering them with a degree of limited authority in order to co-opt them and curb their unruliness. It was an admirable practice, and I was one of the beneficiaries of it in 1969 and 1970. But that, surely, is not how we want the empowerment of loyal opposition to be understood—as a form of political co-option, like the party-approved version of the Catholic Church in China, or (a more sinister example) the party-approved version of the Lutheran Church in Nazi Germany against which Dietrich Bonhoeffer struggled so courageously. We also have memories of the dignifying of certain parties close in spirit to the Communist Party as pathetic approved "opposition" figures in the Soviet Bloc in the 1950s and 1960s.[80] When Cam Hobhouse first used the term "His Majesty's Loyal Opposition" in 1826, another MP, George Tierney, said that it was an apposite phrase because "we [the Opposition] are, certainly, to all intents and purposes, a branch of his Majesty's government."[81] Nevil Johnson has described the Loyal Opposition in Britain as "a state agency."[82] So, is co-option a problem?

It has occasionally been said in British political circles that the Loyal Opposition has a duty to support the government. They are loyal to the Queen, it is said, and that means supporting her authority wielded by her ministers. As one opposition peer put it in 1979: "[I]t is our duty . . . to give such constructive help as we can to the newly-formed Government in the carrying out of policies for which they have received the decisive support of the electorate as a whole."[83]

The duty to support the government has often been thought to be particularly important in matters of foreign policy. For example, it is said that the Opposition should not criticize treaties that the government has entered into.[84] (Correlative to this is a duty on the part of the government to consult with Opposition leaders.)[85] Also, although the Leader of the Opposition is entitled to meet with foreign heads of state and heads of government when they make official visits to the United Kingdom, it was long thought inappropriate for him to maintain separate lines of communication with foreign powers.[86] But there are now serious limits on this doctrine. Potter notes that in 1937 a Conservative MP put down a motion of censure against the Leader of the Opposition for speeches he had made during a visit to the Spanish Republican government. (The Conservative government's policy was—at best—indifference between the Republican government and Franco's "Nationalist" rebels.) Clement Atlee responded with this personal statement in the House of Commons: "The Leader of the Opposition . . . owes no allegiance to the Government. No action of his can in any way implicate the Government. He is responsible only to his constituents and to the Members from whom he derives his position."[87] Apparently that was the end of the matter. Potter infers from this that, even in this area of foreign relations, "Her Majesty's Opposition is not a 'licensed' opposition: the status of being the official opposition is not in the gift [or under the control] of the Government."[88]

11. LOYAL TO WHAT?

What, then, does the word "loyal" mean in the phrase "loyal opposition"? The relatively abstract idea that one can oppose but still be loyal is made more concrete when we ask "loyal to what?" What, if anything, is one not entitled to oppose if one's opposition is to be described as "loyal"? I am going to explore several possibilities before concluding that the question is misguided.

(i) The Queen

In Britain, the opposition is described as *"Her Majesty's* Loyal Opposition." Is the monarch then the focus of loyalty?[89] It seems an attractive idea. Indeed, it might be thought to be an advantage of having a (constitutional) monarchy that the monarch can serve the function of providing, in Jennings's phrase, a safe "focus for patriotism."

> This is of particular importance in a democracy, for the Government for the time being, though supported by a section of the people only, is the instrument of the whole. It is possible, therefore, for opposition to the Government to be attacked as opposition to the nation. The Government, too, does nothing to destroy the idea. It parades the national flag and uses every opportunity to take to itself the title of "National." The ordinary individual appears to be on the horns of a dilemma. Either he must support the Government, or he must oppose the nation. The monarchy provides a simple means of demonstrating that the dilemma does not exist. A person can be loyal to his King and yet oppose the Government.[90]

Certainly, the monarchy is one focus of the cooperation between government and opposition: the prime minister must by convention consult with the Leader of the Opposition on any matter concerning the monarchy or the royal family.[91]

But does this mean that in order to be accounted loyal the Opposition must be monarchist in its principles? That would be a problem because even in Britain and elsewhere in the Commonwealth there are respectable politicians who want the monarchy to be done away with.

In fact, the issue can be finessed. In the United Kingdom, before a Member of Parliament can receive any of the public money allocated to support the activities of opposition parties, he must swear allegiance to the Crown: "I . . . swear by Almighty God that I will be faithful and bear true allegiance to Her Majesty Queen Elizabeth, her heirs and successors, according to law. So help me God."[92] David Fontana reports that the House of Commons has found ways to fund Sinn Fein, the Irish nationalist group, as an opposition party despite the fact that its members refuse to take this oath.[93]

(ii) The Constitution

In the United States, we might expect the focus of loyalty in "loyal" opposition to be adherence to the Constitution.[94] Article VI of the U.S. Constitution requires state and federal legislators and all executive and judicial officers to "be bound by Oath or Affirmation" to support the Constitution.

But again we have to contemplate the possibility of opposition statesmen who oppose various provisions of the Constitution. The U.S. Constitution hasn't always been the object of unconditional worship as it is now. There were abolitionists in the antebellum period who regarded it as a "covenant with death" and "an agreement with Hell."[95] Yet there might still be a distinction of loyalty between them and the insurgent John Brown, who actually rose up forcibly against the government on this basis.

Less apocalyptically, we might also note (and deplore) the tendency of modern American politicians to try to insert controversial party positions into the constitutional structure (of a state constitution or the federal constitution) in an attempt to outflank or outfox one's opponents—whether it is prohibitionists with the Eighteenth Amendment in 1919 or conservatives who for a while contrived the insertion of bans on the legal recognition of same-sex marriage in thirty state constitutions. The politics of this may be understandable, but, of course, the more we do things like this on controversial issues on which reasonable people in the polity disagree, the less the Constitution can function as a focus of allegiance to define the supposed loyalty of the political opposition.

Nancy Rosenblum's position seems more sensible. She is skeptical about a constitutional focus of loyalty, and about insisting that "parties operate within an agreed-on constitutional framework." She writes:

> I see no reason to . . . say that by definition parties operate within a settled constitutional framework or constitutional consensus and that interpreting and challenging constitutional bounds or the character of the regime is no business of parties. Often enough parties are organized over or against it, advocate and effect constitutional change, sometimes radical.[96]

(iii) "Constitutional essentials"

Can we solve the problem by "slimming down" the constitutional focus of loyalty? Consider, for example, John Rawls's notion of "constitutional essentials" in *Political Liberalism* and elsewhere.[97] Rawls is actually one of the few political philosophers who bothers talking about loyal opposition, and his theme is that "[t]he government and its loyal opposition agree on . . . constitutional essentials. Their so agreeing makes the government legitimate in intention and the opposition loyal in its opposition."[98] (In his account, constitutional essentials include "the fundamental principles that specify the general structure of government and the political process" as well as "basic rights and liberties . . . that legislative majorities are to respect.")[99] He includes the principle of loyal opposition itself among these constitutional essentials.

This idea of constitutional essentials played a major role in Rawls's work. It is the focus of his controversial doctrine of public reason: his insistence that arguments by officials and among citizens on constitutional essentials are to be conducted within the limits of reasoning that is intelligible to the whole public,[100] and that people are not to cite religious or other deep philosophical grounds for their views on these matters that might not make sense to others who come at them from a different perspective. He also holds the view that "[p]ublic political discussion[s], when constitutional essentials and matters of basic justice are at stake, are always, or nearly always, reasonably decidable on the basis of reasons,"[101] and he thinks it follows that this sets them apart from the normal hurly-burly of politics as being matters on which deliberative consensus is available and on which we should not expect very much change.[102] And he thinks it follows also that we should not expect them to be changed very often, certainly not in a way that reflects the temporary ascendancy of party.

I applaud Rawls for taking the principle of loyal opposition seriously, but I think he is wrong about all this. The fact (if it is a fact) that everyone can approach constitutional essentials in terms of public reasons that seem to compel a certain conclusion does not demonstrate that reasonable disagreement on these matters is impossible. There are many views on these matters, and each of dozens of contesting views puts itself forward as a cogent working through of public reasons, as though no other conclusion were possible. We must not let this style of philosophical presentation lure us into insisting, as a focus of loyalty, on doctrines that, whether we like it or not, are still subject to the reasonable disagreements with which we are familiar in real-life politics.

I know many political philosophers and some constitutional theorists are attracted by the idea that not everything should be up for grabs in politics, and many are convinced that the things that should not be up for grabs are normally to be found in the Constitution. The Constitution is supposed to represent a consensus that transcends politics and that can therefore be designated the focus of social unity and political allegiance for the system as a whole.[103] But those who take this view must surely understand that, in the real world, people disagree about many of these formulations. The burdens of judgment are such that we must expect such disagreement.[104] Rawls said that he himself had objections to certain features of the U.S. Constitution under which he lived,[105] and presumably he would have had no difficulty voting for a party that swore to alter the Constitution in this regard. He might also say that the idea of a loyal opposition—loyal to the constitutional essentials of the society in which it operates—is a conception for a well-ordered society, and the United States as presently constituted is not well ordered in his view.[106] To that extent, his work on this is mildly utopian. Fair enough. But we need a concept of loyal opposition for the imperfect real world here and now. This is especially so if we are imagining it as a principle whose acceptance will help build a democratic constitutional society in countries that have not hitherto enjoyed those advantages.

(iv) The rules of the game

Even more minimally, can we say that a loyal opposition party must at the very least accept the basic ground rules of the political game—the "fundamental tenets of the democratic system"[107] (i.e., the rules that designate a party as the winner or the loser in a democratic contest)? Lord Campion suggested that it is important for the Loyal Opposition not to be "anxious to win at the expense of ruining the game."[108] There is something to this, though again we are well advised not to look for a doctrinal formulation, a sort of loyalty test that must be administered to any party before it can be admitted to this status. Many Democrats thought that the "rules of the game"—at least as administered by the Supreme Court in *Bush v. Gore*[109]— were illegitimate; they didn't rise up against the Bush administration, but many did not concede its legitimacy either. Do we want to say that they were not "loyal" in their opposition to the Bush regime? What about people—say, supporters of a radical change to proportional representation—who believe that the present electoral system is quite unjust? Are they to be excluded from being described as a loyal opposition if they propound this view and do what they can to undermine and replace the rules of the game by which they are supposed to be playing?

We might say that if an opposition party does not like the current system, the rules of the game as it is currently played, they must work within the system to change the rules. That is what it takes to be "loyal" in a system like ours. So, for example, the U.S. Constitution envisages that certain changes may take place, and it ordains a process for that. Should we say that a party counts as loyal if, even though it criticizes some aspects of our constitutional system, it is nevertheless willing to work through Article V of the Constitution to amend it? Attractive, but even this will not do. Many people think Article V ordains a process that is outrageously difficult for a constitution most of whose terms were laid down hundreds of years ago in radically different circumstances. Bruce Ackerman has reminded us that many of the most important changes in our constitution have taken place through irregular means.[110] I do not mean this to be the basis of a thoroughgoing constitutional skepticism—just to indicate that once again it is a mistake to think we can isolate certain norms or certain provisions as the focus of unequivocal loyalty.

(v) The nation

I am afraid much the same has to be said about other less formal suggestions about what the opposition must be loyal to. Maybe it is loyalty to the nation that is important. But opposition parties can be secessionist or anti-Unionist—as with Sinn Fein in Northern Ireland, Parti Québecois in

Canada, or the Scottish National Party in the United Kingdom. People might disagree with the particular basis on which their nation is constituted, and may be unable to take loyalty oaths that draw attention to that principle. Avigdor Lieberman's suggestion that loyalty oaths be administered to all Israel's citizens, including Arab citizens, was rightly criticized on this ground.[111] Wherever we look, we see difficulties with any doctrinal test for loyalty.

In all of this, maybe we should look less to what the opposition has to say, in order to be counted as loyal, and more to what a loyal opposition is supposed to *do*. In the British House of Lords, the Earl of Lauderdale put it this way: [W]e respect the Government even if we disagree with them; we obey them; we obey the laws; . . . even though we form part of Her Majesty's loyal Opposition."[112] A responsible opposition party does not try to seize the government benches when the majority members' backs are turned or counsel disobedience in the community. They are loyal to the ruling party (or to the system that designates a party as the ruling party) to that extent. But even here, we will run into antinomies having to do with "civil" modes of disobedience and resistance. Few of us, I think, will want to say that a party is disqualified from being designated a "loyal" opposition party simply because some of its members or even its leadership engage in civil disobedience.

Or think of the paradoxes that Otto Kirchheimer got into in trying to distinguish between loyal opposition parties and parties whose ideology or behavior "indicates the desire for a degree of goal displacement incompatible with the constitutional requirements of a given system."[113] He called the latter an "opposition of principle"—which was a curiously respectful label, given that he wanted to associate it, for example, with the Nazis and Communists in the Weimar period.[114] But he acknowledged the indeterminacy of the concept in less extreme cases, where you have in a given party, say the German Social Democrats, some oscillation between two tendencies: (1) treating elections as a temporary "ready-made battleground, where they might integrate and exploit their gains and then proceed [perhaps violently] to more far-reaching political action" and (2) a more patient state of mind where it is accepted that electoral politics is the only field of action for the medium term, even though in the long run the seizure of the state cannot be ruled out.[115] In both cases, we have a party whose engagement in the "game" of electoral politics seems strategic at best, a way of biding their time until they can launch themselves into more activist and determined opposition. But do we want to characterize all such tendencies as "disloyal" or to use the difference in timescale to indicate some important distinction so far as the loyalty of an opposition party is concerned? I must admit, I do not know what to say about that.

Clearly, there is difficulty pinning down the focus of loyalty in the principle of loyal opposition. Whatever work "loyal" is doing in this regard, it has to do it in the context of plurality, in the context of reasonable disagreement about virtually everything, which has been our starting point in this analysis. The circumstances of modern politics are such that different people are bound to have different accounts of what everyone needs to be loyal to. So this is inevitably going to be a basis of contestation, and we have to deal with it as such.

I think what I want to say is that it is probably a mistake to regard "loyal" in the concept of loyal opposition as denoting some sort of doctrinal or behavioral test that a party has to pass before it can be dignified with this appellation. It is probably a mistake to distract ourselves with the question of what it is that goes into the test (i.e., what are the essential commitments that are supposed to stand above party competition). Instead of saying that the word "loyal" in "loyal opposition" refers to a stipulated focus of allegiance, we might say instead that it indicates the way in which the opposition party *must be regarded* in a constitutional system. The word "loyal," in my view, works as a sort of admonition to the ruling party. Their opponents are to be regarded for all purposes as loyal; their loyalty is not to be questioned but is to be assumed. You may ask, "Their loyalty to *what* is not to be questioned? I answer loosely: their loyalty to *anything* whose perceived absence might be cited as grounds for suppressing their criticism or disempowering them from the oppositional role that I have been talking about. They are assumed to be loyal not in the sense that there are certain things they may not criticize and certain things they may not propose but in the sense that none of their criticism is ever to be regarded as a reason for regarding them as subversive. They are assumed to be loyal in the sense that the prospect of their becoming a government is constitutionally and politically thinkable and is to be respected as such, no matter what the nature of their program. This principle is an open and inclusive one, and the benefit of its application is to be open to any party that has the capacity to fulfill the role ordained by the principle. Under favorable conditions, this attitude can create the reality of loyalty that it postulates.[116]

12. A PARADOX?

Loyal opposition has the appearance of a paradox,[117] but if it is, I hope I have shown that it is a productive paradox and one of the more interesting things that constitutions do, one of the more interesting roles and plays that the political game makes provision for.

According to Ludger Helms, "It has long been acknowledged by democratic theory that the principle of legitimate political opposition belongs to the most fundamental components of any liberal democracy."[118] I wish that were true; I wish that the people Helms calls democratic theorists would devote some time to acknowledgment of and reflection on this principle. Most of them—most self-described political theorists in the academy—ignore the principle of loyal opposition (in the same way that, as Nancy Rosenblum reminds us, they ignore political parties). In fact, in my experience, too many political theorists ignore the principles of political institutions altogether. They say it is not philosophical enough. They say we should leave it to the law professors, the empirical political scientists, or the comparativists; the theorists are too busy writing pamphlets on global justice.

As I said in Chapter 1, I think there are all sorts of things wrong with this asserted division of labor within the study of politics. Of course, there is an important place for more philosophical reflection on political issues, including—I readily concede—philosophical reflection on matters such as justice, rights, and equality, which represent the content of the work done within the housing that constitutions provide. But there is theoretical work to be done on the housing as well, on the structures that accommodate our politics. I have tried, in these reflections on the idea of loyalty in politics, to give some indication of this work both in the very idea of opposition and in the way various principles operate in our system—principles such as political competition, Aristotelian turn-taking, the toleration of dissent, the importance of parties, the separation of powers, the principle of checks and balances—to recognize and dignify opposition with an empowered role of criticism and the positing of an alternative within an orderly democratic system.

At its best, officially empowered opposition involves what George Kateb has called a "radical chastening" of political authority.[119] It is not just about free speech or the toleration of dissent, though those are important. A theory of human rights or constitutional rights is not all we need to understand this principle. We have to look to the way in which political opposition is empowered in a democratic system, and the way in which doing that pays tribute to and teaches lessons about what Nancy Rosenblum calls "the provisional nature of political authority" in circumstances of plurality.[120] As I said at the beginning, quoting Hannah Arendt, politics exists because not one person but people inhabit the world—people in all their diversity with all their disagreements. Even if the objective truth about justice or the common good is singular, here on earth there are still many of us with many views, and ways must be found to accommodate us all in a political system.

CHAPTER SIX

Representative Lawmaking

WHAT MAKES LEGISLATION an attractive mode of lawmaking? You may ask, "Attractive compared to what?" Attractive compared to lawmaking by judges and lawmaking by decree or executive agency (though in a broader inquiry we might contrast it also with lawmaking by treaty and also lawmaking by custom).

1. DEMOCRACY

One answer is that, in the modern world, legislation is associated with democracy. Legislatures are mostly elective and accountable bodies. Their members are elected as legislators, and they can be replaced at regular intervals if their constituents dislike what they or their party are doing in the legislature. This gives their lawmaking a legitimacy that lawmaking by judges lacks. In a lot of my work, I have emphasized this aspect of the matter: I have said that one of the main objections to judicial review is that it allows the decisions of unelected officials to trump the legitimate decisions of elected officials.[1]

But this can't be all there is to it. In many American jurisdictions, state judges *are* elected officials; they, too, can claim democratic credentials. And the same might be said of an elected president. If we are faced with a choice between rule by legislation and rule by presidential decree, we are not choosing between democratic and nondemocratic lawmaking; we are choosing between two different sets of democratic credentials. There is also the point that some legislatures have nonelective components. The British House of Lords, for example, and the upper house of the Canadian legislature are appointed rather than elective bodies (and indeed the House of Lords still has a residual hereditary, not to mention an ecclesiastical, component). So, some legislative bodies do not have democratic credentials, and some bodies that do not identify themselves as legislative do have democratic credentials. It follows that democracy cannot be the key to what makes lawmaking by a legislature attractive compared to lawmaking by other entities.

2. TRANSPARENT DEDICATION TO LAWMAKING

A legislature is a particular kind of lawmaking institution. What are its distinctive features? The first feature—in my view a very significant feature—is that a legislature is an institution *publicly dedicated to making and changing the law.*

Parliaments, congresses, and state assemblies are set up and publicly identified as lawmaking bodies. We tell our citizens, "This is where the laws are made and changed. If you have a lawmaking proposal or if you want to see lawmaking going on, this is where it's at." Now this may not distinguish parliaments, congresses, and state assemblies from entities within executive agencies that are set up as rulemakers. But it certainly distinguishes parliaments, congresses, and state assemblies from courts. For although we (insiders) know that an awful lot of legal change and adaptation takes place through the activities of courts, we are also uncomfortably aware that courts do not present themselves as lawmaking institutions, nor are courts publicly presented that way in official constitutional discourse. Quite the contrary, any widespread impression that judges were acting as lawmakers rather than lawappliers would detract radically from the legitimacy of their decisions in the eyes of the public. And this popular perception is not groundless. Courts are not set up in a way that is calculated to make lawmaking legitimate. They are not publicly provided with the structures, resources, and personnel that are needed for a lawmaking role. They have to cobble together resources for lawmaking from the briefs they consider and the arguments they hear in relation to the discharge of the functions they perform that *are* publicly acknowledged—namely, the interpretation and application of existing laws and the settlement of disputes.

The English positivists put this rather well when they distinguished between oblique and direct lawmaking. Judge-made law, according to nineteenth-century jurist John Austin, is an "oblique" form of lawmaking. The judge's "direct and proper purpose is not the establishment of the rule, but the decision of the specific case. He legislates *as properly judging*, and not *as properly legislating*."[2]

Similarly, because the decision-making members of these institutions—the judges—are not officially understood to be lawmakers, they are not evaluated for this role at the time of their appointment or selection. Quite the contrary, both the judicial candidates and those who nominate and support them are at pains to assure the public that nothing is further from their thoughts than that they should be making and changing the law. This is true both of judicial appointments through a process like the one ordained in Article III of the U.S. Constitution and also of elections to judicial office (in states where that takes place). Candidates for election to the judiciary do not announce to the voters what laws they would like to make or change when they are in office. They don't campaign in the way that wannabe legislators do. Quite the contrary, they outdo one another in assuring the voters that they will definitely not act as lawmakers.

Of course, it cannot be denied that judges *are* lawmakers. Courts make and change the law all the time. But they do not do so transparently. And transparency is the first virtue of what I am calling legislative institutions. These are institutions publicly dedicated to lawmaking. That means no one is under any misapprehension about what they are doing in this regard. Legislatures exist explicitly for the purpose of lawmaking, and they are known to exist for that purpose. Sure, they also have other functions.[3] But lawmaking is their official raison d'être, and when we evaluate the structures, procedures, and membership of legislatures, we do so with this function in the forefront of our minds.[4] (If you want to have a debate about parliamentarians' lawmaking intentions and to elicit commitments from them in this regard, there is no official ideological obstacle to such a discussion. True, legislators have other tasks to perform, and we might quiz them about those tasks also. By contrast, the official line in the case of judges is that this is not one of their tasks at all; indeed, this is a task they are supposed to be prohibited from performing; and they are most reluctant to talk about it.)

I do not want to be misunderstood when I say that transparency is the first virtue of legislatures. I mean transparency about what their function is, not necessarily transparency about *how* it is performed. No doubt, all sorts of legislative deals are made in back corridors, in what we used to call in Britain "smoke-filled rooms." For all I know, the same is true of courts. But at least in the case of legislatures, we know what the back-room deals are about: they are about lawmaking. In courts, there are back-room deals too, but the public is officially assured—quite misleadingly in many cases—that they are deals about the application, not the making or changing, of the law.

Elsewhere I have referred to this transparency advantage as "the very idea of legislation."[5] The idea of legislation is not the same as the idea of lawmaking. Lawmaking is any activity that has the effect of making or changing the laws. Legislation, however, is the business of making or changing law *explicitly, in an institution and through a process publicly dedicated to that task.* The idea of legislation embodies a commitment to explicit lawmaking, a principled commitment to the idea that on the whole it is good, if law is to be made or changed, that it should be made or changed in a process publicly dedicated to that task.

How important is this principle? It is not just a matter of giving notice to those who are to be bound by a given law; that is the function of the rule-of-law principle of promulgation, and it, too, is very important for those on whom the law casts its burdens. But the transparency I am talking about is important for the whole community. The idea of legislation is an application of the general liberal principle of publicity, recognized by John Rawls and others, that the legitimacy of our legal and political institutions should not depend on any misapprehensions among the people about how their society is organized.[6]

It is particularly important in a democracy that the place where laws are made be publicly known and identified. If we are sure that this is where our laws are made, then *this* will be the place where we will want to focus our attention so far as democratic principles are concerned. This also affects the way citizens discharge their participatory powers. Those who advocate changes in the law have a responsibility to orient that advocacy to a forum where their proposal can be explicitly discussed for what it is rather than to other forums where it will be presented under the guise of (say) constitutional interpretation. A forum such as a constitutional court may be politically more promising for a given group, but that is only because less care has been taken with the legitimacy conditions of lawmaking in that forum (precisely because it has not been thought officially to be a forum for lawmaking). I think there is a responsibility not to try and "steal a march" on one's political opponents in this way but instead to submit one's proposals for honest debate and evaluation in a forum that everyone knows is the place to go to reach decisions about whether and how the law should be changed.

All this affects the way we organize and repair our political system. To the extent that laws are made in courts, which are not publicly acknowledged as lawmaking institutions, then attempts to enhance the responsiveness and accountability of judges as lawmakers will be haphazard and confused, with one side seeking to bring policy considerations to bear, another side denying that any improvement is needed, and a third side denying that these values are even relevant in light of the public's ideological commitment to the proposition that the judiciary's role is not to make law but only find, interpret, and apply it (which are roles whose performance is to be evaluated in light of a quite different set of values).

I have argued elsewhere that the lack of candor and transparency associated with judicial lawmaking contributes to what some commentators have called the rather arid and contentless character of judicial argument, especially in regard to the moral values that ought to be in play when the making of law is at stake. Because they are at pains to conceal the fact that lawmaking is what they are engaged in, courts are not as open to the sort of reasons and argumentation that any reasonable person would regard as indispensable for rational and responsible lawmaking. Instead, a mélange of reasons is deployed, with the relevant moral considerations often heavily compromised or attenuated behind the elements of text, precedent, and interpretive doctrine that are supposed to provide cover for the entire exercise. What goes on in the legislative chamber may be cacophonous and unsophisticated, but better a noisy and cacophonous debate of the considerations that are actually relevant to the task of lawmaking than a sophisticated but morally distracting rehearsal of esoteric legalisms.

So, to go back to our starting point, the very idea of legislation provides a specific gloss on the democratic character of parliaments, congresses, and assemblies that relates to their democratic legitimacy, to the important principle of institutional candor and transparency in politics.

3. LARGE NUMBERS

Another distinctive way in which legislatures serve democratic values, when they do, has to do with their *size*.[7]

Unlike other democratic institutions, the typical legislature comprises—at its highest decision-making level—hundreds (in some cases thousands) of individuals. Compare that to the leadership of the executive. Even though the executive in most countries comprises a huge bureaucratic apparatus, we assume that it is headed by one person—or, if you reject the theory of the unified executive, by a small cabinet of twenty or so members.

The decision-making membership of legislatures is also usually one or two orders of magnitude higher than the decision-making membership of most apex courts. The Supreme Court of the United States consists of nine justices, while the federal legislature, comprising the House of Representatives and the Senate, has a total high-decision-making membership of 535. In the United Kingdom, the Supreme Court usually sits in panels of five.[8] The British legislature, by contrast, had until recently a membership of about 1,900, almost three orders of magnitude higher than the number of justices sitting on the highest court. Of course, that high figure counted everyone in both houses, and I should say that since the reforms of the House of Lords that took place a few years ago, the British Parliament has shrunk to around 1,425 members. (The House of Lords now includes only 26 bishops and archbishops, and 90 or so hereditary dukes, marquesses, earls, and viscounts, along with 600 or so life peers.) Even if the noble and ecclesiastical elements are neglected, and focus is placed only on the House of Commons, which is the dominant branch in the British legislature, the total is 650.

Political scientists often remark that real legislative power is vested in a much smaller number of people than the full membership of Parliament or the full membership of Congress. They emphasize the power of the cabinet in Westminster-style systems, under which the Parliament very seldom fails to enact any bill proposed by the cabinet and very seldom enacts any bill not proposed by the cabinet. Or, in American legislatures, political scientists point to the power of committee chairs as the effective legislative power. This might suggest that the disparity of numbers to which I have called your attention is more a matter of what Walter Bagehot called a "dignified" characteristic of constitutional custom rather than an "efficient" aspect of constitutional reality.[9] In some countries, no doubt, that is true.[10] But, in the end, this debunking gambit will not do, for I have no doubt that if the very same political scientists were called to advise a new democracy on the reconstruction of its constitution, they would say, among other things, that the country should have a structure of courts with a high court sitting in panels of five or so; that it should have a small and decisive executive body of about twenty ministers or secretaries of state; and that it should have a legislative chamber of some hundreds of members to enact and amend its laws. This insistence on a parliament of some hundreds of members would not be seen as just a quaint concession to antiquarianism. It would seem more or less obvious as a feature of working constitutional structure. We have a sort of *constitutional instinct* that the lawmaking branch, above all the other branches of government, should consist of large numbers of people. We take it for granted that if there is explicit lawmaking or law reform to be done in society, it should be done in or under the authority of a large assembly consisting of hundreds of individuals, ranked roughly as equals.

I said in *The Dignity of Legislation* that political theorists historically have cited the large size of legislatures as the basis of their unwieldy and dysfunctional behavior: noise, insults, people talking at cross purposes, each legislator pursuing his own agenda on the basis of his unscrupulous ambitions. What gets done in these circumstances, what emerges from the maelstrom, seems likely to be "an unprincipled, incoherent, undignified mess."[11] I have never been entirely convinced by this critique, preferring Niccòlo Machiavelli's observation that good laws may arise "from those tumults that many inconsiderately condemn" and that those who condemn them pay too much attention to "the noises and the cries that arise in such tumults more than the good effects that they engendered."[12]

Why exactly do we value the large numbers in our legislatures? Why not reduce the mess and the incoherence by electing just one man as a lawmaker or a small legislative team, a dozen or so?

One possible explanation is that political scientists continue to toy with Condorcet's Jury Theorem, which provides an arithmetical account of the value of larger rather than smaller numbers of people voting on a proposal. The basic idea is that when all the members of a group are reasonably competent, then the chances that a majority will reach the right answer by voting increases toward certainty as group size increases.[13] But this cannot be the real explanation. Condorcet certainly did not think it was. He believed that average individual competence tended to decline independently as group size increased (and then of course the arithmetic of majority decision worked in the other direction): "A very numerous assembly cannot be composed of very enlightened men. It is even probable that those comprising this assembly will on many matters combine great ignorance with many prejudices."[14] So the Condorcet effect, for all its mathematical interest, may be a bit of a nonstarter in our account of why we have this constitutional instinct for large assemblies rather than small bodies to undertake the task of lawmaking.[15]

If we want a model from the canon of political theory to capture the value of large legislatures, it is to Aristotle rather than to Condorcet that we must turn. Aristotle insisted in Book III of the *Politics* that a multitude

> when they meet together may be better . . . *if regarded not individually but collectively,* just as a feast to which many contribute is better than a dinner provided out of a single purse. For each individual among the many has a share of excellence and practical wisdom, and when they meet together, just as they become in a manner one man, who has many feet, and hands, and senses, so too with regard to their character and thought.[16]

The key here is diversity. Different people bring different perspectives to bear on the issues under discussion, and the more people there are, the greater the richness and diversity of viewpoints is going to be. When diverse perspectives are brought together deliberatively in a collective decision-making process, that process will be informed by much greater informational resources than those that attend the decision-making of any single individual.

What sort of diversity are we talking about here? Diversity of opinion? Certainly. But it is not just diversity of opinion; it is diversity of experience and also diversity of interests. The first two seem appropriate, but the third may be a problem for some theorists of democracy. Certainly, in lay discussion if not in political and legal theory, it is often thought that it would be an improvement if legislators were to concentrate on what are said to be "the issues" rather than what is in it for them or what is in any particular legislative proposal to affect the interests of their constituents.

A moment's reflection, however, indicates that this cannot be right. Legislation affects people's interests, and the effect it has on their interests is surely important; in many, perhaps most, cases, that effect is of the essence. The aim of the legislature is to promote the interests of the members of society, or the interests of one particular sector in some particular regard as part of an overall strategy of promoting the common good. Also, if a legislative proposal seems likely to have a negative impact on certain interests, then that surely ought to be a matter of concern for those who are making our laws. Theorists who say that legislative deliberation should be addressed only to "the issues" forget that *the impact on interests is often the main issue.* Those who think that legislative discussion should be conducted at the level of high principle forget that it is the point of many of our principles to insist that certain interests be taken seriously or that certain interests should not be neglected. Even when we think a decision should not be made on the basis of pure consequentialist reasoning, even when the relevant principles are not utilitarian or wealth-maximizing, it is still a rare moral or political principle that makes no reference to interest at all or that is impervious to the impact on people's interests of its being applied.

In any case, even legislation on morally significant matters—matters of individual rights, for example—is never just the embodiment of principle. Principles may be in the background, but each piece of legislation must be framed so that technical provisions—with their attendant definitions, procedures, exceptions, and administrative clauses—will actually have the effect of promoting the principles that we think are morally important. The task of converting principles into statutory provisions is not an easy one. Sometimes we want to compare various possible provisions to consider the different ways in which they will impact people, and there we do need information about interests, in particular information from those who are familiar with the conditions under which interests are served or disserved under particular conditions—in a specific kind of transaction, for example, or in a particular kind of profession or business. In our high-flown enthusiasm for principled deliberation, we are sometimes in danger of forgetting that information about interests and about the likely impact of laws on interests does not reach the legislature automatically or by magic. It is not something that can be taken for granted as though members were able to concentrate all their deliberative attention on the more abstract issues of principle.

For these reasons, one might value the presence of an array of persons in the legislature acquainted with all walks of life, all types of interest and experience in the community. If the community is geographically diverse, for example, with different conditions in the north compared with those in the south, then one would value the presence of legislators from both ends of the country. If there is diversity of interests between town and country, again one would value the presence of people from rural and urban sectors. If there are differences and conflicts between the interests of the workers and the interests of their employers, then we would want labor unionists as well as oligarchs in the legislature, and so on. Where measures impact men and women differently, one would hope there were women in the legislature to bear witness to those differences. And finally, if there are ethnic differences in the community, one might want the legislature to include members of different ethnicities so that various—and, from the point of view of the dominant group, unanticipated—impacts can be assessed.

I say all this because it is often assumed that proportional representation along lines of political opinion is a good thing, with the proportion being entirely between popular support for general parties and numbers in the legislature. The Aristotelian diversity we look for is diversity of theory and moral viewpoint—like organizing a panel at a philosophy conference. But it is also important to see the point of other modes of representation as good-faith attempts to represent the diversity of various communities of interest in the society.

4. REPRESENTATION

The fourth distinctive and attractive feature of legislatures that I want to consider is representation. Legislatures are not just democratic institutions, not just transparent institutions, not just large assemblies, but large *representative* assemblies. What I have to say about this is going to involve some rather abstract political theory—in fact, much of it is about the value of abstraction. This theme of abstraction is extremely important in our theory of legislation and our theory of the distinctive significance of representative assemblies in a modern society.

It is often thought by those who dabble in political philosophy that lawmaking by a representative assembly must be regarded—at least from a democratic point of view—as a "second best." Surely, the democratic ideal should be some sort of plenary legislature of the people. People assume that Jean-Jacques Rousseau's conception of direct popular sovereignty in lawmaking is the ideal from a democratic point of view, and that even if we are not as scathing about representation as Rousseau was, we should nevertheless deplore representative lawmaking as a very distant second best.[17] It is thought that if only we could have a direct democracy that was fully inclusive (in a way that Athenian democracy, for all its direct and participatory virtues, was not), then that would be the democratic ideal. Or, if only we could have a California-style system of plebiscitary legislation, shorn of all the corruption and manipulation that it presently involves, then that would be preferable ideally from a democratic point of view, preferable to lawmaking by an elected Congress or Parliament, or assemblies of elected state representatives. If we want information about interests, then surely the ideal has to be the literal presence in the lawmaking process of all interested parties. And if we want deliberation among opinions, theories, and ideologies, then surely the ideal is the literal presence in the lawmaking process of each adherent of an ideology or theory, each partisan of a view, principle, or hypothesis, so that every shade of opinion in the community can really and truly speak for itself.

People have assumed from my own work on judicial review, based as it is on principles of democratic legitimacy and political equality, that I, too, must favor the people themselves voting directly as equals on the laws that are to govern them.[18] It is sometimes said that if a democrat accepts anything short of that—any form of indirectness or representation—then they have effectively given the game away because both representative authority and judicial authority involve the exercise of political power at some remove from the participation of ordinary citizens.

All this, in my view, is wrong, at least as far as legislation is concerned. Legislation is a function for which representation, rather than direct participatory choice, is the better democratic alternative. And the charge against judicial power is not only that it is insulated from popular accountability but that it does not have the democratic representative credentials required for legislation.

This is a counterintuitive view, so I had better explain it. In doing so, I am going to draw on some of the recent work of Nadia Urbinati, a distinguished theorist of politics at Columbia University. Professor Urbinati's article "Representation as Advocacy," published some years ago in *Political Theory*, and her 2006 book *Representative Democracy: Principles and Genealogy*, represent major contributions to democratic political philosophy.[19] Urbinati is interested in a body of thought that emerged in France not long after Rousseau had put his frenzied pen to paper, a body of work that suggested that representative democracy might be the best option for political institutions and that anything like direct democracy might run a very distant second. I think Urbinati's work is very important, as are the writings of the French *philosophes* she draws on, such as Sièyes and Condorcet. I said earlier that I was interested in abstraction. The part of their work that intrigues me is a connection between two sorts of abstraction: (1) the abstraction that is exhibited by enacted laws, insofar as they satisfy rule-of-law requirements of generality (I call this *content abstraction*); and (2) the abstraction that is involved in the task of representation whereby a single political actor may represent a certain kind of constituent, a constituent from a given locality, for example, or a constituent who holds a party allegiance of a certain sort (I call this *agent abstraction*). The connection that interests me relates these two kinds of abstractions to one another in a democratic rule-of-law society. Here is my hypothesis: whatever its relevance in other functions of government, the abstraction that representation involves is particularly appropriate for lawmaking, which is a domain in which we are striving to produce abstract norms, abstract in the sense of *general,* rather than directives focused on some particular person or situation in the way that a bill of attainder is focused or in the way that a judicial decision might be focused, at least in the first instance.

The idea of such a connection was mooted famously by Rousseau, though it is the burden of the work that I am drawing on that Rousseau did not get the connection quite right. According to Rousseau, it is important that laws be general in character, applicable equally to everyone in the society.[20] That law should be general in its formulations is not just Rousseau's insight; it is, as I said, commonly cited as one of the foremost principles of the rule of law.[21] Now Rousseau thought it was important to match this generality with generality of source or provenance, and this is why he insisted that lawmaking was properly the work of all the members of the relevant society acting together not just as subjects (affected by the general character of its provisions) but as active elements of the sovereign (who contribute to the generality of its source). The plenary provenance of law is the proper match to its general form:

> [W]hen the people as a whole makes rules for the people as a whole, it is dealing only with itself; and if any relationship emerges, it is between the en-

tire body seen from one perspective and the same entire body seen from another, without any division whatever. Here the matter concerning which a rule is made is as general as the will which makes it. And *this* is the kind of act which I call a law.[22]

He went on, "law unites universality of will with universality of the field of legislation."[23] And this is why Rousseau disparaged representation.

But, notoriously, the fact that all subjects are implicated in the sovereign act of lawmaking is no guarantee that they are motivated by the appropriate spirit. The will of all is not the same as the general will. Rousseau tried to wrestle with this difficulty in his political theory, with—as we all know—very mixed results.

I would argue, as many of the thinkers that Nadia Urbinati studies believed, that it makes more sense to associate content abstraction with the abstraction involved in representation. A representative stands *for* something. In a sense, in a democratic system, she stands for a whole array of constituents who have voted for her or participated (for or against her) in the voting process by which she was chosen. But she stands for the persons *under certain auspices:* she stands for them geographically, in constituency based systems; she stands for them jurisdictionally, in federal systems; she stands for them ideologically, in systems of party representation, particularly party-proportional representation. And because she stands for them under those auspices, her standing for them involves abstraction from their (and her) personal decision-making. She stands for the interests of the northeast district, or she stands as the junior senator from New York, or she stands as a representative of the Liberal Democratic Party.

Rousseau asked indignantly how a representative could possibly stand for the *personal will* of his constituents, considered severally, when it is only their willing that can possibly make a law legitimate: "[W]ill does not admit of representation."[24] But the sense in which will does not admit of representation is the sense in which will is unique and personal to each individual—like the will that is involved in the consent that one gives to sex, for example, or the consent that one gives to some medical procedure.[25] It is a further question whether *this* sense of will or consent is what is required for the legitimacy of making laws, where it is part of the understanding of the very idea of law that we are trying to move away from a direct focus on the unique identity of each person and consider them instead in the light of what they have in common.

We know that a bill of attainder, directly imposing a penalty or disqualification on a known individual by legislative fiat, is an abuse of lawmaking power. But the difference between that and the generality of a law—a norm formulated in general terms, according to the requirements of the rule of law—is not just a difference of numbers, as though it would be alright to govern a society of a hundred million people with a hundred million bills of attainder. We want our laws to consider people universalizably under certain aspects, and as we embark on lawmaking, we want our representatives to present people's interests, concerns, and ideals, universalizably, under certain aspects.

Let me illustrate this with a crude example. Suppose a society is planning to introduce universal conscription, national military service. It is going to be a general law, though of course there may be all sorts of conditions and exceptions built into it, each stated in general terms. There may be a question, for example, about whether there should be certain exemptions, not for identifiable individuals but for classes of people, for instance people involved in education or in certain areas of employment such as labor-intensive farming or horticulture. It may be important that the people of the country, who are going to be subject to this law, should be considered in its making not just as potential conscripts but as potential conscripts from the cities, or potential conscripts from the northern rural areas where farming is difficult and potential conscripts from the ranches out west where farming is not so labor-intensive. Geographic representation seems to make this possible, for now the law has to be scrutinized in an assembly that represents the very classes of interest, understood in general terms, that may be relevant to the complexity—though still the generality—of its content. There will be representatives from the north, from the west, from the cities, and so on, and their presence, influence, and interaction, as representatives, will determine the configuration of general requirements and universalizable exemptions that the law finally embodies. The idea is that the presence of these various interests, not directly in the role they play in the personal will and wishes of those whose interests they are but the presence of the interests as such, is what is necessary for appropriate legislative debate. No doubt, the proposed exemptions will be controversial, but it may be easier to deliberate in the midst of that controversy in a representative forum, where the rivalry of interests is seen not just as a zero-sum game among the personal bearers of the respective interests but as an interaction between types of interests considered abstractly under the auspices of a matrix of representation that covers the society as a whole.[26] As Urbinati points out, representation "helps to depersonalize claims and opinions" in a way that makes deliberation easier.[27] It represents what various classes of people have in common and thus operates "as a simplifier of interests and an assimilator of subjects."[28]

Of course, my conscription example is contrived and highly simplified: the array of relevant kinds of interest that the law in question needs to accommodate matches the basis of representation in the society. Usually, there will not be anything like this straightforward match. For one thing, the representative matrix for the legislature will not be able to reproduce the diversity of relevant interests for just one enactment, let alone those that are germane to all the bills that need to be considered in a given session. But it is important to see that if there is a falling short of an ideal here, it is a falling short of a *representative* ideal. A utopian legislature would represent interests with great specificity, so that not only farmers would be represented, or farmers from the north and the west, but woman farmers, poor farmers who have been in the business for a long time, poor farmers in the business for a long time with children available to work the farm, and so on. But the limit of this idealization is a very fine-grained representation; it is not the literal presence of each person in a plenary legislature. Specificity is not the same as particularity,[29] and it is the particular, not the specific, that we are seeking to abstract from in our insistence that laws must be general and that they should be considered in the light of types of interests, not in light of personal presence.

In real-world legislatures, we have compromised on this ideal specificity by making arrangements for all-purpose representation, using rather crude indices of geography, mainly leavened by party affiliations. We also hope that through the law of large numbers various dimensions of representation will emerge informally, on the back of geographical representation, so that there will be a balance of black and white, men and women, professionals and working people, and so on in the legislature. (Sometimes we adjust geographical representation to ensure this as a more or less formalized objective.)

We also compromise on the specificity of our laws. Even though a highly specific law would not necessarily violate the requirement of generality, we do in fact legislate with reasonably coarse-grained distinctions, albeit not nearly as coarse-grained as our matrix of representation. The more elaborate and specific the terms of a law, the harder it is to promulgate and administer.

Once again, though, it is important to understand what the contrast is here. The contrast is not with an ideal piece of legislation that would make provision for the particularity of each individual; it is with an ideal piece of legislation that would refer to each and every relevant *type* of individual circumstance or consideration, no matter how specific. But we do not approach that ideal; instead we leave it to the realm of particularized equitable decision-making to determine specific cases that general legislation really cannot take account of.[30]

Let me return now to the matrix of representation. Many political systems also set out to represent opinions, not just interests, where the relevant opinions are bodies of doctrine or ideology about the way in which interests in society are properly dealt with and balanced against one another. Systems of pure proportional party representation, like that of Israel, do this directly. Mixed systems, with both a party-proportional and a constituency basis of representation (such as New Zealand), do it alongside geographic representation, and in addition New Zealand also has a dimension of direct ethnic representation in the provision for Maori seats).[31] Most legislative systems, even those like the American one or the British Parliament, which do not admit of any formal proportionality element, still use parties to organize representation in the legislature, so that there is a useful matrix of party-political categories cutting across the geographical ones.

Once again, there are limits on specificity. Not every shade of opinion is represented, partly because not all have significant support in the country and the number of members allocated to the legislature is not large enough to provide a more fine-grained sample. But also—and significantly—it is the function of political parties to organize opinion into a relatively small number of comprehensive and well-thought-through programs and proposals, drawing on the experience as well as the political enthusiasm of their members. In this way, there is a more or less well-organized process of abstraction from the particular opinions held from time to time by any individual to a type of opinion—or rather several types of opinions—about legislation and policy generally, which can then address and deal with the various types of interests that are also represented. And so we get a combination of a broad array of types of interest along with an array of well-organized political ideologies to address these interests. The whole thing of course is organized on the basis of individual voting and thus is permeated with the impact of fundamental principles of political equality, but the processes of representation built on this foundation add up to a viable and responsible politics.

What I have said about representation has been quite sketchy and abstract; mostly I am trying to show why lawmaking as such might have a special affinity with representation more than other structures and functions of government. I want to show why a large representative assembly, of the sort that we are familiar with in the legislative context, is a better environment for lawmaking than other institutions or agents that might conceivably perform that task.

The points that Nadia Urbinati and others have made about representation are slightly more familiar when they address the promotion of genuine deliberation in politics. They are familiar from a tradition of political moderation that is apprehensive about the pressure and immediacy of plenary decision-making.

Legislation requires time and careful deliberation, but a large gathering of the populace can barely contrive for itself the space, let alone the time, for genuine engagement. The crowd we have assembled will melt away unless a decision is made simply and quickly. Yet simplicity and haste are the obverse of responsible legislative decision-making, precluding, as they do, the time and space for thought and speech—and, within the realm of speech, for successive rounds of proposal, reply, amendment, and reconsideration that genuine engagement with legislative issues requires.[32] That is simply not possible in a gathering of tens or hundreds of millions of citizens, and any attempt to make it possible would involve a radical attenuation and "dumbing-down" of legislative debate. Representation, on the other hand, "creates distance between the moments of speech and decision and, in this sense, enables a critical scrutiny while shielding the citizens from the harassment of words and passions that politics engenders."[33]

There is an ancient contrast in political philosophy between a politics based on will and a politics based on judgment, and a contrast between respecting people simply in a voluntaristic sense, as the bearers of a will, and respecting them as capable of political judgment. It has always seemed to me that it is the latter respect, not the former—respect for judgment, not respect for will—that is most affronted when we assign lawmaking to a nondemocratic institution. It is people's capacity for judgment that is at stake when we look for a democratic mode of lawmaking, and if we are to respect that capacity, we must respect the forms, structures, and processes that can house and frame it. Like Professor Urbinati, I believe that structures of representation provide processes for judgment formation and for the deliberative engagement of judgments both among the people and among their representatives. In Urbinati's own words, representation involves a comprehensive filtering, refining, and mediating process of political will formation and expression, shaping "the object, style, and procedures of political competition."[34]

It is a position that, as Hannah Arendt noticed, was held also by the American Framers, who suggested that we need representation in politics to pass opinions "through the sieve of an intelligence which will separate the arbitrary and the merely idiosyncratic, and thus purify them into public views."[35] Arendt pursued this in *The Origins of Totalitarianism*, contrasting the discipline of representative politics with the fragmentation of political parties, their supersession by mass movements, and the growth of public irresponsibility, procedural impatience, and general contempt for parliamentary institutions in the interwar period.[36] In these circumstances, there was a "chaos of unrepresented and unpurified opinions," which could produce nothing in politics except an array of dangerous impulses waiting for a strong man to mold them into the slogans and ideologies of a mass movement, which in Arendt's view would spell death to all genuine opinion, all genuine judgment in politics.[37] To diminish these dangers, she looked to two-party systems (like that of Great Britain) where effective participation in politics required both cooperation with others in "broad-church" arrangements and a degree of shared responsibility for the public world, born of the constant possibility that one might have to take office at the next election.[38]

The idea of representative party politics as a process of "opinion formation, reflection, revision, and amendment,"[39] as a way of transforming impulse and sentiment into judgment, by and for the sake of the interplay of representative with constituent, constituent with party, representative with representative, representative with party, party with party, and citizen with citizens generally, all adds up to a model of politics that I find enormously attractive.[40] And in the grip of that picture, it is impossible to see direct democracy as an ideal, of which we have tragically fallen short. We should see direct democracy instead as a wrong turn, which only representative structures can redeem. No doubt, a case can be made along these lines in favor of framing and filtering political decisions of every kind through representative processes and representative institutions. But it seems to me that the case has a particular importance in regard to legislation.

5. CONCLUSION

I have been in the business of defending the dignity of legislation long enough to expect that there will be complaints about the highly idealized picture of legislatures that I have painted. There is something to this criticism. But we cannot undertake intelligent disparagement or criticism of our actually existing legislative institutions if we do not have a well-thought-through ideal that we can hold up to them for comparison. I don't mean a utopian ideal, one that cannot possibly be realized in practice. I mean a realistic normative account that shows us the moderate standards to which we ought to be holding our lawmaking. Otherwise—if we are not in possession of a well-thought-through normative ideal—our criticisms will be intuitive gut reactions rather than intelligent assessments based on some articulate sense of what a good set of legislative institutions ought to be.

I have been concerned that, to the extent that people ever think about this ideal, they carelessly fall into a couple of misapprehensions. From the fact that our normative theory of lawmaking is broadly democratic, they assume that our ideal must say, "The more democracy the better," and they assume this pushes us in the direction of direct democracy and in the direction of treating everything else as a shabby compromise. I have tried to answer that with my account of the relation between the representative character of our institutions and the generality that is required of our statutes under the rule of law. There is also a tendency to assume that although, in the real world, legislative politics is about preferences and interests, with special-interest groups lobbying and jockeying for pressure and advantage, an ideal legislature would brush off such sordid distractions and concentrate on matters of principle, deliberating about them in the manner of a philosophy colloquium. This, too, I think is a mistake. A politics of principle is no doubt desirable, but the important thing about principles is that they are addressed to interests, they guide us in the equitable treatment of interests, and they indicate for us which interests it is morally important to take into account and when, and which kinds of impacts on interests are or ought to be matters of moral concern. That sort of work cannot be done in our legislatures unless they serve as clearinghouses for information about interests and for the pressing of the claims of interests, of various sorts, on the conscience of the nation. That's what needs to go on in politics, and it is in relation to that ideal—not an impossibly philosophical ideal—that we ought to develop our assessment of actual legislative institutions.

CHAPTER SEVEN

Principles of Legislation

A LEGISLATURE IS a place for making law, and because law is a serious matter affecting the freedom and interests of all the members of the community, legislating is an activity we ought to take seriously. It is like marriage in *The Book of Common Prayer*[1]—not to be enterprised nor taken in hand carelessly, lightly or wantonly, but discreetly, advisedly and soberly, duly considering the purposes for which legislatures have been instituted and considering also the harm and injustice that poorly conceived or hastily enacted legislation may do. In this chapter, I want to consider some principles that I believe ought to govern the activities that take place in and around legislative institutions.

My title—"Principles of Legislation"—is familiar enough. But I am going to be using it in a rather unfamiliar way. The principles of legislation that I will be talking about need to be distinguished from two other sorts of legislative principles—the principles of a utilitarian such as Jeremy Bentham and the principles of a theorist of justice such as John Rawls.

The year 1802 saw the publication of a work by Jeremy Bentham, whose first volume was called "Principles of Legislation."[2] Chapter 1 of Bentham's book opened with the following ringing words, less familiar then than they are now:

> THE PUBLIC GOOD ought to be the object of the legislator; GENERAL UTILITY ought to be the foundation of his reasonings. To know the true good of the community is what constitutes the science of legislation; the art consists in finding the means to realize that good.[3]

For Bentham, the pursuit of the general good was the key principle for lawmaking. His volume continued in a utilitarian vein, telling us how to determine the general good and instructing us to measure pleasure and pain in terms of their intensity, duration, certainty, proximity, productiveness, purity, extent, and so on. His account culminated in the startling claim that provided we keep the principle of utility in view and apply our minds rigorously to these measurements, "legislation . . . becomes a matter of arithmetic" and "[e]rrors . . . in legislation . . . may be always accounted for by a mistake, a forgetfulness, or a false estimate . . . in the calculation of good and evil."[4] Actually, there is much more to Bentham's "Principles of Legislation" than this: there are also excellent discussions of the difference between law and morals, the reasons for making or not making something an offense, the issues of liberty that are almost always at stake when legislation is contemplated, and the compromises that the legislative imposition of sanctions necessarily involves.

The volume ends with a critique of the principles that were actually used by Englishmen to evaluate legislation in Bentham's time. The headings of this critique are a delight: "Antiquity is not a Reason," says Bentham, "The Authority of Religion is not a Reason," "Reproach of Innovation is not a Reason," "Metaphors are not Reasons," "An Imaginary Law is not a Reason," and so on.[5] This chapter reminds us that although Bentham's principles were set out as principles for legislators, they were not only for legislators. They were also principles for those who call for and oppose legislation. Bentham recognized that in the evaluation of proposed laws there is always a back-and-forth relation between the prejudices of the people and the fallacies of their representatives.[6] In the new world of law dominated by statute that Bentham helped usher in, the education of the public was as much an imperative as the education of the legislators themselves.[7]

We owe a tremendous debt to Jeremy Bentham for embarking as he did on the science of legislation. But we are not comfortable these days with the character of his contribution. The arithmetical calculus of the general good seems a bit one-dimensional, and we object to the aggregative logic of general utility. It seems to us that by adding everything up, Benthamite utilitarianism does not properly address issues of the distribution of the goods and evils that are the currency of legislation. This is sometimes expressed by saying that the calculus "does not take seriously the distinction between persons."[8] To put it another way, we think principles of legislation should include principles of justice.

The emphasis on justice has been characteristic of much recent political philosophy. In John Rawls's theory, for example, the basic work of evaluation is done by egalitarian principles. Rawls tells us that legislators ought to be particularly preoccupied with what he calls the Difference Principle and the Principle of Equal Opportunity.[9]

Rawls acknowledges that implementing this principle at the legislative stage will often involve disagreement and indeterminacy: "[J]udgment frequently depends upon speculative political and economic doctrines and upon social theory generally."[10] But the task of the legislator—and, again, of those in the public who call for or oppose legislation—is to do the best they can from this perspective. Also, Rawls's principles of justice as fairness are not just recipes for statesmen to use. They help define a well-ordered society in which "everyone accepts, and knows that everyone else accepts, the very same principles of justice" (even if they disagree about their application) and in which this provides a common ground from which the claims that people make on their political institutions can be considered and debated.[11]

Rawls's opponents include modern-day Benthamites,[12] but he also has opponents who espouse alternative theories of justice (i.e., alternative accounts, rival to his, of why Benthamite utilitarianism is wrong).[13] I guess very few real-world legislators think of their tasks as being guided explicitly by either Rawlsian or Benthamite principles, or indeed by any principles stated at that level of abstraction. Legislators approach their tasks with a much less rigorously formulated approach to public policy and social justice than that. Still, they disagree with one another in rather the way in which Rawls disagrees with Bentham or in a very loose and informal version of the disagreement between Rawls and his other philosophical competitors. Legislation is a controversial business. The inevitability of disagreement, which I have tried to emphasize in all my work on the subject,[14] leads to the question: "Are there any principles of legislation which can be shared by the adherents of rival theories of justice or among rival agendas for public policy?"

One well-known answer looks to principles that govern certain abstract characteristics of legislation—rule-of-law principles or the principles of Lon Fuller's "internal morality of law."[15] In *The Morality of Law*, Fuller tells a story of how an inept legislator went wrong by failing to respond properly to the need for generality, stability, intelligibility, consistency, practicability, and publicity in the statutes he enacted. Quite apart from Rawlsian, utilitarian, or other "external" principles that compete to govern their content, Fuller argued that laws need to be enacted *in a certain form* to be effective, to be fair, and to respect the dignity of those to whom they are addressed. In regard to these principles, Fuller says:

> What I have called the internal morality of law is in this sense a procedural version of natural law.... The term "procedural" is ... broadly appropriate as indicating that we are concerned, not with the substantive aims of legal rules, but with the ways in which a system of rules for governing human conduct must be constructed and administered if it is to be efficacious and at the same time remain what it purports to be.[16]

I think this is a mischaracterization, born of the assumption that anything that is not substantive must be procedural. In fact, there are three kinds of principles that might be relevant to the legislative task: (i) substantive principles, like Rawls's or Bentham's; (ii) formal principles (i.e., principles having to do with the form of legislation, like Fuller's); and (iii) procedural principles, having to do with the institutions and processes we use for legislation (as well as those we use for adjudication). Principles of all three kinds are important, but in this chapter I will focus mainly on (iii)—procedural principles, having to do with the institutions and processes we use for legislation. Just as Fuller argued that his formal principles were not just instrumental but in an important sense moral, so shall I argue something similar for my seven principles of legislative due process. Though they do not go to substantive moral justifications of law, they address important moral issues of legitimacy. And just as Bentham and Rawls argued that their principles of legislation were principles to govern action and debate among members of the public as well as among those in power, so shall I argue that my procedural principles should discipline the kinds of demands we place on our legislators and the choices we make about the lawmaking we clamor for.

There's a temptation to think that procedural and formal principles are unimportant compared with substantive ones.[17] Certainly, substantive principles are important because they go to the heart of the matter. But it has been the great achievement of modern rule-of-law jurisprudence to emphasize the importance of formal principles, and I think the importance of procedural principles needs to be understood in this way as well. Procedures in politics are not just ceremonies, red tape, or mindless bureaucratic hoops we have to jump through. They relate specifically to issues of legitimacy, particularly in circumstances where there is deep-seated disagreement as to which substantive principles should be observed. I mentioned legitimacy a moment ago, and I want to say that the importance of addressing issues of legitimacy cannot be overestimated. Suppose a citizen asks: "Why should I comply with or support this law, when I think its content is wrong?" Appealing in response to a substantive principle may be reassuring for the sponsors of the law, but it will carry no weight for this citizen. For this citizen, one has to appeal to something about the way the law was enacted in the circumstances of disagreement, so that he can see its enactment as fair even if he does not see its substance as just. The procedural principles of legislation that I will identify are all related to that burden of legitimacy in various ways. They concern the processes by which laws should be enacted, the question of who should participate in those processes, the spirit in which they should participate, and the various forms of care that should be taken with a process this important. In summary, the principles I will consider are the following:

1. The principle of explicit lawmaking (i.e., the principle that holds that when law is made or changed, it should be made or changed explicitly).
2. The duty to take care when legislating, in view of both the inherent importance of law and the interests and liberties that are at stake.
3. The principle of representation, which requires that law should be made in a forum that gives voice to and gathers information about all important opinions and interests in the society.
4. The principle of respect for disagreement, and concomitant requirements like the principle of loyal opposition.
5. The principle of deliberation and the duty of responsiveness to deliberation.
6. The principle of legislative formality, including structured debate and a focus on the texts of the legislative proposals under consideration.
7. The principle of political equality and the decision procedure it supports in an elective legislature (i.e., the rule of majority decision).

There is nothing sacred about this list. Others may come up with different principles, organized in a different way. But I think this way of setting them out is illuminating.

Before proceeding to the details of my seven principles, there are some general points to be made. Procedural considerations seldom stand on their own: they are usually predicated on some sense of the importance of what the procedures are used for or what they are supposed to produce. We do not argue for democracy, for example, because participation is valued as an end in itself. We argue for democracy in the light of what political systems do: they exercise power; they have an impact on people's lives; they bind whole communities; they impose costs and demand sacrifices. It is because of all this that we make demands about voting and enfranchisement: we say that each person is entitled to a vote, for example, because of the potential momentousness for him or her of the decisions that are being made. Apart from these considerations, an insistence on democratic enfranchisement might be seen as frivolous. Something similar is true of legislation. It would not be worth taking so much care with legislation, paying attention to the processes by which laws were made in the various ways that I will consider, if *law* were not an important mode of governance. If law were just a game, or if the realities of political power or political impacts had little to do with law, then principles of legislation would matter less and their content might be different. I therefore begin my discussion with an account of why law as such is important. If we understand *that*, then we will better understand why the making of law is important, and we will also understand why it is important to have a place dedicated to the making of law in the way that legislatures are dedicated.

The concept of law is not the same as the concept of governance, and a people does not enjoy the rule of law just because they are ruled. Of course, any ruling or being ruled is a serious matter. When people are ruled, power is exercised, freedom is limited, penalties are threatened, force is used, sacrifices are demanded, costs and benefits are allocated, people are elevated or degraded, and actions reputable and disreputable are undertaken in the name of the whole community. To be ruled by law, however, is to be ruled in a particular way. It is to be ruled under the auspices of what John Locke referred to as "settled standing Rules, indifferent and the same to all Parties"[18] (i.e., general rules laid down, promulgated, and then applied impartially to particular cases). The function of these rules is, in the first instance, to guide and govern the conduct of members of the community in various regards for the sake of justice and the general good, and, second, to direct and govern official interventions, particularly official responses (like sanctions) to the situations to which the norms are directed in the first instance. The positing and promulgation of these rules establishes them as a sort of publicly recognized morality, laying down duties and creating rights. Citizens no doubt differ in their personal moral views, including their personal views about justice and the general good. But the promulgated rules of law are supposed to constitute a code to which all of us can orient ourselves despite our differences. The sheer fact of law's public presence gives it salience for us in our dealings with one another, and it stands as a focal point of our allegiance and obligation to the political community. Our primary political obligation is to obey the law, and the primary basis of legitimacy in a society ruled by law for any power that is exercised on us is its being authorized and governed by these "settled standing Rules." I don't mean that the claims of law are absolute or that their legitimating effect is unlimited: I mean that they offer themselves as the primary basis of obligation and legitimacy, and the claim they purport to make on us and on our rulers is that they are to be treated with the greatest respect by those who have the well-being of the community in mind. Law, as we know, claims finality and supremacy in social affairs. What is settled in lawmaking is what finally is to prevail in our society, and this means that our laws present themselves as already taking account of everything that might be important about the matters that they govern. Again, this doesn't mean that they always succeed in doing so: a law may be criticized for imposing a prohibition or establishing a distribution that fails to take this or that into account. My point is that making law represents a particularly comprehensive exercise of power, one that seeks to transform and redirect in quite a broad and permanent way people's sense of what is required of them in society. In view of the sort of intervention it claims to be, lawmaking ought to be taken seriously.

Edward Rubin has argued that the image of law set out in the previous paragraph is obsolete.[19] Most law, he says, is not like this; certainly most legislation is not. Much of it does not aim to govern the conduct of ordinary citizens at all, at least not directly. It does not impose obligations or establish rights. Instead, it gives directions to officials and agencies, indicating goals to be pursued and the broad types of rule-making that they should engage in. Rubin observes:

> We speak of legislative enactments as laws, as in the high school civics phrase about "how a bill becomes a law," and we refer to legislators as lawmakers. But this usage is quite old and bears the imprint of the pre-administrative state. . . . At present, a large proportion of legislation does things other than regulate human conduct, and many direct regulations of conduct are enacted by other governmental institutions, most often administrative agencies.[20]

Rubin thinks we need to "desanctify" the notion of law, and not assume it has the sort of normative force or "metaphysical kick" that it seems traditionally to have had. If we do this, he says, we will be in a position to develop realistic principles to apply to lawmaking.[21] We should evaluate laws as mere instrumentalities, as policy initiatives, Rubin says, and understand lawmaking as nothing much more than the initial stage of the mobilization of public resources. It doesn't follow that law is unimportant. But if we take Rubin's advice, we will see lawmaking as less of a big deal from the moral point of view and attribute less importance to grand-sounding principles regarding its form or the procedures by which it is enacted.

Rubin has a point about much modern legislation. But I think he underestimates the traditional character of much modern law. Though much of it is directed in the first instance to officials, this aspect of it does not necessarily detract from its effective public normativity. It is true that if a legislature increases the penalties for marijuana use, or directs that officials shall no longer regard assisted suicide as an offense in certain circumstances, a literal reading will tell us that its primary addressees are prosecutors and judges; no one is literally being told not to smoke marijuana, nor is anyone actually being given permission to help their loved ones end their lives. *Still,* people will read the directions to officials as part of a code of publicly recognized morality on drug use and end-of-life issues. And they will be right to do so. They will debate the measures solemnly as though they were norms for citizens and they will treat them, once enacted, as settled standing rules on these matters, despite the point about their literal addressees. These are examples from criminal law, but the same is true of private law: people are aware that major changes in private law doctrine—a new set of rules on class actions or punitive damages, for example—have broad normative implications for the arrangements that structure our lives together.

Earlier, I quoted the Lockean formula: "settled standing Rules, indifferent and the same to all Parties." The last phrase is particularly important. Governance by law is governance on the basis of general rules, and that is what gives it its moralistic flavor. Jurists sometimes write as though the generality of law were simply a pragmatic advantage so far as administrability is concerned.[22] But it is more than that. Generalization across acts and across persons is a token of assurance that legal decisions are made and imposed for reasons (and that those reasons are being followed where they lead), rather than arbitrarily or on a whim. It is important, moreover, for its promise of impartiality and as an intimation of justice;[23] H. L. A. Hart observed that both law and justice embody the formal idea of "treating like cases alike."[24] Generality connotes reciprocity, and this may be valued as expressive of what Ronald Dworkin has called the *integrity* of a system of governance.[25] In all these ways, law presents itself in the image of morality. Though positive law can be morally misguided and though it is undeniable that unjust laws can also be general in form, there is something morally, not just pragmatically, attractive about a determination to govern according to this form even when that is inconvenient for the purposes of those in power. To make law, then, is not just to exercise power; it is (so to speak) to make a public morality for a particular community, something that purports to have the status among a people that moral principles have in their individual consciences.

What I have said so far is true of all law, common law doctrine and customary law as well as statutes, treaties, and constitutions. We now need to consider the more particular question of what it is for law to be legislated; that is, created explicitly by an institution formally dedicated to that purpose. Bearing in mind all that has been said as to the general significance of law, it is time to turn to the principles that should inform our understanding of legislation as a particular form that law may take.

1. THE VERY IDEA OF LEGISLATION

My first principle refers to the very idea of legislation. The idea of legislation is not the same as the idea of law. Others have drawn this distinction ideologically;[26] here I am drawing an institutional distinction. The idea of legislation is the idea of making or changing law *explicitly, through a process and in an institution publicly dedicated to that task*. The distinction takes notice of the fact that legislation is not the only means by which law is made or changed. Law is also made and changed by the decisions of judges as they interpret existing legal materials, including the work of other judges. This is unavoidable and no doubt in some cases also desirable. But it has drawbacks. Although the lawmaking role of the courts is well known to legal professionals, judicial decision-making does not present itself in public as a process for changing or creating law. Quite the contrary, any widespread impression that judges were acting as lawmakers, rather than as law appliers, would detract from the legitimacy of their decisions in the eyes of the public. And this popular perception is not groundless. Courts are not set up in a way that is calculated to make lawmaking legitimate. Legislatures, by contrast, exist explicitly for the purpose of lawmaking, and they are known to exist for that purpose. Sure, they also have other functions. But lawmaking is their official raison d'être, and when we evaluate the structures, procedures, and membership of legislatures, we do so with this function in mind.

So, our first principle embodies a commitment to explicit lawmaking. Underlying any theory of legislation is the idea that on the whole it is good that, if law is to be changed, it should be changed openly in a transparent process publicly dedicated to that task. When courts change the law, this transparency is often lacking. Courts perform their lawmaking function under partial cover of a pretense that the law is not changing at all. The English positivists put this rather well when they distinguished between oblique and direct lawmaking. Judge-made law, according to John Austin, is an "oblique" form of lawmaking. The judge's "direct and proper purpose is not the establishment of the rule, but the decision of the specific case. He legislates *as properly judging*, and not *as properly legislating*."[27]

How important is this principle commanding explicit rather than oblique lawmaking? It is not just a matter of giving notice to those who are to be bound by a given law. Publicity is important for the whole community, for it indicates what is being done in their name and gives them information regarding the appropriate deployment of their political energies. It is also a matter of the general liberal principle of publicity that people should not be under any misapprehension about how their society is organized, and the legitimacy of our legal and political institutions should not depend on such misapprehensions.[28] This has particular importance in the case of law, because of the connection between law and a certain ideal of political autonomy.

The law of a people is often presented as something to which they have committed themselves rather than as something thrust on them.[29] No doubt, this is partly mythology. But the demand for explicit lawmaking, along with the demand that legislation be a democratically representative process, pays tribute to the importance of these ideas.

I noted at the outset that principles of legislation are for citizens, not just for legislators. This is particularly true of my first principle, which is *primarily* a principle for citizens. Those who advocate changes in the law have a responsibility to orient that advocacy toward a forum where their proposal can be explicitly discussed for what it is rather than toward other forums where it will be presented under the guise of a matter of interpretation. A forum such as a constitutional court may be politically more promising for a given group, but that is only because less care has been taken with the legitimacy conditions of lawmaking in that forum (precisely because it has not been thought to be a forum for lawmaking). Access to a constitutional court may be attractive opportunistically. But there is a responsibility not to try and "steal a march" on one's political opponents in this way but to submit one's proposals for honest debate and evaluation in a forum that everyone knows as the place to go to reach decisions about whether and how the law should be changed.

2. A DUTY OF CARE

In view of the inherent importance of law and of the interests and liberties that are at stake in their decision-making, lawmakers have a duty to *take care* when they are legislating. We want our laws to be efficient devices for promoting the general good, and we want them to be fair in the burdens they impose and solicitous of the rights as well as the interests of all whom they affect. Reckless or hasty lawmaking may impose oppressive constraints or unfair or unnecessary burdens on people. Lawmaking is not a game: the consequences of failure to satisfy this second principle are real harms and injustices to real people.

This principle has a number of implications. The general duty of care in this regard means that people in a position to modify the law have a responsibility to arrive at a sound view about what makes a legal change a good change or a bad change. They need principles of legislation in the very first sense I identified—a theory of the sort that Rawls offered or a theory of the sort that Bentham offered; or, if those theories are thought inadequate, a better alternative theory of justice and of the general good.

Beyond that, responsible lawmakers ought to pay careful attention to the relation between their own individual decisions and the eventual effects, on citizens and on society, of the law that they make (or fail to make). Laws are seldom made by a single Solon or Pericles. Lawmaking is collective action, in two dimensions. First, laws are often made and changed by a collectivity,[30] so individual lawmakers have to consider the relation between their participation—their proposals, their speeches, their votes—and the eventual outcome of the lawmaking process. Second, the making or unmaking of any particular law affects the whole body of laws, so attention needs to be paid not just to the particular measure under consideration but also to the way in which it will affect the broad impact of the legal system on the interests and rights of citizens.[31]

In principle, this applies to all lawmaking, not just legislating. But aspects of it are worth particular emphasis in the legislative context. Unlike judges, legislators are not necessarily versed in the background law that they are changing or adding to. And legislators also have other distractions that perhaps judges do not have. After all, lawmaking is just one among many activities performed in legislatures, and, from the point of view of political power or prestige, it may not be the most important. Members of the legislature may be preoccupied with things like the mobilization of support for the executive, the venting of grievances, the discussion of national policy, processes of budgetary negotiation, the ratification of appointments, and so on. It is easy for them to regard lawmaking as a distraction. Legislatures have hundreds of members, but often you will be hard put to find ten or twenty on the floor of the chamber during the middle stages of an average legislative debate. For these reasons, we need to place particular emphasis on the duty of care that is associated with the lawmaking part of a legislator's business.

Many structural and procedural attributes of legislatures embody a sense of the need for care in making law. Proposals for new laws are not just introduced and voted on in the legislative assembly. Usually, they are debated and voted on several times—sometimes in their general character, sometimes clause by clause. Often there are public hearings; almost always there is consideration by a dedicated committee of the legislature. Many legislatures, moreover, are bicameral. They comprise different assemblies, in some cases appointed as well as elective, in other cases elected on different schedules from one another.[32] Usually a bill must satisfy majorities in both houses. Now we may see all this simply as an opportunity for politicking and delay, and citizens sometimes call for a more efficient legislative procedure that would eliminate these features. Such proposals, however, are almost always reckless in regard to the duty of care I am talking about.

3. THE PRINCIPLE OF REPRESENTATION

A new law may be formulated and drafted by an elite—by the political executive, for example, or by a Law Reform Commission, or by specialist parliamentary counsel. However, we expect these officials will not try simply to impose their ideas by virtue of their own expert assessment. However important the innovation is perceived to be, and however well drafted the measure, we still expect it to be submitted for scrutiny, debate, and decision by a large representative assembly, comprising hundreds of representatives drawn from all sections of society.

This is partly a reflection of our commitment to democracy: we want lawmaking to be democratic, and accordingly we expect it to take place in an institution whose members have been elected by the people. I will consider the democracy aspect under Principle 7. But the principle of representation in lawmaking is older than democracy.[33] Elsewhere, I have written on the sheer *numbers* of persons that deliberate lawmaking involves. Supreme courts have eight or nine voting members; legislatures have hundreds.[34] I think these numbers are valued not just because more is better for, say, the reasons elaborated in Condorcet's Jury Theorem[35] but because more gives us the opportunity to diversify the membership, to have legislators from a variety of places, representing a diversity of interests and opinions. Legislatures are formally structured to ensure diversity, and the modern idea of legislation rests philosophically on an insistence that society, being pluralistic, is in essence incapable of representation by a single voice or by reference to a small set of interests. Of course, there are disputes about what the axes of legislative diversity should be. In almost all countries, geographical diversity is represented; sometimes there are formal structures to ensure ethnic or religious diversity, but increasingly political diversity is valued in a sense that seeks some sort of rough comparability between the proportion of a given body of opinion in the legislature and the proportion of people who support that opinion in the community.

Why is this diversity so important for *lawmaking?* Partly it is informational. We hope that representatives will come from different parts of the country, bringing with them knowledge of the special needs and circumstances of different groups. We want to ensure an adequate representation of the diversity of *interests* in society. (Even if the legislature is passing general laws, universalizable in form and applicable to all, it will still need information about how particular provisions affect different sectors of the society in order to determine a fair allocation of benefits and burdens.) But the value of diversity also has to do with heterogeneity of opinions. The legislature is a place where we argue and debate, and we want to ensure a hearing for the largest possible variety of opinions concerning the issues that are raised when a change in the law is being contemplated. The idea is that new law emerging from this institution cannot claim its authority on the basis of any cozy consensus among like-minded people (whether in the community or in the legislature). Instead, its claim to authority must make reference to the controversies surrounding its enactment. If a citizen who disagrees with the new law asks why she should obey it, we want to be able to say to her that disagreements (along the lines that she is expressing) were aired as fiercely and as forcefully as possible at the time the law was considered and that it was enacted nevertheless in a fair process of deliberation and decision.

4. RESPECT FOR DISAGREEMENT

Few legislative proposals are likely to meet with unanimous agreement. John Rawls wrote about "the many hazards involved in the correct (and conscientious) exercise of our powers of reason and judgment in the ordinary course of political life" that make it likely that we will disagree with one another on important issues:[36]

> Different conceptions of the world can reasonably be elaborated from different standpoints and diversity arises in part from our distinct perspectives. It is unrealistic . . . to suppose that all our differences are rooted solely in ignorance and perversity, or else in the rivalries for power, status, or economic gain.[37]

Rawls used this account to characterize ethical and religious disagreements. He spoke about the burdens of judgment that stand in the way of easy or eventual consensus. But the idea of the burdens of judgment might characterize disagreements about justice and public policy as well.[38] Of course, what distinguishes justice and public policy is that we need settlement on these issues, whereas we do not need settlement on all the ethical and religious issues that Rawls associates with the burdens of judgment. But the need for settlement doesn't make disagreement evaporate; instead, it means that settlements have to be forged in the heat of disagreement and not on a basis that wishes disagreement away.

Real-world legislatures differ in the extent of disagreement that is aired in their debates. Whenever any large group of people gather together to perform a civic function, there will be pressures of various sorts to conform, to refrain from rocking the boat, and to show solidarity with widely accepted ideas. For example, American legislatures used to be overwhelmed on occasion by enthusiastic consensus of one sort or another, and dissenting views were sometimes informally suppressed so that resolutions could be passed quickly before the public face of the consensus dissolved. Given the vicious polarization of recent years, some may yearn for this era of lost consensus. My fourth principle, the principle of respect for disagreement, aims to combat the tendency to concoct consensus artificially. It conceives of legislatures as institutions set up specifically to enable rival views to confront one another in debate, so that all of those involved in lawmaking hear all that is to be said against, as well as all that is to be said in favor of, the legislative proposals in front of them. Various things can facilitate expressions of dissent. In some circumstances, strong party structures can help by giving dissenting views a solid presence in politics that is not simply identified with the conscience or opinions of particular individuals. Even with minority status, a socialist *party* is much less vulnerable to the pressures of national consensus than two or three individuals scattered as members throughout the chamber, each of whom happens to hold socialist views. (On the other hand, where parties are few—e.g., where there is a simple two-party or, worse, a one-party system—then some other basis needs to be found whereby dissident members can give voice to their views without fear of intraparty retaliation.)

Above all, what is indicated under this fourth principle is the need for a pervasive doctrine of *loyal opposition* of the sort we discussed in Chapter 4. A person is not to be regarded as a subversive or as disloyal to the society merely on account of his public disagreement with some social consensus. A party is not necessarily to be regarded as a threat because it establishes and makes solidly present in the society views on public policy that most people regard as undesirable. Loyal opposition is not just a matter of free-speech guarantees. There are all sorts of ways in which legislative structures can give the principle some real embodiment, including the establishment of an officially recognized "Opposition" (say, in a Westminster-style system) with established and paid posts such as "Leader of the Opposition" and "Shadow Minister," as well as the official majority/minority arrangements that are associated with American legislatures. These are structural embodiments of the principle I have been discussing, establishing the legislature as a place where dissenting voices have a real opportunity to test their persuasiveness and the extent of their support.

5. THE PRINCIPLE OF RESPONSIVE DELIBERATION

In a well-known article, Lon Fuller argued that courts are distinguished from other political institutions as forums of reason not because reasoning does not go on in other institutions but because courts are set up specifically to ensure that the reasoned arguments presented there are heard and responded to. A judge has not only a duty to let each side present its case but a duty, which (in Fuller's account) a legislator does not have, to stay awake and listen and respond to the presentation.[39] I am not sure whether Fuller is right about the formal structures; the debating rules of legislatures often allow members to put questions to one another in debate and insist on a response. But assuming he is mostly right, then it is all the more important that the ethos of legislation be suffused with a normative principle of responsiveness in deliberation. It is not enough that voice be given to a variety of conflicting views. The legislature is a place for debate, not just display, and as recent theories of "deliberative democracy" have emphasized, debate requires an openness to others' views and a willingness to be persuaded.

It is therefore important that the views voiced in the legislature not be held as frozen positions, with no possibility of change or compromise. Opinions must be held as opinions, and therefore open to elaboration, argument, correction, and modification. If (as I have been arguing) the basic argument for the legitimacy of an enacted statute is that all the alternatives had the opportunity to put their case and failed to win majority support, then we are presupposing at least in principle the possibility that people might have their minds changed through argument. This does not mean that people must be willing to abandon their interests or give up their principles.[40] They might be persuaded to take a different view of the respect required for their interests in relation to the interests of others, or a different view of what follows from their fundamental principles so far as particular legislative proposals are concerned. But I am not saying that political opinion must be fickle for deliberation to work. The point is that opinions should be held and defended in a spirit of openness to argument and consideration. Sometimes this will mean that individuals must be prepared to abandon positions they have taken, at other times it will mean that parties of legislators must be willing to reconsider positions they have staked out. The principle of responsiveness does not condemn that second, more ponderous and collective mode of reconsideration. On the contrary, reconsideration by a party may take the reevaluation of a public political position more seriously than the faltering uncertainty of an individual member.

The requirement of responsiveness is directed in the first instance to the legislators themselves. But Edmund Burke is famous for having directed it also to the people who elect the legislators, reminding the electors of Bristol that they ought not to demand that their representative sacrifice "his unbiassed opinion, his mature judgment, his enlightened conscience" to the views of his constituents:

> Parliament is not a congress of ambassadors from different and hostile interests; which interests each must maintain, as an agent and advocate, against other agents and advocates; but . . . a deliberative assembly of one nation, with one interest, that of the whole; where, not local purposes, not local prejudices, ought to guide, but the general good, resulting from the general reason of the whole.[41]

Certainly, it is reasonable for electors to expect their representative to communicate to the legislative body important facts about their interests, especially if those would otherwise be overlooked. And it is also important that if there are opinions peculiar to a particular constituency, then the system of representation should be such that these are heard. But Burke is also right that the whole point of those demands is to allow for a process of deliberation in which views may be formed about the merits of legislation that would not have been formed apart from the *bringing together* in the legislature of all this peculiar information and all these distinctive voices.

6. THE PRINCIPLE OF LEGISLATIVE FORMALITY

At the end of my discussion of Principle 2, I referred to those large structural features of legislatures like bicameralism that respond to the duty of care incumbent on any group that takes it on itself to make law. My sixth principle is concerned less with structures and more with the microfeatures of legislative debate and with their sometimes exasperating formality. Legislation is not supposed to be an informal process, and under the heading of this sixth principle, I want to explain why.

One of the reasons we take such care with the electoral system, the composition of legislative chambers, the rules about parties, and the debating and decision procedures is that these features enable a political system to make use of the diversity represented in the legislature. Legislatures are supposed to be large gatherings of disparate individuals who do not understand one another particularly well.[42] This is a normative, not just a factual, observation. It follows partly from what we said about Principle 3: whatever differences of ideology, value, culture, opinion, and interests are found in the community are also supposed to be represented in the legislature. If this normative expectation is fulfilled in a diverse society, it follows that the potential for mutual misunderstanding in any interaction among legislators is great. No doubt, it is mitigated to some degree by the personal collegiality of the legislators as they go about their business, growing out of their common experience of a life in politics. But if there is too much of that, we start to lose exactly what we value about diversity.

How then is it possible for legislators to interact in the institutional mechanics of legislation? The answer lies in the highly stylized rules of procedure that govern the formal details of their interaction: *these are rules for people who have very little else in common.* Unless it is structured by tight rules of order, deliberation is always liable to fall into futility, as people misunderstand one another, talk past one another, or lose the thread of the discussion. Formal rules of procedural order go a long way toward mitigating these dangers, and I believe they are therefore entitled to respect, not just as any old formalities might be but as formalities that make possible precisely the debate-among-diversity that we value among our lawmakers.

I have argued elsewhere that there is an important connection between procedural formality and the formal respect that is accorded to a legislative text. In any deliberative context, the key to rules of procedural order is a tight focus on a particular resolution under discussion—a resolution formulated clearly and publicly, established as a criterion of relevance in a particular debate, amended only in a carefully controlled way, and subject in the end to formal voting. Without that reference to a given form of words, a disparate body of representatives of the sort we have postulated would find it difficult to share a view about exactly what they have been debating, exactly what they have voted on, exactly what they have done, as a collective body, acting in the name of the community.[43]

This principle should make a difference not only to the way legislators behave but also to the way in which legislative outcomes are received and understood. In the United States, lawyers sometimes look behind the text to what was said in debate for evidence as to how a statute is to be interpreted. When legislative history is used in this way, certain interventions in debate are given authority even though the procedural rules of debate never made them the focus of deliberation. So we see lobbyists urging representatives to insert language into the debate that will be useful for later interpretation,[44] and we see judges and lawyers according interpretive authority to speeches in debate even though that authority has not been acquired through voting or deliberation focused on those speeches. Now these practices depend for their manageability on the text of the statute remaining the formal focus of deliberation and voting; they depend on legislators' proceeding in debate as though the text of the bill were all that mattered. For if it were openly acknowledged that speeches given in debate were also potentially authoritative, and if an attempt were made—through deliberation and voting—to determine which of them should *be* authoritative, then the whole process of deliberation would degenerate into something unwieldy. Those who use legislative history in this way should think about the procedural implications of what they are doing (and about the extent of their free-riding on conventions that formally facilitate debate on a different basis altogether).

7. POLITICAL EQUALITY AND MAJORITY DECISION

My seventh principle is ultimately the most important, for it governs the procedures by which binding decisions are finally made concerning controversial legislative proposals. Sometimes we need law in an area even though we have been unable to resolve disagreement about what that law should be; in these circumstances, we need a decision procedure that will involve a mode of participation like voting and a decision rule such as the rule of majority decision (MD). Of course, voting in a legislature should not be sharply separated from debate. But equally the importance of deliberation should not obscure or sideline the need on most occasions for voting.[45] Deliberation does not always eliminate disagreement, and eventually decisions need to be made.

Legislatures, I have already said, are not the only lawmaking entities in a modern state. Courts also make law. But modern legislatures, much more than courts, organize their decision procedures around the ideal of fairness and political equality. The legislature is set up to respect the fact that, in principle, each permanent member of the community liable to be bound by its laws is entitled to participate, directly or indirectly, in the processes by which the laws are made. It is the respecting of this entitlement that gives legislation its special claim to legitimacy in modern democratic societies.

MD is used in most legislatures for determining whether a bill is adopted finally as law or not.[46] Political theorists have posited alternatives to it,[47] but a plausible alternative would have to satisfy a number of important constraints that seem to be satisfied by the rule of majority decision: it is neutral between outcomes, it gives equal weight to each participant's input, and it gives each participant's input as much weight as possible in the direction that their input indicates as is compatible with equality.[48] It seems fundamentally fair; it satisfies the principle of political equality. The point of my seventh principle is not to defend MD in particular but to insist that some such rule satisfying conditions like these must be used in order to respect the principle of political equality in regard to legislation.

The application of MD in legislation needs to be understood carefully. Legislatures, we know, are far from fully inclusive. Though, as I have said, they are large bodies compared (say) to courts, they are still minuscule compared to the populations of the societies they govern. A few hundred participate directly in the actual business of lawmaking; the other tens of millions do not. So when we are talking about the application of political equality in the legislature, we must not talk as though *the equality of the representatives* was ultimately what mattered. The representatives have a derivative claim to be treated as one another's equals, but that arises only because their individual constituents—the millions of them—have an *ultimate* claim to be treated as one another's equals, and only because their own status as legislators rests on the votes of their constituents in a certain way. We design the representative structure, the system of elections, and the procedures of the legislature so that *as a package* they satisfy political equality. Neither MD among the electors nor MD among the legislators does it by itself; it is the package that works.

People will say that even conceived in this complicated way, political equality is a utopian ideal. I admit that it is an ideal, but it has undoubted real-world influence. It is what we appeal to when we worry that campaign finances or first-past-the-post electoral systems undermine the ideal of one person, one vote. We need a norm of fair representation in a legislative assembly, along with principles of democratic enfranchisement and basic political equality that go with it, in order to think sensibly about the apportionment of legislative constituencies, about redistricting, about the electoral system itself, and about the rules, particularly the voting rules, of the legislative process. We need all of this in order to relate what happens in the legislature to the fair conditions of decision for a society whose ordinary members disagree with one another about the laws that they should be governed by.

In all of this, I have talked about *principles* of legislation rather than *rules*. Of course, legislation is a minutely rule-governed enterprise, and there is a dense procedural thicket of rules on all sorts of things that go on in the legislature. Elsewhere I have discussed the theoretical relation between this thicket of rules and principles of legislation of the sort I have been talking about.[49] Briefly, the principles underlie the detailed rules and explain why the detailed rules are important. An analogy with the rules that govern criminal trial proceedings may help here. What happens in the courtroom is minutely governed by detailed rules of evidence and rules of procedure. These rules don't just constitute a game. They serve deep and complex principles about truth-seeking, fairness, and respect for persons, and they are supposed to be imbued with a suitable awareness of what the parties have at stake in the matter.[50] As we frame the rules of courtroom procedure, we have these underlying principles in mind; they determine the way in which we evaluate the rules and urge changes in them; and they should also inform the spirit in which we conform our behavior, and demand that others conform their behavior, to the rules. The same—I want to suggest—is true of legislation. The principles I have mentioned may not be mentioned in the detailed rulebooks that govern the legislative process. But they help explain the point of the rulebooks; they provide a basis for evaluating and criticizing the rulebooks; and they offer an account of why holding ourselves and others to the requirements of the legislative rulebooks should be regarded as something more than mindless proceduralism.

It is worth mentioning again, finally, an even deeper value that underlies not just the rules but also the principles I have mentioned and that pervades them all. That is the value of legitimacy—the importance of the political legitimacy of the final output of the legislature, the laws that it enacts. By legitimacy I mean the laws' claim to acceptance and compliance even by those who oppose them so far as their contents are concerned. Of all the modes of making law—the emergence of custom, the development of doctrine by courts, the framing of a constitution, the enactment of statutes—it seems to me that legislation is the one that takes legitimacy most seriously. This is evident not just in the pains that are taken to establish decision procedures that respect political equality. It is evident also in our principle of explicitness in lawmaking and our insistence on the representation in the legislature of all substantial competing opinions. We cannot understand the work that these principles do or the detailed rules that they support without understanding the importance of legitimacy. Any laws that we enact must do their work in a community of people who do not necessarily agree with them and who will therefore demand that something other than the merits of their content—something about the way they were enacted—be cited in order to give them an entitlement to respect. The explicit and articulate process of legislation in the modern state responds to that demand and takes seriously the demand for legitimacy. And it is with an eye to that demand—as well as to the general norm of fair and responsible conduct in the discharge of this most important civic function—that I have developed my suggestions about principles of legislation and about the distinctive features of this way of making law.

CHAPTER EIGHT

Accountability and Insolence

1. TWO CONCEPTIONS OF ACCOUNTABILITY

Accountability is a popular idea, though for political scientists it can sometimes seem a tiresome and clichéd aspect of democratic theory.[1] I think we are in danger of underestimating its importance. Too often, accountability is simply identified with elections or with "catching out" those who are charged with public responsibilities, without any sense of its exact contribution to our understanding of democracy.[2]

In order to see how much it contributes, we need to focus on a narrow conception of accountability. Accountability is used in two main ways in political theory, only one of which has the fundamental importance for democracy that I want to discuss. The first meaning is

> (1) *Forensic accountability*. In this conception, "accountability" denotes the liability of a person to have his actions assessed by a tribunal on the basis of some established norm, such liability being predicated on the availability of a process, formal or informal, to assess his actions in that way. The classic case is that of a person who may be brought before a court: a tyrant or a kleptocrat may be brought before a tribunal to answer for some offense against the people subject to his rule.

I call conception (1) "*forensic* accountability" because of the judicial paradigm that it involves. The tribunal need not be a court in the strict sense. Forensic accountability applies to any situation where a person's actions are assessed impartially on the basis of a preestablished standard. But "accountability" may also mean something rather different, and this second meaning is the one I want to concentrate on.

> (2) *Agent accountability*. In this conception, "accountability" denotes the duty owed by an agent to his principal, whereby the principal may demand from the agent an account of the work that the agent has been doing in the principal's name or on the principal's behalf, enabling the principal if she sees fit to sanction or replace the agent or terminate the agency relationship. My relation to my realtor is of this character: he makes certain arrangements for the purchase of a house on my behalf; he may even have a power of attorney to act in my name. But I am entitled to insist that he give me a full account of what he has done and what he is doing, and if I judge it adversely I may dispense with his services.

I call conception (2) "*agent* accountability" for obvious reasons. Conception (2) is basically a legal idea.[3] What I want to pursue in this chapter is the light that the legal idea of agent accountability can cast in democratic theory.[4]

One key difference between the two conceptions is that agent accountability involves accountability *to* someone: it indicates the privileged position of someone to whom another person is accountable. Forensic accountability is not really accountability to anyone. The real accountability is to the law. True, one might say that the person held accountable is accountable to the relevant tribunal, or perhaps accountable to the prosecutor who brings him before the tribunal, but neither of these has much in common with an agent's accountability to his principal. Another key difference concerns the basis of assessment. In forensic accountability, the basis of assessment is given: there is a standard and something like a tribunal charged with administering it. But in agent accountability, the principal herself decides the basis on which she will assess the actions of her agent.

The two may be connected. It is possible that agent accountability might also involve forensic accountability (for example, when an agent's conduct discloses some criminal malfeasance). The principal may have to bring the agent before a court. One of the things I will emphasize is that agent accountability is often highly complex, layered, and mediated, especially in its political manifestations. A forensic component may be part of that layering. But this is by no means necessary. A principal may hold an agent accountable when there is no question of the intervention of any prosecutor or tribunal. And forensic accountability need not involve any form of agent accountability: someone may be forensically accountable for the violation of a given norm even though he was not acting as an agent on behalf of anyone else. So the two ideas are distinct. I guess what they have in common is the insistence that a given person is not a law unto himself; he may have to answer for his actions in a setting not necessarily of his own choosing; and he has to provide a justification of his conduct, which will be assessed authoritatively by someone other than himself.

2. AGENT ACCOUNTABILITY

The elementary accountability of an agent to his principal goes as follows. One person who is unable or unwilling to do something herself that she wants done (for example, because it demands skills she does not have or time and attention she cannot afford to devote to it) empowers another person—for instance, a realtor, an attorney, a broker, or an accountant—to do that thing on her behalf (to find out what is required or what would be best and to do it). The first person is the principal, and the second person is her agent, and when the agent's task is complete (or perhaps at regular periods while the task is being performed), the agent is required to give the principal an account of what he has done or what he is doing, and the principal is empowered to modify or terminate the agency relation in the light of this account.

Political theory uses all sorts of legal models—contract and trust, for example. Is the relationship of *agency* different from a relation of *trust* for our purposes? I think it is different, and in Section 3 I will say something about the use of what appears to be a trust model in political theory by John Locke and others. At this early stage, I would like to emphasize the following difference. In a trust model, we distinguish three roles: the settlor (who sets up the trust), the beneficiary (for whose benefit the trust is set up), and the trustee (the person empowered by the settlor to act for the benefit of the beneficiary). Lines of accountability are much more rigid in this relationship than they are in the agency model. The beneficiary is mostly passive. The conditions under which the beneficiary (or anyone else) can hold the trustee to account are quite limited, and the terms of reference for accountability are those laid down by the settlor—all of which lends a rather unpleasantly originalist cast to any attempt to apply the trust model in politics.

So I am inclined to stick with the model of agent accountability, so far as our understanding of accountability in a democracy is concerned. Of course, there is nothing inherently democratic or even political about agency (except in the very broad sense that "politics" can cover any human relation that is freighted with power). I believe that agent accountability is key to our understanding of democracy. But that does not mean it is in essence a democratic idea. Agent accountability can operate in a variety of contexts, many of them nonpolitical. And, in its political uses, it need not be associated with democracy, though democracy, as I will argue, cannot do without it. Of course, terms such as "trust" and "entrust" are sometimes used loosely without any sense of the technical differences between trustee and agent. It is the form of the relation that is important for my purposes—the more active role of the principal in the agency relation—not any particular terminology.

So, in the basic agency model, the principal actively demands an account from the agent, as she is entitled to do, because it is her business that is being transacted by the agent. Her money is being spent, her property is being dealt with, her affairs are being negotiated or litigated, her obligations are being fulfilled. What is being done by the agent is being done in her name and she, the principal, may have to take responsibility for it. That is the basic idea. Now for some further analytic points.

Accountability and fear. Sometimes it is said that our insistence on holding political officials accountable is part of "the liberalism of fear."[5] We fear the worst that our rulers can do, so we set up mechanisms of accountability as a way of "limiting the inherent hazards of political subjection."[6] No doubt, it is wise to make provision against the dangers of political authority, but not all such provision involves agent accountability. And the liberalism of fear approach might equally be used to justify forensic accountability where the standards whose violations one fears are already well established. (Rights-based judicial review is a mechanism of this kind.) No doubt, agent accountability can also be used to identify and respond to egregious abuses on the part of the agent. But its use is not confined to that. Even if the principal has the greatest confidence in her agent, even if that confidence is justified, and even if there is no question of gross mismanagement or abuse, the principal is *still* owed an account from the agent of what he (the agent) is doing with her resources, about her business, and in her name. And this is true in the political case as well. Equally, there is no reason to say that accountability applies only where there is fear of venality or corruption.[7] Even if there is no reason for suspecting that political officials are abusing their authority, *still* if they are the agents of the people, going about the people's business, not their own, then they owe the people an account of even their wisest and most impeccable behavior. And it is not impertinent—rather it goes to the essence of the political relationship—for the people to demand such an account.

Accountability and interests. In commercial relations between agent and principal, it is the principal's own interests that are at stake, and I guess an economist would say that "the agency problem" is to put the agent's self-interest at stake in the relationship also. But it may be a mistake to treat this as an essential feature.[8] A principal may have interests other than his own for the agent to take care of. Sometimes this may justify our modeling the relationship in terms of a trust. At other times, the agency model is sufficient, provided we realize that the principal's business, which the agent is about, need not be restricted to the principal's *self-interested* business.

Accountability and sanctions. People sometimes say that accountability is an inherently punitive idea. They say that we talk of accountability only when there is a question of the principal bringing sanctions to bear on the agent.[9] Again, this is certainly true of forensic accountability. And it may be involved in many cases of agent accountability: agent accountability may involve the principal dismissing the agent or seeking recompense from him. But the demands of agent accountability are present even where there is no question of sanctions.[10] The agent is not entitled to say that the only condition under which he has to give an account is when his firing is in prospect. He is about the principal's business, so he has to give an account when the principal demands it for whatever reason.

Disagreement. Sometimes there is more than one principal in an agency relationship. When my wife and I hire a realtor, we may disagree sometimes about what we want him to do, about what standards we should use to assess what he has been doing, and about the application of those standards.

The same is true of any partnership that hires an agent. This may leave the agent in a difficult position. Sometimes he has to defer to me; sometimes he has to defer to my wife. For many purposes, this indeterminacy just stands where it is, and the agent has to make the best of it, for he may never know which of us is going to prove the more powerful in determining his fate as our agent. But eventually there may have to be clarity and explicit resolution of the disagreements between the principals: either we are to bid on this house or not, and we do need to settle on an upper limit on what we will pay for it. Also, if there is a question about whether we should drop this man and get another realtor, there will have to be resolution of the disagreements between me and my wife. My wife and I will need a decision procedure. This, as we will see, is one of the reasons democracies need elections; elections are not just ways of holding rulers accountable; they are ways of resolving disagreements among citizens about holding rulers accountable.

Information. What the agent owes his principal(s) in the first instance is an account of what he has been doing. Confronted with the demand for such an account, the agent may not say: "Well, it is up to *you* to find out what I have been doing, and then you see if you can understand it and if you are in a position to assess it." That sort of response is wholly inappropriate in an agent–principal relationship; it is what I mean by "insolence" in the title of this chapter. It is not up to the principal to find out what the agent has been doing. The agent *owes* her an account, and the *agent* must provide the necessary information on demand. Moreover, in commercial agent–principal relations, we say not only that the agent has an obligation to faithfully render his account of what he has been doing but also that he must find a way of doing so in a form that can be understood by the principal (if that is at all possible). That is what my realtor must do, and my lawyer, and my accountant. They are not entitled to sit back and see if I have the capacity to piece together what they have been doing from sources of my own. They have a responsibility to tell me, explain to me, and (if humanly possible) make sure I understand what I have been told. And all this, by the way, is part of the essence of the agent-accountability relation. It is not just a means to the principal's holding the agent accountable; it is part of what it is for the agent to be held accountable.

I emphasize this because it is sometimes said that the main problem with democratic accountability is that the people do not know and cannot find out what their rulers are doing. This is said as though it were *a problem for the people* that only they can solve (e.g., by getting more information, paying better attention, or bringing better understanding to the information they have). Practically, it may be a problem for the people, but normatively it represents a dereliction on the part of their rulers. If the rulers are truly the agents of the people, then they have a responsibility (owed to the people) to give the people the information that is required concerning what they have been doing.[11] Accountability, in other words, provides a premise for a normative requirement of open and transparent governance.

I suppose there is a further issue about whether the people, as principal, have what it takes to understand and assess information concerning what their agents, rulers, or officials have been doing. Later in the chapter, I will talk about various ways in which democratic accountability can be mediated. For now, though, we should note that this is not a problem unique to politics. It applies to all agency relations, and one virtue of focusing, early on, on the commercial examples is that we see more clearly—more clearly than political scientists have been willing to acknowledge—that this, too, involves normative obligations on the part of the agent. So far as possible, the agent must find and learn ways of communicating honestly with his principal that aid and permit the principal to understand what the agent is telling her. This is what my realtor owes me when he describes a difficult lease; it is what my accountant owes me when he has to pass on the significance of complicated tax changes; and it is what my lawyer owes me when he has to explain some plea bargain he has negotiated on my behalf. In these contexts, it is obvious that the assessment difficulties faced by the principal are, normatively speaking, a challenge that the agent, as a professional, must find ways of overcoming; the agent is not entitled to sit back and refuse an account in a way that takes no responsibility for what some critics of democratic accountability have called "apocalyptic levels of ignorance" on the part of the principal.[12]

Instructions. In agent accountability, does the principal necessarily give instructions to the agent, and is it on the basis of those instructions that the agent is held accountable? Sometimes the answer is "Yes," though if we also say that the principal can use only the instructions she has given as the basis of the agent's accountability, we are heading more toward something like forensic accountability. In any case, instructions can be more or less specific and can leave room for more or less independent action and discretion on the part of the agent. But even when there are no explicit instructions, the agent is still accountable to the principal for what he has done.[13]

With these preliminary ideas in place, let us turn to political accountability and thence to democratic accountability.

3. KINGDOMS, REPUBLICS, AND DEMOCRATIC ACCOUNTABILITY

Agent accountability, I said, is not inherently a political ideal. I have illustrated it with a model of the relation between a realtor and his client. I hope we have already seen that lessons can be drawn from this model for the context we are trying to illuminate. Our eventual aim is to shed light on democratic accountability. To do that, we must move from the commercial context to the political context.

But we have to move slowly, for even in political settings, agent accountability may have nothing to do with democracy. In certain monarchies, the state, its resources, and its people are conceived of as *belonging to the king*. They are part of his patrimony: what is done with them is done in his name; it is done in the first instance for his benefit; and what is done with the state, its resources, and its people is his business. But a king, personally, has only so much time and energy to devote to this business. He must act in large part through servants and appointed officials who are, in effect, his agents. And these agents owe their master an account of what they are doing.

Now monarchy, even of this patrimonial kind, might involve some obligation on the part of the monarch to take care of his people. He might promise to do this in his coronation oath, and his legitimacy in the eyes of the people may depend on it. But this does not make *him* accountable to the people in the sense of agent accountability. If the king does not perform the obligations he owes in respect of the people, they may criticize and denounce him, and in extremis they may rise up against him. He may even be held forensically accountable for this. But this is not agent accountability, for neither the people nor the king hold that the king is supposed to be acting as an agent on the people's behalf. Maybe the king owes agent accountability to God for the way he treats God's people. He may say, with King David, "Against thee, thee only, have I sinned,"[14] meaning not just that he is forensically accountable on the basis of Divine Law but that he is God's agent in dealing with the people committed by God to his care. Also, the king's servants may be accountable to the king in an agency sense for the way they treat the people. As I indicated when I sketched the basic model, the agent often has to take care of the principal's obligations. Just as my accountant may be accountable to me for failing to file my taxes on time, so the king's sheriff may be accountable to the king for failing to carry out the king's obligation to look after the welfare of the people. But this in itself does not establish a relation of agent accountability between the king and the people.

Patrimonial monarchy has not lasted, and the growth of something like agent accountability may have played a part in its demise. In the monarchy that I have been considering, the people may begin to question the premises of their political relation to the king. They may previously have been accustomed to thinking of themselves as the king's property, to dispose of as he pleases (though hopefully for their benefit), and the king may continue to insist on this view. But some members of the community may question it. And, after a while, they may start to develop alternative theories of politics—theories in which the fundamental business of the realm is understood to be *the people's business, not the king's*—which, to be sure, the king takes responsibility for, but which he now pursues *as their agent on their behalf.* On this basis, the people may begin to insist that he be accountable to them in the sense of agent accountability, and his servants should be accountable to the people also (perhaps through lines of accountability that the king mediates but that ultimately end up with the people as principal). No doubt, the king will resist this line of reasoning and say, with Charles I,

> For the people, I must tell you that their liberty and freedom consist in having of government, those laws by which their life and their goods may be most their own. It is not for having share in government, Sirs, that is nothing pertaining to them. A subject and a soveraign are clean different things.[15]

In this view, the monarch's undoubted obligations to the people do not put them in a position to hold him to account as their agent. But King Charles said this on the scaffold, and it was the contrary view that eventually prevailed in England.

Republicanism is the frank acknowledgment that the business conducted by government is the public business of the realm and of everyone in it rather than the patrimony of any privileged individual or family, and it is the exploration of what follows from that premise for the whole of the theory of politics.[16] Republicanism thus provides a premise for any doctrine that those who conduct the business of government are accountable to the people. But republicanism does not necessarily embody that doctrine. I mean it does not necessarily involve the specific doctrine that the people are actively entitled to demand an accounting, in the sense of agent accountability, of how public business is being conducted. Public business might be conducted as such by nobles, aristocrats, judges, senators, and other notables, with various officials and servants ranged under them. And it may not be thought that the occupants of any of these roles are *agents* of the public in whose name official business is conducted.

There may be internal lines of something *like* agent accountability, with generals or tax collectors being required to give an account of their actions to a senate, say.[17] And this may happen without the senators themselves being regarded as those whose business the generals or the tax collectors are conducting. Everyone may accept that this is the business of the public generally, not of its ruling elite. But relative to that business, the senators are more like trustees than agents, and the people are more like the beneficiaries of a trust than like the principals of an agency relationship—and pretty passive beneficiaries at that.[18] After a while, perhaps, the precision of these legal distinctions will become unhelpful. But here it does help us distinguish between republicanism as simply the static conviction that the business entrusted to officials is public business and the active relation of accountability of the rulers to those whose business it is.

The kind of republic I have in mind here is the Venetian republic,[19] where the conception of governmental business as public business was not really associated with any idea of active entitlement by ordinary members of the public to demand an account from officials of how public business was being conducted. There was scrutiny by the Senate, but this was not accountability *to* the Senate because the business being conducted by the officials was not conceived by anyone as inherently the business of the nobles who made up the Senate. Both officials and senators were trustees for the publicness of public business, but the publicness of public business was not personified in any entity conceived of as entitled to actively demand an account. Instead, officials were held to the rule of law, and both they and those who evaluated their actions were expected to exercise and apply standards of civic virtue. It was in the rule of law and in the standards of virtue that the publicness of the republic was represented.[20]

Some republics, however, *do* use active forms of agent accountability, and to do this—while keeping active faith with the idea of a republic—they really have to be or become *democratic* republics. What they do is empower the whole body of those in whose name and for whose sake the business of republican government is undertaken to insist that government officials give an account to them and to insist that the officials bear and accept the people's response to this account.

Terminology is again a slight difficulty here. James Madison famously insisted in *The Federalist Papers* that there was an important contrast between republics and democracies.[21] But his distinction is not the one I am making.[22] In fact, he regarded both republics and democracies as forms of "popular government,"[23] and he thought that in both forms there would be ways of exposing the conduct of government to the verdict of popular voting. A democracy, in Madison's terminology, was what we would call "direct democracy," operating in a small polity such as ancient Athens without any system of representation. A republic, by contrast, according to Madison, was a species of popular government adapted to a country of large extent and enjoying the benefits of representative government. And although Madison did not label the system of government he envisaged as "democratic," still he said that "the elective mode of obtaining rulers is the characteristic policy of republican government."[24]

> [T]he House of Representatives is so constituted as to support in the members an habitual recollection of their dependence on the people. Before the sentiments impressed on their minds by the mode of their elevation can be effaced by the exercise of power, they will be compelled to anticipate the moment when their power is to cease, when their exercise of it is to be reviewed, and when they must descend to the level from which they were raised; there forever to remain unless a faithful discharge of their trust shall have established their title to a renewal of it.[25]

This account of the elective aspect of legislative representation is a fine statement of what *we* should call the democratic principle of agent accountability. It signifies that the state belongs to the people and that it is not just something set up for the public benefit. It presents the people of a country as genuine living principals in relation to the tasks and conduct of state officials, who are their agents.

As acknowledged earlier, I have chosen not to approach political accountability in terms of a formal model of trusteeship, bearing in mind that trust and agency are different ideas. I explained the formal advantages of the agency idea in Sections 1 and 2. But the notion that government and governmental officials act as trustees for the people is quite common in political theory: it is pervasive in Locke's political theory, for example, and in Sieyès's too.[26] It is a superficially attractive idea, and Locke uses it in ways that closely resemble the ways I use agent accountability: those who have set up the legislature, say, as a trustee are entitled to overthrow it when it acts "contrary to their Trust."[27] Formally, however, it is difficult to get the legal idea of trust to do this work. Locke does it only by being quite loose in his use of its legal connotations.[28] In a trust relationship, neither the settlor nor the beneficiary of the trust has the right to control or to demand an account from the trustee. If they do demand an account, they have to do it through a court, under certain quite rigid conditions, and on the basis of just the terms laid down when the trust was established. All this makes the kind of legal accountability that a trust involves much more like a form of forensic accountability. The agency notion is sharper and more powerful in the authority and discretion that is deemed to be possessed by the principal in relation to his agent.[29] I should mention also, once again, that the language of political theory is not always precise. Jean-Jacques Rousseau spoke of a class of people being entrusted *(confiée)* with the powers of government by the people, but I don't think he meant to indicate the technical idea of a trust,[30] for he was also perfectly happy to speak of the government as an "agent" of the people.[31]

4. THE PEOPLE, JOINTLY AND SEVERALLY

Like Madison, we associate accountability with elections and representation. There is no doubt that elections are the main means of holding legislators and other officials accountable. But the connection between accountability and elections is very complicated, and before addressing it directly in Section 5, I want to say something about aspects of plurality or multiplicity in connection with democratic accountability.

In the simple model of agent accountability set out in Section 1, we envisaged a single agent being held accountable by and to a single principal. But in modern politics there is multiplicity on both sides of this agency relationship. In a modern state, there are tens or hundreds of thousands of officials, accountable sometimes individually and more or less directly (like a U.S. president),[32] sometimes in arrays (like congressional or parliamentary representatives), sometimes only indirectly (like civil servants), and sometimes not at all (like members of the federal judiciary). Agent accountability in modern democracies is often mediated: a civil servant may be accountable to a minister, the minister to the parliament, and the parliamentarians to voters in their constituencies. Often there is even more complexity than this linear formulation suggests, and there are genuine questions about where "the buck stops" so far as ultimate accountability is concerned.[33] It is also worth mentioning that in these intermediate layers of accountability, those who play the part of principals have not only the right but also the duty—owed to the ultimate principals—to hold the subordinate agents accountable.[34]

On the other side of the relation, of course, the multiplicity is massive.[35] In democratic agent accountability, the principal consists of millions of people—in the United States, for example, more than a quarter of a billion, all of them voluble and opinionated with diverse interests and preferences and conflicting expectations of those they vote for. For the rest of this section, I will focus on this issue of the multitude of principals. This will pave the way for our discussion of elections and representation in Section 5.

We use phrases like "accountable to the people" as though the singularity of the noun phrase "the people" could take care of this problem of multiplicity. But it cannot. Thomas Hobbes took this problem so seriously that he denounced the very idea of a ruler's accountability to the people as a confusion. The very circumstance that gives rise to their need for an agent in the first place—diversity of interests and the potential for conflict among them—precludes them from acting as a united principal to hold that agent accountable. They need an agent in the first place, Hobbes argued, because apart from such an agent they—the people—have no agency, no ability to act as a unitary entity at all. They are unable to even act like a principal apart from the work of their agent. So they need an agent, but having secured one, they have no independent agency of their own to use in holding their agent accountable.[36]

It is a powerful and intriguing argument. But it ignores the possibility that, having been united in one political system by their sovereign, the people might find themselves with an ability to act as a single entity in a way that outstrips the sovereign representation that first made that possible. Hobbes may be right in his claim that it is the sovereign that first constitutes the people as an entity, but he is wrong in his suggestion that once this has happened, that entity can only act through the sovereign. By melding his subjects into a political community, the sovereign may have established paths of communication and unity among them that have a life of their own, that can operate independently of the sovereign's will, and that conceivably can be turned against him.

In any case, even in democratic theory, we should not be too obsessed with this entity called "the people." Democratic accountability may be conceived of as something owed to the people severally as well as jointly. It is owed to persons individually, to persons arrayed in ragged and sometimes ad hoc subsets of "the people," as well as to "the people" itself as a notionally and occasionally unified entity. There is no reason why the theory of democratic accountability should be held hostage to any particular political ontology—"the people" as a singular entity, the general will, the will of the people, the majority, and so on.

I do not want to preclude such ontology out of hand; perhaps there is a place in political theory for such reification. But the liberal tradition—in which I believe the theory of democratic accountability should be located—is much looser and more open than that. Suppose we stick with the straightforward reality of individual men and women—millions of them. In some theoretical models, government and its officials may be accountable to each and every one of them. Hobbes recognized this in a very rudimentary form when he acknowledged that each individual is entitled to insist on her own survival (considered just by itself, apart from anyone else's survival or security) as an elementary term of her relation to the sovereign.[37] And along these lines, something much broader is true in modern contractarian theory, such as Rawls's theory, for example.[38] The contract idea is not majoritarian. The contractors are individuals, and the thing about contracts is that nothing but one's own individual signature will do: one cannot be voted into a contract. So there is nothing theoretically implausible about saying that there is a relation of accountability to each and every contractor so far as the reasons for her entering into the contract are concerned. If her interests and her liberty are not protected, then she has a legitimate complaint, and the contractarian conception explains why it is not unfair of her to make that complaint on her own behalf. Even apart from contractarian theory, we do say that individuals have rights and that in a sense the government is accountable to each person in regard to the respecting, protection, and promotion of her rights.

This sort of individualism is by no means all there is to be said about accountability, but it is not implausible to think of it as one layer among many. A more socially realistic approach will emphasize that people think, act, and work together as collectivities, not just as individuals, in their relation to government. But it is a serious mistake to rush from that acknowledgment to the proposition that therefore we should concentrate on the artificial entity called "the people." In between, there are many layers of partial collectives; interest groups; factions; the inhabitants of provinces, states, and regions; and members of various corporate entities. Some of these entities act as mediators and facilitators of government accountability to the whole people, but some of them also act as mediators and facilitators of government accountability to individuals or to small groups considered on their own account.

I think, by the way, that all this is very helpful with a problem that John Ferejohn identifies:[39] if we concentrate just on accountability to a collective entity called the people, we make it difficult to see how our rulers are accountable to minorities. (Obviously, this is also a cost of concentrating too rigidly on accountability through elections.) But if we accept that "the people" comprises groups of all sorts, we can have a multifaceted conception of democratic accountability, albeit one that is less tidy than a rigidly collectivized one. The point I want to stress is that both in its agency aspect and in its accountability aspect, democratic accountability displays multiple layers of responsiveness. In some respects, the government is the agent of each and every one of us, and we are entitled to hold it to account on that basis. In some respects, it is the agent of groups and minorities, and they too are entitled to insist on an account. In some respects, it is the agent of us all, but when we hold it accountable to us all, we do so in a way that is also cognizant of these other layers among us.

True, individuals and minorities don't have the formal power to throw politicians out of office. But they have a right to embarrass them with questions, and that embarrassment is often politically (and electorally) consequential. And, as I emphasized in Section 2, demanding an account—demanding that the agent (like a realtor) indicate what he has been doing so far as the principal's business is concerned and that he justify it to his principal—is part and parcel of agent accountability, not just as a preliminary to the sanctioning of an agent. Sanctioning may or may not be an immediate prospect. And so too in politics: our rulers are answerable (as agents) to their subjects (their principals) in this sense even when there is no immediate prospect of an election to toss them out of office. And their accountability in this sense is not restricted to responding to demands that can be identified as coming formally from the whole people. They come from here, there, and everywhere—sometimes from individuals, sometimes from groups, sometimes from regions, sometimes a welling up of querulous demands from the whole nation: "Tell us all—or some of us or any of us—what you have been doing about the public business that is ours (in numerous joint and several senses)." In response to such demands, wherever they come from, the government and its officials are not entitled to say: "This is none of your business; we owe no account to *you*."[40] And nor are they entitled to say, "You are nothing to us; we owe only an account to some vague abstraction called *the people*."

No doubt, this is all very untidy; rich accounts often are. And here is one other dimension of untidiness. I said in Section 1 that one of the things that distinguishes agent accountability from forensic accountability and the accountability of trustees is that principals are entitled to choose their own criteria for assessing the work of their agents. They are not like a court that has to use criteria established in rules of law, for example, or like the beneficiary of a trust who has to proceed on the terms laid down in the trust deed. This is especially important in *informal* democratic accountability.[41] People, whether individually or in groups, will often voice the concerns they have when they demand an account from their agent. In formal elections, they need not do so, but informal accountability often involves an explicit confrontation between the agent's account of what he has done and criteria for assessing his performance that the principal(s) have come up with. There is no reason to suppose that people hold their rulers accountable only at the bar of their self-interest. Sometimes one person or one group may hold an official responsible for the way other persons or other groups are treated. When overlapping groups, large and small, and individuals and whole nations hold politicians accountable at the bar of public opinion, it may be for reasons that are as diverse and overlapping as the political principals themselves. They may even be downright inconsistent. We should not worry about this at a conceptual level. It is just one of the standard risks of the political vocation: one purports to act as an agent for the public business of a whole people. The business is multifaceted and hydra headed, and inevitably so are the opinions of the people who will assess what one has done. Inconsistency and unwieldiness in this are business as usual.

So, accountability in politics involves millions of principals acting for various reasons, individually, in groups, and (in complicated ways) as a whole people, to assess, directly and indirectly, many thousands of officials. There is raggedness, there is redundancy, there are overlaps, and there are continuities; all of this is what one would expect in regard to the democratic supervision of the conduct of public business in a large polity.

All of this complicates *but it does not compromise or qualify* what I said in Section 3. Democratic accountability is predicated on a fundamental *republican* idea: the business of government is public business. And it adds to that the following strong and active democratic idea: ordinary members of the public, in all sorts of modes and combinations, are entitled to participate actively in supervising the conduct of government business because it is *their* business conducted in *their* name. Democratic accountability is the accountability of officials to the people whose business—the public business—the officials are conducting. People relate to the activity of government, as members of the public whose business the government is supposed to be conducting, in all sorts of capacities and in a variety of ways. The relation is not monolithic or unitary, and neither is the agent accountability that it involves.

5. ELECTORAL ACCOUNTABILITY

With all this in hand, let us turn now to electoral accountability. Elections are not all there is to democratic accountability. In ancient Athens, which was a kind of democracy, certain political officials were selected from the body of the people by lot. They carried out their tasks as the people's agents, and at the end of their term of office each of them was accountable to the people through a formal process called *euthynai:* upon leaving office, they were subject to a sort of obligatory scrutiny and audit, and any complaints against them were heard and resolved at this stage.[42] At the end of the *euthynai*, there was voting, but it was more like the voting of a jury than that of an election. We have no such formal process in modern democracies, but we do have informal versions of it. Departing political officials are held accountable to public opinion. They may have nothing to hope or fear so far as future office is concerned, but we should not be blinded by political scientists' emphasis on electoral sanctions into ignoring the importance of reputational and "legacy" considerations at this stage. We should not underestimate the importance of pride, vanity, honor, and an awareness of one's place in history (legacy) in people's political motivations or the significance of shame and damage to reputation as sanctions.

Still, electoral accountability *is* massively important. That is why I am devoting this whole section to it, along with the relation between accountability and representation.

In Section 4, I considered informal accountability relations between officials in a democracy and individual citizens and clusters and groups of citizens, large and small. When we turn to formal accountability through elections, it may seem as if we are now, at last, in the arena of accountability to the people as a whole. But even here it is complicated. For one thing, there is the small matter of local politics: municipalities and states, provinces, and regions. I hope I may be forgiven for putting this to one side.

Even in national politics, legislative accountability relates lawmakers to particular separated groups (constituencies) of citizens. In most democracies, lawmakers operate in a representative system: the members of a large legislature represent their constituents on a basis of various axes of representation, such as geographic interest, party sympathy, ethnicity, and so on. They may be accountable to their constituents for this representation, among other things.[43] They may be asked: "How good a representative have you been? Have you ensured that perspectives and experiences like ours are represented in Washington, D.C., or at Westminster?" But that accountability is layered with considerations of national party politics as well. In theory, a British MP from a particular constituency in Bristol, say, is directly accountable only to the voters in that constituency. Indirectly, of course, the voters' choice in, say, Bristol North West is a way of participating in holding the government of the whole of the United Kingdom formally accountable. The voting of their representative in Parliament after all helps determine national policy.

Thus, in the 2015 election, many will vote for or against the Conservative incumbent in Bristol North West as a way of assessing the record of the present coalition government. But some may value or condemn the incumbent for her personal qualities, not just her party affiliation. And also, whether they focus on the candidate or the party, they may vote on the basis of interests or opinions particular to their part of Bristol or on the basis of interests or opinions relevant to the government of the United Kingdom as a whole. They will be making complicated judgments, and different citizens in the constituencies may make these complicated judgments in different ways.

I said in Section 2 that when my wife and I hire an agent, we have to establish a decision procedure among ourselves, as principals. Now families have all sorts of decision procedures; in my family, "Carol decides" is mostly the procedure we use. Polities mostly use some version of majority rule ranging over a defined array of citizens. When the citizens of Bristol North West disagree, as they certainly will, about whether to replace their Conservative MP, a majoritarian decision procedure is used, assigning the post to her or to whoever among her competitors secures the most votes. Sometimes people say that this means the MP is accountable to "the majority," but that is misleading. The MP is accountable to the people of Bristol North West, and they use a majoritarian decision procedure to resolve their disagreements about what to do about their MP. This procedure is valued because it is fair and because it treats all citizens as equals. So, elections are not just a mode of accountability; they represent a fair way of settling disagreements that arise among the people who are seeking to hold their agents accountable.

I used Bristol as an example because I also wanted to consider the relation between electoral accountability and instructions. Edmund Burke famously told the electors for the Bristol seat that he won in 1774 that a parliamentary representative should not take instructions from his constituents.[44] However, it is a mistake to infer from this that Burke's speech is "a classic defense of not holding representatives accountable to their narrow constituencies."[45] Instruction is one thing; accountability is another. Even if the MP's role is determined on a Burkeian theory of representation—rejecting the idea that the MP should take instructions from or conform his judgment to the interests of his constituents—still the MP might be held accountable for all the judgments he makes and for the exercise of his "unbiassed opinion, his mature judgment, his enlightened conscience" (even when these relate to the general interest of the country, not just the interests of his constituents). As I said at the very end of Section 2, an agent is accountable to his principal whether she has given him specific instructions or not. Indeed, in the absence of instructions, accountability is likely to be more rather than less important. In 1777, Edmund Burke *did* feel constrained to give to his constituents a lengthy account of his parliamentary votes and speeches in the American crisis.[46] And, of course, he accepted the electoral verdict of his constituents in 1780 when they found fault with these actions and judgments and voted him out of office.[47]

Let me now return to the main theme of this section. Electoral accountability is not straightforward so far as the relation between the people and their government is concerned. It is layered, and it is entangled with the accountability of particular representatives: there are many of us, and we hold many officials accountable at the same time. Overall, whether the Labour Party replaces the present coalition in the United Kingdom in 2015 (as I write) will depend on patterns of voting over the whole 650 constituencies. We may call this *accountability of the British government to the British people,* but as I emphasized in Section 4, it will not do to infer from that anything about the importance of *the people* as a solidly unitary entity given the complexities of the electoral system. But if we have a more relaxed notion of the people, we do not have to abandon the idea of popular accountability just because of these complexities.

Some complexities, however, cannot be handled so easily: some of them generate objections, not just striated layers in the account. A first point is that not all elections involve accountability. Formally, the function of an election is to choose a high official and to resolve disagreements about that choice. When the cardinals elect a pope or when the nobles used to elect a king in Poland,[48] there was no question of holding anyone accountable: these offices were held for life. Even apart from elective monarchy, elections may not seem to have any accountability aspect in a situation where someone's tenure in office is term limited. At the end of his term, how can the voters sanction him?[49] Suppose that, in the United States, an incumbent president has finished his second term. Then the election for his successor is not really a way of holding him accountable—or at least not directly. It is just the choice of a new president. In terms of our agency model, it is more like the choice of an agent than the holding of an existing agent to account. But we should be careful with these cases. We should not underestimate the earlier point that even a term-limited candidate may be held accountable in informal ways and that reputation and legacy may be important to him. We should also remember that elections are often about the accountability of parties, not just the accountability of individuals. The verdict on an official facing a term limit may be conveyed in the way we vote for or against candidates bound to him by bonds of party.

To be sure, even in cases where we are not dealing with term limits or elections for life, even in cases where there *is* an opportunity to sanction an incumbent, we cannot assume that voters think of themselves as taking that opportunity even when they vote against the incumbent. As James Fearon insists, the function of their voting this way may be to transmit policy preferences into the political system or simply to choose a good type of representative or president for the future, irrespective of their verdict on his predecessor.[50] And, of course, if some voters are voting this way while others are voting for accountability, there may be no telling what it all adds up to.

But perhaps it is wrong to draw lines too sharply here. I have already argued against the idea that accountability is just a matter of sanctions. It is a mistake to proceed on the basis that only the punitive use of the ballot counts as democratic accountability. Equally, it is a mistake to distinguish the sanctioning of an electee too sharply from forward-looking electoral choice.[51] At least when there are no term limits, choosing a better agent will be a way of, or will involve, holding the earlier agent accountable. Certainly, that is how it will seem from the agent's point of view: like any agent who values his position, an electee will be concerned about replacement, whether that replacement is intended in a strictly punitive sense or not.

I hope readers will not think that I have complicated the link between elections and accountability out of all recognition. Elections are and remain massively important for democratic accountability: the importance is not diminished, though it is complicated, by the fact that *the people* is not treated as a unitary entity for the purposes of elections, and by the fact that voting has other uses besides holding officials accountable. The fact is that we embed the means of holding officials accountable in a complex practice that serves other functions as well. This sort of embedding is not unknown in social and political life. Moreover, none of the other functions that elections serve is utterly independent of accountability. We choose our rulers, we distinguish ourselves agonistically as citizens, we transmit policy preferences to the government, we make it possible for politicians to rotate in and out of office in a Schumpeterian way without continual coups d'état, and we sort out disagreements among ourselves. All of this is related to the key premise of accountability in a democracy—namely, that government business is *our* business and we are entitled to be treated as *principals* in regard to the agency of our rulers.

6. ACCOUNTABILITY AND POWER

This is all very well. But it is not easy to hold governments and political officials accountable in a real-world democracy. Considered abstractly, accountability implies an asymmetry of authority between principal and agent: the principal has the real authority; the agent is just acting on his behalf and is ultimately supposed to be under the principal's control; and the agent has no authority over the principal (though he may have authority to bind her in some transaction he undertakes on her behalf).[52]

This normative scheme works well for some forms of political accountability, such as the accountability of a tax gatherer to a king in the example we imagined at the beginning of Section 3. The king, the principal, already holds very considerable real power over his agent. But, in a modern democracy, people actually confront their rulers in almost the reverse relation of power. The rulers are there; they are already empowered; and they are strong and in control. For the people to be in the position of principal(s), they have to be empowered in ways that are certainly not *given* in their political relations to their rulers, as things stand. John Dunn makes much of this point. He says quite rightly that accountability arises under conditions of vertical power. It presupposes what any modern theory of government has to presuppose: namely, that there is a powerful and well-organized state ruling over a population and a territory, a state standing distinct as an entity from the people over whom it rules. But Dunn makes too much of this when he says that any theory of accountability "will be parasitic on a well-entrenched and effective practice of subjection" or that we must give priority to subjection over accountability and treat accountability as a sort of *arrière-pensée*.[53] That is like saying we must give danger priority over courage.

Still, we do have to reckon with the asymmetry of actual power. Even from a normative point of view, anything we say about accountability is said also in the presence of strong doctrines of political authority and political obligation. The point of these doctrines is to emphasize and explain what people owe to their governments, not vice versa. But this last point at least we may be able to mitigate. Political obligation (owed by citizens) is a separate issue and, by and large, should not be thought to contradict or diminish democratic accountability.[54] It does not affect accountability: certainly it would be quite wrong to say that citizens in a democracy have a political obligation not to try to hold their rulers to account.[55] Nothing remotely like that is true. The normative position is that accountability establishes clear lines of obligation in the other direction—obligations owed by the rulers to the people—and these co-exist with, and are not diminished by, any theory of the political obligations of citizens. We should also remember that accountability sometimes operates in circumstances where an official has no authority of any sort over the people holding him accountable. An official with a job to do that involves no element of command may still be accountable directly or indirectly to the people for his share of the carrying out of public business.

Still, the de facto asymmetry remains. Whatever the juridical characteristics of agent and principal, democratic accountability requires the empowerment of people who would otherwise be powerless—the empowerment of the common people, bereft of the money, prestige, power, and means of coercion that are in the hands of government officials. Democratic accountability purports to confer authority on those who are otherwise powerless over those who are already well endowed with power. It takes those who have the wherewithal to protect themselves and seeks to make them vulnerable to the verdicts and assessments of those who are, factually speaking, among the least powerful members of society. This vulnerability of the powerful at the hands of the powerless does not come into existence by magic. It has to be constructed, and unless something is done to sustain it, it will not last.

Obviously, there are various things that can be done, structures and institutions that can be put in place, to constitute the proper power relation that accountability requires. Some of these support and constitute accountability in a positive sense. Electoral arrangements are the most obvious: though, as I have argued, the electoral sanctioning of rulers is not all there is to democratic accountability, it is a large part of it and it requires the institution of a system for free, fair, and frequent elections. In addition, there need to be well-constituted forms of intermediate accountability even when an election is not in the offing.[56] Ministers, cabinet officials, and heads of agencies need to be accountable to committees of legislative representatives, for example, not because the latter are the principals in this relation but because they act on the principals' behalf in holding these officials accountable.[57] Other formal arrangements are protective of accountability and its mechanisms in a negative sense: I mean they protect accountability against various standard threats. So there must be freedom of speech and freedom of the press. There must be widespread freedom of association and agitation at the level of civil society. There must be no question of reprisal or retaliation for those who monitor and criticize, or who get together to monitor and criticize, the government or any of its officials.

Above all, there must be free access to information about what the government is doing—not (I emphasize again) as a prerequisite of accountability but as part and parcel of what accountability involves. *In a democracy, the accountable agents of the people owe the people an account of what they have been doing, and a refusal to provide this is simple insolence.* It is like my realtor refusing to provide me with an account of the transactions he has been undertaking on my behalf. There should be no question of tolerating such insolence in democratic politics.

This brings me to a broader point that is very important for democracy. Formal democratic arrangements, including formal structures of accountability, are important. But they need to be supported by an ethos of accountability, and a certain change of perspective in the way we think about politics.[58] For example, a refusal to provide information to the people is not just a wily political strategy that officials are entitled to use in the "agency game" if they can get away with it. And for the people, for their part, a failure to receive information is not just an unfortunate strategic failure—as though they had been outfoxed by their adversaries in the agency game. Rulers and officials are not entitled to taunt their constituents with the constituents' inability to find out what rulers and officials are doing; they are not entitled to congratulate themselves on the relative immunity that follows from the constituents' lack of information. And positive political theory—however hard-headed—should not be echoing that taunting or that celebration.

Theory is not everything, but it makes some difference to the atmosphere in which practices like democratic accountability flourish or wither. If these practices are to flourish, *we* need to play our part in developing and disseminating theoretical conceptions that present such attitudes—e.g., the celebration, by the government, of the people's lack of information—not just as undesirable but as insolent and as something approaching criminality.[59] At the very least, we need to treat them as they would be treated in any other agency relationship in legal or commercial life. I believe some political scientists, who rather abjectly crave recognition as "realists," have done democracy a great disservice by presenting knowledge asymmetry as a brute matter of fact that simply conditions the agency game rather than as the consequence of something comparable to malfeasance in office, corruption, or electoral fraud.

7. APPROPRIATING DEMOCRATIC ACCOUNTABILITY

As I indicated at the beginning of this chapter, the term "accountability" is quite loose in ordinary usage. I distinguished two senses, (1) forensic accountability and (2) agent accountability, and I concentrated on the latter. But "accountability" may also have a third sense:

> (3) *Consumer accountability.* In this conception, "accountability" denotes the fact that it is deemed desirable for an organization to take the views or preferences of specified others into account in deciding how to act.

This sense of accountability is used sometimes in business—with firms regarding themselves as "accountable" to their customers. It is also sometimes used in government—with entities such as hospitals and police forces being "accountable" to those whom they serve or supervise.[60] Though consumer accountability may involve elements of forensic accountability and elements of agent accountability, it need not. It may convey little more than a sense that it is a rather good idea—perhaps as a matter of management, perhaps as a matter of marketing—for an organization to be seen to be taking people's preferences into account, irrespective of the basis on which this sense is founded. It definitely does not embrace the point—common to both of the other conceptions—that consequences may follow from the assessment of the conduct of the person or organization said to be accountable, consequences that the person or organization cannot and is not supposed to be able to control. A business that receives feedback from its customers itself decides what to do with that feedback; the gathering of that feedback does not empower the customers or represent any sort of genuine vulnerability on the part of the business.

In political and administrative contexts, consumer accountability may involve an attempted appropriation of the moral force of one or both of the more specific conceptions—particularly the conception of agent accountability—that, as I have argued, is a crucial component of democratic theory. I hope I have been able to show that democratic accountability, understood as a version of agent accountability, is a rich, sharp, interesting, and powerful idea, and that it is an attractive idea when it is properly understood. A government agency may think it advantageous to give the impression that they are operating under the auspices of this rich, sharp, interesting, and powerful idea when in fact all they are doing is deploying some weak sense of consumer accountability. And they may take advantage of the looseness of the term "accountability" to enable them to do this.[61] When there are calls for, say, a government medical service to be held accountable, the agency may point proudly to the fact that its patients fill in service-review cards after their dealings with the agency are complete. But this makes a mockery of the call for accountability. At least in a democratic sense, accountability for an entity of this kind requires that it give an account of its operations directly or indirectly to the people in whose name it acts (not just the patients it deals with) and that it hold itself vulnerable to their assessment. An arrangement for receiving consumer feedback is not a way of doing this.

I wonder if there is a similar element of conceptual misappropriation when people substitute forensic accountability for democratic agent accountability. The agent accountability that characterizes democratic politics is—as I said—a rich, sharp, powerful, and attractive idea. In the perennial debate between those who favor a greater role for courts in assessing legislation and those who have democratic misgivings about this, the former may argue that judicial review is just another version of the accountability that democratic theorists are supposed to value. But this is an equivocation unless it is understood clearly that forensic accountability and agent accountability are two quite different things, not necessarily substitutable for one another. One of the key differences I mentioned earlier is that in agent accountability the principal gets to set the basis on which the agent's actions are assessed, whereas in forensic accountability the basis of assessment is given independently. This may make all the difference to defenders of democratic accountability, and they will—quite rightly—not want to regard any freestanding form of forensic accountability as an adequate substitute. Another difference is that in the agent accountability of electoral politics, disagreements about what the government is doing are resolved fairly among all the citizens acting as equals, not in a way that singles out five or nine judges to decide the matter by voting among themselves. I do not want to disparage forensic accountability, but it should not be allowed to distract us from the very particular demands and the very particular empowerment that democratic accountability involves.

That said, I should offer a couple of concessionary points. It is possible to view judicial review of legislation as a mediated form of democratic accountability, with scrutiny by a court helping to focus a broader process of democratic accountability and with court procedures operating insistently to require legislators and other officials to give an account of themselves, which is then made available to the people.[62] It is analogous to accountability of cabinet officials and others under oath to a legislative committee.

Also, any full account of these matters would acknowledge John Dunn's point that the dangers we apprehend from our rulers—dangers that in Dunn's view motivate accountability as a sort of liberalism of fear—are sometimes dangers that are urged on by the very majorities that are involved in democratic accountability. "[H]orizontal hazards between groups of citizens . . . are transposed into vertical hazards."[63] Sometimes a subset of the principals—a subset of the people—gang up on a minority, in cahoots with those who are supposed to be the people's agents. There has to be a way of preventing this, and forensic accountability in courts may be the answer. But that doesn't make forensic accountability a form of democratic accountability.

8. A JACOBIN CONCEPTION?

Maybe my view of accountability will be judged too extreme. John Dunn talks of certain conceptions of accountability requiring "Jacobin levels of surveillance."[64] That sounds unpleasant until we realize that he is referring to surveillance over political officials, not ordinary citizens. The idea is that, in the performance of public business, the government and its officials do not have a legitimate *general* interest in concealing from the people information about what they have been up to. Official secrecy may be necessary in very specific areas. But, as a general rule, transparency is required, and people are entitled to insist on it. We are not required (or permitted) to subject *each other* to this scrutiny, but we are permitted to apply it to our rulers.

In this chapter, I have tried to locate transparency—the publicity of public business—at the foundation of our conceptions of democracy and democratic accountability. I have been preoccupied with agent accountability, for I believe that if we focus that conception on democratic politics, we will begin to see some of the real or alleged difficulties of democratic accountability in a different light. Though democratic accountability is indeed a demanding idea, it makes a difference where its normative demands are supposed to fall. Critics sometimes exaggerate its impracticability under the circumstances of modern governance. Accountability requires transparency and the diffusion of information about government, and this can be difficult to achieve. But in a proper understanding, the agent accountability that is involved in democracy puts the onus of generating that transparency and the conveying of the information that accountability requires *on the persons being held accountable*. It is not for the principal to come up with ways of keeping track of what its agents are doing: the agents owe the principal an account.

CHAPTER NINE

The Core of the Case against Judicial Review

WE TURN NOW to consider the power of the judiciary. Should judges have the authority to strike down legislation when they are convinced that it violates individual rights? In many countries, they do. The best-known example is the United States. In November 2003, the Supreme Judicial Court of Massachusetts ruled that the state's marriage licensing laws violated state constitutional rights to due process and equal protection by implicitly limiting marriage to a union between a man and a woman.[1] The decision heartened many people who felt that their rights were unrecognized and that, as gay men and women, they were treated as second-class citizens under the existing marriage law. The plaintiffs and their supporters were able to feel that at least the issue of rights was now being confronted directly. A good decision and a process in which claims of right are steadily and seriously considered[2]—for many people these are reasons for cherishing the institution of judicial review. They acknowledge that judicial review sometimes leads to bad decisions—such as the striking down of 170 labor statutes by state and federal courts in the *Lochner* era[3]—and they acknowledge that the practice suffers from some sort of democratic deficit. But, they say, these costs are often exaggerated or mischaracterized. The democratic process is hardly perfect and, in any case, the democratic objection is itself problematic when what is at stake is the tyranny of the majority. We can, they argue, put up with an occasional bad outcome as the price of a practice that has given us decisions like *Brown v. Board of Education, Roe v. Wade,* and *Lawrence v. Texas,*[4] which upheld our society's commitment to individual rights in the face of prejudiced majorities.

That is almost the last good thing I will say about judicial review. (I wanted to acknowledge up front the value of many of the decisions it has given us.) However, in this chapter I argue that judicial review of legislation is inappropriate as a mode of final decision-making in a free and democratic society.

Arguments to this effect have been heard before, and often. They arise naturally in regard to a practice of this kind. In liberal political theory, legislative supremacy is often associated with popular self-government,[5] and democratic ideals are bound to stand in an uneasy relation to any practice that says elected legislatures are to operate only on the sufferance of unelected judges. Alexander Bickel summed up the issue in the well-known phrase "the counter-majoritarian difficulty."[6] We can try to mitigate this difficulty, Bickel said, by showing that existing legislative procedures do not perfectly represent the popular or the majority will. But, he continued,

> nothing in the further complexities . . . of the system, which modern political science has explored with admirable and ingenious industry, and some of which it has tended to multiply with a fertility that passes the mere zeal of the discoverer—nothing in these complexities can alter the essential reality that judicial review is a deviant institution in the American democracy.[7]

In countries that do not allow legislation to be invalidated in this way, the people themselves can decide finally, by ordinary legislative procedures, whether they want to permit abortion, affirmative action, school vouchers, or same-sex marriage. They can decide among themselves whether to have laws punishing the public expression of racial hatred or restricting candidates' spending in elections. If they disagree about any of these matters, they elect representatives to deliberate and settle the issue by voting in the legislature. That is what happened, for example, in Britain in the 1960s, when Parliament debated the liberalization of abortion law, the legalization of homosexual conduct among consenting adults, and the abolition of capital punishment.[8] On each issue, wide-ranging public deliberation was mirrored in serious debate in the House of Commons. The quality of those debates (and similar debates in Canada, Australia, New Zealand, and elsewhere) makes nonsense of the claim that legislators are incapable of addressing such issues responsibly—just as the liberal outcomes of those proceedings cast doubt on the familiar proposition that popular majorities will not uphold the rights of minorities.

By contrast, in the United States, the people or their representatives in state and federal legislatures can address these questions if they like, but they have no certainty that their decisions will prevail. If someone who disagrees with the legislative resolution decides to bring the matter before a court, the view that finally prevails will be that of the judges. As Ronald Dworkin puts it—and he is a *defender* of judicial review—on "intractable, controversial, and profound questions of political morality that philosophers, statesmen, and citizens have debated for many centuries," the people and their representatives simply have to "accept the deliverances of a majority of the justices, whose insight into these great issues is not spectacularly special."[9]

In recent years, a number of books have appeared attacking judicial review in America.[10] For years, support for the practice has come from liberals, and opposition from conservative opponents of the rights that liberal courts have upheld. But liberal opposition to judicial review has grown in recent years, as the Rehnquist Court struck down some significant achievements of liberal legislative policy.[11] However, there have been spirited defenses of the practice as well.[12] The two hundredth anniversary of *Marbury v. Madison* elicited numerous discussions of its origins and original legitimacy, and the fiftieth anniversary of *Brown v. Board of Education* provided a timely reminder of the service that the nation's courts performed in the mid-twentieth century when they spearheaded the attack on segregation.

So the battle lines are drawn, the maneuvering is familiar, and the positions on both sides are well understood. What is the point of this present intervention? I have written plenty about this myself already.[13] Why another piece attacking judicial review?

What I want to do is identify a core argument against judicial review that is independent of both its historical manifestations and questions about its particular effects—the decisions (good and bad) that it has yielded, the heartbreaks and affirmations it has handed down. I want to focus on aspects of the case against judicial review that stand apart from arguments about the way judges exercise their powers and the spirit (deferential or activist) in which they approach the legislation brought before them for their approval. Recent books by Mark Tushnet and Larry Kramer entangle a theoretical critique of the practice with discussions of its historical origins and their vision of what a less judicialized U.S. Constitution would involve.[14] This is not a criticism of Tushnet and Kramer. Their books are valuable in large part precisely because of the richness and color they bring to the theoretical controversy. As Frank Michelman says in his blurb on the back cover of *The People Themselves,* "Kramer's history . . . puts flesh on the bones of debates over judicial review and popular constitutionalism." And so it does. But I want to take off some of the flesh and boil down the normative argument to its bare bones so that we can look directly at judicial review and see what it is premised on.

Charles Black once remarked that in practice opposition to judicial review tends to be "a sometime thing," with people supporting it for the few cases they cherish (like *Brown* or *Roe*) and opposing it only when it leads to outcomes they deplore.[15] In politics, support for judicial review is sometimes intensely embroiled in support for particular decisions. This is most notably true in the debate over abortion rights, in which there is a panic-stricken refusal among pro-choice advocates to even consider the case against judicial review for fear this will give comfort and encouragement to those who regard *Roe v. Wade* as an unwarranted intrusion on the rights of conservative legislators. I hope that setting out the core case against judicial review in abstraction from its particular consequences can help overcome some of this panic. It may still be true that judicial review is necessary as a protection against legislative pathologies relating to sex, race, or religion in particular countries. But even if that is so, it is worth figuring out whether that sort of defense goes to the heart of the matter or whether it should be regarded instead as an exceptional reason to refrain from following the tendency of what, in most circumstances, would be a compelling normative argument against the practice.

A connected reason for boiling the flesh off the bones of the theoretical critique is that judicial review is an issue for other countries that have a different history, a different judicial culture, and different experience with legislative institutions than the United States has had. For example, when the British debate the relatively limited powers their judges have to review legislation, they are not particularly interested in what the Republicans said to the Federalists in 1805 or in the legacy of *Brown v. Board of Education.* What is needed is some general understanding, uncontaminated by the cultural, historical, and political preoccupations of each society.

My own writing on this has been more abstract than most. But still I have managed to discuss judicial review in a way that embroils it with other issues in jurisprudence and political philosophy.[16] I am not satisfied that I have stated in a clear and uncluttered way what the basic objection is, nor do I think I have given satisfactory answers to those who have criticized the arguments I presented in *Law and Disagreement* and elsewhere.[17]

I am going to argue that judicial review is vulnerable to attack on two fronts. It does not, as is often claimed, provide a way for a society to focus clearly on the real issues at stake when citizens disagree about rights; on the contrary, it distracts them with side issues about precedent, texts, and interpretation. And it is politically illegitimate, so far as democratic values are concerned: by privileging majority voting among a small number of unelected and unaccountable judges, it disenfranchises ordinary citizens and brushes aside cherished principles of representation and political equality in the final resolution of issues about rights.

1. WHAT IS JUDICIAL REVIEW?

This chapter is about judicial review of legislation, not judicial review of executive action or administrative decision-making.[18] The question I want to address concerns primary legislation enacted by the elected legislature of a polity. (For the United States, it includes state and federal legislation.) It might be thought that some of the same arguments apply to executive action as well: after all, the executive has elective credentials of its own with which to oppose decision-making by judges. But it is almost universally accepted that the executive's elective credentials are subject to the principle of the rule of law, and, as a result, officials may properly be required by courts to act in accordance with legal authorization. The equivalent proposition for legislators has been propounded also: judicial review is just the subjection of the legislature to the rule of law. But, in the case of the legislature, it is not uncontested; indeed, that is precisely the contestation we are concerned with here.

There are a variety of practices all over the world that could be grouped under the general heading of judicial review of legislation. They may be distinguished along several dimensions. The most important difference is between what I will call strong judicial review and weak judicial review. My target is strong judicial review.[19]

In a system of strong judicial review, courts have the authority to decline to apply a statute in a particular case (even though the statute on its own terms plainly applies in that case) or to modify the effect of a statute to make its application conform with individual rights (in ways that the statute itself does not envisage). Moreover, courts in this system have the authority to establish as a matter of law that a given statute or legislative provision will not be applied, so that as a result of stare decisis and issue preclusion, a law that they have refused to apply becomes in effect a dead letter. A form of even stronger judicial review would empower the courts to actually strike a piece of legislation out of the statute book altogether. Some European courts have this authority.[20] American courts do not,[21] but the real effect of their authority is not much short of it.[22]

In a system of weak judicial review, by contrast, courts may scrutinize legislation for its conformity to individual rights, but they may not decline to apply it (or moderate its application) simply because rights would otherwise be violated.[23] Nevertheless, their scrutiny may have some effect. In the United Kingdom, the courts may review a statute with a view to issuing a "Declaration of Incompatibility" in the event that "the court is satisfied that the provision is incompatible with a Convention right" (i.e., with one of the rights set out in the European Convention on Human Rights as incorporated into British Law through the Human Rights Act). The latter statute provides that a declaration of this kind "does not affect the validity, continuing operation or enforcement of the provision in respect of which it is given; and . . . is not binding on the parties to the proceedings in which it is made."[24] But still it has an effect: a minister may use such a declaration as authorization to initiate a fast-track legislative procedure to remedy the incompatibility.[25] This is a power the minister would not have but for the process of judicial review that led to the declaration in the first place.

A form of even weaker judicial review would give judges not even that much authority. Like their British counterparts, the New Zealand courts may not decline to apply legislation when it violates human rights (in New Zealand, the rights set out in the Bill of Rights Act of 1990), but they may strain to find interpretations that avoid the violation.[26] Although courts there have indicated that they may be prepared on occasion to issue declarations of incompatibility on their own initiative, such declarations in New Zealand do not have any legal effect on the legislative process.[27]

There are some intermediate cases. In Canada, there is provision for the review of legislation by courts, and courts there, like their U.S. counterparts, may decline to apply a national or provincial statute if it violates the provisions of the Canadian Charter of Rights and Freedoms. But Canadian legislation (provincial or national) may be couched in a form that insulates it from this scrutiny: Canadian assemblies may legislate "notwithstanding" the rights in the Charter.[28] In practice, however, the notwithstanding clause is rarely invoked.[29] Thus, in what follows I will count the Canadian arrangement as a form of strong judicial review, with its vulnerability to my argument affected only slightly by the formal availability of the override.[30]

A second distinction among types of judicial review pays attention to the place of individual rights in the constitutional system of a society. In the United States, statutes are scrutinized for their conformity to individual rights as set out in the Constitution. Rights-oriented judicial review is part and parcel of general constitutional review, and the courts strike down statutes for violations of individual rights in exactly the spirit in which they strike down statutes for violations of federalism or separation of powers principles.[31] This gives American defenses of judicial review a peculiar cast. Though philosophical defenses of the practice are often couched in terms of the judiciary's particular adeptness at dealing with propositions about rights, in reality that argument is subordinate to a defense of the structural role the courts must play in upholding the rules of the Constitution. Sometimes these two defenses are consistent; other times, they come apart. For example, textualism may seem appropriate for structural issues, but it can easily be made to seem an inappropriate basis for thinking about rights, even when the rights are embodied in an authoritative text.[32] In other countries, judicial review takes place with regard to a Bill of Rights that is not specifically designated as part of the (structural) constitution. Weak judicial review in the United Kingdom on the basis of the Human Rights Act is of this kind. Because most cases of strong judicial review are associated with constitutional review, I will focus on these cases. But it is important to remember not only that an approach oriented toward structural constraints might not be particularly appropriate as a basis for thinking about rights but also the additional point that many of the challenges that are posed to rights-oriented judicial review can be posed to other forms of constitutional review as well. In recent years, for example, the Supreme Court of the United States has struck down a number of statutes because they conflict with the Supreme Court's vision of federalism.[33] Now everyone concedes that the country is governed on a quite different basis so far as the relation between the states and the federal government is concerned than it was at the end of the eighteenth century, when most of the Constitution's text was ratified, or in the middle of the nineteenth century, when the text on federal structure was last modified to any substantial extent. But opinions differ as to what the new basis of state/federal relations is or ought to be. The text of the Constitution does not settle that matter, so it is settled instead by voting among justices—some voting for one conception of federalism (which they then read into the Constitution), the others for another, and whichever side has the most votes on the Court prevails. It is not clear that this is an appropriate basis for the settlement of structural terms of association among a free and democratic people.

A third distinction is between a posteriori review of the American kind, which takes place in the context of particular legal proceedings, sometimes long after a statute has been enacted, and ex ante review of legislation by a constitutional court specifically set up to conduct an abstract assessment of a bill in the final stages of its enactment.[34] There are questions about how to understand ex ante review. Something that in effect amounts to a final stage in a multicameral legislative process, with the court operating like a traditional senate, is not really judicial review (though the case against empowering an unelected body in this way may be similar).[35] I will not say much more about this. For some defenses of judicial review, the a posteriori character of its exercise—its rootedness in particular cases—is important, and I will concentrate on that.

A fourth distinction is connected with the third. Judicial review can be carried out by ordinary courts (as in the Massachusetts case we began with), or it can be carried out by a specialized constitutional court.[36] This may be relevant to an argument I will make later, that the ability of judges in the regular hierarchy of courts to reason about rights is exaggerated when so much of the ordinary discipline of judging distracts their attention from direct consideration of moral arguments. Perhaps a specialist constitutional court could do better, though experience suggests that it too may become preoccupied with the development of its own doctrines and precedents in a way that imposes a distorting filter on its rights-based reasoning.

2. FOUR ASSUMPTIONS

To focus my argument, and to distinguish the core case in which the objection to judicial review is at its clearest from noncore cases in which judicial review might be deemed appropriate as an anomalous provision to deal with special pathologies, I will set out some assumptions.[37]

Certain of these assumptions may strike some readers as question-begging, but I am not trying any sort of subterfuge here. The reasons for beginning this way will be evident as we go along, and the possibility of noncore cases, understood as cases in which one or more of these assumptions does not hold, is freely acknowledged and will be considered in Section 7. In effect, my contention will be that the argument against judicial review is conditional; if any of the conditions fail, the argument may not hold. Let me add that part of what I want to combat in this chapter is a certain sort of bottom-line mentality toward the issue of judicial review.[38] I fully expect that some readers will comb quickly through my assumptions to find some that do not apply, say, to American or British society as they understand it, leading them to ignore the core argument altogether. What matters to them is that judicial review be defended and challenges to it seen off; they don't particularly care how. That is an unfortunate approach. It is better to try and understand the basis of the core objection, and see whether it is valid on its own terms, before proceeding to examine cases in which, for some reason, its application may be problematic.

Here are the four assumptions I will make. We are to imagine a society with: (i) democratic institutions in reasonably good working order, including a representative legislature elected on the basis of universal adult suffrage; (ii) a set of judicial institutions, again in reasonably good order, set up on a nonrepresentative basis to hear individual lawsuits, settle disputes, and uphold the rule of law; (iii) a commitment on the part of most members of the society and most of its officials to the idea of individual and minority rights; and (iv) persisting, substantial, and good-faith disagreement about rights (i.e., about what the commitment to rights in (iii) actually amounts to and what its implications are) among the members of the society who are committed to the idea of rights.

I will argue that, relative to these assumptions, the society in question ought to settle the disagreements about rights that its members have using its legislative institutions. If these assumptions hold, the case for consigning such disagreements to judicial tribunals for final settlement is unconvincing, and there is no need for decisions about rights made by legislatures to be second-guessed by courts. And I will argue that allowing decisions by courts to override legislative decisions on these matters fails to satisfy important criteria of political legitimacy.

Let's go through the assumptions now, one by one.

(i) Democratic institutions

I assume that the society we are considering is a democratic society and that, like most societies in the modern Western world, it has struggled through various forms of monarchy, tyranny, dictatorship, or colonial domination to a situation where its laws are made and its public policies are set by the people and their representatives working through elective institutions. The society has a broadly democratic political system with universal adult suffrage, and it has a representative legislature to which elections are held on a fair and regular basis. I assume that the legislature is a large deliberative body, accustomed to dealing with difficult issues, including important issues of justice and social policy. The legislators deliberate and vote on public issues, and the procedures for lawmaking are elaborate and responsible (along the lines set out in Chapter 7), and they incorporate various safeguards, such as bicameralism, robust committee scrutiny, and multiple levels of consideration, debate, and voting. I assume that these processes connect both formally (through public hearings and consultation procedures) and informally with wider debates in the society. Members of the legislature think of themselves as representatives in a variety of ways, sometimes making the interests and opinions of their constituents key to their participation, sometimes thinking more in terms of virtual representation of interests and opinions throughout the society as a whole. I assume also that there are political parties and that legislators' party affiliations are key to their taking a view that ranges more broadly than the interests and opinions of their immediate constituents.

None of this is meant to be controversial; it picks out the way in which democratic legislatures usually operate. I am assuming that the democratic institutions are in reasonably good order. They may not be perfect, and there are probably ongoing debates as to how they might be improved. I assume these debates are informed by a culture of democracy, valuing responsible deliberation and political equality. The second of these values—political equality—is worth particular emphasis. I assume that the institutions, procedures, and practices of legislation are kept under constant review from this perspective, so that if there are perceived inequities of representation that derogate seriously from the ideal of political equality, it is understood among all the members of the society that this is an appropriate criticism to make and that, if need be, the legislature and the electoral system should be changed to remedy it. And I assume that the legislature is capable of organizing such change, either on its own initiative or by referendum.[39]

I emphasize these points about a democratic culture and electoral and legislative institutions in reasonably good working order because they will be key to the argument that follows. The initial structure of the argument will be to ask the following question: once we have posited this first assumption, what reason can there be for wanting to set up a nonelective process to second-guess and sometimes override the work that the legislature has done?[40] On the other hand, I don't want to beg any questions with this initial assumption. I will balance it immediately with an assumption that the society we are postulating also has courts in good working order—this will be the second assumption—doing reasonably well what courts are good at doing. The society we are contemplating has what it takes to have a system of judicial review, if judicial review can be shown to be appropriate.

One note of caution: When I say that the institutions are in good working order, I am not assuming that legislation enacted by a reasonably democratic legislature is by and large good or just so far as its content is concerned. I assume that some of the legislation is just and some of it is unjust—people will disagree about which is which—and that this is true both of the measures that might conceivably be subject to judicial review and of the measures that nobody is proposing to subject to judicial review. What I have said about the legislative and electoral arrangements being in good working order applies to process values rather than outcome values.

(ii) Judicial institutions

I assume that the society we are considering has courts—that is, a well-established and politically independent judiciary, again in reasonably good working order, set up to hear lawsuits, settle disputes, and uphold the rule of law. I assume that these institutions are already authorized to engage in judicial review of executive actions, testing them against statutory and constitutional law.

I assume that the courts are mostly not elective or representative institutions. By this I mean not only that judicial office is not elective but also that the judiciary is not permeated with an ethos of elections, representation, and electoral accountability in the way that the legislature is. Many defenders of judicial review regard this as a huge advantage because it means courts can deliberate on issues of principle undistracted by popular pressures and invulnerable to public anger. Sometimes, however, when it is thought necessary to rebut the democratic case against judicial review, defenders of the practice will point proudly to states where judges *are* elected. This happens in some states in the United States. But even where judges are elected, the business of the courts is not normally conducted, as the business of the legislature is, in accordance with an ethos of representation and electoral accountability.

I am going to assume that, in the society we are considering, courts are capable of performing the functions that would be assigned to them under a practice of judicial review. They could review legislation; the question is whether they should and, if so, whether their determinations should be final and binding on the representative branches of government. I assume that if they are assigned this function, they will perform it as courts characteristically perform their functions. There is an immense law review literature on the specific character of the judicial process and on the tasks for which it does and does not seem institutionally competent.[41] I do not want to delve deeply into that here. I will assume that we are dealing with courts that (1) do not act on their own motion or by abstract reference but rather respond to particular claims brought by particular litigants; (2) deal with issues in the context of binary, adversarial presentation; (3) give reasons for their decisions, responding to the arguments presented before them; and (4) refer to and elaborate their own past decisions on matters that seem relevant to the case at hand. I further assume (5) a familiar hierarchy of courts, with provisions for appeal, and with larger multimember bodies (perhaps five or nine judges) addressing cases at the highest level of appeal, with lower courts being required largely to follow the lead of higher courts in the disposition of the matters that come before them.

In some societies, judges are specially and separately trained; in other societies, they are chosen from the ranks of eminent lawyers and jurists. In either case, I assume that they have high status in the political system and a position that insulates them from specific political pressures. In other regards, I assume they are typical of the high-status and well-educated members of their society. This is important to emphasize for two reasons. First, inasmuch as the society prides itself on being largely democratic, I will assume that the judges share some of that pride and so are likely to be self-conscious about the legitimacy of their own activity if they engage in judicial review of legislation. This may affect how they exercise such authority.[42] Second, although judges are likely to be at least as committed to rights as anyone else in the society, I assume that like other members of the society, judges disagree with one another about the meaning and implications of individual and minority rights. That is, I assume they are subject to my fourth assumption about rights disagreement and that this too affects how they exercise powers of judicial review (if they have such powers). Specifically, just like legislators, modes of decision-making have to be developed for multijudge tribunals whose members disagree about rights. The decision procedure most often used is simple-majority voting. Later in this chapter and also in Chapter 10, I will address the question of why this is an appropriate procedure for judges to use.

(iii) Commitment to rights

I assume that there is a strong commitment on the part of most members of the society we are contemplating to the idea of individual and minority rights. Although they may believe in the pursuit of the general good under some broad utilitarian conception, and although they believe in majority rule as a rough general principle for politics, they accept that individuals have certain interests and are entitled to certain liberties that should not be denied simply because it would be more convenient for most people to deny them. They believe that minorities are entitled to a degree of support, recognition, and insulation that is not necessarily guaranteed by their numbers or by their political weight.

The details of the prevalent theory of rights need not detain us here. I assume that this society-wide commitment to rights involves an awareness of the global idea of human rights and of the history of thinking about rights. I assume that this commitment is a living consensus, developing and evolving as defenders of rights talk to one another about what rights they have and what those rights imply. I assume that the commitment to rights is not just lip service and that the members of the society take rights seriously: they care about them, they keep their own and others' views on rights under constant consideration, and they are alert to issues of rights in regard to all the social decisions that are canvassed or discussed in their midst.

No doubt, there are skeptics about rights in every society, but I assume that this position is an outlier. Some reject rights as they reject all political morality; others reject rights because they hold utilitarian, socialist, or other doctrines that repudiate them for (what purport to be) good reasons of political morality—for example, rights are too individualistic, or their trumping force undermines the rational pursuit of efficiency or whatever. But I assume that general respect for individual and minority rights is a serious part of a broad consensus in the society, part of the most prevalent body of political opinion, and certainly part of the official ideology.

To make this third assumption more concrete, we may assume also that the society cherishes rights to an extent that has led to the adoption of an official written bill or declaration of rights of the familiar kind. I will refer to this throughout as "the Bill of Rights" of the society concerned. This is supposed to correspond, for example, to the rights provisions of the U.S. Constitution and its amendments, the Canadian Charter of Rights and Freedoms, the European Convention on Human Rights (as incorporated, say, into British law in the Human Rights Act), or the New Zealand Bill of Rights Act. Those familiar with the last of these examples will recognize that I am making no assumption that the "Bill of Rights" is entrenched or part of a written constitution. I want to leave that open. All I assume at this stage is that a Bill of Rights has been enacted to embody the society's commitment to rights. Thus, it may have been enacted sometime in the past on the society's own initiative, it may be the product of imitation, or it may be a fulfillment of the country's external obligations under human rights law.

Readers may be puzzled by these assumptions. On the one hand, I appear to be arguing against interest, stacking the deck in favor of judicial review by assuming a Bill of Rights. On the other hand, it may seem that something sneaky is in the offing. Readers may be aware that I have argued in the past that judicial review should not be understood as a confrontation between defenders of rights and opponents of rights but as a confrontation between one view of rights and another view of rights.[43] What I want to emphasize in response to both these observations is that there is a distinction both at the cultural and at the institutional levels between a commitment to rights (even a written commitment to rights) and the various institutional forms (e.g., judicial review of legislation) that such a commitment may take. I am tired of hearing opponents of judicial review denigrated as being rights skeptics. The best response is to erect the case against judicial review on the assumption of a strong and pervasive commitment to rights.

This third assumption defines as noncore cases societies where the commitment to rights is tenuous and fragile. It may seem strange or unfair to proceed in this way, for defenders of judicial review do sometimes argue that we need the practice to help shore up our commitment to rights, to teach participants in a new democracy to value rights, or to give guarantees to minorities that might not be forthcoming in a pure majority-rules system. Such arguments are interesting, but they do not go to the heart of the case that is made for judicial review in countries such as the United States, Britain, or Canada. In those countries, we are told that judicial review is an appropriate way of institutionalizing or administering a society's existing and long-established commitment to rights. These formulations should be taken at face value, and that is what I am doing with my third assumption.[44]

(iv) Disagreement about rights

My final and crucial assumption is that the consensus about rights is not exempt from the incidence of general disagreement about all major political issues that we find in modern liberal societies. So I assume that there is substantial dissensus as to what rights there are and what they amount to. Some of these disagreements are apparent at a philosophical level (e.g., whether socioeconomic rights should be included in the Bill of Rights), some become apparent when we try to relate abstract principles of rights to particular legislative proposals (e.g., whether the free exercise of religion demands exemptions from otherwise generally applicable laws), and some become apparent only in the context of hard individual cases (e.g., how much tolerance for dissident speech there should be in a time of national emergency).

I assume that most rights disagreements are not issues of interpretation in a narrow legalistic sense. They may present themselves in the first instance as issues of interpretation, but they raise questions of considerable practical moment for the political community. Elsewhere I have referred to these as "watershed" issues of rights.[45] They are major issues of political philosophy with significant ramifications for the lives of many people. Moreover, I assume that they are not idiosyncratic to the society in which they arise. They define major choices that any modern society must face, choices that are reasonably well understood in the context of existing moral and political debates and that are focal points of moral and political disagreement in many societies. Examples spring quickly to mind: abortion, affirmative action, the legitimacy of government redistribution or interference in the marketplace, the rights of criminal suspects, prisoner voting, the precise meaning of religious toleration, minority cultural rights, the regulation of speech and spending in electoral campaigns, and so on.

As these examples suggest, disagreements about rights are often about central applications, not just marginal ones. Because I am already assuming a general commitment to rights, it is tempting to infer that this general commitment covers the core of each right and that the right only becomes controversial at the outer reaches of its application. That is a mistake. A commitment to rights can be wholehearted and sincere even while watershed cases remain controversial. For example, two people who disagree about whether restrictions on racist hate speech are acceptable may both accept that the right to free speech is key to thinking through the issue, and they may both accept also that the case they disagree about is a central rather than marginal issue relative to that right. What this shows, perhaps, is that they have different conceptions of the right,[46] but that is no reason to doubt the sincerity of their adherence to it.

Generally speaking, the fact that people disagree about rights does not mean that there must be one party to the disagreement who does not take rights seriously. No doubt, some positions are held and defended disingenuously or ignorantly by scoundrels (who care nothing for rights) or moral illiterates (who misunderstand their force and importance). But I assume that in most cases disagreement is pursued reasonably and in good faith. The issues involved are serious issues on which it is not reasonable to expect that there would be consensus. In other words, I assume something like John Rawls's "burdens of judgment," but applied (where Rawls hesitated to apply the doctrine) to issues of the right as well as issues of the good.[47] It is not reasonable to expect that people's views on complex and difficult issues of rights will always converge to consensus. And, as Rawls emphasizes, it is "unrealistic . . . to suppose that all our differences are rooted solely in ignorance and perversity, or else in the rivalries for power, status, or economic gain."[48]

The assumption of disagreement has nothing to do with moral relativism. One can recognize the existence of disagreement on matters of rights and justice—one can even acknowledge that such disagreements are, for practical political purposes, irresolvable—without staking the meta-ethical claim that there is no fact of the matter about the issue that the participants are disputing. The recognition of disagreement is perfectly compatible with there being a truth of the matter about rights and the principles of constitutionalism—assuming that our condition is not one in which the truth of the matter discloses itself in ways that are not reasonably deniable.[49]

If there is a Bill of Rights, I assume that it bears on, but does not resolve, the issues at stake in the disagreements. I mentioned some examples a few paragraphs back. In the United States, it is indisputable both that the provisions of the Bill of Rights have a bearing on how each of these issues is to be resolved and that the provisions of the Bill of Rights do not themselves determine a resolution of the issue in a way that is beyond reasonable dispute. Thus, I assume that the extent of these disagreements belies our ingenuity at devising abstract formulations. Disagreement does not prevent the enactment of a Bill of Rights.[50] But the disagreements remain unresolved, leaving us in a situation in which—when an issue about a possible rights violation arises—it is beyond dispute that a Bill of Rights provision bears on the matter, but what its bearing is and whether it prohibits (or should limit the application of) the legislative provision that is called into question remains a matter of dispute among reasonable people.

This is not to deny that arguments can be made that seem conclusive—at least to those who make them—as to the bearing of the Bill of Rights on the issue in question. If judicial review is set up in the society, then lawyers will argue about these issues using both the text and the gravitational force of the text of the Bill of Rights as reflected in the precedents of the relevant court. In fact, lawyers will have a field day. Each side to each of the disagreements will claim that its position can be read into the bland commitments of the Bill of Rights if only those texts are read generously (or narrowly) enough. Neither will be prepared to acknowledge what I am assuming now will be obvious: that the bland rhetoric of the Bill of Rights was designed partly to finesse the real and reasonable disagreements that are inevitable among people who take rights seriously for long enough to see such a bill enacted. Instead of encouraging us to confront these disagreements directly, judicial review is likely to lead to their being framed as questions of interpretation of those bland formulations. Whether that is a desirable context in which to deliberate about the moral issues that they pose is one of the things we consider in Section 5.

3. THE FORM OF THE ARGUMENT

So these are our assumptions. What do we do with the situation they define? The members of the community are committed to rights, but they disagree about rights. Most issues of rights are in need of settlement. We need settlement not so much to dispose of the issue—nothing can do that[51]—but to provide a basis for common action when action is necessary. Now there are all sorts of issues on which we do not need society-wide settlement—transubstantiation, the meaning of *Hamlet,* the value of a purely contemplative life—and that is fortunate because there is little prospect of agreement in these areas. Unfortunately, on issues of rights, where we do need settlement, there is little prospect of agreement either. The need for settlement does not make the fact of disagreement evaporate; rather, it means that a common basis for action has to be forged in the heat of our disagreements.

In the real world, the need for settlement confronts us in the legislative arena. We legislate in certain areas, and the legislation we enact raises issues of rights. Those issues may not be facially prominent in the legislation. The legislation may be on marriage formalities, minimum working hours, campaign finance reform, or the historic preservation of city centers, but what happens is that somebody notices that its application happens to raise an issue of rights, and it is in connection with that issue—is the legislation to be applied according to its terms or not?—that the need for settlement arises.

An argument, which I respect, for some sort of power of judicial review goes as follows. It may not always be easy for legislators to see what issues of rights are embedded in a legislative proposal brought before them, and it may not always be easy for them to envisage what issues of rights might arise from its subsequent application. So it is useful to have a mechanism that allows citizens to bring these issues to everyone's attention as they arise. But this is an argument for weak judicial review only, not for a strong form of the practice, in which the abstract question of right that has been identified is settled in the way that a court deems appropriate. It is an argument for something like the system in the United Kingdom, in which a court may issue a declaration that there is an important question of rights at stake. Alternatively, it is an argument for the arrangement we find in systems of even weaker review, whereby the attorney general has the nonpartisan duty to scrutinize legislative proposals and publicly identify any issues of rights that they raise.[52] Such an arrangement is a kind of institutionalization of the alertness to issues of rights that was embodied in Assumption 3 here.

Let us assume, for now, that the legislature is broadly aware of the issues of rights that a given bill gives rise to and that, having deliberated on the matter, it resolves—through debate and voting—to settle those issues in a particular way. The legislature takes sides, as it were, on one or more of the disagreements we imagined in Assumption 4. The question we face is whether that resolution of the legislature should be dispositive or whether there is reason to have it second-guessed and perhaps overruled by the judiciary.

How should we answer this question? I have heard people say that the decision rule should be that the legislature's decision stands, except when it violates individual rights. But clearly this will not do. We are assuming that the members of the society disagree about whether a given proposal violates rights. We need a way of resolving that disagreement. The point is as old as Hobbes. We must set up a decision procedure whose operation will settle, not reignite, the controversies whose existence called for a decision procedure in the first place.[53] This means that even though the members of the society we are imagining disagree about rights, they need to share a theory of legitimacy for the decision procedure that is to settle their disagreements. So, in thinking about the reasons for setting up such a procedure, we should think about reasons that can be subscribed to by people on both sides of any one of these disagreements.

I am presenting the need for legitimate decision procedures as a response to the problem of moral disagreement. But I have heard philosophers say that because disagreement is pervasive in politics we should not let it throw us off our stride. Because we disagree as much about legitimate decision procedures as we do about the justification of outcomes, and because (in my own account) it is plain that we have to take a stand on something—namely, decision procedures—despite such disagreement, why can't we just take a stand on the issue of substance and be done with it?[54] The response to this is that we must go to the issue of legitimacy whether we are likely to find disagreement there or not. For one thing, we do need to design a decision procedure, and we need to consider reasons relevant to that design. For another thing, there are important reasons relating to legitimacy (e.g., fairness, voice, participation) that arise because of disagreement and do not arise apart from our addressing the question of decision procedures. Even if we also disagree about these, we have no choice but to consider them. The fact that we will disagree about them is not a proper ground for pushing them to one side and simply taking a stand on one side or the other in the prior (or substantive) disagreement.

No decision procedure will be perfect. Whether it is a process of unreviewable legislation or a process of judicial review, it will sometimes come to the wrong decision, betraying rights rather than upholding them.[55] This is a fact of life in politics. Everyone must concede that there will sometimes be a dissonance between what they take to be the right choice and what they take to be the choice yielded by the decision procedure they regard as legitimate. Richard Wollheim called this "a paradox in the theory of democracy"[56] because it allows one and the same citizen to assert that A ought not to be enacted, where A is the policy he voted against, and A ought to be enacted, because A is the policy chosen by the majority. But Wollheim was wrong to ascribe this paradox to democracy. It is a general paradox in the theory of politics affecting any political theory that complements its account of what ought to be done with an account of how decisions ought to be made when there is disagreement about what ought to be done.

With that caution in mind, what are the reasons that need to be taken into account in designing or evaluating a decision procedure for settling disagreements about rights? Two sorts of reasons may be considered. I call them *outcome-related* and *process-related reasons,* though they are both relevant to the issue of decision procedures.

Process-related reasons are reasons for insisting that some person make, or participate in making, a given decision that stand independently of considerations about the appropriate outcome. In personal life, we sometimes say that a parent has the right to make the decision as to whether her child should be disciplined for a given infraction. It is not for an interested passerby to make that decision. We may say this while reserving judgment on whether the child should be disciplined. Indeed, we may say this even though we think the passerby is likely to make a better decision on this than the parent. In politics, the most familiar process-related reasons are those based on political equality and the democratic right to vote, the right to have one's voice counted even when others disagree with what one says.

Outcome-related reasons, by contrast, are reasons for designing the decision procedure in a way that will ensure the appropriate outcome (i.e., a good, just, or right decision). Our subject matter is disagreements about rights. Because rights are important, it is likewise important that we get them right, and so we must take outcome-related reasons very seriously indeed. Wrong answers may be tolerable in matters of policy, but on matters of principle, if the wrong answer is given, then rights will be violated. The members of the society we are imagining understand how important it is to avoid such outcomes or minimize them to the extent they can.

Of course, it may not be easy to identify outcome-related reasons that people on opposing sides of rights disagreements can agree on. As I said earlier, the design of a decision procedure must be independent of the particular disagreement it is supposed to settle; it is no good if it simply reignites it. So we must avoid outcome-related reasons that aim specifically at particular controversial outcomes (e.g., favoring a decision procedure because it is more likely to generate a pro-choice outcome than a pro-life one). A decision procedure chosen on this basis will hardly command the allegiance of the pro-life advocates. Given the disagreement, the whole point here is to set up a procedure for generating settlements in a way that can be recognized as legitimate on both sides.

It is possible, however, to garner outcome-related reasons on a more modest basis. Instead of saying (in a question-begging way) that we should choose those political procedures that are most likely to yield a particular controversial set of rights, we might say instead that we should choose political procedures that are most likely to get at the truth about rights, whatever that truth turns out to be. As Aileen Kavanagh puts it:

> [W]e do not need a precise account of what rights we have and how they should be interpreted in order to make some instrumentalist [i.e., outcome-related] claims. Many instrumentalist arguments are not based on knowledge of the content of any particular rights. Rather, they are based on general institutional considerations about the way in which legislatures make decisions in comparison to judges, the factors which influence their decision and the ways in which individuals can bring their claims in either forum.[57]

Reasons of this kind deserve to be taken seriously. Joseph Raz has gone further and suggested that these kinds of outcome-related reasons are the only reasons worth considering.[58] This dogmatism is based, presumably, on the importance of the issues at stake. The outcomes of decisions about rights are important. But there are also all sorts of important reasons that are not outcome related that we should not hesitate to also apply to the choices we make about the design of procedures for the resolution of disagreements about rights. I have given a few examples already, but another one is the principle of self-determination. There is a reason for having these disagreements settled for each society within its own political system rather than by diktat from outside (e.g., by a neighboring government or a former colonial power). Some think this is not a conclusive reason. They say that national self-determination and sovereignty should sometimes give way to international authority on questions of human rights.[59] But few deny that it has some importance. Raz has paid insufficient attention to the point that although outcome-related reasons are very important in this area of decision-making about rights, reasons of other kinds may be important too.

Once we see that there are reasons of all sorts in play, we have to consider their normative character because this will affect how they relate to one another. The term "outcome-related" sounds consequentialist. But because the consequences we are trying to avoid are rights violations, their avoidance has some of the deontological urgency associated with rights. They may not be quite as compelling as the principle that prohibits direct violations. The designers of a decision procedure are indirectly, not directly, responsible for the violations that might be involved in an exercise of that procedure. But their responsibility is still a rights-based responsibility—there is a duty to take care in this regard.[60]

What about the normative character of the process-related reasons? Process-related reasons are often matters of deontological urgency also. Ronald Dworkin, I think, misstates the character of participatory reasons when he refers to them as "[t]he participatory consequences of a political process."[61] He suggests that allowing individual citizens the opportunity to play a part in the community's political decision-making has the consequence—a good consequence—that it confirms their equal membership or standing in the community. It reassures them that they are regarded by others as persons whose opinions and choices have value. Allowing people to participate also has the good consequence of helping citizens to identify with the results of political decisions and to view those decisions as in some sense theirs, with good knock-on effects for legitimacy (in the sociologist's sense of that word).[62] All this is no doubt important. But it has the flavor of a headmaster noting the advantages that may accrue from giving his pupils a say in educational affairs through a school council. Dworkin's account radically underestimates the notion of a *right* to participate, the imperative that one be treated as an equal so far as a society's decision-making is concerned, the sense of principle that is at stake when someone asks, "Why has *my* say been excluded from this decision, which affects me and to which I am subject?"

So, how do we weigh these process-related and outcome-related considerations? We face the familiar problem of trying to maximize the value of two variables, like asking someone to buy the fastest car at the lowest price. There are various ways we can set up the question. We could ask: "What method is most likely to get at the truth about rights, while at the same time adequately respecting the equal claim to be heard of the voices of those affected?"[63] Or we could ask: "What method best respects the equal claim to be heard of the voices of those affected, while at the same time being reasonably likely to get at the truth about rights?" I think I can cut through this Gordian knot. What I will argue is that the outcome-related reasons are at best inconclusive. They are important, but they do not (as is commonly thought) establish anything like a clear case for judicial review. The process-related reasons, however, are quite one-sided. They operate mainly to discredit judicial review while leaving legislative decision-making unscathed. Thus, it seems to me that the legislative side wins in either formulation of the question. And that will be the core of the case against judicial review.

4. OUTCOME-RELATED REASONS

According to Raz, "[a] natural way to proceed is to assume that the enforcement of fundamental rights should be entrusted to whichever political decision-procedure is, in the circumstances of the time and place, most likely to enforce them well, with the fewest adverse side effects."[64] I guess the discussion at this point ought to be continuous with the broader debate about the institutional competence of courts, initiated by the legal process school.[65] Courts are good at deciding some issues and not others. Technically, we use the term "rights" to denote the issues that courts characteristically decide, because a plaintiff has to state a claim of right to be heard in a court at all. But, as Lon Fuller observed, it does not follow that courts are therefore the appropriate forum for dealing with claims of rights in the less technical sense under consideration here.[66] Some claims of rights have the character of the sort of binary issue that courts might be competent to address; others have a multifaceted character that has usually been regarded as inappropriate for decision in a judicial structure. Though this matter bears further consideration, I will not say much more about it now. I will turn instead to the more specific claims that are made about the competence of courts and legislatures on the important moral issues that are the subject of this chapter.

It is tempting to associate outcome-related reasons with the case for judicial review and process-related reasons with the case against it. In my view, this is a mistake. It is true that many of the more important process-related reasons are participatory and therefore favor elective or representative institutions. But it does not follow that all or most outcome-related reasons argue the other way. Outcome-related reasons, as we will see, cut in both directions. There are things about legislatures that make them vulnerable sometimes to the sorts of pressures that rights are supposed to guard against, but there are also things about courts that make it difficult for them to grapple directly with the moral issues that rights disagreements present.

Raz acknowledges that outcome-related reasons may weigh on both sides. On the one hand, he argues in familiar fashion that

> [i]n many countries there are ample reasons to suspect that members of the legislature are moved by sectarian interests to such a degree that they are not likely even to attempt to establish what rights (some) people have. . . . We may know that certain factors are likely to cloud people's judgments. They may be, for example, liable to be biased in their own interest. We may therefore prefer a procedure in which those charged with a decision are not affected, or not directly affected, by their own decision. There are other factors known to bias judgment, and their nature and presence can be established even without knowledge of the content of the rights concerned.[67]

Now, in considering a charge like this, we have to ask about its compatibility with our third assumption: Is this sort of sectarian prejudice typical of legislatures in all societies? Or should we associate it with the noncore case of a society whose members are largely indifferent to rights? I will say more about this later. But even taken at face value, Raz's argument is not univocal in its tendency. The same sectarian pressures often explain judicial neglect of rights as well. We have seen this in the United States in cases as diverse as *Prigg, Dred Scott, Schenck,* and *Korematsu.*[68] More recently, Laurence Tribe (usually a stalwart defender of judicial review) observed that in the panic that afflicted America after 9/11, "it would be a terrible mistake for those who worry about civil rights and liberties to pin too much hope on the judiciary in times of crisis."[69]

In any case, Raz acknowledges that sometimes outcome-related reasons also argue in the opposite direction:

> Sometimes . . . there are reasons for thinking that those whose interests are not going to be affected by a decision are unlikely to try honestly to find out what is just in the circumstances. Sometimes one may be unable to appreciate the plight of classes of people unless one belongs to the same class oneself, and therefore rather than entrusting the decision to those not affected by it, it should be given to those who are so affected.[70]

Legislatures are set up with structures of representation precisely in order to foster this sense of appreciation.

It is sometimes suggested that structures of democratic participation take no cognizance at all of the independent importance of securing appropriate outcomes—they just blindly empower the majority. This is nonsense. All democracies limit the franchise in various ways in order to secure a modicum of mature judgment at the polls. They exclude children from voting, for example, even though children are affected by the decisions under consideration. Democracies are almost everywhere associated with systems of free public education. Moreover, legislatures are constituted in a way that ensures that information about the tolerability of various options to different sections of the society is fed into the decision process. And, as we saw in Chapter 4, legislative decisions are usually made in the context of bicameral institutions, so that each proposal for a change in the law has to secure majority support in each of two houses on slightly different elective schedules. Furthermore, systems with weak judicial review or no judicial review sometimes make specific provision in the legislative process for issues of rights to be highlighted. Specific provision is made in most democracies for carefully orchestrated debate around election time, as well as a whole array of connections between formal debate in the legislature and informal debate outside the legislature. All these are outcome-related adjustments to democratic procedures. Thus, what we see, on the participatory side, is not what Rawls called a claim of pure procedural justice but something more like imperfect procedural justice.[71] In general, what I notice when I read outcome-related arguments in favor of judicial review is that people assume that an outcome-related case must be able to be made in favor of courts, if only because the most familiar arguments against judicial review are not outcome related. People strain to associate outcome-related reasons with the judiciary, and in so doing they often peddle a quite unrealistic picture of what judicial decision-making is like.[72] Opponents of judicial review are often accused of adopting a naively optimistic view of legislatures. But sometimes we do this deliberately, matching one optimistic picture with another in the face of the refusal of the defenders of courts to give a realistic account of what happens there.[73]

I now want to consider in more detail three outcome-related advantages that are sometimes claimed for courts: (A) that issues of rights are presented to courts in the context of specific cases; (B) that courts' approach to issues of rights is oriented toward the text of a Bill of Rights; and (C) that reasoning and reason-giving play a prominent role in judicial deliberation. These are said to weigh in favor of judicial review. On all three counts, however, I will argue that there are important outcome-related defects in the way courts approach rights and important outcome-related advantages on the side of legislatures.

A. Orientation to particular cases

People sometimes say that the wonderful thing about judicial reasoning on rights (as opposed to legislative reasoning on rights) is that issues of rights present themselves to judges in the form of flesh-and-blood individual situations. Rights, after all, are individual rights, and it helps focus the mind to see how an individual is affected by a piece of legislation. As Michael Moore puts the point, "[J]udges are better positioned for . . . moral insight than are legislatures because judges have moral thought experiments presented to them everyday [*sic*] with the kind of detail and concrete personal involvement needed for moral insight."[74]

But this is mostly a myth. By the time cases reach the high appellate levels we are mostly talking about in our disputes about judicial review, almost all traces of the original flesh-and-blood rightsholders have vanished, and argument such as it is revolves around the abstract issue of the right in dispute. Plaintiffs or petitioners are selected by advocacy groups precisely in order to embody the abstract characteristics that the groups want to emphasize as part of a general public policy argument. The particular idiosyncrasies of the individual litigants have usually dropped out of sight by the time the Supreme Court addresses the issue, and the Court almost always addresses the issue in general terms.[75]

The process of legislation is open to consideration of individual cases, through lobbying, in hearings, and in debate. Indeed, there is a tendency these days to initiate legislation on the basis of notorious individual cases—Megan's Law, for example.[76] Hard cases make bad law, it is sometimes said. To the extent that this is true, it seems to me that legislatures are much better positioned to mount an assessment of the significance of an individual case in relation to a general issue of rights that affects millions and affects them in many different ways.[77]

B. Orientation toward the text of a Bill of Rights

We are imagining a society with a Bill of Rights, and if there is to be judicial review of legislation, it will presumably center on the Bill of Rights. The Bill of Rights, we have assumed, has been adopted in the society pursuant to members' shared commitment to the idea of individual and minority rights, notwithstanding the fact that they disagree about what these rights are and what they entail. Now, when rights disagreements erupt in regard to legislation, there is a question about the role that the established Bill of Rights should play in the decision process in which the issue is posed. From an outcome-related point of view, is it a good idea or a bad idea that rights disagreements be fought out in relation to the terms of a Bill of Rights?

One reason for thinking it is a good idea is that the written formulations of the Bill of Rights help disputants focus on the abstract rights issues at stake. But there are powerful reasons on the other side. The forms of words used in the Bill of Rights will not have been chosen with rights disagreements in mind. Or, if they were, the forms of words will have been chosen in order to finesse the disagreements about rights that existed at the time the Bill of Rights was set up so as to secure support from its institution. They will be platitudes, and platitudes may be exactly the wrong formulations for focusing clear-headed, responsible, and good-faith explorations of rights disagreements.

The written formulations of a Bill of Rights also tend to encourage a certain rigid textual formalism. A legal right that finds protection in a Bill of Rights finds it under the auspices of some canonical form of words in which the provisions of the bill are enunciated. One lesson of American constitutional experience is that the words of each provision tend to take on a life of their own, becoming the obsessive catchphrase for expressing everything one might want to say about the right in question. This may be less of a danger in a system of legislative supremacy, because legislators can pose the issue for themselves if they like without exclusive reference to the formulations in the Bill of Rights. But it is part of the modus operandi of courts to seek textual havens for their reasoning, and they will certainly tend to orient themselves toward the text of the Bill of Rights in a rather obsessive way.

At the very least, courts will tend to be distracted in their arguments about rights by side arguments about how a text like the Bill of Rights is best approached by judges. American experience bears this out: the proportion of argument about theories of interpretation to direct argument about the moral issues is skewed in most judicial opinions in a way that no one who thinks the issues themselves are important can possibly regard as satisfactory. This is partly because the legitimacy of judicial review is itself so problematic. Because judges (like the rest of us) are concerned about the legitimacy of a process that permits them to decide these issues, they cling to their authorizing texts and debate their interpretation rather than venturing out to discuss moral reasons directly.[78]

Let me make one final point under this heading. The text of a Bill of Rights may distort judicial reasoning not only by what it includes but also by what it omits. Suppose the members of a given society disagree about whether the Bill of Rights should have included positive (socioeconomic) as well as negative (liberty) rights.[79] Those who think positive rights should have been included may think the present Bill of Rights distorts moral reasoning by excluding them. A response may be that, at worst, this omission just leads to a possible failure to review legislation in cases in which review would be appropriate, but it is not an argument against judicial review as such. Unfortunately, that's too simple. A failure to include positive rights may alter (or distort) judges' understanding of the rights that *are* included. Judges may give more weight to property rights or to freedom of contract, say, than they would if property and freedom of contract were posited alongside explicit welfare rights. And giving them greater weight may lead judges to strike down statutes that ought not to be struck down—statutes that are trying to make up the deficiency and implement by legislation those rights that failed to register in the formulations of the Bill of Rights.

C. Stating reasons

It is often thought that the great advantage of judicial decision-making on issues of individual rights is the explicit reason-giving associated with it. Courts give reasons for their decisions, we are told, and this is a token of taking seriously what is at stake, whereas legislatures do not. In fact, this is a false contrast. Legislators give reasons for their votes just as judges do. The reasons are given in what we call debate and they are published in *Hansard* or the *Congressional Record*. The difference is that lawyers are trained in close study of the reasons that judges give; they are not trained in close study of legislative reasoning (though they will occasionally ransack it for interpretive purposes).

Perhaps this argument is not really about the presence or absence of reason-giving but rather about its quality. In my view, however, the reasons that courts tend to give when they are exercising powers of judicial review of legislation are seldom the reasons that would be canvassed in a full deliberative discussion, and the process of searching for, citing, assessing, and comparing the weight of such reasons is quite different for courts than for an ideal political deliberator. Partly this is the point mentioned earlier—that the reasons will be oriented toward the terminology of the Bill of Rights. If one is lucky enough to have a fine and up-to-date Bill of Rights, then there may be some congruence between judicial reason-giving and the reason-giving we would expect in moral or political deliberation. But if one has an antiquated constitution, two hundred years old, for example, then the alleged reason-giving is likely to be artificial and distorted. In the United States, what is called "reason-giving" is usually an attempt to connect the decision the court is facing with some antique piece of ill-thought-through eighteenth- or nineteenth-century prose.

Courts' reason-giving also involves attempts to construct desperate analogies or nonanalogies between the present decision they face and other decisions that happen to have come before them (and in which they were engaged in similar contortions). There is laborious discussion of precedent, even though it is acknowledged at the highest levels of adjudication that precedent does not settle the matter.[80] (So there is also laborious discussion of the circumstances in which precedent should or shouldn't be overridden.[81]) And, all the time, the real issues at stake in the good-faith disagreement about rights get pushed to the margins. They usually take up only a paragraph or two of the twenty pages or more devoted to an opinion, and even then the issues are seldom addressed directly. In the Supreme Court's fifty-page opinion in *Roe v. Wade,* for example, there are but a couple of paragraphs dealing with the moral importance of reproductive rights in relation to privacy, and the few paragraphs addressed to the other moral issue at stake—the rights status of the fetus—are mostly taken up with showing the diversity of opinions on the issue.[82] Read those paragraphs; the result may be appealing, but the "reasoning" is threadbare.

I actually think there is a good reason for this. Courts are concerned about the legitimacy of their decision-making, and so they focus their "reason-giving" on facts that tend to show that they are legally authorized—by constitution, statute, or precedent—to make the decision they are proposing to make. This is an understandable thing to do. But it counts heavily against courts in the outcome-related argument about the preferability of judicial review over legislation.[83] Distracted by these issues of legitimacy, courts focus on what other courts have done, or what the language of the Bill of Rights is, whereas legislators—for all their vices—at least tend to go directly to the heart of the matter.[84]

In this regard, it is striking how rich the reasoning is in legislative debates on important issues of rights in countries without judicial review. I recently read through the British House of Commons debates on the Medical Termination of Pregnancy Bill from 1966. This was a bill proposing to liberalize abortion law. The second reading debate on that bill is as fine an example of a political institution grappling with moral issues as you could hope to find. It is a sustained debate—about 100 pages in *Hansard*[85]—and it involved pro-life Labour people and pro-choice Labour people, pro-life Conservatives and pro-choice Conservatives, talking through and focusing on all of the questions that need to be addressed when abortion is being discussed. They debated the questions passionately, but also thoroughly and honorably, with attention to the rights, principles, and pragmatic issues on both sides. It was a debate that in the end the supporters of the bill won; the pro-choice faction prevailed. One remarkable thing was that everyone who participated in the debate, even the pro-life MPs (when they saw which way the vote was going to go), paid tribute to the respectfulness with which their positions had been listened to and heard in that discussion.[86] Think about that. How many times have we ever heard anybody on the pro-life side in the United States pay tribute to the attention and respectfulness with which their positions were discussed, say, by the Supreme Court majority in *Roe v. Wade?*[87]

In the United States, we congratulate ourselves on consigning issues of individual rights to the courts for constitutional adjudication on the ground that courts may be regarded as forums of principle, to use Ronald Dworkin's famous phrase.[88] Indeed, we sometimes say the British are backward for not doing things that way.[89] But the key difference between the British legislative debate and the American judicial reasoning is that the latter is mostly concerned with interpretation and doctrine, while in the former decisionmakers are able to focus steadfastly on the issue of abortion itself and what it entails—on the ethical status of the fetus, on the predicament of pregnant women and the importance of their choices, their freedom, and their privacy, on the moral conflicts and difficulties that all this involves, and on the pragmatic issues about the role law should play in private moral questions. Those are the issues that surely need to be debated when society is deciding about abortion rights, and those are the issues that are given most time in legislative debates and least time in judicial deliberations.

I am sure there is more to be said on the outcome-related question.[90] It is certainly the case that just as courts address questions of rights in ways that distort what is really at stake, so can legislative reasoning also be a disgrace, as legislative majorities act out of panic, recklessly, or simply parrot popular or sectarian slogans in their pseudo-debates. The question is, "Which defects in deliberation should be regarded as normal and which as aberrations in the way that the respective institutions—courts and legislatures—are supposed to behave?" Despite Dworkin's rhetoric about "forums of principle," I think courts are expected to behave in the ways that I have criticized, focusing on precedent, text, doctrine, and other legalisms. Our assumption about courts—Assumption 2—is about institutions that behave in that way, indeed behave well by these (legalistic) standards. In the case of legislatures, however, hasty or sectarian legislating is not part of the normal theory of what legislatures are set up to do. It is not what we should assume for the core case of legislative decision-making in a society most of whose members respect rights. There may be some countries—perhaps the United States—in which peculiar legislative pathologies have developed. If that is so, then Americans should confine their noncore argument for judicial review to their own exceptional circumstances.

5. PROCESS-RELATED REASONS

Among the reasons we have for setting up decision procedures one way or another, some may have little to do with outcomes, either particular outcomes or outcomes in general. They are concerned instead with voice or fairness, or other aspects of the process itself. As I said earlier, it is often assumed that process-related arguments weigh unequivocally against judicial review. This is not quite true. Some feeble process-related arguments have been concocted by defenders of the practice, and I will say something about these. But it is mostly true: the preponderance of process-related reasons weigh in favor of legislatures.

The question of the political legitimacy of decision procedures in the face of disagreement about outcomes may be posed as follows. (I am afraid this is going to be quite abstract.)

We imagine a decision being made by a certain process, and we imagine a citizen C_n—who is to be bound or burdened by the decision—disagreeing with the decision and asking why she should accept, comply, or put up with it. Some of those who support the decision may try to persuade C_n that it is right in its substance. But they may fail not because of any obtuseness on her part but simply because C_n continues (not unreasonably) to hold a different view on this vexing and serious matter. What then is to be said to C_n? A plausible answer may be offered to her concerning the process by which the decision was reached. Even though she disagrees with the outcome, she may be able to accept that it was arrived at fairly. The theory of such a process-based response is the theory of political legitimacy.

Political decision procedures usually take the following form. Because there is disagreement about a given decision, the decision has to be made by a designated set of individuals $\{C_1, C_2, \ldots C_m\}$ using some designated decision procedure. The burden of legitimacy theory is to explain why it is appropriate for these individuals, and not some others, to be privileged to participate in the decision-making. As C_n might put it, "Why them? Why not me?" The theory of legitimacy will have to provide the basis for an answer to that question. Because the problem is general—it is not just a matter of C_n's idiosyncratic perversity—it will have to give a similar answer to similar questions from C_o, C_p, and all the other C's not included in the set of privileged decisionmakers. But even if this answer is accepted, the struggle is not over. The theory of legitimacy also has to provide an answer to an additional question that C_n may pose: "In the decision procedure that was used, why wasn't greater weight given to the views of those decisionmakers who felt as I do about the matter?" There must be a defense of the decision procedure used by $\{C_1, C_2, \ldots C_m\}$, not just defense of its membership.

Let us now make this abstract algebra more concrete. Suppose a citizen who disagrees with a legislative decision about rights poses the two questions I have envisaged. She asks: (1) "Why should this bunch of roughly five hundred men and women (the members of the legislature) be privileged to decide a question of rights affecting me and a quarter billion others?"; and (2) "Even if I accept the privileging of this five hundred, why wasn't greater weight given to the views of those legislators who agreed with me?"

In democracies, legislatures are set up in ways that provide reasonably convincing answers to these two questions. The answer to the first question is provided by the theory of fair elections to the legislature, elections in which people like C_n were treated equally along with all their fellow citizens in determining who should be privileged to be among the small number participating in decisions of this kind. The answer to the second question is given by the well-known fairness arguments underlying the principle of majority decision (MD). It is not my task to defend this here. The fairness/equality defense of the majority-decision rule is well known.[91] Better than any other rule, MD is neutral between the contested outcomes, treats participants equally, and gives each expressed opinion the greatest weight possible compatible with giving equal weight to all opinions. When we disagree about the desired outcome, when we do not want to bias the matter up front one way or another, and when each of the relevant participants has a moral claim to be treated as an equal in the process, then MD—or something like it—is the principle to use.[92]

But what if someone responds as follows: I can see why individual citizens like C_n have a right to be treated as equals in a decision-making process on a matter that affects them all. But why do the five hundred representatives in the legislature have a right to be treated as equals in this process? What justifies their use of MD?

We dealt with a version of this question in Chapter 6. The answer refers to the continuity as between the answers to the first and second questions in the case of legislatures. For legislatures, we use a version of MD to choose representatives, and we use a version of MD for decision-making among representatives. The theory is that together these provide a reasonable approximation of the use of MD as a decision procedure among the citizenry as a whole (and so a reasonable approximation of the application of the values underlying MD to the citizenry as a whole).

In general, then, what we say to C_n goes roughly as follows: You are not the only one who makes this challenge to the decision procedures we use. As a matter of fact, millions of individuals do. And we respond to each of them by conceding her point and giving her a say in the decision. In fact, we try to give her as much of a say as we can, though of course it is limited by the fact that we are trying to respond fairly to the case that can be made along the same lines for taking into account the voice of each individual citizen. We give each person the greatest say possible compatible with an equal say for each of the others. That is our principle. And we believe that our complicated electoral and representative arrangements roughly satisfy that demand for political equality—that is, equal voice and equal decisional authority.

Of course, in the real world, the realization of political equality through elections, representation, and legislative process is imperfect. Electoral systems are often flawed (e.g., by unsatisfactory arrangements for drawing district boundaries or a lack of proportionality between districts), and so are legislative procedures (e.g., by a system of seniority that compromises fairness in the legislature). All this can be acknowledged. But remember our first assumption: a set of legislative institutions—including a system of elections to the legislature and a system of decision-making within it—that are in reasonably good shape so far as these democratic values of equality and fairness are concerned. We are assuming also that legislators and their constituents keep this system under review for its conformity to these principles. For example, in many democracies there are debates about rival systems of proportional representation, districting, and legislative procedure. C_n may complain that these systems are not perfect and that they have not been reformed to the extent that they ought to have been. But a good theory of legitimacy (for real-world polities) will have a certain looseness to accommodate inevitable defects. It will talk about reasonable fairness, not perfect fairness. No doubt, some electoral and legislative systems fail even these generous criteria. But our core case is not supposed to address situations in which the legislative and electoral systems are pathologically or incorrigibly dysfunctional.

Let's return to our core case and to the confrontation we are imagining with our recalcitrant citizen C_n. That something along the lines described earlier can be said in response to C_n's complaint about the decision of a reasonably well-organized legislature is important for legitimacy, but it is not conclusive, C_n may envisage a different procedure that is even more legitimate than the legislative procedure. Legitimacy is partly comparative. Because different institutions and processes might yield different results, defending the legitimacy of a given institution or process involves showing that it was or would be fairer than some other institution or process that was available and might have reached the contrary decision.[93]

So now we imagine—or, in a system like that of the United States, we observe—decisions being made not by a legislature but by a court (let's make it the U.S. Supreme Court) on a vexing issue of rights on which the citizens disagree. And a citizen—again we'll call her C_n—who disagrees with the substance of one of the court's decisions complains about it. She asks, "Why should these nine men and women determine the matter? And even if they do, why should they make their decision using the procedure that they use rather than a procedure that gives more weight to justices with a view that I favor?"[94]

These are much tougher questions for the Court to answer than they were for legislators to answer. We have it on good authority that challenges like these are often voiced noisily outside the Court and that the justices are sometimes distressed by them. Some of them, however, reflect on that distress. (It is time to roll your eyes now and pay no attention for a few minutes because I am going to quote Justice Antonin Scalia and quote him at length.)

> In truth, I am as distressed as the Court is . . . about the "political pressure" directed to the Court: the marches, the mail, the protests aimed at inducing us to change our opinions. How upsetting it is, that so many of our citizens (good people, not lawless ones, on both sides of this abortion issue, and on various sides of other issues as well) think that we Justices should properly take into account their views, as though we were engaged not in ascertaining

an objective law but in determining some kind of social consensus. The Court would profit, I think, from giving less attention to the fact of this distressing phenomenon, and more attention to the cause of it. That cause permeates today's opinion: a new mode of constitutional adjudication that relies not upon text and traditional practice to determine the law, but upon what the Court calls "reasoned judgment," . . . which turns out to be nothing but philosophical predilection and moral intuition.[95]

Justice Scalia continued:

What makes all this relevant to the bothersome application of "political pressure" against the Court are the twin facts that the American people love democracy and the American people are not fools. As long as this Court thought (and the people thought) that we Justices were doing essentially lawyers' work up here—reading text and discerning our society's traditional understanding of that text—the public pretty much left us alone. Texts and traditions are facts to study, not convictions to demonstrate about. But if in reality, our process of constitutional adjudication consists primarily of making value judgments . . . then a free and intelligent people's attitude towards us can be expected to be (ought to be) quite different. The people know that their value judgments are quite as good as those taught in any law school—maybe better. If, indeed, the "liberties" protected by the Constitution are, as the Court says, undefined and unbounded, then the people should demonstrate, to protest that we do not implement their values instead of ours.[96]

So, as Scalia says, the legitimacy questions are front and center, and the defenders of judicial review have to figure out a response.

First, why should these judges and these judges alone decide the matter? One answer might be that the judges have been appointed and approved by decisionmakers and decision-making bodies (the president and the Senate) who have certain elective credentials. The president is elected, and people often know what sort of person he is likely to appoint to the Supreme Court, and the U.S. senators who have to approve the appointments are elected also, and their views on this sort of thing may be known as well. True, the judges are not regularly held accountable in the way legislators are, but, as we have already remarked, we are not looking for perfection.

So, the defender of judicial review is not altogether tongue-tied in response to our citizen's challenge; there is something to say. Nevertheless, if legitimacy is a comparative matter, then this is a staggeringly inadequate response. The system of legislative elections is not perfect either, but it is evidently superior as a matter of democracy and democratic values to this indirect, and limited basis of democratic legitimacy for the judiciary. Legislators are regularly accountable to their constituents, and they behave as though their electoral credentials were important in relation to the overall ethos of their participation in political decision-making. None of this is true of judges.

Second, even if we concede that vexing issues of rights should be decided by these nine men and women, why should they be decided by simple majority voting among the justices? I will address this issue in full in Chapter 10. What I can say here is that the situation gets worse for defenders of judicial review. I know the justices deliberate and produce reasons and so forth. But in the end it comes down to head-counting: five votes defeat four in the U.S. Supreme Court, irrespective of the arguments that the justices have concocted. If MD is challenged in this context, can we respond to it in roughly the same way that we imagined a response on behalf of legislatures? Actually, no, we cannot. Majority decision is appropriate for persons who have a moral claim to insist on being regarded as equals in some decision process. But I cannot see any moral basis for this claim in the case of Supreme Court justices. They do not represent anybody. Their claim to participate is functional, not a matter of entitlement. And so, as we will see in Chapter 10, their use of a majoritarian methodology remains a mystery.

In all of this, we should remember that the various responses we have been imagining to C_n's challenge to legislative and judicial procedures do not stand alone. We may also make an outcome-related case to respond to her challenge. But I think I have been able to show that the outcome-related case is inconclusive (or it argues in favor of legislatures), while the process-related case is almost wholly on the legislative side. If one institution or the other were clearly superior at determining what rights people really have, then that would weigh very heavily indeed in favor of that institution. But that is not the case. On the process side, institutions giving final authority on these matters to judges fail to offer any sort of adequate response to the fairness complaint of the ordinary citizen based on the principle of political equality. That failure might be tolerable if there were a convincing outcome-based case for judicial decision-making. Defenders of judicial review pretend that there is. But, as we have already seen, it is mostly unsupported assertion.

Perhaps aware of all this, defenders of judicial review have tried a number of last-ditch attempts to reconcile their favored institution to democratic values. I will consider these briefly because there is not much to them.

First, defenders of judicial review claim that judges do not make their own decisions about rights; they simply enforce decisions of the people that are embodied in a Bill of Rights, which itself has democratic credentials, either as legislation or as part of a constitution. This claim does not undermine the core case against judicial review. One of our assumptions has been that the Bill of Rights does not settle the disagreements that exist in the society about individual and minority rights. It bears on them, but it does not settle them. At most, the abstract terms of the Bill of Rights are popularly selected sites for disputes about these issues. The question we have been considering is who is to settle the issues that are fought out on those sites.

Second, and in much the same spirit, defenders of judicial review claim that judges are simply enforcing the society's own preexisting commitment (precommitment) to rights. The society has bound itself to the mast on certain principles of right, and, like Ulysses's shipmates, the judges are just making sure the ropes remain tied. This common analogy has been thoroughly discredited in the literature.[97] Briefly, the response is that the society has not committed itself to any particular view of what a given right entails, so when citizens disagree about this, it is not clear why giving judges the power to decide should be understood as upholding a precommitment. If someone insists nevertheless that society has committed itself to a particular view about the right in question (and the judges, by voting among themselves, somehow ascertain that precommitment), once an alternative understanding of the right is in play, it is not clear why the existing precommitment should hold. The Ulysses model works only when the precommitment guards against various aberrations, not when it guards against changes of mind in relation to genuine disagreement as to what a reasonable outcome would be.[98]

Third, defenders of judicial review claim that if legislators disagree with a judicial decision about rights, they can campaign to amend the Bill of Rights to explicitly override it. Their failure to do this amounts to a tacit democratic endorsement. This argument is flawed because it does not defend the baseline that judicial decision-making establishes. Amending a Bill of Rights characteristically involves a supermajority; or if it is a British- or New Zealand-style statute, it will have credentials in the political culture that raise the stakes and increase the burden associated with the amendment effort. If our disgruntled citizen C_n asks why the deck should be stacked in this way, the only answer we can give her refers back to the legitimacy of a judicial decision. And that has already been found wanting.

Fourth, defenders of judicial review insist that judges do have democratic credentials: they are nominated and confirmed by elected officials, and the kind of judicial nominations that a candidate for political office is likely to make nowadays plays an important role in the candidate's electoral campaign.[99] This is true, but (as I have already remarked) the issue is comparative and these credentials are not remotely competitive with the democratic credentials of elected legislators. Moreover, to the extent that we accept judges because of their democratic credentials, we undermine the affirmative case that is usually made in favor of judicial review as a distinctively valuable form of political decision-making.

Fifth and finally, defenders of judicial review claim that the practice may be justified as an additional mode of access for citizen input into the political system. Sometimes citizens access the system as voters, sometimes as lobbyists, sometimes as litigants. They say we should evaluate the legitimacy of the whole package of various modes of citizen access, not just the democratic credentials of this particular component. The point is a fair one, as far as it goes. But embedding judicial review in a wider array of modes of citizen participation does not alter the fact that this is a mode of citizen involvement that is undisciplined by the principles of political equality usually thought crucial to democracy. People tend to look to judicial review when they want greater weight for their opinions than electoral politics would give them. Maybe this mode of access can be made to seem respectable when other channels of political change are blocked.[100] We will discuss this later in the chapter. But the attitude toward one's fellow citizens that judicial review conveys—stealing a march on them by finessing the restraint of political equality—is not respectable in the core case we are considering, in which the legislature and the elective arrangements are assumed to be in reasonably good shape so far as democratic values are concerned.

6. THE TYRANNY OF THE MAJORITY

I want to give defenders of judicial review—for the core case—one last bite at the apple. The concern most commonly expressed about the work of a democratic legislature is that, because they are organized on a majoritarian basis, legislative procedures may give expression to the "tyranny of the majority." So widespread is this fear, so familiar an element is it in our political culture, so easily does the phrase "tyranny of the majority" roll off our tongues,[101] that the need for judicially patrolled constraints on legislative decisions has become more or less axiomatic. What other security do minorities have against the tyranny of the majority?

I believe this common argument embodies a confusion. Let us grant, for now, that tyranny is what happens to someone when their rights are denied. The first thing to acknowledge is that, according to this definition, tyranny is almost always going to be at stake in any disagreement about rights. In any disagreement about rights, the side in favor of the more expansive understanding of a given right (or the side that claims to recognize a right that the other denies) will think that the opposite side's position is potentially tyrannical. For example, the peyote smokers will think their subjection of their sacraments to generally applicable narcotics laws is tyrannical. Opponents of restrictive campaign finance laws will think those laws are tyrannical. But it is an open question whether they are right. Some of these claims about tyranny may be correct. But they do not become correct simply because they are asserted. Indeed, in some cases, there will be allegations of tyranny on both sides of a rights issue. Defenders of abortion rights think the pro-life position would be tyrannical to women, but the pro-life people think the pro-choice position is tyrannical to another class of persons (fetuses are persons in their account). Some think that affirmative action is tyrannical; others think the failure to implement affirmative action programs is tyrannical. And so on.

Let us grant what we acknowledged in our discussion of Wollheim's paradox. Democratic institutions will sometimes reach and enforce the incorrect decision about rights. This means they will sometimes act tyrannically in the sense we have defined. But the same is true of any decision process. Courts will sometimes act tyrannically as well.[102] Tyranny, in the definition we are using, is more or less inevitable. It is just a matter of how much tyranny there is likely to be, which was the subject of our discussion in Section 4.

Is the tyranny of a political decision aggravated by the fact that it is imposed by a majority? I leave aside the pedantic point that a court may also reach its decision by majority voting. Is tyranny by a popular majority (e.g., a majority of elected representatives, each supported by a majority of his or her constituents) a particularly egregious form of tyranny? I do not see how it could be. Either we say that tyranny is tyranny irrespective of how (and among whom) the tyrannical decision is made or we say—and this is my view—that the majoritarian aspect actually mitigates the tyranny, because it indicates that there was at least one nontyrannical thing about the decision: it was not made in a way that tyrannically excluded certain people from participation as equals.

That may seem a little flippant, so let me address the question less provocatively. The most commonly expressed misgiving about unrestrained legislative authority is that minorities or individuals may suffer oppression in relation to the majority. They may be oppressed, discriminated against, have their rights denied and violated compared to those of the majority, or have their interests unduly subordinated to those of members of the majority (for example, harmed or neglected in a way that justice condemns). In describing these forms of tyranny, oppression, or injustice, we use the terms "majority" and "minority." But in this particular context they are not necessarily terms related to political decision processes. Let me explain.

Injustice is what happens when the rights or interests of the minority are wrongly subordinated to those of the majority. Now, we have conceded that this *may* happen as a result of majoritarian political decision-making. When it does, however, we need to distinguish at least in the first instance between the *decisional* majority and minority and what I will call the *topical* majority and minority[103] (i.e., the majority and minority groups whose rights or interests are at stake in the decision). In some cases, the membership of the decisional majority may be the same as the membership of the topical majority, and the membership of the decisional minority—those who voted against the injustice—may be the same as the membership of the topical minority. This is often true in the case of racial injustice, for example: white legislators (decisional majority) vote for white privilege (topical majority); black legislators lose out in the struggle for equal rights for blacks. These are the cases, I submit, that we should be particularly concerned about under the heading of "the tyranny of the majority."

With this distinction in mind, let us return to cases of rights disagreement. Suppose there is disagreement in a society about what the rights of a topical minority are. Assuming this disagreement has to be settled, the society will have to deliberate about it and apply its decision procedures to the issue. Suppose the society uses MD to settle this matter, I take part in this decision-making, using my vote, and the side that I vote for loses. I am therefore a member of the decisional minority on this issue. But so far it has not been shown that anything tyrannical has happened to me. To show that, we would have to show two additional things: (1) that the decision really was wrong and tyrannical in its implications for the rights of those affected; and (2) that I was a member of the topical minority whose rights were adversely affected by this wrong decision.

The point to remember here is that nothing tyrannical happens to me merely by virtue of the fact that my opinion is not acted on by a community of which I am a member. Provided that the opinion that is acted on takes my interests properly into account along with everyone else's, the fact that my opinion did not prevail is not itself a threat to my rights, my freedom, or my well-being. None of this changes necessarily if I am also a member of the topical minority whose rights are at issue. People—including members of topical minorities—do not necessarily have the rights they think they have. They may be wrong about the rights they have; the majority opposed to them may be right. Responsible talk about "tyranny of the majority" will keep these analytic points in mind.

To sum up, tyranny of the majority is possible. But the term should not be used simply to mark the speaker's disagreement with the outcome of a majority decision. The most fruitful way of characterizing tyranny of the majority is to say that it happens in cases when topical minorities are aligned with decisional minorities. In Section 7, I will consider the application of this to what are called "discrete and insular minorities." For now, though, we may note that this sort of alignment is exactly what we should not expect under the core assumptions we are considering. Our third assumption was that most people, and therefore most members of any given decisional majority, care about rights just as much as the members of a given decisional minority. And our fourth assumption about disagreement was that disagreement is not usually driven by selfish interests. Disagreement is sufficiently explained by the complexity and difficulty of the issues themselves. What Rawls called "the burdens of judgment"[104] argue precisely against the sort of alignment between opinions and interests that, we have just seen, responsible talk of the tyranny of the majority ought to presuppose.

The conclusion is not, however, that tyranny of the majority is something we need not worry about. Rather, the conclusion is that tyranny of the majority—if that term is being used responsibly—is a characteristic of non-core cases, in which people care little for minority or individual rights other than their own. I do not want to deny that this happens, but I think it is important to emphasize its incompatibility with my third assumption and not to try to talk *simultaneously* about a society committed to rights in which tyranny of the majority is nevertheless an endemic possibility.

The distinctions made in this section can help us deal with two other arguments about judicial review. First, Ronald Dworkin argues in *Freedom's Law* that democratic decision-making is inherently tyrannical if people's rights are not respected. This is not just because it may generate tyrannical outcomes, he argues, but because respect for rights is a background condition for the legitimacy of any system of political decision-making. Dworkin is not just making the familiar point that democracy depends (constitutively) on certain rights, like the right to vote or, indirectly, the right to free speech or freedom of association. His point is more sophisticated than that. He maintains that processes like MD have no legitimacy at all in a democratic context (or any other context) unless each voter is assured that the others already regard him with equal concern and respect. A bunch of terrorists deciding my fate by majority decision (even an MD process in which I myself am given a vote) has no legitimacy at all, because this background condition is not met. In general, Dworkin argues, a person can hardly be expected to accept majority decisions as legitimate if she knows that other members of the community do not take her interests seriously or if the established institutions of the community evince contempt or indifference toward her or her kind.[105]

Dworkin thinks this refutes the democratic objection to judicial review.[106] Suppose a piece of legislation is enacted by an elected assembly and then challenged by a citizen on the ground that it undermines right R, a right that is a condition of democratic legitimacy. We imagine that others will disagree, some because they think R is not a condition of democracy, others because they understand R in a quite different way. And suppose the issue is assigned to a court for final decision and the court strikes down the statute, accepting the citizen's challenge. Is there a loss to democracy? The answer, Dworkin says, depends entirely on whether the court makes the right decision. If it does—that is, if the statute really was incompatible with the rights required as conditions for legitimate application of MD—then democracy is surely improved by what the court has done, because the community is now more democratically legitimate than it would have been if the statute had been allowed to stand.[107]

There are many things wrong with this argument, some of which I have pointed out elsewhere.[108] For one thing, Dworkin seems to be suggesting that if a political decision is *about* democracy, then there is no interesting question to be raised about the institutional process by which the decision is made. This seems wrong to me. If a decision about the majoritarian process (or about the conditions of its legitimacy) were made using some procedure that, for example, precluded the participation of women, equality-based objections to that procedure would not be disqualified simply because the legitimacy of the majoritarian process was actually the matter at issue. We care about process values even when process is what is at stake in our disagreements.

But the most telling objection is this: Let us grant Dworkin's premise—that democratic procedures are legitimate only among people who respect one another's rights. That may be read in two ways: (1) democratic procedures are legitimate only among people who hold and act upon the correct view of one another's rights; or (2) democratic procedures are legitimate only among people who take one another's rights seriously and who in good faith try as hard as they can to figure out what these rights are. The first reading is far too strong; no imaginable political system satisfies it. I cannot see any objection to the second reading of Dworkin's premise. But if we read it this way, then Dworkin's premise *is* satisfied for the sort of society we are considering in this chapter. Even if people disagree about rights, they may take one another's rights seriously. Decisional majorities may prevail. Sometimes they will be right about rights and sometimes they will be wrong. But that is something they have in common with all systems of decision-making, and that alone cannot undermine their legitimacy, so long as topical minorities have an assurance that most of their fellow citizens take the issue of their rights seriously.

Second, we can also use the distinctions developed in this section to help deal with the allegation that unreviewable legislative decision-making about rights involves the majority being the judge in its own case. Those who invoke the maxim *nemo iudex in causa sua* in this context say it requires that a final decision about rights should not be left in the hands of the people. Rather, it should be passed on to an independent and impartial institution such as a court.

It is hard to see the force of this argument. Almost any conceivable decision rule will eventually involve someone deciding in his own case. Unless we envisage a literally endless chain of appeals, there will always be some person or institution whose decision is final. And of that person or institution we can always say that because it has the last word, its members are ipso facto ruling on the acceptability of their own view. Facile invocations of *nemo iudex in sua causa* are no excuse for forgetting the elementary logic of legitimacy: people disagree and there is need for a final decision and a final decision procedure.[109]

What this second argument for the necessity of judicial review might mean is that the members of the topical majority (i.e., the majority whose rights and interests are at stake) should not be the ones whose votes are decisive in determining whether those rights and interests are to remain ascendant. And there are legitimate grounds for concern when topical majorities align with decisional majorities. (If this alignment is endemic, then I think we are dealing with a noncore case, for reasons I will explain in a moment.) But it is striking how rarely this happens, including how rarely it happens in the kinds of cases that are normally dealt with by judicial review in the United States. Think of the two examples I mentioned earlier: abortion and affirmative action. In neither case is there the sort of alignment that might be worrying. Many women support abortion rights, but so do many men; and many women oppose them. Many African Americans support affirmative action, but so do many members of the white majority; and many African Americans oppose affirmative action. This is what we should expect in a society in which our third and fourth assumptions are satisfied. People who take rights seriously must be expected to disagree about them, but it is a sign of their taking rights seriously that these disagreements will be relatively independent of the personal stakes that individuals have in the matter.

7. NONCORE CASES

The arguments I have made so far are based on the four quite demanding assumptions set out in Section 2. What becomes of my arguments when these assumptions fail, or for societies in which the assumptions do not hold? I have in mind particularly my first assumption, that a society has democratic and legislative institutions in good shape so far as political equality is concerned, and my third assumption, that the members of the society we are considering are by and large committed to the idea of individual and minority rights. For many people, I think the case for judicial review rests on the refusal to accept these assumptions. Judicial review is in part a response to perceived failures of democratic institutions, or it is in part a response to the belief that many people do not take rights sufficiently seriously (so they need a court to do it for them). In sum, supporters of the practice will say we need judicial review of legislation in the real world, not the ideal world defined by my assumptions.

A number of things need to be said in response to this before turning to a couple of specific issues about noncore cases. First, the assumptions on which I have been proceeding are not utopian or demanding. Assumption 3, for example—a general commitment to rights in the society—is not unreasonable, given that the case for judicial review almost always assumes that somehow the society for which judicial review is envisaged has a Bill of Rights that stands in some real relation to the views of citizens. The first assumption was about electoral and legislative arrangements being in reasonably good shape, bearing in mind that even in the name of political equality we are not entitled to demand perfection. Also in Section 5, when I talked about the legitimacy of legislatures and courts, I again stressed that my argument did not turn on there being a perfect response to individual citizens' demands for voice and participation. The case for the legitimacy of legislative decision-making does not depend on any assumption of the utopian perfection of legislative institutions, nor on their perfectly embodying the principle of political equality in their elective and procedural aspects. It turns on these institutions being explicitly oriented toward this principle, organized in a way that is designed to satisfy the principle, and making a reasonable effort to do so. Not only that, but I took care to cite the actual deliberations of an actual legislature—the House of Commons on the Medical Termination of Pregnancy Bill (1966)—as an example of how legislatures might work, not some concoction of the philosophic a priori.

Having said all this, we still must ask what happens to the argument against judicial review if the assumptions fail. In cases in which the assumptions fail, the argument against judicial review presented in this chapter does not go through. As I emphasized in Section 2, my argument is a conditional one. However, it does not follow that judicial review of legislation is defensible whenever the assumptions fail. There may be other good arguments against judicial review that are not conditioned on assumptions like mine. Or it may be the case that judicial review offers no hope of ameliorating a particular situation. It may not be appropriate to set up judicial review of legislation if judicial decision-making in a society is no less corrupt or no less contaminated with prejudice than the society's legislative decision-making. The arguments we entertained for the core case were in large part comparative, and this logic applies to noncore cases as well.

Suppose we are dealing with a case that is noncore by virtue of the failure of my first assumption. In this case, legislatures are inadequately representative or deliberative, the system of elections is compromised, and the procedures used in the legislature no longer bear any credible relation to political legitimacy. Two questions then arise. Is it possible to improve the situation so far as the legislature is concerned? And should a final power of decision for important issues of rights be vested in the courts, assuming that the courts would handle those issues better? The questions are independent, for we may reasonably think that some issues of rights are too urgent to await the emergence of a more responsible and representative legislature. But they are not utterly independent. Vesting the final power of decision in courts may well make it more difficult to reform the legislature or more difficult to develop the legislative ethos that the first assumption and perhaps also the third assumption presuppose. I have heard speculation to this effect about the United States. The idea is that U.S. legislatures, particularly state legislatures, operate irresponsibly and in a way that fails to take rights seriously because the knowledge that the courts are there as backup constitutes a moral hazard, making it harder to develop a responsible culture among legislators. How far this is true I don't know. It is certainly worth considering.

I want to end by discussing one well-known way in which my first assumption might be thought to fail. I have in mind Justice Stone's suggestion in the famous *Carolene Products* footnote four: "[P]rejudice against discrete and insular minorities may be a special condition, which tends seriously to curtail the operation of those political processes ordinarily to be relied upon to protect minorities."[110] This it seems to me is an excellent way of characterizing the sort of noncore case in which the argument for judicial review of legislative decisions has some plausibility. Minorities in this situation may need special care that only nonelective institutions can provide—special care to protect their rights and special care (as John Hart Ely points out) to repair the political system and facilitate their representation.[111]

We have to be cautious about this argument, however. It follows from what I said in Section 6 that not every minority deserves this special treatment: certainly not every decisional minority, and not even every topical minority.[112] There is no reason to suppose even that every chronic minority deserves this special treatment, certainly not chronic decisional minorities—Bolsheviks in the United States, for example.

Too often, the phrase "discrete and insular" is used thoughtlessly. Not every distinct and identifiable minority is discrete and insular. There is nothing magical about Justice Stone's language. But, if taken seriously, "discrete" and "insular" are useful adjectives, for they convey not just the idea of a minority that exists apart from political decision-making—in other words a topical minority—but also a minority whose members are isolated from the rest of the community in the sense that they do not share many interests with nonmembers that would enable them to build a series of coalitions to promote their interests. The alignment of decisional and topical minorities that we warned against in Section 6 is a good example of "insularity" in this sense. And it is a cause for concern.

What about the other criterion that Justice Stone mentioned—that the minority is the victim of prejudice? Pervasive prejudice is certainly incompatible with my third and fourth assumptions; it connotes indifference or hostility to the rights of the group's members, and it may lead members of the majority to differ unreasonably from the minority members' estimation of their own rights. But the term "prejudice" may be too narrow, and its connotations may fail to capture the depth of entrenched and unconscious antipathy between one group and another. The point is not to insist on any particular mode of antipathy but to distinguish between its various modes and the phenomenon of reasonable disagreement about rights.[113]

In cases where there is such antipathy, the core argument against judicial review that I have outlined may not be able to be sustained. But, again, this is not the same as saying that a case has been made in favor of judicial review. Everything depends on whether judicial majorities are infected with the same prejudice as legislative majorities. If they are, then the case may be not only noncore but hopeless. A practice of judicial review cannot do anything for the rights of the minority if there is no support at all in the society for minority rights. The affirmative case that is often made for judicial review in these circumstances assumes that there is some respect for the relevant minority's rights outside the minority's own membership but that it is largely confined to political elites. The idea is that most ordinary members of the majority do not share this sympathy. Now the elite members who do share it—I'll call them elite sympathizers—may be in the legislature or they may be in the judiciary. The argument for giving final authority to judges is that elite sympathizers in the judiciary are better able than elite sympathizers in an elected legislature to protect themselves when they accord rights to the members of an unpopular minority. They are less vulnerable to public anger and need not worry about retaliation. They are therefore more likely to protect the minority. Of course in the American case there are strong counter-examples: the U.S. Supreme Court never lifted a finger against slavery, for example, and raised several fists in its defense. Slavery was abolished as a result of the actions of ordinary men and women, elected politicians, and soldiers fighting for the union in the Civil War.

Notice also how the argument for judicial review developed in the last paragraph depends on a particular assumption about the distribution of support for the minority's rights. The sympathy is assumed to be strongest among political elites. If that is false—if the sympathy is stronger among ordinary people—then there is no reason to accept the argument of the previous paragraph. On the contrary, elective institutions may be better at protecting minority rights because electoral arrangements will provide a way of channeling popular support for minority rights into the legislature, whereas there are no such channels into the judiciary. No doubt, the distribution of support for minority rights varies from case to case. But I find it interesting that most defenders of judicial review, when they assume that there will be some support for minority rights in a society, are convinced that in all cases it will be found among elites if it is found anywhere. They will have to defend this as an empirical claim, but I must say it is entirely consonant with ancient prejudices against democratic decision-making.

One other factor to take into account is whether an established practice of judicial review will make it easier or harder in the long term to remedy the elective and legislative dysfunctions we are imagining here. In certain circumstances, discrete and insular minorities may benefit from judicial intervention to protect their rights. But institutionally, judicial solicitude may make things worse, or at least fail to make them much better. As the United States found in the 1950s and 1960s, for all the excitement of judicial attacks on segregation in *Brown* and other cases, what was needed in the end was strong legislative intervention (in the form of the 1964 Civil Rights Act), and it turned out that the main difference was not courts versus legislatures per se but federal institutions versus state institutions, with the federal legislature finally playing the decisive role.

Overall, we should not read the *Carolene Products* footnote or any similar doctrine as a way of "leveraging" a more general practice of judicial review into existence.[114] The problem of discrete and insular minorities is not to be seen as a sort of Trojan Horse for judicial review or as a basis for embarrassing the arguments against it. The aim of considering such cases is not to defend judicial review; rather, it is to do whatever best secures the rights of the minorities affected. We should aim directly at that, conscious of the fact that there is no convincing *general* argument for judicial review of which this could be treated as a sort of ideological vanguard.

I have not argued that the practice of judicial review of legislation is inappropriate in all circumstances. Instead, I have tried to show why rights-based judicial review is inappropriate for reasonably democratic societies whose main problem is not that their legislative institutions are dysfunctional but that their members disagree about rights.

Disagreement about rights is not unreasonable, and people can disagree about rights while still taking rights seriously. In these circumstances, they need to adopt procedures for resolving their disagreements that respect the voices and opinions of the persons—in their millions—whose rights are at stake in these disagreements and treat them as equals in the process. At the same time, they must ensure that these procedures address, in a responsible and deliberative fashion, the tough and complex issues that rights disagreements raise. Ordinary legislative procedures can do this, I have argued, and an additional layer of final review by courts adds little to the process except a rather insulting form of disenfranchisement and a legalistic obfuscation of the moral issues at stake in our disagreements about rights.

Maybe there are circumstances—peculiar pathologies, dysfunctional legislative institutions, corrupt political cultures, legacies of racism, and other forms of endemic prejudice—in which these costs of obfuscation and disenfranchisement are worth bearing for the time being. But defenders of judicial review ought to start making their claims for the practice frankly on that basis—and make it with a degree of humility and shame in regard to the circumstances that elicit it—rather than preaching it abroad as the epitome of respect for rights and as a normal and normatively desirable element of modern constitutional democracy.

CHAPTER TEN

Five to Four: Why Do Bare Majorities Rule on Courts?

WHY, IN MOST appellate courts, are important issues of law settled by majority decision? Why, when judges disagree, do they use the same method of "counting heads" that is used in electoral and legislative politics? Some scholars call this the problem of "judicial majoritarianism,"[1] though that phrase is also used by Barry Friedman and others to describe the inclination of judges to follow majority opinion in the wider society.[2] In this chapter, I am not interested in "judicial majoritarianism" in Friedman's sense. What I want to address is the decision procedure used internally in our appellate courts.

Judges vote when they disagree and—as we all know—many important U.S. Supreme Court cases are settled by a vote of five to four among the justices, even when the Court is reviewing legislation and deciding whether to overturn the result of a majority vote among elected representatives. Consider, for example, *Citizens United v. Federal Election Commission*,[3] which overturned a piece of federal legislation, the Bipartisan Campaign Reform Act of 2002. The judicial vote to overturn it was 5–4; the legislative votes to enact it were 240–189 in the House of Representatives and 60–40 in the Senate. Majorities, everywhere you look. This leads to my question, "Why is majority decision[4]—I am going to abbreviate it as MD—an appropriate principle to use in an institution that is supposed to be curing or mitigating the defects of majoritarianism?"[5] Of course, it is not only in constitutional cases that majorities rule in court. It is pretty much universal among multi-member judicial panels, in private law appeals as well as in public law, at least in our tradition. It is simply how judges decide when they disagree. But that is not an answer; it is an indication of how pervasively the question arises.

So, why is MD used in judicial decision-making? And why do people put up with it? Let me say at once that my pressing these questions is not intended as a way of discrediting judicial decision-making, not even with respect to questions of judicial review. (As we saw in Chapter 9, there are ample grounds for opposing judicial review of legislation whatever decision procedure judges use.) Even for those who favor judicial review, the absence of a clear theory of judicial MD constitutes a gap in our understanding of our most important legal institution.

1. WHY ASK?

I think my question is worth asking, for several reasons. First, it is worth asking simply out of interest. MD in court is something we take for granted, but it would be interesting to know whether this practice has ever been made the focus of explicit justificatory argument in the history of the modern judiciary. I suspect the answer is "no," and I wonder why that has been the case, especially in light of the theoretical attention—much of it critical—that is paid to MD in democratic settings. When we consider electoral or representative institutions, we ask questions about the justification of MD all the time, and we devote a lot of effort to elaborating and discussing the answers. Is the justification of MD in democratic politics epistemic? I mean, is MD an appropriate decision procedure to use because it promises to get us more often to the right answer (e.g., to the election of good representatives or the making of good legislative choices)?[6] Or is it appropriate only as a fair procedure, one that respects the principle of political equality (one person, one vote)?[7] Is MD in electoral or legislative contexts just "natural" in some sense that does not require justification? Do we use it simply because it's efficient?[8] These are good questions to ask about voting in elections and in legislatures. They are also good questions when we turn our attention to courts.

Here's a second reason. Defenders of judicial review often say they are opposed to majoritarianism as such. But because they seem to have no trouble with MD in court, that can't really be their position. It must be *democratic* majoritarianism that they oppose, not judicial majoritarianism. Opportunistically, however, they will sometimes seize on certain difficulties with majoritarian decision-making as such in order to discredit democratic majoritarianism. Whether or not they are disingenuous in this, we ought to take these difficulties seriously. So, for example, critics of democratic majoritarianism sometimes allege that MD can lead to incoherent decision-making (e.g., through Arrow's paradox).[9] And so it can. But this may also be true of appellate courts using MD (unless there is something about courts that keeps their decision-making within the parameters where Arrow's paradox does not arise). Dan Farber and Philip Frickey pointed this out in their excellent study *Law and Public Choice*. They said that if we think (for reasons associated with social choice paradoxes) that "chaos and incoherence are the inevitable outcomes of majority voting, then appellate courts ... are equally bankrupt.... If we accept the thesis as to legislatures, we are left with nowhere to turn."[10] Justifying a given decision procedure is partly a matter of answering what can be said against its use, so we ought to investigate whether what is said against MD in other contexts can be said against its use in court and, if so, whether such criticisms can be answered.

Our question is also worth asking—this is my third point—because we can imagine other decision rules for judicial settings, and it might be worth considering why these are (mostly) dismissed out of hand for decision-making among judges on appellate courts.[11] For a long time, the practice of trial by jury proceeded on the basis that unanimity was required to convict a criminal defendant. Nowadays, in some jurisdictions (England, for example), a majority verdict is sufficient, but it still must be a heavy supermajority—something like ten to two. A bare majority is never sufficient (except for grand juries). Why is nothing similar envisaged for disagreements among judges? One might imagine a supermajority rule for judicial review. Actually, imagination is not necessary: the Constitution of the State of Nebraska ordains that Nebraska's "Supreme Court shall consist of seven judges" and that "[a] majority of the members sitting shall have authority to pronounce a decision except in cases involving the constitutionality of an act of the Legislature. No legislative act shall be held unconstitutional except by the concurrence of five judges."[12] The Constitution of North Dakota is even more stringent, requiring four out of five justices to strike down legislation.[13] These seem like good rules, embodying as they do a sort of presumption in favor of the constitutionality of legislation.[14] So why is a supermajority rule not the decision procedure on the Supreme Court of the United States?[15]

Fourth, there is an anomaly in the absence of theoretical discussion, given the fact that, in the United States and other common law countries, MD seems to be accepted *explicitly* as the basis for appellate judicial decision-making. Other legal systems—most civil law systems, for example—present only a consensus judgment and do not allow the public expression of dissenting opinions.[16] In these systems, judges don't appear to vote. Presumably, there is often dissensus in their private deliberations, and maybe MD (or something like it) is used behind closed doors to determine what will be the consensus position.[17] Yet the public does not perceive the judges as voting; they don't perceive the outcome as depending on counting heads. In contrast, in common law systems, we do. And in the United States, the fact that courts use MD is the crucial assumption on which the whole politics of judicial appointments turns. This is particularly so because many areas of constitutional decision are potentially unsettled—abortion, of course, is the best-known example. The issue may be decided by MD one year, but justices of the Supreme Court come and go, and partisans hope that a bare majority on one side of a given issue may be replaced in time by a bare majority on the other side.[18] So, for example, since 1973, it has been an important feature of presidential politics to try to secure judicial appointments to the Supreme Court that—on the assumption of MD—will either secure (for a while) or overturn *Roe v. Wade*.[19] The matter is always on a knife-edge, and pro-choice advocates are vividly aware that one or two conservative appointments might upset the 5–4 balance on which they rely. In this sense, MD explicitly frames the politics of judicial nomination and confirmation. Oddly, though, despite its explicit presence as a frame, the use of MD in court is never itself made a topic of argument. In abortion politics, for example, no pro-life faction ever argues that anti-abortion legislation in the states should be protected from federal review by a Nebraska-style rule. No pro-choice faction ever argues that a supermajority should be required to overturn a precedent of long standing. People just assume MD and argue around it.

Fifth, it would be useful to have a good account of the use of MD in courts to complement and illuminate scholarly discussion of other issues about judicial decision-making. As I will shortly show, there is very little in the law review literature addressing the exact question that I have posed. (The few exceptions will be discussed in Section 2.) But there is considerable literature on other aspects of judicial decision-making.[20] Scholars talk frequently about how judges, individually, should approach the exercise of their power on multimember courts. When a judge disagrees with her colleagues, should she defend her position in the way that people defend their interests, in the way a member of a political party defends a plank in the party platform, or in some other way? There are debates about whether judges ought to trade votes, compromise, logroll, and so on.[21] Should judges switch their votes when there is no majority on the disposition of a case?[22] There is some literature on when a high appellate court like the United Kingdom's Supreme Court should hear appeals with a larger-than-usual panel of justices. Some arguments on this focus on the possibility that MD might produce a 3–2 outcome on a small panel (e.g., of five members) that might have been quite different if the panel had been constituted from among the other available justices.[23]

There is also interesting literature on the relation between judges' voting and the reasons they give in their opinions. Should judges vote only on outcomes (and is that the vote that should be decisive), or should we be seeking consensus or a majority on the various reasons that justify their votes?[24] At the moment, in common law systems, we do not insist on MD or any decision procedure regarding the reasons that are given for outcomes determined by courts. It seems we can afford to leave that undecided. But it is not clear whether MD for the outcome makes sense in the absence of a complementary procedure governing choice of reasons. These are all important questions of institutional design or institutional practice. But we may not be able to answer them adequately without some sense of why MD is thought appropriate for the judiciary in the first place.

There is one last reason I want to mention for our interest in this question. Paying explicit attention to the use of MD in courts may redound to the credit of its use elsewhere in our political system. For example, it is tempting to disparage MD in a legislative context, where it seems like a decision procedure fit only for the aggregation of preferences and for the bargaining and logrolling that involves. But when we see judges using it, what we are seeing is the application of MD to matters of principle as well as policy and preference, and we see the use of MD in court as the upshot of a deliberative process rather than as something that obstructs or usurps deliberation. I hope my discussion in this chapter will make us more open to the idea that majority voting is not opposed to principled deliberation but part and parcel of what principled deliberation involves in the modern political world.

2. A LACK OF DISCUSSION

The question I am asking about the use of MD in court has not been much addressed in the law review literature. I may be wrong, but I don't think there is any article-length treatment of judicial MD.[25] I have occasionally raised the matter in discussions of judicial review, challenging defenders of that practice to explain why a supposedly counter-majoritarian institution uses this method of majority voting. When I originally published "The Core of the Case against Judicial Review" (Chapter 9 of this collection), I said that the topic is one that "I have never, ever heard a defender of judicial review introduce . . . into discussion himself or herself, let alone undertake to explain why it is a good idea."[26] And, in a more recent piece, I said that after years of raising the question, "Why do judges use simple majority decision among themselves to determine whether to overturn statutes passed by majoritarian institutions?" "I have long since given up any expectation of an honorable answer."[27] A couple of people have attempted to respond to these provocations, and I will discuss their answers in a moment.

Some have misinterpreted my challenge. It is not itself intended to discredit judicial review; it is not supposed to add anything to the critique that already exists. One set of authors, Krishnamurthi et al., has said that "[i]f Waldron's intuition is correct, and defenders of judicial review cannot justify the use of judicial majoritarianism, then judicial review might also be without justification."[28] And their response was to show that that conclusion wouldn't follow.[29] They were right about that. A failure to explain why courts use majoritarian decision-making would not undermine judicial review. It just leaves us with a puzzle. Obviously, courts have to use some method of decision. Maybe MD is as good as any other; perhaps it doesn't need justification. (I will deal with this possibility in Section 3.) However, by leaving the matter there, Krishnamurthi and his coauthors really do not answer my question. They do not themselves provide anything in the way of a justification—though they gesture in certain directions as to where a justification may be found.

In 2010, my late colleague Ronald Dworkin offered the following as an answer to the question "Why, if majority rule is not intrinsically fair, is it appropriate on final appellate courts like the Supreme Court, which decides many very important cases by a 5–4 vote?" I am going to quote his answer at length:

The choice among checks on majoritarian procedures must of course depend on which options are available. Judicial review is an available option for checking legislative and executive decisions. It is also an available option for checking judicial review itself through a hierarchal system of appellate courts. But of course judicial review is not available to check the decision of the highest appellate court; if it were the court would not be the highest. It does not follow that if the judges in this series of reviews disagree the disagreement should be settled by a vote among them. A Supreme Court's 5–4 decision might overrule the unanimous decisions of a great many more judges on lower courts.

But the head-counting procedure does hold on the Supreme Court itself, and it makes perfect sense to ask what alternatives, beyond judicial review, are available. We can easily imagine some. Constitutional courts might give more votes to senior judges because they have more experience. Or more votes to junior judges because they are likely better to represent popular opinion. The Supreme Court does give each justice an equal vote, but it also gives some justices much more power than others in shaping constitutional law. When the Chief Justice is in the majority, he decides the often crucial question who will write the opinion for the Court; when he is not the senior justice in the majority does. No vote decides that issue. The Court's practice of adopting majority rule for the verdict itself can sensibly be challenged. But since judicial review is logically not an option at that stage, the choice of a majority decision procedure hardly suggests that that procedure is intrinsically fairer than a different process that includes judicial review.[30]

All of this is interesting, but I don't see any explanation here of why bare-majority decision is the appropriate procedure—or even *an* appropriate procedure—to use. As far as I can tell, Dworkin does not even want to claim that it is: much of his account entertains possibilities for judicial decision-making that are at odds with MD (e.g., more weight to be accorded to the views of some justices than others). Dworkin does make an important point when he says that there is nothing inconsistent about (i) opposing the use of MD standing alone in the legislative context in light of the availability in that context of MD complemented by judicial review and yet (ii) embracing MD standing alone in the context of the highest court, where (by definition) MD complemented by further judicial review is unavailable. That is a fair point, but it only takes care of an ad hominem argument of inconsistency. It provides no affirmative explanation of why MD standing alone is an appropriate procedure for courts to use.

The only other scholarly engagements with this issue that I am aware of are by Akhil Amar, in a recent book titled *America's Unwritten Constitution*;[31] by Jed Shugerman, in an article arguing for a supermajority rule;[32] and by Rick Hills, in a very thoughtful couple of paragraphs in a 2002 essay.[33]

Amar notes that "[f]rom its first day to the present day, the [U.S. Supreme] Court has routinely followed the majority-rule principle without even appearing to give the matter much thought."[34] He believes that it was just obvious to those who set up our judicial system that MD was the rule to use; it seemed natural, he says, and he cites John Locke, Benjamin Franklin, and Thomas Jefferson to that effect.[35] The position seemed to be that MD was taken for granted, and decision procedures were stipulated in the Constitution's text only when there was to be a departure from MD.[36]

Jed Shugerman's article is mainly an account of the inadequacy of bare MD and an argument for a 6–3 supermajority rule. But Shugerman does consider some arguments for MD in the course of trying to show that a 6–3 rule would do better at promoting the values that MD is supposed to promote. He suggests that MD is based on a combination of practical efficiency and a "consensus theory of truth" among experts.[37]

Rick Hills's contribution comes in the course of a symposium essay on Chris Eisgruber's book *Constitutional Self-Government*.[38] Eisgruber's book is a defense of the role of principled judicial decision-making on constitutional matters and the appropriateness of its being able to override the majoritarian decision-making of legislators. Hills says that Eisgruber's work is underpinned by an anti-majoritarian assumption "that there cannot be a connection between quality of argument and numbers of persons who are persuaded by an argument."[39] But, says Hills,

> [t]his contrast between the weight of numbers and the quality of reasons . . . is confused: the assumption of any regime of political equality is that the arguments that persuade the largest number of adherents are the best arguments. Where political equality reigns, the weight of numbers is regarded as the best available proxy for the quality of argument. Thus, on that ultimate forum of principle, the United States Supreme Court, five votes decides a case and sets precedent. Why? Because the Justices are political equals: we assess the quality of argument by counting noses. Likewise, in every philosophy department, hiring decisions which rest largely on the "quality of reasons" in the published work of a candidate are determined by a majority or supermajority vote of the faculty (or their elected representatives on an executive

committee). Why? Again, because the community is a community of equals, "counting heads" is regarded as the only acceptable way to determine quality of argument.[40]

This passage definitely points us toward an affirmative argument in favor of MD. Indeed, maybe there are two arguments here. In Section 4, I will tease out the difference between (i) the argument that "the weight of numbers is . . . the best available proxy for the quality of argument" and (ii) the argument that, because judges are regarded as one another's equals, MD is required as a matter of fairness. Hills runs these two lines together in an interesting way, suggesting that fairness might require us to treat the weight of numbers *as if* it were the best proxy for the quality of argument (even if it is not).

As far as I know, that's all the serious discussion there is in the literature. I am not sure why there has been so little analysis of this issue of MD in court. Perhaps it is because the use of this decision procedure strikes people as so obvious that it needs little discussion. But, in other contexts, legal theorists are not deterred from discussing the obvious; that's what philosophers do. Or it may be because the use of MD in this context is something of an embarrassment to people who predicate their support for the empowerment of judges on the perceived disrepute of MD in other contexts. I indicated at the beginning of Section 1 that this might be one reason for scholarly silence on the issue. Or it may be just happenstance. This is a question that has been hiding for some time in plain sight. It is now time to come to terms with it explicitly.

3. DOES THE USE OF MD IN COURT REQUIRE A JUSTIFICATION?

I am asking, "What is the justification for the use of MD in multimember judicial panels?" My question talks of "*the* justification for the use of MD." That suggests a sort of single official justification. But there may not be anything of the sort: neither the U.S. Constitution nor the Judiciary Act makes any reference to the use of MD. Perhaps it is better to ask whether the use of MD in court be justified (whether our officials have signed up for such a justification or not). And we may find that there is more than one line of possible justificatory argument.

Our question assumes that the use of MD requires an argument. Occasionally, one finds suggestions in the literature that it does not—that it is simply something obvious and beyond justification. Hannah Arendt, in *On Revolution,* stated that "the principle of majority is inherent in the very process of decision-making" and is "likely to be adopted almost automatically in all types of deliberative councils and assemblies."[41] The paucity of scholarly discussions suggests that this might be the prevailing view in the legal academy: MD needs no justification.

But really that won't do, not for me at any rate. It is the job of philosophers to question the obvious and to try to come up with arguments for things that practical people take for granted, whether they "need" a justification or not. Sometimes the request for justification is answered with a rhetorical question—"What's the alternative?"—with the implication that MD is the least bad decision procedure (after minority rule, supermajority, and unanimity are rejected). But even if one accepts this as a starting point, one wants to know more: least bad on what dimensions? What is the reason that MD is better than minority rule, and is that the same reason that makes it better than unanimity, decision by lot, or a supermajority requirement?

Throughout this chapter, I will argue that the demand for justification is connected to the issue of legitimacy. Decision procedures like MD operate in circumstances of disagreement:[42] some people in society believe fervently that a given issue currently before a court should be resolved one way; others believe with equal fervor that it should be resolved the other way. One side is going to lose as a result of the court's decision, and which side that is may be affected by the decision procedure that is used. The legitimacy of a decision procedure is partly a matter of whether support can be mobilized for the decisions that are made under its auspices. But legitimacy also has a more focused aspect: it has to reconcile the losing party in particular to the decision that has been made. The decision procedure has to carry with it some sense of justification that enables the losing party to say, "It is right for me to accept this decision, not because I agree with it on the merits, but because of some characteristic of the process by which it was made."

What characteristic can that be? Some theorists say that MD is "natural." This is not the same as a claim that the use of MD is obvious. A claim of naturalness does not imply that MD is beyond justification; rather, it points toward a justification of a certain kind. Akhil Amar believes the American founders must have held a view of this kind. He cites John Locke (whom he says the American founders must have studied on this point):

> [I]n assemblies impowered to act by positive laws where no number is set by that positive law which empowers them, the act of the majority passes for the act of the whole, and of course determines as having, by the law of Nature and reason, the power of the whole.[43]

But Locke's naturalistic case for this is unsatisfactory, depending as it does on a claim that each "[b]ody move[s]" by a sort of physical necessity "that way whither the greatest force carries it, which is the consent of the majority."[44] There is little reason to suppose that we can analogize the consent given by each individual to an equal quantum of physical force, certainly not for the purposes of a normative argument.[45]

Anyway, elsewhere in political theory—for example, when democracy is being discussed—MD is not treated as obvious or natural. Its use is regarded as an open question.[46] There is an active and considerable literature on MD in political theory, and it is surely worth considering how that literature bears on its use in this particular domain.[47]

Having said that, we must be careful not to think that arguments that purport to make sense of MD in an electoral or legislative context can necessarily be transferred to the judicial context. Some may; some may not. Here are a couple of examples that do not survive the transfer.

It is sometimes said that MD is a sort of proxy for combat in the political arena. In an essay entitled "Minimalist Conception of Democracy: A Defense," Adam Przeworski says this: "Voting constitutes 'flexing muscles': a reading of chances in the eventual war. If all men are equally strong (or armed) then the distribution of vote is a proxy for the outcome of war."[48] The party that wins an election, says Przeworski, is in a position to "inform the losers—'Here is the distribution of force: if you disobey the instructions conveyed by the results of the election, I will be more likely to beat you than you will be able to beat me in a violent confrontation.'"[49] This is a pretty threadbare argument, even for electoral politics.[50] It makes no sense at all in the judicial context. Judges use MD to decide issues not just for themselves but (in our system) for more than 300 million people. It is imaginable, I guess, that if some of these issues are not decided in an orderly manner, they will have to be decided by fighting. (This happened with some important issues about race in the United States 150 years ago.) But if fighting does break out, on an issue like abortion for example, it will not be confined to the nine justices of the U.S. Supreme Court. And so the existence of a majority (one way or the other) *among the justices* is no indication at all of who is likely to win a civil war about abortion in the country at large.

Here is another example of an argument for MD that cannot survive the transition from electoral to judicial politics. Suppose that voters are self-interested: they vote their pocketbook; they vote for policies that they think will bring them personally a greater balance of happiness over suffering. And suppose, too, that they are well enough informed to make this calculation wisely (strong assumptions, I know, but common in positive political theory). Then the use of MD to make political decisions in an electorate of this kind may be justified on utilitarian grounds.[51] The majority view corresponds (roughly) to the greatest balance of happiness over suffering in society as a whole. It is a rough correspondence at best.[52] But, rough or not, it will not survive the transition to judicial politics, for not even the staunchest rational choice theorist thinks that judges vote primarily for what will promote their personal benefit.[53] And even if they did, there is no conceivable ethical theory that could make the greatest happiness of the greatest number of judges into an ideal for the whole society.[54]

The failure of the utilitarian argument to survive the trip from electoral to judicial politics reminds us of a couple of important features of the judicial terrain. First, if the use of MD is to be justified on this terrain, it has to be justified on the basis that a majority of votes represents a majority of opinions rather than a majority of interests. Judges end up with different views, not just different preferences on the matters of principle and interpretation they are called on to address. So we can't use anything like a calculus of interests to address the problem posed by judicial dissensus. It is not that sort of problem.

A second point is that judges are supposed to be experts in the areas on which they disagree. We are not talking about the use of MD to resolve disagreements among amateurs. Both the judges in the majority and the judges in the minority are supposed to know what they are talking about. In this regard, we should bear in mind other features of judicial decision-making. Judges don't just "come up with" a view on the matter before them and vote in its favor. They are trained in the law. They hear hours of oral arguments back and forth and they read volumes of written submissions and precedential cases. They deliberate thoughtfully both among themselves and each in the solitude of his or her own chambers. They (or their clerks) write elaborate essays to spell out their reasons for adopting one or another view. And yet, as often as not, they still disagree—quite sharply in the American judiciary. So the question is why—after all this training, argument, thought, deliberation, and looking things up and testing them out—the simple procedure of "counting heads" that MD involves is still the appropriate way to resolve disagreements in these circumstances.

4. THE MAIN LINES OF JUSTIFICATION FOR MAJORITY DECISION

How is MD justified in political theory generally, and can any of these justifications be applied to its use in courts? I will consider four possible lines of justification—(A) arguments about efficiency, (B) epistemic arguments, (C) arguments from fairness, and (D) Rick Hills's epistemic-fairness hybrid argument.

A. Efficiency arguments

The first kind of argument is the most common. When I raise questions about MD in courts, some of my colleagues claim it needs no justification. When I say (as I said in Section 3) that is not good enough, they retreat to the view that MD is justified on the grounds of its decisional efficiency. They say MD lowers decision costs compared with any other method, it is decisive, and it is easy to apply.

Those who say this are usually puzzled by my continued refusal to accept this as all that needs to be said for jurisprudential purposes. But more does need to be said, for there are other decision procedures we could use that would be equally if not more efficient. A coin could be tossed as soon as an appeal comes before a multimembered court (either in all cases or when the court reveals itself as divided). The outcome could be determined in that way. This would lower or eliminate decision costs, it would be decisive, and it is even easier to apply than MD. My interlocutors respond by saying, "Don't be silly. Of course we can't just toss a coin." And if they are asked why, they swallow their exasperation and say, "Coin-tossing would be ridiculously unresponsive to the merits of the appeal and the arguments and precedents put forward," or they say, "Coin-tossing would be ludicrously unfair, and you know it." And they conclude, "So, be realistic: MD is the most efficient of the *acceptable* methods of decision-making."

I think this trajectory of call-and-response indicates that there is indeed much more to be said about MD in the courtroom than that it is efficient. We must ask ourselves, "How and why exactly is MD properly responsive to the merits of the case, to precedents and arguments, etc., in a way that coin-tossing is not?" Or we have to ask, "How and why exactly is MD a fairer (e.g., more respectful) decision procedure than coin-tossing?" These are the questions we need to answer, and only answers to these questions will illuminate the problems that motivated our inquiry (in Section 1). They take us, respectively, to the second and third lines of argument: (B) the epistemic argument and (C) the argument based on fairness.

I cannot emphasize enough how important it is to get beyond the lazy response that MD is just more efficient. The crucial thing is to establish why it is *legitimate* for us to decide cases on the basis of this procedure. The legitimacy issue is particularly important in regard to judicial decisions that overturn legislation, for there a question seems to be raised about MD in one context that is not raised about its use in another context. Discussion in terms of fairness and responsiveness to the merits might help address the issue of legitimacy, but a stubborn insistence on efficiency as the only criterion suggests misleadingly that the problem of legitimacy here is simply a matter of cost.

Having said all that, I don't deny the importance of efficiency. All I am saying is that it cannot be the whole story. I have said that efficiency includes, among other things, decisiveness: the ability to settle a contested matter with some finality. It is possible to interpret this particular element of efficiency in a way that gives MD an advantage over coin-tossing. If a given issue is settled by coin-tossing, everybody involved knows that applying the same procedure again—even if it is applied again immediately following the first settlement—might yield a different outcome. By contrast, and as a matter of political sociology, the division of the decisional body into majority and minority is likely to be more stable than that, and so the first settlement is more likely to "stick." Of course, majorities can come undone; perhaps this is true mostly of large assemblies,[55] though, even on a small judicial panel, a key member—a sort of Justice Kennedy figure—may waver. And maybe this is an advantage. We want a degree of settlement in the law but not absolute settlement.[56] I have heard it said that settling contested matters by judicial decision on a multimember court using MD provides the modicum of finality and settlement that the rule of law requires, but it does not preclude the prospect that the matter may be revisited sometime in the future and reversed. This prospect would be much dimmer if judicial decisions were protected by supermajority requirements against variance. MD may be valuable, in other words, precisely because it affords an optimal combination of decisiveness and nonfinality.[57]

B. Epistemic arguments

Let us now consider the idea that MD may be an epistemically reliable way of getting at or near the truth, a way of responding better than any other available method to the objective merits of the arguments presented before a court. Rick Hills invited us to consider the proposition that "the arguments that persuade the largest number of adherents are the best arguments."[58] Certainly there is something intuitive about this, especially when the voting constituency consists of experts, and its intuitive appeal is reflected in ancient doctrine.[59] Who is not persuaded by the slogan, "Four out of five dentists choose Colgate for their families"?[60] But it is surprisingly hard to account for the intuition once it is put under pressure.

Let's take it step by step. That any given expert is persuaded by a proposition in his or her area of expertise is surely evidence, though not conclusive evidence, that the proposition is true. This we can accept. That any given expert denies a proposition in his or her area of expertise is surely evidence that the proposition is false. This we have to accept also. So far, so good. But we have not yet begun to grapple with majorities and minorities. We can perhaps advance a step or two further. If a majority among experts is overwhelming (say 4–1 like the dentists or 5–2 like the Nebraska Supreme Court striking down a statute), then the contrary view of one or two experts can be dismissed as an aberration. No expert is infallible, and for any expert there is some small chance that he or she might have made a mistake. If there is something short of a dissensus, we may want to ask ourselves, "Which is more likely, that the one or two outliers have made a mistake or that all the members of the large and expert majority have made a mistake?" We may think it is much less likely that the majority view is mistaken. (Perhaps this is how something like judicial MD began. Maybe the earliest cases of dissensus on judicial panels were cases of an overwhelming majority of judges versus one or two dissenters.)

But it is not at all clear that an expertise theory can survive for cases in which there is a *bare* majority, say five to four.[61] Five experts believe that a certain proposition is true and four believe it is false. I don't think the dynamics of expertise and fallibility help us at all in this situation.[62] Which is more likely—that the five fallible experts are mistaken or that the four fallible experts are mistaken? Who knows? Would we be better off, epistemically, tossing a coin if there was no budging the five-to-four vote?[63]

Perhaps I should not be so absolutist about this. Maybe it is better to say that the argument from expertise *diminishes* for these cases, not that it disappears altogether. We might still be better off betting that the majority is right, particularly over a large number of instances, even when the majority margin is very small. But I am not convinced that this is so. The expertise argument with which we began was not about bare numbers. It was about overwhelming majorities versus outliers. That is why I doubt that it has any application when majorities cease to be overwhelming and dissenters cease to be outliers.

Can the position be retrieved? Can we associate an epistemic argument with the weight of numbers as such, even the bare weight of numbers? In recent years, political theorists have become interested in something called "the Jury Theorem," associated with an eighteenth-century theorist, the Marquis de Condorcet.[64] As a matter of arithmetic, Condorcet proved that if a group like a jury faces a binary choice (say, guilty or not guilty), and if each of the individual jurors is more likely than not to arrive at the right answer when he votes (that is, if the probability of his getting the right answer is greater than 0.5)—I'll call this individual competence—then the likelihood that a *majority* of the jurors will reach the right answer is greater than the likelihood of any one of them getting the right answer.[65] Moreover, the likelihood that a majority will get the right answer increases as group size increases. So, for example, if there are three jurors, each with an individual competence of 0.6, the chance that a majority of them will be right is 0.648. (And that latter chance increases quite sharply as group size increases.)[66]

Can we apply Condorcet's Jury Theorem to the judiciary? Maybe. The judges are experts, so let us say that each of them surely has a greater than 0.5 chance of coming up with the right answer in a given case. And if that is true, then the Condorcet arithmetic ensures that the chance that a majority of judges—even a bare majority of judges—is right will be quite high. Indeed, it will be higher, the higher up the judicial hierarchy you go: as we move from one federal district court judge, to a three-judge panel on a court of appeals, and then to a nine-judge panel on the Supreme Court. Even if the expertise does not increase on the way up—and we hope and expect that it does through the seniority and experience of judges in the higher courts, and through deliberation and the hearing of submissions[67]—Condorcet's theorem would seem to justify the use of MD on the multijudge panels.[68] QED?

I have to say that I am uncomfortable with this result. There is something gimmicky about it. Consider first that there is nothing *epistemological* in Condorcet's Jury Theorem, which could justify MD as truth-enhancing. *It is just arithmetic.* It works best for an urn that happens to contain sixty black balls and forty white balls: the chance that a majority of three balls drawn at random from the urn will be black is 0.648. There is nothing about truth or knowledge in that. Certainly the theorem can be *applied* to cases where truth is at issue. It can be applied to cases where *anything* is at issue. If there is a better than 0.5 chance that a given opinion will be φ, then the chance that a majority of three opinions will be φ is greater than that, and the chance that a majority of opinions will be φ increases as the number of opinions given increases. The value of φ may be "true" or "high-quality," or the value of φ may be "long-winded," "melodious," "printed in pink," or "beginning with the definite article." The result still holds. Condorcet's theorem has nothing to do with objective truth or right answers; those terms just happen to be within the domain of its arithmetic applicability.

Defenders of MD might respond that we should just take the epistemic enhancement where we find it and not worry about how mindlessly Condorcet's theorem generates the result. If the assumption of our application of the theorem is correct—namely, that judges really are (individually) more likely to get their decisions right than to get them wrong—then MD applied to judicial panels will enhance the quality of their decisional output, just as Condorcet predicted. It is an arithmetical certainty.

Whether this furnishes us with a justification that will satisfy the demands of political legitimacy is another matter. It depends in no small part on how the losers in a political struggle regard the competence of the judges who voted against them. It is important to remember that most people do not approach decisions by the Supreme Court using the dispassionate language of objectivity and expertise in the way that a philosopher might. They certainly do not attribute undifferentiated levels of expertise to the justices. The liberals I know think that at least four of the justices currently on the U.S. Supreme Court are likely (unerringly and maybe willfully) to come up with the wrong answer on most important issues. And the conservatives I know think the same about at least four other justices. Now let's suppose that the Court has made a decision by a bare majority (five to four) about some controversial issue like abortion. How should people think about this exercise in judicial majoritarianism? Specifically, how should people who oppose the decision that the Court has made think about this method of making a decision? Bear in mind that judicial decision-making has long since left the era of consensus behind, certainly in the United States. It is bitterly divisive. If we want to justify a decision procedure in these circumstances of controversy, we must understand that we are doing it not as an academic exercise but in order to confer some legitimacy on the decision in the eyes of people who would otherwise bitterly oppose it.

So let us suppose that five liberal justices have voted to uphold some pro-choice position. Can the fact that this was determined by MD possibly make the decision legitimate in the eyes of conservative pro-life advocates? Specifically, can Condorcet's Jury Theorem contribute anything to the decision's legitimacy in their eyes? I think not. The pro-life citizens will be convinced that the liberal justices are incompetent on this issue: they will think that the probability of liberal justices' coming up with the right answer on abortion is well below 0.5 (probably they think it is something approaching zero). And since, ex hypothesi, there are five liberal justices out of nine involved in this decision, it is likely that our pro-life citizens will attribute to the panel as a whole an average individual competence lower than 0.5. In that case, no Condorcetian arithmetic will be able to persuade them to accept the legitimacy of bare MD as a way of making this decision. (Remember that when average individual competence falls below 0.5, the Condorcet effect goes into reverse.) At best, they will end up where we were a page or two ago: when five alleged experts line up against four alleged experts on a matter like this, who knows where the truth lies? At worst, they will be where Justice Scalia was in *Planned Parenthood of Southeastern Pennsylvania v. Casey:* all talk of judicial expertise and objectivity in this area of basic values is nonsense.[69] And if this is the likely reaction of the pro-life citizenry to pro-choice decisions of the Court, it is also likely to be the reaction of the pro-choice citizenry to pro-life decisions. On any controversial decision by the Court taken on the basis of bare-majority decision, it is likely to be the reaction of the very group that most needs to be persuaded that this method of decision-making is legitimate.

C. Fairness arguments

In democratic theory, the most powerful case that can be made for MD is that it is required as a matter of *fairness* to all those who participate in the social choice. Fairness can be understood formally and informally.

Informally, people may be persuaded that MD is fair because, although they are losers this time around, they may be winners in the next political cycle, when their faction is in the ascendancy and when their party is in a position to nominate judges and get their appointments confirmed. Alexis de Tocqueville argued in general along these lines: "[E]very American discovers a kind of personal interest in obeying the laws because the man who today does not belong to the majority may tomorrow be among its ranks."[70] Similar sentiments might be applied, albeit indirectly, to the judicial context, though the timeline is longer and more haphazard than the regularized turn-taking among electoral majorities on which Tocqueville's point was predicated.

Formally, we may defend MD as a way of respecting political participants as equals. If a society faces a binary option, and each of its members votes one way or the other, then the advantage of MD is that it is decisive (except in the rare case of a tie); it is neutral between the options (and thus fair to the supporters of the various options); it gives as much weight as possible to each individual's vote, in the direction in which that vote points (so it is fair to each voter); and it gives no greater weight to any one individual's vote than to the vote of any other individual (so that it is fair in the sense of equality). That MD alone satisfies these four conditions—decisiveness, neutrality, highest positive weight, and equality—in the circumstances of a binary choice is a well-established theorem in the theory of social choice.[71] And that is why we should support its use.[72]

In the democratic context, these four conditions seem plausible. In the midst of political disagreement in society, we want a decision procedure that will be decisive but not biased toward any particular political point of view. Respect for individual citizens in the context of a democracy demands that weight be given to nothing but individuals' opinions, but democratic equality—one man, one vote—insists that the opinions of all should be treated equally. These requirements of fairness seem to argue for the use of MD to make social choices not because of any epistemic hypothesis but simply because this is a procedure that respects people as equals, as they are entitled to be treated on democratic assumptions. How do these conditions fare when we move to judicial decision-making?

That we want a decisive decision procedure in court is clear enough: an appeal must be decided one way or the other (even if its value as a precedent is later revisited). But the applicability of the other conditions is not so clear.

The Nebraska rule mentioned in Section 1 invites us to abandon neutrality, at least in cases of judicial review of legislation. Instead of being neutral between the claim that a given statute is constitutionally invalid and the claim that it does not violate the constitution, Nebraska operates instead with a presumption of constitutionality.[73] That is the default position unless a supermajority (≥ 5 to 2) can be assembled. It is by no means a silly position. A presumption of constitutionality used to be part of American constitutional doctrine;[74] and for a while people toyed with the proposition that the unconstitutionality of a piece of legislation could not be thought of as established beyond reasonable doubt if four justices believed it was constitutional.[75] However, quite early on, jurists realized that the two issues of reasonable doubt and substantive dissent could be drawn apart: the issue on which the bench divided five to four might be exactly the issue of whether there was reasonable doubt about a given law's constitutionality.[76] Anyway, I am not urging the adoption of the Nebraska rule;[77] I am just showing that there is room for doubt about the condition of neutrality that MD presupposes.

The other condition whose application might be thought problematic in the judicial context is the crucial condition of equality. Each judge's opinion counts positively in the direction in which it points—that sounds sensible. But on what basis do we insist, as Hills puts it, that "the Justices are political equals"?[78] We saw Dworkin imagining a system in which more votes were given to senior judges because they had more experience, or one in which more votes were given to junior judges because they were likely better to represent popular opinion.[79] As I have said elsewhere, the members of the Supreme Court are ranked by seniority, and the public commonly ranks them by their virtue, learning, and effectiveness, not to mention their politics.

They have an order of precedence in their dealings with one another.[80] But in the authority accorded to their opinions, the rule seems to be that they are equal.[81] When they disagree, the fact that the chief justice or a senior justice takes one side or the other makes no difference to the weight accorded to his vote.[82] Why is this? In the electoral context, the assumption of political equality is fundamental, and the fierceness of our democratic insistence on it gives a sharp and powerful edge to the fairness argument in favor of MD. "One person, one vote" matters enormously, and most of us reject out of hand the plural voting system—more votes for university graduates—that John Stuart Mill envisaged.[83] But we might not be so offended by a similar proposal for judges. The normative principle of political equality does not seem to be applicable to the members of a judicial panel in the same way that it is applicable to the body of citizens.

Perhaps there is a mistake here. We should not be comparing the proposition of equality for judges (on which judicial MD is predicated) with the very fundamental proposition of political equality for citizens; perhaps we should be comparing equality for judges with equality for legislators. How does that comparison come out? Well, legislators have greater or less seniority, greater or less influence in their caucuses and on the floor of the House or the Senate. But when it comes to a vote on legislation, each legislator's vote is equal. Why? Because in a properly apportioned polity, granting equal weight to the votes of each legislator is a rough and indirect way of respecting the equality of their constituents.[84] Political equality for legislators thus conveys something of our fierce and fundamental adherence to political equality for citizens.

Maybe something similar can be said for judges, though it is a lot more indirect than the legislative case. Each justice represents an appointment by the president, and the president of course is elected (indirectly) by the people.[85] So if we were to give greater weight to one judge than to another, we would be disrespecting the president who appointed the latter judge, and the voters who elected that president. Conservatives might like the idea of assigning less weight to the votes of Justice Ginsburg than to the votes of Justice Scalia, but doing that would be a way of according less respect to those who voted for Bill Clinton in 1992 than to those who voted for Ronald Reagan in 1984. This is a pretty indirect argument, but it is the best I can come up with (and maybe something similar can be rigged up for elected judges).

I don't doubt that we could simply *announce* that we propose to treat each judge on a given panel as the equal of every other judge on that panel and just leave it at that. And that could be the equality condition that underpins the use of MD. But remember how much work MD has to do so far as legitimacy is concerned. An awful lot hangs on the use of MD in court, especially when decisions are being made on matters of fundamental principle. And, for the time being, we require passionate advocates for one side or the other to put up with a constitutional position that they regard as an abomination simply because one more justice voted for it than for the contrary view.[86] That's a lot of weight to put on a decision procedure and it is especially a lot of weight to put on a procedure when one of its leading assumptions is just a stipulation. In the case of electoral or legislative politics, we can invoke a powerful ethical premise to convince electoral or legislative losers to put up with adverse outcomes:

> It is an ethical premise of democracy, derived from belief in human equality (i.e., the equality of men as human beings to seek self-development, happiness, God, and fellowship), that each citizen, whether he be learned or barely literate, rich or poor, has the right to have his vote for elected officials counted equally with others.[87]

We plead with them in the name of fairness to their fellow citizens. But what do we offer the losers in 5–4 judicial decisions? I worry that the equivalent equality plea in the case of judicial MD is based on much weaker or perhaps even nonexistent grounds.

D. Hills's hybrid

I don't want to end this discussion of possible grounds for MD without considering the hybrid view intimated by Rick Hills, which I outlined in Section 2. Though Hills talks a lot about MD as a way of "assess[ing] the quality of argument," I think his theory is really more like a fairness argument than an epistemic one. His position is that "[b]ecause the Justices are political equals, we assess the quality of argument by counting noses."[88] A pure fairness argument would say that "because the justices are political equals, we count noses." But Hills's view is that because the justices are political equals, we act as though nose-counting were a way of determining epistemic quality.

I don't want to put too much weight on what might have been quite a loose formulation—and what follows is rather tentative—but perhaps what Hills means is the following. We treat the justices formally as one another's equals, not in the way that we treat citizens as one another's equals but in the deferential way in which experts might be treated as one another's equals. Citizens are to be respected as equals in the way that (say) stakeholders are to be respected as equals; to treat one citizen as less than an equal is to act as though it didn't matter that he too has a stake in what is going on around here. The principle for citizens is *quod omnes tangit ab omnibus decidentur*: what affects all should be decided by all. But that is not the theory of judicial equality. We treat the judges on a panel as one another's equals because of what they represent—the law. We—that is, those who are to be ruled by them—defer to them equally as experts in the law. Though in reality they may differ in their expertise, in court we are supposed to respect them as we would respect the law itself that they represent. It is a sort of artifice: each judge stands for the law and stands for it equally.

This is an interesting way of thinking about the equality that is supposed to underpin the fairness argument. We saw earlier that there is really nothing in judicial decision-making equivalent to the political equality that serves as a normative foundation for electoral and legislative majoritarianism. But maybe we can proceed with something like the following. We might say that a fairness argument for MD in court can be predicated on the idea of an equal deference to each of the judges; that is, to the judicial office embodied, in a purely formal sense, by each of them. We might even go so far as to say it is equal deference to the law as such, of which (in theory) each of the judges is supposed to be a mouthpiece. Whether the principle of this deference can survive the sort of skepticism about expertise that we saw wrecking the application of the Condorcet argument is another question.[89] I do not mean skepticism about judicial expertise as such; I mean skepticism about the significance of a very narrow majority among justices, to each of whom we have reason to defer. Hills intimates a good account of the reason for individual deference, but it is still not clear that it adds up to a hybrid argument for deference to a narrow majority.

I have not been able to come up with any decisive and powerful argument for the use of MD in court. The efficiency argument tells us too little. The epistemic argument falters when MD seems to support a decision by the barest of majorities. The best argument in favor of MD—the fairness argument—is considerably weaker in the judicial context than the equivalent argument is in an electoral or legislative context. Hills's hybrid argument is interesting, but its rationale for a normative principle of judicial equality rests on an admitted fiction and may be vulnerable in exactly the circumstances, fraught with controversy, in which the Court's decision procedure has to do its hardest work for legitimacy.

5. SAYING MEAN THINGS ABOUT MAJORITARIANISM

I want to end with a provocation. Perhaps it is no surprise that American legal scholars have not come up with a convincing defense of the use of MD in court. Many of them have become so used to saying mean and disparaging things about majoritarianism and majority voting (among the citizenry or in the legislature) in their arguments for judicial review that they find themselves a bit tongue-tied when forced to say something about the use of *exactly the same decision procedure* among judges on appellate courts. If we go around saying that a commitment to the use of MD in politics involves a "crude statistical view of democracy,"[90] we will probably want to avoid drawing attention to the fact that ultimately nothing but numbers determines how the Supreme Court, which is supposedly a "forum of principle,"[91] makes its decisions.[92] Statistics don't cease to be statistics just because the numbers are lower and the voters wear robes. That 5 votes beat 4 in a court is as crude and statistical as the proposition that 218 votes beat 217 in the House of Representatives.

Once we face up to this point, it might be a good idea to change the terms in which the question of judicial review is usually stated. Judicial review is said to pose a "counter-majoritarian difficulty,"[93] and of course we all know what that means. But it is, strictly speaking, inaccurate. Entrusting final decisions about important legislation to courts does not involve abandoning or rejecting majoritarianism. It reveals instead what Baker and Knopf call a preference for courtroom majoritarianism over legislative majoritarianism.[94] What changes is the constituency of people whose votes will be counted on the matter: the votes of just nine unelected judges will be counted (to determine a simple majority) rather than the votes of a hundred elected senators,

435 elected representatives, or millions of ordinary voters in a California-style plebiscite. It is a counter-democratic difficulty, not a counter-majoritarian difficulty.[95] Our practice of referring certain matters to the courts for final decision reflects a distrust of democratic decision-making. It is a distrust of persons: we don't trust ordinary voters or their representatives on certain matters; we prefer the judges. It is not a distrust of MD, for that is a principle we continue to deploy.

I am not saying all this to embarrass defenders of judicial review. I do believe, however, that a more open and accurate characterization of the decision procedure that judges use may help us get clear about a few things that are relevant to that debate.

First of all, there is nothing inherently incompatible between the use of MD and the addressing of issues of principle. When we contrast judicial decision-making with majoritarianism, the implication is that majoritarianism is appropriate for bread-and-butter issues, or grubby pork barrels, where crude and inarticulate interests are involved, but that issues of principle should be decided by a more elevated procedure. We must abandon that characterization. The fact that courts address matters of principle by voting tells us that there is nothing inherently inappropriate about these issues being decided in institutional contexts that are more notorious for their majoritarianism.

Second, frank recognition of the role that MD plays and of the circumstances of judicial decision-making that call for a decision procedure of this kind may help us think more tolerantly about disagreement. Part of understanding that matters of principle have to be dealt with in this way involves owning up to the fact that reasonable disagreement on these matters is possible. Judges disagree about rights—there is no way around that—and although they are experts in constitutional law, there is no denying that their disagreements with each other are in many ways just like the disagreements on these matters that ordinary citizens have with one another. On abortion, affirmative action, campaign finance, or the juvenile death penalty, reasonable people disagree. That even the judges, at the end of the day, have no choice but to count heads on these issues shows us that. Acknowledging this, we might be a little more tolerant of our disagreements with one another—not relaxing our opposition necessarily, but refraining from characterizing our opponents' views as positions that are in some sense vicious, corrupt, or beyond the pale.

Third, acknowledging the use of MD in court might make us more judicious in the way we use the phrase "the tyranny of the majority." It's a phrase that rolls easily off the tongue when we are discussing "the countermajoritarian difficulty." But once we see that there is no getting away from majorities and minorities, we may be more careful how we use it. Of course, we must acknowledge the possibility that a majority decision may be tyrannical, whether it is a majority decision by a court or a majority decision by a legislature: *Dred Scott*[96] was tyrannical, and so were the Fugitive Slave Acts. But, in either context, tyranny of the majority does not happen every time someone loses a majority vote. Judicial MD helps us see that: a judicial minority may fervently disagree with the majority on the court, but in almost every case *they*—I mean the dissenting justices—do not suffer from anything that can be called the tyranny of the majority. Justice Scalia does not suffer under the tyranny of the majority in *Dickerson*[97] or in *Planned Parenthood of Southeastern Pennsylvania v. Casey*.[98] Once we realize this, we may want to say the same thing about being a member of a losing faction in democratic decision-making: it does not necessarily mean suffering under the tyranny of the majority. It *may* in cases where members of the decisional minority are also members of a topical minority group who suffer disadvantage as a result of the majority decision.[99] But even in cases like that, the imposition of the disadvantage on the minority by a majority decision is not necessarily tyrannical. The disadvantage may be fair and appropriate, or its fairness and appropriateness may be a matter of dispute; it is not tyrannical just because it is a disadvantage, and it is not tyranny of the majority just because it was imposed through MD.

My fourth and final point takes us out of the judicial context but suggests ways in which judicial MD might help us in democratic theory generally. Facing up honestly to the use of MD in court might help us develop more realistic accounts of what is known in the trade as "deliberative democracy." Democratic theorists these days are quite keen on the idea of a democracy where citizens address the major issues facing the polity in a thoughtful and impartial spirit, not focusing exclusively on their own pocketbooks. They discuss the issues of the day, presenting their opinions to others, and holding themselves open to persuasion and correction when the opinions of others are presented to them.[100] But it is evident that deliberation does not always yield consensus, though consensus (on the truth) might be thought of as its *telos:* sometimes deliberation aggravates dissensus.[101] So there is a question about how deliberative democrats should think about decision-making in the face of disagreement. The problem is that, as things stand, deliberative democracy and majority voting seem like odd bedfellows. There is something embarrassing about voting in a deliberative context—or at least that is the impression we are given; voting seems like an admission of deliberative failure, for it shows that a discussion based on the merits has failed to resolve the issue. When those who write about deliberation turn their attention to voting, the sense of distaste is almost palpable.[102] I think what we need is a theory of democracy that makes voting the natural culmination of deliberation rather than something indicating that deliberation has been in some sense inadequate. We need a theory of deliberation that dovetails with voting, not a theory of deliberation that is embarrassed by it, a theory that explains why it is reasonable to require people to submit to MD not just their self-interest but their most impartial, their most earnest, their most high-minded, and their best-thought-through convictions about what justice, rights, or the common good require.

I suggest that we should take voting on the Supreme Court as our clue for the development of a more general theory that reconciles voting and deliberation. For there is surely no doubt that the Supreme Court is a deliberative body and that it does not cease to be so when its members disagree with one another, even though their disagreement means that, at the end of their deliberation, the matter before them has to be determined by a vote. This, I say, we should regard as our clue—for it indicates that in principle there is nothing incompatible between deliberation, disagreement, and voting. If the combination makes sense in the courtroom, then maybe it also makes sense at the level of a more general theory of deliberative democracy.

These changes in the way we think about judicial decision-making, judicial review, and deliberation in the face of disagreement are the intended normative payoff of my reflections in this chapter. This has been an exercise in exploration rather than advocacy or denunciation. I do think it is a pity that there is not more discussion of MD in court, and it is interesting how difficult it is to transpose into the judicial context arguments for MD that seem to work reasonably well in electoral and legislative politics.

I have mentioned several times the possibility of instituting a supermajority decision rule for striking down legislation. No doubt, it is healthy to think about the possibility of a supermajority rule and to come up with reasons why it might be a good or a bad idea. But it is not the aim of this chapter to advocate such a rule. Even Jed Shugerman said that his discussion of it was primarily by way of thought experiment.[103] Experiments in thought can help fill in gaps in our understanding, and it is primarily with that in mind that I have undertaken this discussion of the use of majoritarian methods by judges.

CHAPTER ELEVEN

Isaiah Berlin's Neglect of Enlightenment Constitutionalism

AFTER ALL THIS talk about institutions—about courts, cabinets, parties, and legislatures—I want to come back to the way we set an agenda for political theory. These final chapters will address the work of two of the most distinguished thinkers of the twentieth-century: Isaiah Berlin and Hannah Arendt. In this chapter, I have a particular claim to make about the work of Isaiah Berlin and a general claim about the Enlightenment.

The general claim is this: one of the most important achievements of the eighteenth century Enlightenment is *Enlightenment constitutionalism*. It is massively important; it transformed our political thinking out of all recognition; and it left as its legacy both the unprecedented achievement of the framing, ratification, and lasting establishment of the Constitution of the United States and also the political repudiation of monarchy and nobility in France in the 1790s. Both of these are now taken for granted as part of our political world. And they grew out of the Enlightenment. That is my general claim.

The particular proposition is about Isaiah Berlin. Berlin, supposedly one of our greatest interpreters of Enlightenment thinking, had very little to say about this heritage of thought and constitutional achievement. I have ransacked his work and I mean it: there is almost nothing on Enlightenment constitutionalism in his writings—some few rags and paltry blurred shreds of paper here and there, but nothing of any significance.

You will balk at this proposition. You will say, what about the insistent theme in all of Berlin's essays cautioning us against perfectionist projects and against the ideation of a perfect society in which all values will be integrated harmoniously and commensurably? What about this warning? Isn't that his verdict on Enlightenment constitutionalism?

No, it is not, In none of that does Berlin really address the idea of constitutional structure, the possibility of institutionalized forms that will house rather than try to abolish human imperfection, protecting liberty and ethical pluralism and providing a modest institutional structure in which security and the general good can be pursued through representation and the rule of law, without anything approaching the hubris of totalitarian utopianism. Isaiah Berlin said next to nothing about any of that. He proceeded in his work as though all attempts at social and political design were on a par, and as though everything invested in the eighteenth-century constitutionalist enterprise was beneath comment.

Why? Well, an unkind interpretation would be that Isaiah Berlin remained silent about Enlightenment constitutionalism because it challenged—it was a most glaring counterexample to—his thesis about the dire consequences of Enlightenment rationalism. Having committed himself to this thesis at an early stage in his career, he was not about to endanger it by identifying the one strain of rationalist constructivism that offered to refute his central concern.

I am sorry to say that one cannot read into this area without entertaining that hypothesis. But it is a frightful thing to say about a public intellectual. Berlin deserves our charity, and maybe the more charitable explanation is that he just wasn't interested in law, constitutions, or institutional politics generally. For some reason, he thought that political philosophers should not be preoccupied with all that. I'll say more about possible biographical explanations at the end of this chapter.

1. ENLIGHTENMENT CONSTITUTIONALISM

But first, what do I mean by Enlightenment constitutionalism? I mean a body of thought that emerged in the eighteenth century, but originated in England in the later decades of the seventeenth century, about forms of government and the structuring of the institutions of government to promote the common good, secure liberty, restrain monarchs, uphold the rule of law, and to make the attempt to establish popular government—representative, if not direct democracy—safe and practicable for a large modern republic.

I have in mind an array of thinkers: James Madison, Emmanuel Sieyès, Voltaire, Denis Diderot, Tom Paine, Thomas Jefferson, the Marquis de Condorcet, Alexander Hamilton, Montesquieu—above all Montesquieu—and of course Jean-Jacques Rousseau. Maybe we could extend it back as far as James Harrington writing in the 1650s or forward to Benjamin Constant in the early decades of the nineteenth century; the boundaries are of course blurred, and there are continuities with later and earlier movements. But my arbitrary bookends are John Locke, who finished writing the second of his *Two Treatises of Government* in the 1680s, and Immanuel Kant in his declining years, putting republican pen to paper in 1795 in *Perpetual Peace* and in the middle sections, the constitutional sections (§§43–50), of the *Rechtslehre* in *The Metaphysics of Morals,* published in 1797.[1]

It is a long list, and I apologize if I have left off the names of anybody's loved ones. I make no apology for populating it with American as well as French names: Madison, Hamilton, Jefferson, and one could add James Wilson, Benjamin Franklin, and John Adams. We need to get over whatever snobbery leads us to separate the work of the American framers from the broader trends of the Enlightenment. Gordon Wood is right when he says in his essay "The American Enlightenment" that "America was the first nation in the world to base its nationhood solely on Enlightenment values."[2] The Americans based their constitutional structures on Enlightenment principles,[3] they thought of themselves as contributing to the constitutional thought of the Enlightenment, and those on the eastern shores of the Atlantic whom we unhesitatingly categorize as Enlightenment *philosophes* thought so too.[4]

2. BERLIN AND MONTESQUIEU

The theorists I have named wrote about many things; other Enlightenment themes—scientific and philosophical—are associated with their work. And I am not saying that Isaiah Berlin neglected these theorists or these other aspects of their work. He wrote about them all, or almost all: there is very little about Sieyès,[5] and I think next to nothing about Madison.[6]

There is plenty on Montesquieu, but most of Berlin's comments tended to be on precisely those aspects of *The Spirit of the Laws* that were furthest from Montesquieu's interest in the structures and processes of government.[7]

When I say "Montesquieu's concerns about the structures and processes of government," I am referring not just to the famous chapter on the constitution of England (Bk. XI, ch. 6)—though that is very important—but also to passages like the following, from Book V of *The Spirit of the Laws,* that followed Montesquieu's characterization of the horrors of life under despotism:

> After what has been said, one would imagine that human nature should perpetually rise up against despotism. But notwithstanding the love of liberty . . . most nations are subject to this very government. This is easily accounted for. To form a moderate government, it is necessary to combine the several powers; to regulate, temper, and set them in motion; to give, as it were, ballast to one, in order to enable it to counterpoise the other. This is a masterpiece of legislation; rarely produced by hazard, and seldom attained by prudence.[8]

By contrast, a despotic government is simple and straightforward; as Montesquieu puts it, "it offers itself . . . at first sight; it is uniform throughout." All that is necessary is the diffusion of terror. But moderate government needs to be carefully designed: "to combine the several powers; to regulate, temper, and set them in motion; to give . . . ballast to one . . . to enable it to counterpoise the other."

That is exactly the theme of Enlightenment constitutionalism that I have in mind. And my point is that Berlin had very little to say to address this theme of the structural intricacy and design of a constitution, even though—as we will see—it has a massive bearing on the plausibility of his well-known and destructive claim that the Enlightenment aspiration to remake society has been a philosophically misbegotten source of totalitarian hubris and terror.

He did not ignore it entirely. Here is what Berlin said in his essay entitled "Montesquieu" in *Against the Current.* (I am going to quote it at length because it represents almost the sum total of Berlin's observations on Enlightenment constitutionalism.)

> Montesquieu advocated constitutionalism . . . put his faith in the balance of power and the division of authority as a weapon against despotic rule by individuals or groups or majorities. . . . His most famous doctrine, that of the separation of powers, an enthusiastic but mistaken tribute to the system that

he had so falsely imagined to prevail in England . . . proved impracticable in France . . . and had been much too faithfully adopted in the United States, with results not altogether fortunate.[9]

That's it: a few lines. That's all he wrote. Nothing more elaborate on Montesquieu's conception of constitutional structure than these airy and dismissive gestures. No attempt to take up Montesquieu's theme of the combining of the several powers, their regulation, their tempering, and the setting of them in motion, the giving of ballast to one enabling it to counterpoise the others. Berlin did say a little bit about Montesquieu's conception of the judiciary.[10] He criticized Montesquieu's mechanical jurisprudence—the judge as the blind and anonymous mouth of the law—and his disparagement of "[t]he entire tradition of judge-made law." But there is nothing on Montesquieu's account of the rule of law or the complexities and procedures of legalism.[11]

Depending on which piece of Berlin you pick up, Montesquieu was guilty or not guilty of ignoring Kant's stricture that nothing straight was ever made from the crooked timber of humanity. In *Against the Current,* we are told that Kant's view was the same as Montesquieu's "as against that of [Montesquieu's] friends, the optimistic planners of his day."[12] In a letter from 1970, however, we are told that Montesquieu was one of a long line of thinkers "all unable to face the proposition that out of the crooked timber of humanity no straight thing was ever made."[13]

The fact is that Berlin was mostly interested instead in Montesquieu as a sociologist and possibly as a sort of relativist; he had no real interest in what Montesquieu said about the intricate design of political and legal institutions.[14]

3. THE CONSTITUTIONAL MACHINE

The conception of a society's constitution as something like a machine with weights, springs, ratchets, ballasts, escapements, and centrifugal governors is present throughout eighteenth-century political philosophy. The Enlightenment constitutionalists were the engineers and scientists of this machinery. They thought of themselves as experimenters—as in James Madison's observations about "the experiment of an extended republic."[15] I don't mean that the approach to constitutionalism is *scientistic* (in the sense that Berlin condemned in his essay "Does Political Theory Still Exist?"), but in the sense that it is a good idea to think of the problem of governance as though it involved the design of a complex machine. If constitutional design is a science, it is a relatively new science, wrote Emmanuel Sieyès, and it has been slow to progress. "It is not the sort of thing . . . despots and aristocrats could have been expected to encourage."[16] But, he insisted, "[i]t will never be possible to understand the social mechanism without first . . . analyz[ing] society as if it is like an ordinary machine, taking each part in turn and joining them together in one's mind to see how they fit together, one by one."[17]

Analysis is indispensable, and so is analytic rationality. "In politics," said Sieyès, "it is the mingling and confusion of powers that constantly make it impossible to establish social order."[18] For example, the case against monarchy in the modern era could only begin to be made when John Locke took apart all the different functions (legislative, executive, prerogative, and federative) that kingship was performing—functions whose legitimacy seemed to depend on their being blurred together——to see how they might be separated, reallocated, or recombined.[19]

So when I talk about the Enlightenment conception of a constitution as something like a well-designed machine, I mean the deliberate disaggregation, in thought first and then insistently in practice, of government into separate agencies understood functionally—a legislature (perhaps the two chambers of a bicameral legislature, with its complex representative relation to social classes); a judiciary in several layers; an executive responsible for government and the enforcement of law; an external executive or (in Locke's words) a federative power; and, in a federation, a fractal reproduction of these distinctions at the state or provincial level, not to mention the complex relation between state and federal arrangements. And I mean a body of philosophic reflection on the values that are served by figuring out how to separate these institutions from one another, man them with separate personnel with separate lines of responsibility, and then reestablish on a rational basis the articulate modes of connection that are necessary to prevent paralysis in a divided commonwealth. Reflection and analysis on the parts and design of the mechanism are what human societies have to do to avoid tyranny and to house the competing concerns that people bring to their politics: that was the theme of Enlightenment constitutionalism.

It is odd that Berlin had so little to say about this, for it was conceived in Enlightenment thought exactly as a response to the human imperfection that he *did* write so much about. I have mentioned already the use Berlin made of Immanuel Kant's saying about *the crooked timber of humanity*. It is a bon mot that he cherished. There is a collection of Berlin's essays with that title, and an essay in it called "The Bent Twig."[20] But Berlin failed to explore what Immanuel Kant did with this insight. In his *Idea for a Universal History*, Kant presented the crooked timber as an observation on the prospects for political leadership among humans: humans need a master because of their "selfish animal inclinations," but any possible master is also human: "such a master is just as much an animal in need of a master."[21] That is precisely why we have to design a constitution. In *Perpetual Peace,* where he also uses the phrase, Kant elaborates the thought:

> [T]he republican constitution is the only one entirely fitting to the rights of man. But it is the most difficult to establish and even harder to preserve, so that many say a republic would have to be a nation of angels, because men with their selfish inclinations are not capable of a constitution of such sublime form.[22]

However, Kant says that this gets things entirely the wrong way around:

> The problem of organizing a state can be solved even for a race of devils. . . . The problem is: "Given a multitude of rational beings requiring universal laws for their preservation, but each of whom is secretly inclined to exempt himself from them, to establish a constitution in such a way that, although their private intentions conflict, they check each other, with the result that their public conduct is the same as if they had no such intentions." A problem like this . . . does not require that we know how to attain the moral improvement of men.[23]

That is Kant in 1795.

Berlin reads the "crooked timber of humanity" passage as saying that "forc[ing] people into the neat uniforms demanded by dogmatically believed in schemes is almost always the road to inhumanity."[24] But Kant said almost exactly the opposite: precisely *because* of the crooked wood of which humankind is made, we have to keep trying to concoct a constitutional scheme. Kant's whole point here is about the need for a constitution and the importance for us of this heritage of thinking about constitutional design.[25]

This theme of constitutional design for men who are not angels is vividly present too in the arguments of James Madison, urging ratification of the U.S. Constitution. Talking about the separation of powers, Madison suggested that

> the great security against a . . . concentration of the several powers . . . consists in giving to those who administer each department the necessary constitutional means and personal motives to resist encroachments of the others. . . . Ambition must be made to counteract ambition.[26]

This echoes Voltaire's observation that "[a] republic is not founded on virtue . . . ; it is founded on the ambition of each citizen, which keeps in check the ambitions of all the others."[27] Perhaps it is "a reflection on human nature," Madison continued, "that such devices should be necessary to control the abuses of government. But what is government itself, but the greatest of all reflections on human nature?"[28]

The archaeology of this facet of Enlightenment constitutionalism does not stop there. In the very first lines of Chapter 1 of this collection, I mentioned David Hume's invitation to us—issued forty years before Madison—to consider ways in which institutional forms can be designed so as to outwit and outflank what Hume called "the casual humours and characters of particular men."[29]

> Political writers have established it as a maxim, that, in contriving any system of government, and fixing the several checks and controuls of the constitution, every man ought to be supposed a knave, and to have no other end, in all his actions, than private interest. By this interest we must govern him, and, by means of it, make him, notwithstanding his insatiable avarice and ambition, co-operate to public good. Without this . . . we have no security for our liberties . . . except the good-will of our rulers; that is, we shall have no security at all.[30]

And of course a version of this is present in Adam Smith's conception of markets—economic mechanisms in which a person "who intends only his own gain . . . is . . . led by an invisible hand to promote an end which was no part of his intention."[31]

None of this interested Isaiah Berlin. There is but one reference in his work to this constitutional economy of self-interested ambition. In *Three Critics of the Enlightenment,* he mentioned the possibility that "[l]egislation can turn private vices into public virtues." But the account he offered was crude by the standards of the constitutionalism we have been examining: he alluded to Helvetius's and Bentham's suggestion that "by dangling rewards and punishments judiciously before men . . . [t]heir egoistic instincts can be canalized by education and laws into doing good."[32] And anyway, it was just an aside, a momentary distraction in a discussion of Vico.

4. DESIGN AND HUMILITY

The thing that is so fascinating in Enlightenment constitutionalism is that all this is presented as a project of deliberate design. True, for much of the eighteenth century, the constitution of England had been held up as a model,[33] despite the fact that in Sieyès's words, it was "more of a product of chance and circumstance than enlightenment."[34] Montesquieu and Voltaire glorified it,[35] though Sieyès said he was "not inclined to prostrate himself before" the English system[36] and Kant wrote acidly about a people who "carry on about their constitution as if it were a model for the whole world."[37] Michael Kammen tells us that after 1789 the French Revolutionaries no longer professed themselves admirers of English constitutionalism but rather, in the words of Joseph Antoine Cerutti, anticipated "the glory of building a Constitution which makes the English in their turn our disciples and imitators."[38] For this is what they had seen the Americans do.

At the beginning of *The Federalist Papers,* Alexander Hamilton observed that if we accept that the British constitution was a product more "of chance and circumstance than enlightenment," then

> it seems to have been reserved to the people of this country [the United States] . . . to decide the important question, whether societies of men are really capable . . . of establishing good government from reflection and choice, or whether they are forever destined to depend for their political constitutions on accident and force.[39]

Constitutional design, in this spirit, was not just speculation or philosophic fantasy. It involved serious proposals by bodies of serious men facing the serious difficulties of actual societies. And those difficulties could be faced down only by the hard and deliberate work of reason, brought to life and put to work in the real world.

According to Berlin, Enlightenment social design was arrogant and monistic, seeking a fatuous reconciliation of all values and a comprehensive solution of all conflicts in a glittering work of reason.[40] As Henry Hardy states the Berlin view, there is simply no possibility of combining all plausible human values and human aspirations "into a single coherent overarching system in which all ends are fully realized without loss, compromise or clashes."[41] And this is seen as an indictment of the Enlightenment agenda, of the "Enlightenment vision of an eventual orderly and untroubled synthesis of all objectives and aspirations."[42] But, for the Americans, constitutional design, though deliberate, was understood to be untidy and pluralistic, setting out to *house* rather than reconcile the pursuit of competing and incommensurable values. Peter Gay called the American design "a political system constructed on distrust of human nature and hostile to utopian optimism."[43] Not only was it a contraption to accommodate the unruliness of human nature, but its establishment also partook of that unruliness. From the outset, it was (to adapt Berlin's own phrase) a provisional and uneasy equilibrium, in need of repair.[44] Most of the states that ratified it did so on the assumption that there would shortly be amendments, and of course there were. It was a product of reason, no doubt, but of many reasons sitting uneasily with one another, offering the citizens of the thirteen states an avowedly flawed and untidy compromise, yet something better than what they had had since 1777 and certainly preferable from the point of view of self-government to the arrangements that were in place before 1776.

In other words, the design of the U.S. Constitution presented itself in a spirit almost entirely contrary to the spirit that Berlin attributed to Enlightenment design. Yet it was an Enlightenment product.[45] It was presented to the American people during the ratification process in a spirit of humility as a modest, pragmatic, and experimental compromise. Nobody said it was perfect. And it was debated in the thirteen ratification conventions from multiple points of view, from town and country, from commerce and agriculture, by scholars, innkeepers, and self-taught politicians; it was voted on, and the votes were often close.[46]

This sense of humility was not confined to the western side of the Atlantic. The best that is to be said for a republican system, said Voltaire, is that it is "the most tolerable of systems." And, he went on, "There has never been a perfect government, because men have passions; and if they did not have passions, there would be no need for government"[47]—again that insistent Enlightenment trope. These voices are sounding back and forth across the Atlantic in tones of humility. Yet there is not a word about that in Berlin's very considerable corpus.

His editor attributes to Berlin the view that "[i]nstead of a splendid synthesis, there must be a permanent, at times painful, piecemeal process of untidy trade-offs and careful balancing of contradictory claims."[48] And another follower tells us that because values and principles clash and come into conflict, there is a need for mechanisms of compromise and tolerance, for no perfect solution is possible."[49] But while Berlin, Hardy, and others wrote in the abstract about processes and mechanisms for conflict and balancing, it was the Enlightenment constitutionalists who sought to actually specify these processes in institutional terms and define the mechanisms and procedures that would frame and furnish a form of governance that could sponsor these trade-offs and compromises.[50]

5. CONSTITUTIONALISM AND LIBERTY

In the late twentieth and early twenty-first centuries, constitutionalism is often associated with limited government and the protection of individual liberty. That was a theme in eighteenth-century constitutionalism too, though by no means the only theme. As I insisted in Chapter 2, we design constitutions to *constitute* governments as well as restrict them, to *empower* as well as to limit—particularly in the case of popular republics, whose aim is to empower people who would ordinarily be without power in a society. But, certainly, constraining government in the interest of liberty is one thing that constitutions do, and of course it was a concern of the constitutionalism of the Enlightenment. And since individual liberty was something that Isaiah Berlin did write about, he might have been expected to approach the topic of constitutionalism at least from this angle; he might have been alert to, and he might have alerted his readers to, what had been done on this front in eighteenth-century political thought.

But no. In fact, Berlin said next to nothing in his published work about the constitutional devices that might be used to uphold the negative liberty that interested him—"freedom from chains, from imprisonment, from enslavement by others . . . the absence of bullying or domination."⁵¹ He wrote next to nothing about the institutional mechanisms that might secure the modicum of liberty he thought was ethically required for each person—"a certain minimum area of personal freedom which must on no account be violated."⁵² He was interested only in debating with the *philosophes* about what liberty *was*, not about how it was to be secured.

He did say that "there must be some frontiers of freedom which nobody should be permitted to cross."⁵³ But he betrayed no scintilla of interest in the question that exercised James Madison and both Madison's friends and Madison's opponents in the American ratification debates: I mean the question about what good "parchment barriers" could do, and whether the frontiers of freedom were better secured by the structural principles of a constitution than by a dedicated Bill of Rights.⁵⁴ He said in an interview, toward the end of his life, that he believed "passionately" in human rights, but there was no discussion at all of the role these might play in law or constitutional arrangements.⁵⁵

One thing we may infer is that Berlin would not have accepted Emmanuel Sieyès's suggestion that "*political rights* are the only guarantee of civil rights and individual liberty," and that we can secure liberty only by "taking possession of our political rights."⁵⁶ Though Berlin sometimes used the phrase "political liberty" to refer to his favored conception of negative liberty, it appears that all he meant by this is that liberty is a value that is studied in the theory of politics—not that it is in and of itself an essentially political activity.⁵⁷ Berlin was happy to accept Bernard Crick's reproach that he was not particularly concerned with political participation.⁵⁸ He offered a grudging acknowledgment of the instrumental value of the exercise of political freedom: "Perhaps the chief value for liberals of political—'positive'—rights, of participating in government, is as a means for protecting what they hold to be an ultimate value, namely individual—'negative'—liberty."⁵⁹ But he was not prepared to say there was anything wrong with political apathy;⁶⁰ he would not say, with Rousseau or with Pericles, that freedom devoted entirely to private pursuits was not really worthy of the name.

The most Berlin would say about institutional provision for liberty was to repeat the Oxford tutorial commonplace that there is "no necessary connection between individual liberty and democratic rule."⁶¹ He wrote: "The connection between democracy and individual liberty is a good deal more tenuous than it [has] seemed to many advocates of both."⁶² He cited

Frederick the Great of Prussia for the proposition that an autocrat may be a better guarantor of liberty than a popular government:⁶³ "[I]t is perfectly conceivable that a liberal-minded despot would allow his subjects a large measure of personal freedom."

But even here, the conceptions that Berlin used were banal and unreflective. He showed no interest in what the Enlightenment constitutionalists made of the idea of a "liberal-minded despot." There might have been plenty to talk about. There were Kant's observations on the possibility that a constitution may be republican in its spirit, being governed by a king on principles analogous to those of a republic.⁶⁴ There were Montesquieu's comments on the structural differences between monarchy and despotism in this regard.⁶⁵ And there was Denis Diderot on the precarious danger of putting all liberty "in absolute dependence on a single person."⁶⁶ Berlin did not even confront the suspicion that enlightened despotism was much more likely than representative or republican government to associate itself with his own nightmare of comprehensive social planning, given all the untidiness and compromise that representative or republican government inevitably involved.

And on the other side of Berlin's comparison between a liberal-minded despot and an illiberal democracy, his comments on "democracy" were equally uncontaminated by reflection on political structure. Berlin held that democracy is not distinguished according to its direct, representative, or republican forms. He did not write about representation, nor did he try to make sense of the design perspective that would build representation into the complex constitutional structures we have been describing. The term "republic" does not figure in any of the indexes to the numerous Berlin volumes that have been cranked out in recent years. "Representation" does, just once—in the volume called *Liberty*, edited by Henry Hardy in 2002, but the page that is referred to (page 3) contains nothing whatever about representation (or any cognate term).⁶⁷ Yet representation was one of the major themes of Enlightenment political thought.⁶⁸

In all of this, it is not Berlin's general hostility to democracy and participatory liberty that concerns me.⁶⁹ That is a matter of record. What concerns me is his failure to consider the subtle and interesting things that were actually said on this score by the Enlightenment thinkers he continually excoriated for their crude perfectionism and their excessive faith in social design. Berlin's general cautionary thesis about the Enlightenment seems to be predicated on his directing us away from any consideration of these themes in Enlightenment constitutionalism.

6. EXPLAINING BERLIN'S NEGLECT

What is the explanation for this neglect? The most damning possibility I have alluded to already. It is that this was not a blind spot at all but deliberate avoidance of an aspect of the Enlightenment heritage that would have falsified Berlin's central proposition that Enlightenment social design was a matter of monistic and bullying perfectionism. That has certainly been the effect of his failure to address this aspect of the matter, and unfortunately those who worship at the Berlin shrine have not thought it worthwhile to undertake any independent exploration of the side of Enlightenment design that he ignored. Whether this was Berlin's intention or not, one really shouldn't try to say. Probably the man deserves better of us than this uncharitable diagnosis.

What other options are there? One possibility, which is almost as discrediting, is that he shied away from this aspect of the Enlightenment because it was already so prominent in the work of his archenemy, Hannah Arendt, particularly in her 1964 book *On Revolution*. But I can't see any connection of this kind in his scattered expressions of lack of respect for that lady's ideas.[70]

Probably the best explanation is that he was just uninterested in this aspect of the Enlightenment. Certainly he was well known for his lack of interest in law and legal structures (though there are those interesting comments about Montesquieu and judge-made law). Berlin considered reading for the Bar after his graduation in 1932 but pursued an All Souls Prize Fellowship instead. Also, despite the years that he spent in the United States during the Second World War, Berlin seemed completely uninterested, as far as I can tell, at least professionally, in American constitutional law and constitutional jurisprudence. In a word-portrait of his friend Felix Frankfurter, in *Personal Impressions,* there is nothing about American constitutionalism.[71] There *is* a throwaway line in a discussion of Alexander Herzen in the *New York Review of Books* in 1968, where he talks casually of "the corrupt constitutionalism in the West":

> He [Herzen] began with an ideal vision of mankind, largely ignored the chasm which divided it from the present—whether the Russia of Nicholas, or the corrupt constitutionalism in the West.[72]

But I don't know what to make of that, not even whether Berlin was intending to use the phrase, in this context, in his own voice. I certainly have not seen it elaborated anywhere. He also wrote disparagingly about constitution-mongering in a letter to Chaim Weizmann upon the founding of Israel in 1948.[73]

Maybe it is just that Berlin had a different conception of the theory of politics, of political philosophy, than the one that has motivated me. I said in my inaugural lecture (to the Chair that he also occupied), which is Chapter 1 of this volume, that Berlin's conception of political theory was far more ethical in its character than political. When Berlin was asked in a 1997 interview, a few months before his death, "What do you think are the tasks of political philosophy?" he replied: "To examine the ends of life,"[74] and he added that "[p]olitical philosophy is in essence moral philosophy applied to social situations."[75] True, he went on to say that the social situations to which moral philosophy is applied "of course include political organization, the relations of the individual to the community, the state, and the relations of communities and states to each other." But he gave no indication that "political organization" or political structures were worth study and reflection in their own right.[76]

To read almost any of Berlin's work, whether it addresses the Enlightenment or not, is to read essays that are resolutely uninterested in the political institutions of liberal society. As I have already said, beyond airy talk of freedom and openness, Berlin was simply unconcerned with the ways in which liberal or democratic political institutions might actually accommodate the pluralism and untidiness he thought so important in human life.

7. THE CONSEQUENCES OF NEGLECT

Whatever the explanation, the blind spot on Enlightenment constitutionalism has done political theory no service. Pedagogically, it has been detrimental to the theory of politics in England. Berlin set an example to his students and followers, and his lack of interest in institutions and constitutions has turned out to be contagious. Today, we study justice and the meaning of liberty; we don't study representation or the separation of powers. I don't want to exaggerate. This is something that probably would have happened anyway, under the influence of Rawls and others. But Berlin's steadfast indifference to questions of institutional politics certainly contributed to the atmosphere—an atmosphere I talked about in Chapter 1—in which political theory (especially in England) is treated more as a branch of ethics than as the theoretical and normative side of the study of the institutional structures that rightly preoccupy our colleagues in political science.

There is also a cost to this sidelining of eighteenth-century constitutional thought that extends beyond the academy. It is something we ought to have been studying because we are in large part the heirs of Enlightenment constitutionalism, and much that is best in our theory of politics and in the real-world application of that theory in the past seventy years is the heritage of the work of thinkers such as Locke, Montesquieu, Condorcet, Sieyès, Madison, and Kant. We believe now in constitutional republics and the design of constitutional republics, even if they are wearing the fancy dress of a monarchy, and we should not be scaring our students away from an inquiry into the intellectual foundations of constitutional republicanism by raising yet again this bogeyman of perfectionist totalitarian design.

This has not been a particularly respectful discussion; it was even less respectful when originally presented as the keynote address for a 2014 conference in Oxford on Isaiah Berlin. But if the price of a greater interest in Enlightenment constitutionalism and a better understanding of it is a bit of disrespect, then so be it. The old man's reputation can take it.

CHAPTER TWELVE

The Constitutional Politics of Hannah Arendt

WE MOVE NOW from Berlin to his nemesis. I want to end with an illustration of what serious theoretical reflection on constitutional structure might be like in modern political theory. It is a bit of a provocation in the circles I move in, but I have chosen to include one of my favorite political theorists—one who is most definitely not an analytic philosopher—Hannah Arendt.

1. A POLITICAL ANIMAL

In what sense (if any) is man a political animal? Hannah Arendt is commonly thought to have made more of the Aristotelean characterization[1] than anyone else in twentieth-century philosophy. I don't mean she is a good expositor of Aristotle; in fact, she is often criticized on that front.[2] I mean she took the content of Aristotle's claim very seriously, particularly the question of what exactly in man's nature is political and what is not.

Historically, Arendt argued, humans have found their greatest fulfillment in politics. For people like Thomas Jefferson and John Adams, "life in Congress, the joys of discourse, of legislation, of transacting business, of persuading and being persuaded, were . . . no less conclusively a foretaste of eternal bliss than the delights of contemplation had been for medieval piety."[3] In politics, such men found something that managed to redeem human life from the cyclical futility of birth, reproduction, and death. Without that something, their existence would be as uniform and pointless as the life of any animal, or its point would be the biological process itself, the endless repetition of generation after generation. In politics, by contrast, our humanity gives us the chance to transcend the merely natural and to undertake unique initiatives that flare up in the public realm and linger indefinitely in memory and history.

It follows (from this contrast between life process and politics) that the sense in which we are political animals must be quite a special sense for Arendt. In common speech, we call someone a political animal if he is hungry for power, and if he has the knack of manipulating people and institutions to get out of them exactly what he wants. (If it is a question of funding or promotion, he knows who to talk to and he gets to them first.) Or, in a slightly different vein, we call someone a political animal if he has a talent for *politicizing* everything. (Things that other people would deal with informally—who pays for dinner, who takes out the garbage—he makes an issue of and forces the rest of us into a huge debate about the fair allocation of responsibilities.) In a third sense, to say that someone is a political animal is to marvel at the way he "struts his stuff" on the political stage; it is to be dazzled by his speeches or his maneuvers as pure performance—as drama or ballet, perhaps—quite apart from their aims or their efficacy.

I am not sure whether any of these types would qualify as a political animal in Arendt's account. Certainly for her they are not paragons or exemplars of the breed. In Arendt's view, a political animal is not someone who politicizes everything or who can manipulate institutions to his personal advantage. Nor is her political animal a mere virtuoso, though, as we will see, her reasons for misgivings about the "performer" image are ambiguous and complicated.

The central case of an Arendtian *zoon politikon* is a person who engages seriously and responsibly in public business under the auspices of public institutions. He has the judgment to discern which issues are political and which are merely social or personal. He can see that what matter in politics are interests and purposes that are shared by all as members of a community. He has the patience to listen to others and to respond to their intelligence in a way that treats them as equals. Above all, he has respect for the structures and procedures that frame the political enterprise and that make possible deliberation and action with others. He takes the framework seriously, and he resists the temptation to dazzle his audience or further his own aims by subverting the formalities it imposes.

This last point—about the importance of structure, formality, and procedure—has not been emphasized nearly enough in recent discussions of Arendt's political thought. Commentators notice what is sometimes referred to as Arendt's *agonistic* conception of politics—politics as a stage for action and distinction, a place where heroic deeds break through the barriers of the mundane and live on in memory as something extraordinary and exhilarating.[4] They portray her as yearning for the public realm of antiquity, perhaps even archaic antiquity—a *polis* "permeated by a fiercely competitive spirit, where everybody had constantly to distinguish himself from all others, to show through unique deeds or achievements that he was the best of all."[5] The whole point of that style of "politics" is an unruly self-disclosure that challenges traditional forms. Alternatively, commentators notice that, in her darker moments, Arendt put almost all her faith in what one might call irregular or extrapolitical action—the spontaneous councils of citizens that spring up at moments of crisis or revolt—and that she doubted whether even the most promising constitutions could contain the human impulse toward freedom.[6] Put these two aspects of her work together, and it appears that Arendt's interest in constitutional structure has little to do with what she valued most about politics. Though no one can deny her interest in "founding moments," it often seems as if these moments are valued primarily for themselves—the 1787 Convention or the Declaration of Independence as archetypes of political action[7]—rather than as the establishment of a framework for subsequent action. That impression is reinforced by what commentators take to be the dominant tone of Arendt's most "constitutionalist" work, *On Revolution,* a tone of elegiac regret that in the American constitution "there was no space reserved, nor room left for the exercise of precisely those qualities which had been instrumental in building it."[8]

I do not want to underestimate the tensions and ambiguities in Arendt's work. Her writing varies in mood, emphasis, and occasion more than that of most political theorists. Even so, the theme of politics as something that requires not just virtuosity but constitution is so insistent in her work that, if we neglect it, we risk trivializing Arendt's real-world concerns about alienation from institutions, first in Europe between the wars[9] and then in modern America.[10] I think, too, that we should not overlook an important genealogical strain in her theory. To the extent that she presents a consistent view, it is not one in which agonistic self-disclosure and the "irregular" politics of councils and civil disobedience are *alternatives* to responsible modes of constitutional politics. Instead, they are presented by Arendt as, in the one case, an archaic precursor to politics in the most fully structured sense and, in the other, a despairing echo of constitutional politics—"strange and sad"—accompanying its lamentable decline.

2. HOUSING, WALLS, AND FURNITURE

That politics needs *housing,* and that building such housing can be equated with the framing of a *constitution*—this is an image that recurs throughout Arendt's writings. Sometimes the metaphor is less of bricks and mortar than of the furniture that enables us to sit facing one another in politics, in just the right way. At other times, Arendt invokes the imagery of construction outside the house: fences and boundary walls, which make politics possible by securing a space for the public realm.[11] Always the emphasis is on artificial structures, which are more rigid and durable than the actions they accommodate, and which exist as features of a world that men have made for themselves.

Arendt stressed this objective aspect of housing, even at some risk to her overall sense of the political nature of constitution-framing. For if constitutions were understood literally as fabrications—in the way she suggests the Greeks understood them—then constitution-framing would be making, not acting, and the framer would be

> like the builder of the city wall, someone who had to . . . finish his work before political activity could begin. He therefore was treated like any other craftsman or architect and could be called from abroad and commissioned without having to be a citizen, whereas the right to . . . engage in the numerous activities that went on inside the *polis,* was entirely restricted to citizens.[12]

That would be misleading for communities whose constitution-building was part of their own politics and no less political than any of the actions it was supposed to house and regulate. The image of fabrication tends also to suggest the singularity of the framer—one man making something out of other men[13]—rather than constitution-building as an activity that arises among men acting and speaking together.[14]

A different image, but more apt to capture these aspects of immanence and plurality, is that of political *grammar* or *syntax*.[15] Rules of grammar are not constructed up front; they are not distinct from usage and certainly they are not established by individual grammarians. They present themselves instead as something implicit in ongoing activity, regulating usage nonetheless and making possible certain forms of life that would be unthinkable without them.[16]

However, grammar does not quite capture an aspect of constitutional structure that Arendt wants to emphasize with her worldly images of housing and furniture. This is the aspect of "the *in-between*"—political structure as something that both separates people from one another and relates them to one another. Like a table or a seating plan, a constitution separates and relates us by putting us in different seats in one another's presence.[17] Now the world of objects does that generally for human life. For politics, however, the in-between is not physical but normative: it consists of rules, not barriers; practices and commitments, not impediments. Citizens are "bound to, and at the same time separated and protected from, each other by all kinds of relationships, based on a common language, religion, a common history, customs, and laws."[18]

True, Arendt did speak of the significance attached to constitutions as written documents, a significance that testified, she said, "to their elementary objective, worldly character."[19] In America, for example, it was important that the Constitution be

> an endurable objective thing, which, to be sure, one could approach from many different angles and upon which one could impose many different interpretations, which one could change or amend with circumstances, but which nevertheless was never a subjective state of mind, like the will. It has remained a tangible worldly entity of greater durability than elections or public-opinion polls.[20]

But paper constitutions by themselves are nothing: she cites the French Constitution of 1791 and the numerous discredited documents—"[t]he constitutions of the experts"—imposed in Europe after the First World War.[21] A constitution, said John Adams (in a passage Arendt quoted with approval), "is a standard, a pillar, and a bond when it is understood, approved and beloved. But without this intelligence and attachment, it might as well be a kite or balloon, flying in the air."[22]

3. WHAT DO CONSTITUTIONS DO?

The abstract idea of the in-between and the imagery of housing, grammar, and furniture are all very well. In literal terms, what is a constitution supposed to do in Arendt's account? Why is politics impossible without this housing? Why are noninstitutional versions of politics so hopeless or so dangerous? What sort of structure, what sort of nexus of relation-and-separation, do we actually need?

There are features of the housing and furniture metaphors that we can take simply at face value. They convey the importance of things like the proper design of legislative chambers or (varying the context slightly) the shape of the table at the Paris peace talks during the Vietnam War. Other aspects are question-begging as they stand. Is it really true, for example, that politics is impossible without boundaries? The men of the eighteenth century "needed a constitution to lay down the boundaries of the new political realm."[23] What sort of boundaries did Arendt have in mind?

She mentions a number of connected issues. In her discussion of jurisdiction in the Eichmann trial, she observes that "the earth is inhabited by many peoples and these peoples are ruled by many different laws."[24] The point of this separation into peoples is partly a matter of preserving identity (though Arendt is ambivalent about the politics of national identity)[25] and partly a matter of the conditions under which a free politics is possible. The state, she said, is not suited for unlimited growth, "because the genuine consent at its base cannot be stretched indefinitely."[26] As Rousseau recognized, there are limits on the scale on which people can deal with one another.[27] Politics depends on freedom and equality, and equality itself, she writes, is "applicable only with limitations and even within spatial limits."[28] I will later examine her view that equality is something constructed, not given. At this stage, it is worth noting, however, that even if we accept her constructivist account, the argument for the separation of states succeeds only if an *un*-bounded equality would necessarily have to rest on some naturalistic theory. Arendt assumes that it would—that is, she assumes that the equality implicit in international charters of human rights presupposes some account of human nature, and she shows the perils of such views in *The Origins of Totalitarianism*.[29] But she does not show that a *constructive* universalism is impossible (indeed her skepticism about the human rights project seems quite dated now). The only hints of argument to that effect seem to rest on a rather unpleasantly Schmittian view about equality: A and B can regard each other as equals only in their enmity toward C.[30]

A second sort of boundary Arendt emphasizes has to do with the scope of politics. It is important, she says, to maintain fences between public and private, and boundaries that separate the world of politics from the life world of labor and subsistence. She says we must sustain a sense of moderation that understands the futility of extending rules and commitments to every aspect of human life.[31] More astute commentators than I have tried and failed to elaborate a defensible version of Arendt's insistence that life-process issues must be forbidden in the public realm.[32] I will say nothing about that in this chapter except that the reconstruction of Arendtian political theory, which is undoubtedly necessary in this regard, will surely leave us still with *some* restrictions on the scope of the political realm for a constitution to patrol—even if it is just the old "wall of separation" between church and state.

Third, Arendt talks of the importance of the fences between individual men, the rules that separate as well as relate them to one another.[33] "Positive laws in constitutional government are designed to erect boundaries and establish channels of communication between men whose community is continually endangered by the new men born into it."[34] Arendt does not flinch from the fact that one of the motives that brings men into community is "their obvious fear of one another."[35] Sure, this is not all there is to human relatedness,[36] but Arendt sees that its mitigation by mutual assurance is the condition for anything more affirmative.

This brings us, then, to the internal aspect of constitutional structure. When *we* (liberals) think of the work that constitutions do, we tend to think of guarantees that are given to individuals, so far as their liberty and security are concerned. In much of her writing, Arendt plays down this aspect, as part of her project of deemphasizing negative liberty and focusing more on the freedom that consists in participation in public affairs.[37] Even when she talks about respect for privacy and property, it is associated as much with the protection of the political realm from life-process issues as it is with the individual (or familial) needs that the private realm represents.[38] Still, civil liberties are not absent from her picture. Though they are not "the actual content of freedom," they are recognized as its sine qua non, and they fade into active political freedom in a way that makes any rigid demarcation unhelpful.[39]

This is one area where it is particularly important to integrate Arendt's concerns in *The Origins of Totalitarianism* into her more abstract philosophy of politics. "Freedom from . . ." various restraints and threats looks uninspiring by contrast with the active participatory freedom of the public realm. But Arendt's study of totalitarianism leaves us with a vivid sense of what in the real world we need security against if freedom is to flourish. True, the terror, torture, madness, and murder described in that work go far beyond anything that constitutional structures could reasonably be expected to protect us against. And Arendt herself draws a distinction between terror and tyranny,[40] which, when coupled with a characterization of tyranny as "merely" a lack of negative freedom, might persuade us that its prevention is beneath the notice of a theory of this kind. Still, tyranny is the precursor of terror (just as liberation is the necessary condition for true freedom),[41] and the fear that is associated with it in the modern world—fear of beatings, torture, and "disappearance"—is, for the people who suffer it, remarkably similar to the dissolving panic that Arendt describes in the total environment of the German concentration camps. Of course, we also suffer forms of tyranny that are well short of that.[42] But, to our shame, we have found it necessary even in modern democratic politics to offer one another assurances against more brutal forms of oppression as well. Moreover, it is not enough for these assurances to be issued in theoretical proclamations. That was Arendt's criticism of the inefficacy of "the Rights of Man."[43] They need to be built into the civic structures of particular states, and enforced as part of the functioning of ordinary law.

Once security is guaranteed, the task is not to limit power but to constitute it, to build the conditions in which political freedom can flourish in an affirmative sense.[44] What sort of housing, what sort of structure, are we looking for here?

It might be thought that the politics of deed, distinction, and display needs very little in the way of constitutive structure. Indeed, structure in the public realm may make men too "well-behaved," diminishing the prospects for virtuosity.[45] What the political animal most needs, in this conception, is for his greatness to be noticed and his deeds to be remembered. I have already expressed my reservations about this take on Arendtian politics. Notice, however, that even at the level of deed and memory there can be nothing political without structure.

Politics orients itself toward action-in-concert and, as Arendt puts it, "action, though it may be started ... by single individuals for very different motives, can be accomplished only by some joint effort, in which the motivation of single individuals ... no longer counts."[46] For concerted action to be possible, men must give their word and play their part, furnishing one another with assurances that the cooperation of each in his assigned role will not be rendered futile by the unreliability of others. "This whole adventure," said the Mayflower compactors, "growes upon the joint confidence we have in each others fidelity and resolution herein, so as no man of us would have adventured it without assurance of the rest."[47] If it is to be anything other than "an extraordinary and infrequent enterprise,"[48] the structuring of action requires permanent arrays of ready-made roles so that provision for action in concert does not have to be invented anew every time an idea is projected.[49] That may sound a little too Weberian for those whose view of Arendt is dominated by her worries about bureaucracy,[50] but those worries, important as they are, must not be construed in a way that condemns all regularized forms of cooperation in the institutional life of actual political communities.

Something similar is true for remembrance as well. Let's say that people do enter public life in order to evince some special excellence. This is something they cannot do unless there are others around to compete with and impress.[51] It might be thought that we do not need much more structure for this than a stage and an audience. Consider, though, what Arendt actually says:

> [N]o remembrance remains secure unless it is condensed ... into a framework of conceptual notions. ... [T]he stories which grow out of what men do ... sink back into the futility inherent in the living word and the living deed unless they are talked about over and over again. What saves the affairs of mortal men from their inherent futility is nothing but this incessant talk about them, which in its turn remains futile unless certain concepts, certain guideposts for future remembrance, and even for sheer reference, arise out of it.[52]

This condensation for reference and memory presupposes a "web of relationships and enacted stories" in which the living deed can take its place as something remembered.[53] George Kateb associates that requirement with the integrity of a community stable enough to evolve traditions of storing and revisiting memories.[54] But one can associate it also with more formal structures. When Arendt discussed the difficulties facing the totalitarian substitution of lies for truthful memory in the modern world, she cited the existence of archives, serials, and anthologies—the mundane apparatus of bibliographical structure—which ensures that it is no easy matter to blot out the achievements of (say) a Trotsky or a Zinoviev from human remembrance.[55]

Focusing on actor, audience, and archive gives us a grip on the requirements for a rather primitive Periclean politics of personal display. But it tells us very little about what is necessary for politics as *inter*-action, the politics that involves debate, deliberation, and the making of decisions. According to Arendt, a well-ordered republic is "constituted by an exchange of opinion between equals."[56] This involves several types of structural arrangements—to begin with, it involves structures that enable us to treat one another as equals, and structures that enable each person's opinion to be exchanged with the opinions of others in a way that is capable of yielding a decision.

The first of these Arendt sometimes labeled *isonomy*[57]—the capacity of positive laws to make people equal in the political realm, even if they are in other respects different and unequal. By nature, we are (depending where you look) either the same in our animality or utterly different in background and character, but by political convention we *hold* ourselves to be one another's equals.[58] In recognition of our engagement in the joint enterprise of politics,[59] the law creates for each of us an artificial *persona* that can take its place on the public stage, presenting us not exactly as the beings we naturally are but as equals for political purposes.[60] Arendt's rejection of all theories of a natural basis for human equality is no doubt the reason that her observations about ancient slavery and other forms of subjugation are expressed with sadness but not surprise.[61] On the one hand, nothing forces a community to extend isonomy to all humans within its orbit, and on the other hand, a theory of natural equality runs the risk of holding that our natural similarities and dissimilarities are the ones that matter, whether they turn out finally to support the notion of equality or not.[62]

What we actually *do* as equals in politics, according to Arendt, is not merely try to impress one another as dramatis personae but talk to one another with a view to action in concert. People come to politics with diverse interests, and as common issues are raised they tend to develop diverse opinions.[63] Now, the formation of an opinion is not a straightforward thing for Arendt. It is not just "happening to hold a view." Instead, it involves a serious effort to see an issue from the point of view of all those affected by it:

> I form an opinion by considering a given issue from different viewpoints, by making present to my mind the standpoints of those who are absent. . . . [T]his is a question neither of empathy, as though I tried to be or feel like someone else, nor of counting noses and joining a majority but of being and thinking in my own identity where I am not. The more people's standpoints I have present in my mind while I am pondering a given issue, . . . the stronger will be my capacity for representative thinking, and the more valid my final conclusions, my opinion.[64]

That last comment about validity might suggest that a valid opinion is, ultimately, the same for everyone. I don't think Arendt means that. She envisages opinion formation by a given individual, A, in the context of A's putting himself into the shoes of B and C, even while B and C are forming their opinions in the same sort of way, and there is no reason why his attempt to put himself in their shoes should end up the same as their attempt to put themselves in his.[65] Since "no one is capable of forming his own opinion without the benefit of a multitude of opinions held by others,"[66] diversity and disagreement are going to be present in this process from start to finish.

If politics is to resolve anything, these various opinions must come together and yield a decision through what Arendt calls "the drawn-out wearisome processes of persuasion, negotiation, and compromise."[67] That cannot happen unless there is a framework in which each person's contribution takes its place and is related to that of each of the others. Now Arendt's remarks at this stage are not as concrete as one would like, but two sorts of structures seem particularly important. The first are the basic rules of political procedure—something like Robert's Rules of Order. By that I mean conventions determining things like how agendas are set; how debates are initiated and concluded; who has the right to speak, how often, and for how long; who may interrupt, who may exact an answer to a question, and who has a right of reply; how a common sense of relevance is maintained; and how deliberation is related to a community's powers of resolution and action. These matters, which I have discussed in detail elsewhere,[68] might seem beneath the notice of a political theory as exotic and exciting as Arendt's. But they are exactly what distinguish structured politics from the sort of undifferentiated welling-up of mass opinion in an extraparliamentary context that so worried her. Moreover, it is in rules like these that we can locate the equality that Arendt associates with citizenship. The right to be heard and the right that there be a system in which one's contributions are registered are exactly what isonomy in politics amounts to.[69] Sure, Arendt also emphasizes the spontaneity with which assemblies spring up whenever they are given the chance to do so. But it is intriguing how everyone seems to know on these occasions that if you constitute a public gathering, no matter how local the basis, no matter how spontaneous the impulse, there are procedures to be followed, chairs elected, motions moved, amendments considered, speakers for and against, points of order, questions put, votes taken, and minutes recorded. (Remember the discussion in Chapter 1 about the use of parliamentary procedure in Stringer Bell's drug enterprise in *The Wire*!) All of this is "second nature" in our political culture—as much a part of our political being as the faculty of speech itself.

The other aspect of structure, about which Arendt says very little, is of course the matter of voting. Her comments on voting tend to be mostly disparaging—along the lines of "[t]he booth in which we deposit our ballots is unquestionably too small, for this booth has room for only one."[70] But if one leaves aside her concerns about self-interested voting (which she associates with negative safeguards against government and, at worst, with blackmail),[71] the disparagement is not of voting as such but of forms of electoral politics that fail to provide people "with more opportunity to make their voices heard in public than election day."[72] Though occasionally she can be heard suggesting that face-to-face politics around a table might yield consensus and thus obviate the need for decision procedures,[73] nothing like that is remotely compatible with her emphasis on diversity of opinion. In fact, she is not at all uncomfortable with the idea of majority decision,

> a technical device, likely to be adopted almost automatically in all types of deliberative councils and assemblies, whether these are the whole electorate or a town-hall meeting. . . . In other words, the principle of majority is

inherent in the very process of decision-making and thus is present in all forms of government.[74]

That is, provided first that it is pursuant to a genuine exchange of opinions and second that it does not degenerate into what she calls majority-*rule,* "where the majority, after the decision has been taken, proceeds to liquidate politically, and in extreme cases, physically, the opposing minority."[75]

Beyond these, Arendt mentions three other structures of a well-organized polity: representation, parties, and federalism. Though political freedom means the right to be a participant in government, "[o]bviously direct democracy will not do, if only because 'the room will not hold all.'"[76] We need federal structures to connect (in a large- or medium-sized polity) the smaller political units in which alone direct participation is possible. Arendt never imagined that everyone in a society would seek the joy of political action. She was interested in structures that would empower "those few from all walks of life who have a taste for public freedom and cannot be 'happy' without it."[77] For this self-selected few, the connections between the "elementary republics" in which they act directly are arguably as important as the internal constitutions of those republics themselves. Such relations work in many ways; Arendt is particularly intrigued by structures of deputization, whereby action on a larger scale becomes possible through the exchange of opinions among deputies, each of whom stands for an opinion formed in roughly the same way among participants at a more "grass-roots" level of politics.[78]

Sometimes Arendt writes as though we need representation in politics to sift opinions, "passing them through the sieve of an intelligence which will separate the arbitrary and the merely idiosyncratic, and thus purify them into public views."[79] In *The Origins of Totalitarianism,* this idea occurs in the context of her concern about the fragmentation of political parties, their supersession by mass movements, and the growth of public irresponsibility, procedural impatience, and general contempt for parliamentary institutions.[80] In these circumstances, there is a "chaos of unrepresented and unpurified opinions." That chaos may crystalize "into a variety of conflicting mass sentiments under pressure of emergency," waiting for a strong man to mold them into a unanimous public opinion, which in Arendt's view spells death to all opinions.[81] To diminish these dangers, she looked to two-party systems (such as that of Great Britain) where effective participation in politics required both cooperation with others in "broad-church" arrangements and a degree of shared responsibility for the public world, born of the constant possibility, which we discussed in Chapter 5, that one might have to take office at the next election.[82]

4. PROMISING AND DURABILITY

The structures we have been discussing are partly a matter of culture (such as the ethos of a two-party system) and partly a matter of law (such as rules governing the way votes are counted). Either way, we have reason to be concerned about their durability, for these structures have to hold their own against all sorts of onslaughts, from self-interest and self-righteous impatience to various forms of communal hysteria.

For Arendt, the solution to the problem of political instability is prefigured in the idea of a promise. There is something crucial for politics in the human capacity to bind oneself in the presence of others and publicly commit oneself, against the unknown exigencies of future circumstances, to play one's part in a scheme agreed on in advance.[83] The paradigm of promise-based politics is the Mayflower compact—the affecting assumption by a group of men and women on the edge of a wilderness that they had the power "to combine themselves into a 'civil Body Politick' which, held together solely by the strength of mutual promise 'in the Presence of God and one another,' supposedly was powerful enough to 'enact, constitute, and frame' all necessary laws and instruments of government."[84] Like a promise, a constitution might appear to limit our freedom, but at the same time it creates something special—the power of political community—whose importance consists precisely in mitigating the incalculability that human freedom gives rise to.

What counts in promising of course is not the making of a promise but the keeping of it; and for the construction of a political community, what matters is not the admirable state of the furnishings when politics begins but the ongoing willingness of citizens to submit to them as regulative structures. The authority of a constitution is not a product of the strength or violence of its framers, or even of their virtue or the perfection of what they have crafted. It consists rather in a willingness on the part of all concerned to treat *this* event (the founding) and *this* body of law (the constitution), rather than any of the other acts and proposals that might crop up from time to time, as the starting point and point of reference for all subsequent politics. And they must do this not because of anything special or perfect about this event or body of law but simply on account of their acknowledgment that there must be such a point of reference, that it is bound to be in some sense arbitrary, and that they are determined nevertheless to act henceforth as though *this one* will do. In that regard, respect for a constitution matches the contingent resolution of promise-keeping. I might have made any one of a number of promises, and some of them might have been excellent, but *this* is the one that I did happen to make, and so *this* is the one I am bound by.[85]

In case that conveys an excessive sense of immutability so far as political structure is concerned, it is worth adding that Arendt associated authority as much with improvement (*augere*—to augment and increase) as with conservation.[86] The order and predictability that we need in political affairs may change with changes in circumstances. A constitution is necessarily a work in progress. Still, the point about the authority of the particular arbitrary beginning remains important. Respect for an established constitution does not mean treating it as sacrosanct and beyond change but means treating *it* as the object of change and augmentation rather than simply purporting to begin again every time we suppose ourselves to have accumulated more wisdom than our ancestors.

Promising is an important clue to constitutional durability, but in one respect it is misleading. In the liberal tradition of government by consent, there is an assumption that each new person can contract anew and that no one need be bound by the promises of a previous generation. But that is incompatible with Arendt's conviction that constitutions must be able to outlast their mortal framers.[87] Law certainly rests on consent, in the sense that it constitutes and therefore cannot presuppose the power that would be necessary to compel obedience. But the rules that make up the public world must also exist before each individual takes his place in that world and they make a claim on him that is prior to anything he might agree to:

> The point of these rules is not that I submit to them voluntarily or recognize theoretically their validity, but that in practice I cannot enter the game unless I conform; my motive for acceptance is my wish to play, and since men exist only in the plural, my wish to play is identical with my wish to live. Every man is born into a community with pre-existing laws which he "obeys"

first of all because there is no other way for him to enter the great game of the world.[88]

5. POLITICS AND DESPAIR

Sometimes when one reads Arendt—and more often when one reads her commentators—the impression one gets is of an obscure and esoteric philosopher, concerned with large and mysterious issues like *dasein* and *the agonal,* who has little to say to the ordinary student of politics. The Arendtian world, it seems, is a world for the initiated, a world of theoretical abstractions largely uncontaminated by mundane things like civil liberties, voting rights, Robert's Rules of Order, and the two-party system. I have not said all there is to say about Arendt's interest in constitutional structure.[89] But I hope I have redressed the balance a little by showing, first, how engaged her work is with quite familiar issues about political institutions, and second, how important structure is, even in her most abstract characterizations of human freedom. If we say Arendt was unconcerned with the formalities of political order, we can make little sense of her preoccupation with foundations, her omnivorous interest in constitution-building, her grasp of the need for patience and discipline in politics, and the orientation of almost all her work to the hard task of sustaining a realm where human freedom can become powerful and not spend itself in the futility she associates with the immediate, the unstructured, and the natural.

I have not forgotten Arendt's political despair, her belief that the American framers failed to provide within their constitution structures that could safeguard the spirit exhibited in their own revolutionary actions.[90] Nor have I forgotten her apprehension about the modern "transformation of government into administration, or of republics into bureaucracies, and the disastrous shrinkage of the public realm."[91] But when she says "it was the Constitution itself, this greatest achievement of the American people, which eventually cheated them of their proudest possession,"[92] that is not a rejection of constitutions, constitutionalism, or constitutional structure as such. It is a lamentation of the failure of the framers and current inhabitants of *this particular constitution* to find a way of structuring for perpetuity the sort of freedom they were exercising. The lament is unintelligible without an understanding of the importance of structure.

Let me return to an observation I mentioned in Chapter 1, by German historian Christian Meier, writing about Julius Caesar in the dying days of the Roman Republic:

> Caesar was insensitive to political institutions and the complex ways in which they operate. . . . Since his year as consul, if not before, Caesar had been unable to see Rome's institutions as autonomous entities. . . . He could see them only as instruments in the interplay of forces. His cold gaze passed through everything that Roman society still believed in, lived by, valued and defended. He had no feeling for the power of institutions to guarantee law and security, but only for what he found useful or troublesome about them. . . . Thus what struck him most about the Senate was the fact that it was controlled by his opponents. It hardly seems to have occurred to him that it was responsible for the commonwealth. . . . In Caesar's eyes no one existed but himself and his opponents. It was all an interpersonal game. He classified people as supporters, opponents or neutrals. The scene was cleared of any suprapersonal elements. Or if any were left, they were merely props behind which one could take cover or with which one could fight. Politics amounted to no more than a fight for his rights.[93]

And by "his rights" Meier meant not Caesar's interests or his wealth but due recognition for his greatness.

Is this the paragon of a political animal? Is this the sort of thing Arendt laments that we have lost? In some readings of her work, one would have to say that it is, for here, in Caesar's case, we have the heroic "wish to excel."[94] Here we have "the self's agonal passion for distinction,"[95] the "unruly" but (nota bene) highly successful pursuit of immortality, breaking through the commonly accepted and reaching into the extraordinary. Caesar might have destroyed the institutions of the republic and created in their place nothing but the splendor of his own deed. But that, surely, is the mark of political *virtu*, "where the accomplishment lies in the performance itself."[96]

In fact, despite some of her rhetoric,[97] I suspect Hannah Arendt's judgment of Caesar would have been the same as Christian Meier's[98]—that there is something reckless, even pathological, about a mode of political action in which the walls and structures intended to house actions of that kind become suddenly invisible, transparent, even contemptible to the actor. In a somewhat different context, she observes:

> The weirdness of this situation resembles a spiritualist séance where a number of people gathered round a table might suddenly, through some magic trick, see the table vanish from their midst, so that two persons sitting opposite each other were no longer separated but also would be entirely unrelated to each other by anything tangible.[99]

Such drastically unmediated proximity—"Now there is just you, and me, and the issue of my greatness"—is alarmingly like the press of bodies against each other that Arendt associates with the destruction of the possibility of thought in mass society. Though thought may be solitary, it must still be articulate.[100] One cannot *think* (not even in a dialogue with oneself) unless there are structures that allow respect for and exchange of opinions with others (which one then might mimic in one's solitude). The ultimate prospect, then, at the end of any road through the public realm that is indifferent to structure, is what Arendt referred to in *The Life of the Mind* as "the possible interconnectedness of non-thought and evil."[101] To saddle her with that indifference, for the sake of a glamorous politics of self-expression, is to neglect the cautionary point of almost everything she wrote about the modern world.

NOTES

1. *POLITICAL* POLITICAL THEORY

1. David Hume, "That Politics May Be Reduced to a Science," in David Hume, *Essays: Moral, Political, Literary,* ed. Eugene F. Miller (Liberty Classics, 1985), p. 14.

2. Ibid., pp. 14–15.

3. Ibid., p. 14n.

4. Max Weber, "Politics as a Vocation," in *From Max Weber: Essays in Sociology,* ed. H. H. Gerth and C. Wright Mills (Oxford University Press, 1958), pp. 120–26.

5. Hume, "That Politics May Be Reduced to a Science," p. 15.

6. David Hume, "On the Independence of Parliament," in Hume, *Essays: Moral, Political, Literary,* p. 42.

7. Alexander Hamilton, John Jay, and James Madison, *The Federalist Papers,* ed. George W. Carey and James McLellan (Liberty Fund, 2001) (Number 51: Madison). See also Immanuel Kant's claim in Immanuel Kant, *Perpetual Peace and Other Essays,* trans. Ted Humphrey (Hackett, 1983), p. 124, that "[t]he problem of organizing a nation is solvable even for a people comprised of devils, if only they possess understanding." According to Kant, the problem is this: "So order and organize a group of rational beings who require universal laws for their preservation—though each is secretly inclined to exempt himself from such laws—that, while their private attitudes conflict, these nonetheless so cancel one another that these beings behave publicly just as if they had no evil attitudes" (ibid.). For some skepticism about Madison's version of this idea, see Daryl Levinson and Richard Pildes, "Separation of Parties, Not Powers," *Harvard Law Review* 119 (2006), 2311, at p. 2317: "Madison's vision of competitive branches balancing and checking one another has dominated constitutional thought about the separation of powers through the present. Yet it has never been clear exactly how the Madisonian machine was supposed to operate."

8. Hume, "That Politics May Be Reduced to a Science," p. 16.

9. Machiavelli, *The Prince,* ed. Quentin Skinner and Russell Price (Cambridge University Press, pp. 54–72 (chs. 15–19).

10. See, e.g., Montesquieu, *The Spirit of the Laws,* ed. Anne M. Cohler, Basia Carolyn Miller, and Harold Samuel Stone (Cambridge University Press, 1989), pp. 22–24 (Bk. III, ch. 3).

11. Terminology can be a problem here. Of course, we can use the language of virtue to refer to something like justice. We can say with Rawls that justice is the first virtue of social institutions [*A Theory of Justice* (Harvard University Press, 1971), p. 3], but then we are not talking about personal characteristics in the way that Hume was, although we may be talking about them in the way that Cohen was.

12. See, e.g., Robert Nozick, *Anarchy, State and Utopia* (Basic Books, 1974); Ronald Dworkin, *Sovereign Virtue: The Theory and Practice of Equality* (Harvard University Press, 2002) and *Justice for Hedgehogs* (Harvard University Press, 2002); Amartya Sen, *The Idea of Justice* (Penguin Books, 2009); Michael Walzer, *Spheres of Justice: A Defense of Pluralism and Equality* (Basic Books, 1983); and G. A. Cohen, *Rescuing Justice and Equality* (Harvard University Press, 2008).

13. See Jeremy Waldron, "The Primacy of Justice," *Legal Theory,* 9 (2003), 269.

14. Ramin Jahanbegloo, *Conversations with Isaiah Berlin,* second edition (Perseus Books, 2007), p. 46. He also observed that "political theory is about the ends of life, about values, about the goals of social existence, about what men in society live by and should live by, about good and evil, right and wrong" (ibid., pp. 57–58).

15. Ibid., K912.

16. I am told—by Peter Pulzer, in conversation—that Berlin had a considerable interest in political institutions, in the United States, the United Kingdom, and elsewhere, even if it did not make its way into his published writings.

17. Jahanbegloo, *Conversations with Isaiah Berlin,* pp. 46–47.

18. See, e.g., Isaiah Berlin, "Political Ideas in the Twentieth Century," in Isaiah Berlin, *Liberty,* ed. Henry Hardy (Oxford University Press, 2002), 55.

19. See also the discussion in Chapter 11.

20. Jahanbegloo, *Conversations with Isaiah Berlin,* p. 143.

21. See Bernard Williams, "Realism and Moralism," in a posthumous collection of his papers, *In the Beginning Was the Word: Realism and Moralism in Political Argument,* ed. Geoffrey Hawthorn (Princeton University Press, 2006), p. 8.

22. Ibid., p. 3.

23. Again, there is nothing inappropriate about Williams's emphasis on values such as security. For an attempt to analyze it using some of Williams's own work, see my essay "Safety and Security" in Jeremy Waldron, *Torture, Terror and Trade-offs: Philosophy for the White House* (Oxford University Press, 2010), 111, esp. at p. 150. Still, one wants it to be complemented by an account of the institutional contexts in which this value might be pursued.

24. The same is true, I think, for Raymond Geuss's book *Philosophy and Real Politics* (Princeton University Press, 2008), which is a refreshing tilt away from what the author calls an "ethics-first" conception of political philosophy (ibid., p. 9); but it is a tilt more toward a philosophy of political action than toward a philosophy of the structures and processes that are needed to house our acting together under circumstances of moral and political disagreement.

25. I have argued this at length in Jeremy Waldron, *Law and Disagreement* (Oxford University Press, 1999).

26. See Nancy Rosenblum, *On the Side of the Angels: An Appreciation of Parties and Partisanship* (Princeton University Press, 2008), where the author excoriates the lack of interest in political parties in modern political theory.

27. I stress "*British* political theory" because there is much more emphasis on these topics in American legal and political theory than there is in the United Kingdom. This is largely because of the prominence of constitutional politics in the United States.

28. S. E. Finer, *The Man on Horseback: The Role of the Military in Politics* (Pall Mall Press, 1962).

29. Lon Fuller, "Positivism and Fidelity to Law: A Reply to Hart," *Harvard Law Review,* 71 (1959), 630, at p. 637. See also Lon Fuller, *The Morality of Law,* revised edition (Yale University Press, 1969).

30. For criticisms, see H. L. A. Hart, *The Concept of Law,* second edition (Oxford University Press, 1994), pp. 206–7; Matthew Kramer, *In Defense of Legal Positivism* (Oxford University Press, 1999).

31. Cf. Waldron, *Law and Disagreement,* pp. 224–31.

32. Daron Acemoglu and James Robinson, *Why Nations Fail: The Origins of Power, Prosperity, and Poverty* (Crown Publishing, 2012).

33. See, e.g., David Austen-Smith and Jeffrey S. Banks, *Positive Political Theory I: Collective Preference* (University of Michigan Press, 2008).

34. Rawls, *A Theory of Justice,* p. 230.

35. John Stuart Mill, *Considerations on Representative Government,* in John Stuart Mill, *On Liberty and Other Essays* (Oxford University Press, 1998), pp. 238–56; Carole Pateman, *Participation and Democratic Theory* (Cambridge University Press, 1970).

36. See, most recently, "House of Lords Reform 'will Cost Taxpayers £500 Million,'" *Daily Telegraph,* July 3, 2012.

37. See the account in William Keith Jackson, *The New Zealand Legislative Council: A Study of the Establishment, Failure and Abolition of an Upper House* (University of Toronto Press, 1972).

38. For a broad and critical account, see Jeremy Waldron, *Parliamentary Recklessness: Why We Need to Legislate More Carefully,* The 2008 John Graham Lecture, Auckland (Maxim Institute, 2008), available at http://www.maxim.org.nz/site

/DefaultSite/filesystem/documents/Monograph%20web.pdf (last visited June 13, 2015) and (on video) at http://www.maxim.org.nz/Policy_and_Research/Parliamentary_Recklessness__Why_we_need_to_legislate_more_carefully (last visited June 13, 2015).

39. See the discussion in Jeremy Waldron, "How Law Protects Dignity," *Cambridge Law Journal,* 71 (2012), 200, esp. pp. 208–12.

40. Mill, *Considerations on Representative Government,* pp. 329 and 335.

41. Cf. Immanuel Kant, *Groundwork of the Metaphysics of Morals,* ed. Mary Gregor (Cambridge University Press, 1998), pp. 42–43 (4: 435 in the Prussian Academy Edition of Kant's works). See also Jeremy Waldron, *Dignity, Rank and Rights* (Oxford University Press, 2012), pp. 23–27.

42. Elizabeth Gaskell, *Mary Barton* (Oxford University Press, 2006), pp. 83–84 (ch. viii).

43. Ibid., p. 84.

44. Ibid., pp. 95–96.

45. Ibid., p. 98.

46. Ibid., p. 96.

47. William Forbath, *Law and the Shaping of the American Labor Movement* (Harvard University Press, 1991). Professor Forbath lists more than 170 instances in which state or federal statutes of this kind were struck down during this period (pp. 177ff.).

48. Ibid., pp. 47 and 56.

49. Ibid., p. 47n.

50. See, e.g., Ajume Wingo, *Veil Politics in Liberal Democratic States* (Cambridge University Press, 2003), ch. 1.

51. Here I have in mind Edmund Burke's admonition, in *Reflections on the Revolution in France,* ed. J. C. D. Clark (Stanford University Press, 2001), p. 259, against too frequent change: "By this unprincipled facility of changing the state as often, and as much, and in as many ways, as there are floating fancies or fashions, the whole chain and continuity of the commonwealth would be broken. No one generation could link with the other. Men would become little better than the flies of a summer."

52. Hannah Arendt, *On Revolution* (Viking Press, 1963), p. 199.

53. Jahanbegloo, *Conversations with Isaiah Berlin,* p. 182. See also Jeremy Waldron, "What Would Hannah Say?" *New York Review of Books,* March 15, 2007.

54. Hannah Arendt, *The Human Condition* (University of Chicago Press, 1958), p. 52.

55. Cf. Jeremy Waldron, "Arendt's Constitutional Politics," in *The Cambridge Companion to Hannah Arendt,* ed. Dana Villa (Cambridge University Press, 2000), p. 205. This essay is reprinted here as Chapter 12.

56. Mill, *Considerations on Representative Government,* p. 283.

57. Ibid.

58. See Waldron, *Law and Disagreement*, pp. 69–87 (ch. 4).

59. David Simon et al., *The Wire* (HBO Television), Series 3, Episode 1: "Time after Time."

60. Weber, *Politics as a Vocation*, p. 120: "We must be clear about the fact that all ethically oriented conduct may be guided by one of two fundamentally differing and irreconcilably opposed maxims: conduct can be oriented to an 'ethic of ultimate ends' or to an 'ethic of responsibility.' . . . [T]here is an abysmal contrast between conduct that follows the maxim of an ethic of ultimate ends—that is, in religious terms, 'The Christian does rightly and leaves the results with the Lord'—and conduct that follows the maxim of an ethic of responsibility, in which case one has to give an account of the foreseeable results of one's action. . . . Politics is a strong and slow boring of hard boards."

61. Christian Meier, *Caesar*, trans. David McLintock (Basic Books, 1995), pp. 358–59.

62. Ibid., pp. 360–63.

63. Arendt, *On Revolution*, p. 89.

64. The decision of the European Court of Human Rights in *Hirst v. United Kingdom (No 2)* [2005] ECHR 681, requiring the U.K. Parliament to revisit the provisions of its electoral legislation that disenfranchised prisoners, provoked a considerable backlash in Britain against the interference of courts in domestic constitutional issues.

65. Mill, *Considerations on Representative Government*, ch. 13 ("Of a Second Chamber"), and *Jeremy Bentham to His Fellow-Citizens of France, on Houses of Peers and Senates* (Robert Heward, London, 1830), pp. 39 and 44 (XII, §1 and XIII, §8). The latter text is available online in the Liberty Fund's *Online Library of Liberty* at http://oll.libertyfund.org/?option=com_staticxt&staticfile=show.php%3Ftitle=1925&chapter=116768&layout=html&Itemid=27. I discuss both of these texts in Chapter 4.

66. I discuss this further in Chapter 3.

67. Cf. Eric Posner and Adrian Vermeule, *The Executive Unbound: After the Madisonian Republic* (Oxford University Press, 2011).

68. See David Estlund, *Democratic Authority: A Philosophical Framework* (Princeton University Press, 2008); Tom Christiano, *The Rule of the Many: Fundamental Issues in Democratic Theory* (Westview Press, 1996) and *The Constitution of Equality: Democratic Authority and Its Limits* (Oxford University Press, 2008).

69. See Jeremy Waldron, "The Core of the Case against Judicial Review," *Yale Law Journal*, 115 (2006), 1346; Ronald Dworkin, *Freedom's Law: The Moral Reading of the American Constitution* (Oxford University Press, 1996), Introduction and chs. 17–18.

70. See, e.g., John Ferejohn, Jack Rakove, and Jonathan Riley (eds.), *Constitutional Culture and Democratic Rule* (Cambridge University Press, 2001); Stephen

Holmes, *Passions and Constraint: On the Theory of Liberal Democracy* (University of Chicago Press, 1997); Sanford Levinson, *Our Undemocratic Constitution* (Oxford University Press, 2008); Posner and Vermeule, *The Executive Unbound*.

71. Charles Beitz, *Political Equality: An Essay in Democratic Theory* (Princeton University Press, 1989); Dennis Thompson, *Just Elections: Creating a Fair Electoral Process in the United States* (University of Chicago Press, 2002). Some comments in Thompson's "Preface" (ibid., pp. viii–ix) about the importance of institutional political theory exactly match the sentiments in this chapter.

72. See Isaiah Berlin, "John Stuart Mill and the Ends of Life," in Berlin, *Liberty*, 218; Isaiah Berlin, "Montesquieu," in Isaiah Berlin, *Against the Current: Essays in the History of Ideas* (Princeton University Press, 2001), 130.

73. Montesquieu, *The Spirit of the Laws*, pp. 59–63 (Bk. V, ch. 14).

74. Ibid., p. 63 (Bk. V, ch. 14).

75. The letter is cited in the introduction to David Carrithers, Michael Mosher, and Paul Rahe (eds.), *Montesquieu's Science of Politics: Essays on The Spirit of Laws* (Rowman and Littlefield, 2001), p. 3.

76. Hume, "That Politics May Be Reduced to a Science," p. 24.

77. Ibid., p. 15.

78. Again, for a view of this sort, see Posner and Vermeule, *The Executive Unbound*.

2. CONSTITUTIONALISM

1. John Stuart Mill, *On Liberty*, ed. Elizabeth Rapaport (Hackett, 1978), p. 50: "[E]ven if the received opinion be not only true, but the whole truth; unless it is suffered to be, and actually is, vigorously and earnestly contested, it will, by most of those who receive it, be held in the manner of a prejudice, with little comprehension or feeling of its rational grounds."

2. George E. Connor and Christopher W. Hammons (eds.), *The Constitutionalism of American States* (University of Missouri Press, 2008).

3. Akhil Reed Amar, "America's Constitution, Written and Unwritten," *Syracuse Law Review* 57 (2007), 267, at p. 269.

4. *Oxford English Dictionary* online: "Constitutionalism—1. A constitutional system of government."

5. For instances of these usages, see John McGinnis and Michael Rappaport, "A Pragmatic Defense of Originalism," *Northwestern University Law Review* 101 (2007), 383, at p. 392; James Fleming, "Living Originalism and Living Constitutionalism as Moral Readings of the American Constitution," *Boston University Law Review*, 92 (2007), 1171; and William Eskridge, "*Lawrence v. Texas* and the Imperative of Comparative Constitutionalism," *International Journal of Constitutional Law*, 2 (2004), 555.

6. Compare the observation of Walter Murphy in "Designing a Constitution: Of Architects and Builders," *Texas Law Review,* 87 (2009), 1303, at p. 1308: "Labeling a document 'the constitution' does not thereby imbue it with any of the norms of constitutionalism."

7. *Oxford English Dictionary* online. The instances given are "1871 Daily Tel. 2 Nov., They persuaded the King that Constitutionalism was his natural *rôle*" and "1889 Times 19 Feb. 9/2, The frigid and negative constitutionalism of M. Carnot."

8. A. V. Dicey, *Introduction to the Study of the Law of the Constitution* (Liberty Classics, 1982), p. 386, uses "constitutionalism" in this sense when he writes that "the aim of Australian statesmen has been to combine . . . ideas borrowed from the federal and republican constitutionalism of the United States . . . with ideas derived from the Unitarian and monarchical constitutionalism of England."

9. Roger Scruton, *A Dictionary of Political Thought* (Macmillan, 1982), p. 94.

10. As in *"princeps ab legibus solutus:* the prince is not bound by the laws." The best-known version of absolutism is that of Thomas Hobbes, *Leviathan,* ed. Richard Tuck (Cambridge University Press, 1996), chs. 18 and 26.

11. Cf. Aristotle, *Politics,* trans. Stephen Everson (Cambridge University Press, 1996), p. 92 (Bk. IV, ch. 1): "[a] constitution is the organization of offices in a state, and determines what is to be the governing body."

12. Alexander Hamilton, John Jay, and James Madison, *The Federalist Papers,* ed. George W. Carey and James McLellan (Liberty Fund, 2001), p. 1.

13. So compare the response of Paul J. Magnarella, "The Comparative Constitutional Law Enterprise," *Willamette Law Review,* 30 (1994), 509, at p. 510: "By definition, every state, even one with a dictatorship, has a constitution—a set of legal norms and procedures that structure its legal and governmental systems. . . . In the absence of the ruling elite's commitment to limited governmental powers under the rule of law, a state may have a constitution without constitutionalism. In such a case, comparativists would label its constitution 'nominal,' rather than 'normative.'"

14. I take up this theme again in Chapter 11.

15. *Marbury v. Madison,* 5 U.S. 137 (1803), at p. 177.

16. *Dr. Bonham's case,* 8 Co. Rep. 114 (Court of Common Pleas [1610]): "And it appears . . . that in many cases, the common law will control acts of parliament, and sometimes adjudge them to be utterly void: for when an act of parliament is against common right and reason, or repugnant, or impossible to be performed, the common law will control it, and adjudge such act to be void."

17. Walton H. Hamilton, "Constitutionalism," in *Encyclopedia of the Social Sciences,* Vol. 4, ed. Edwin Seligman and Alvin Johnson (Macmillan, 1931), p. 255, cited in Richard S. Kay, "American Constitutionalism," in *Constitutionalism: Philosophical Foundations,* ed. Larry Alexander (Cambridge University Press, 1998), at p. 16.

18. For James Madison's observation, see Hamilton, Jay, and Madison, *The Federalist Papers,* ed. Carey and McClellan, p. 256 (Number 48: Madison):

> Will it be sufficient to mark, with precision, the boundaries of these departments, in the constitution of the government, and to trust to these parchment barriers against the encroaching spirit of power? This is the security which appears to have been principally relied on by the compilers of most of the American constitutions. But experience assures us, that the efficacy of the provision has been greatly overrated; and that some more adequate defense is indispensably necessary for the more feeble, against the more powerful, members of the government.

For Hamilton's view, see ibid., p. 380 (Number 73: Hamilton):

> The propensity of the legislative department to intrude upon the rights, and to absorb the powers, of the other departments, has been already suggested and repeated; the insufficiency of a mere parchment delineation of the boundaries of each, has also been remarked upon; and the necessity of furnishing each with constitutional arms for its own defense, has been inferred and proved.

See also the comments of Madison together with Hamilton on the hapless inefficacy of the parchment on which the Belgian constitution is written, ibid., p. 96 (Number 20: Madison).

19. Hannah Arendt, *On Revolution* (Viking Books, 1964), p. 157.

20. Jeremy Bentham makes a similar point about bodies of unwritten law, such as the Common Law, in his book *Of Laws in General,* ed. H. L. A. Hart (Athlone Press, 1970), pp. 194–95n. See also Jeremy Waldron, "Custom Redeemed by Statute," *Current Legal Problems,* 51 (1998), 93, at pp. 111–12.

21. I have argued this point for textual law and textualism generally in Jeremy Waldron, *Law and Disagreement* (Clarendon Press, 1999), pp. 69–87.

22. Cf. Lon L. Fuller, *The Morality of Law,* revised edition (Yale University Press, 1969), p. 96; and Joseph Raz, "The Rule of Law and Its Virtue," in his book *The Authority of Law: Essays on Law and Morality* (Oxford University Press, 1979).

23. Scott Gordon, *Controlling the State: Constitutionalism from Ancient Athens to Today* (Harvard University Press, 1999); and András Sajó, *Limiting Government: An Introduction To Constitutionalism* (Central European Press, 1999).

24. Sajó, *Limiting Government,* p. x.

25. Cass R. Sunstein, "Constitutionalism after the New Deal," *Harvard Law Review* 101 (1987), 421, at pp. 434–36.

26. C. H. McIlwain, *Constitutionalism Ancient and Modern* (Cornell University Press, 1940), p. 24 (quoted in Gordon, *Controlling the State,* p. 5). For most writers, constitutionalism equals constraint. They accept McIlwain's characterization or that of Carl Friedrich, who spoke of constitutionalism as "effective regularized restraint" on government. Carl J. Friedrich, *Constitutional Government and Democracy: Theory and Practice in Europe and America,* fourth edition (Blaisdell, 1968), pp. 35–36.

27. Judith N. Shklar, "The Liberalism of Fear," in a collection of her essays, *Political Thought and Political Thinkers,* ed. Stanley Hoffman (University of Chicago Press, 1998), p. 3.

28. U.S. Constitution, Article I, section 10.

29. Cf. Linda Bosniak, "Constitutional Citizenship through the Prism of Alienage," *Ohio State Law Journal,* 63 (2002), 1285, at p. 1287. See also Douglas Sturm, "A Prospective View of the Bill of Rights: Toward a New Constitutionalism," *Journal of Law and Religion,* 13 (1996–1998), 27, at pp. 29–30: "[C]onstitutionalism, a tradition of political theory and practice with which the idea of human rights is often associated, has the connotation of limited government. At one extreme, constitutionalism is linked with the concept of a laissez faire state."

30. *Government of the Republic of South Africa v. Grootboom,* 2001 (1) SA 46 (CC).

31. See Jeremy Waldron, "Legislation and the Rule of Law," *Legisprudence,* 1 (2007), 91; and Jeremy Waldron, *The Rule of Law and the Measure of Property* (Cambridge University Press, 2012).

32. Richard S. Kay, "American Constitutionalism," in *Constitutionalism: Philosophical Foundations,* ed. Alexander, p. 19.

33. *Jackson v. City of Joliet,* 715 F2d 1200 (1983), at p. 1203.

34. This is what Stephen Holmes, Sotirios Barber, and others have called "positive constitutionalism." See Stephen Holmes, *Passions and Constraints: On the Theory of Liberal Democracy* (University of Chicago Press, 1997), pp. 6–8; and Sotirios Barber, *Welfare and the Constitution* (Princeton University Press, 2003), pp. 147–53.

35. Sajó, *Limiting Government,* p. 2.

36. See also the argument about the relation between the separation of powers and the rule of law at the end of Chapter 3.

37. See also the argument about the representational advantages of bicameralism in Chapter 4.

38. Cf. A. V. Dicey's account of separation of powers in his attempt to reconcile parliamentary sovereignty and the rule of law: Dicey, *Introduction to the Study of the Law of the Constitution,* pp. 268–73. That the legislature may not control what happens to an act once it passes into the hands of the courts is not just a method for preventing oppression (by ensuring that the legislators themselves are subject to the force of what they have enacted), though it is that; it is also a way of marking something about what has been done in the legislature. By virtue of the legislature's solemn decision, what has been produced comes to have the special status of *law;* it is not just another governmental measure. And its handling after it leaves the legislature is the tribute paid to that fact through institutional articulation.

39. For an excellent account of how constraints on political participation may have, in the long run, an affirmatively empowering and structuring effect, see Samuel Issacharoff, "Fragile Democracies," *Harvard Law Review,* 120 (2007), 1405.

40. The themes I have mentioned here are particularly prominent in the constitutional theory of Hannah Arendt; see Chapter 12.

41. I am thinking of Colonel Rainsborough's exclamation in 1647 at Putney: "[T]ruly I think that the poorest he that is in England has a life to lead as the greatest he; and therefore truly, sir, I think it's clear that every man that is to live under a government ought first by his own consent to put himself under that government." See "The Debates at the General Council of the Army, Putney, 29 October 1647," in Andrew Sharp (ed.), *The English Levellers* (Cambridge University Press, 1998), p. 103.

42. Robert A. Schapiro, "Polyphonic Federalism: State Constitutions in the Federal Courts," *California Law Review,* 87 (1999), 1415, at p. 1438.

43. Sandra Schultz Newman and Daniel Mark Isaacs, "Historical Overview of the Judicial Selection Process in the United States: Is the Electoral System in Pennsylvania Unjustified?" *Villanova Law Review,* 49 (2004), 1, at p. 16.

44. John Stuart Mill gives this impression at the beginning of *On Liberty,* pp. 2 and 15–16.

45. Ronald Dworkin, *Freedom's Law: The Moral Reading of the American Constitution* (Harvard University Press, 1996), p. 71.

46. I have criticized Dworkin's position in *Law and Disagreement,* ch. 13.

47. *Marbury v. Madison,* 5 U.S. 137 (1803), at p. 176.

48. See Locke, *Two Treatises,* pp. 329–30 and 354–56 (II, §§94 and 132–33); and Thomas Hobbes, *De Cive: The English Version,* ed. Howard Warrender (Oxford University Press, 1983), pp. 37 and 131ff.

49. See Bernard Manin, *The Principles of Representative Government* (Cambridge University Press, 1996), for the argument that republican and even representative ideas often involve something of an aristocratic celebration of political virtue.

50. Larry Alexander, "Constitutional Rules, Constitutional Standards, and Constitutional Settlement: *Marbury v. Madison* and the Case for Judicial Supremacy," *Constitutional Commentary,* 20 (2003), 369, at p. 373.

51. See Waldron, *Law and Disagreement,* pp. 255–81, for a critique of this precommitment idea. See also Jon Elster, *Ulysses Unbound: Studies in Rationality, Precommitment, and Constraints* (Cambridge University Press, 2000).

52. This was James Madison's approach to separation of powers in Hamilton, Madison, and Jay, *The Federalist Papers,* ed. Carey and McClellan, p. 268 (Number 51: Madison): "Ambition must be made to counteract ambition. The interest of the man must be connected with the constitutional rights of the place."

53. See Chapter 9.

54. I develop this argument further in Jeremy Waldron, "Judicial Power and Popular Sovereignty," in Mark Graber and Michael Perhac (eds.), *Marbury versus Madison: Documents and Commentary* (CQ Press, 2002), 181. The argument is based on principles enunciated by Emmanuel Joseph Sièyes, *What Is the Third Estate?* trans. M. Blondel (Frederick A. Prager, 1964).

55. See, e.g., Larry D. Kramer, *The People Themselves: Popular Constitutionalism and Judicial Review* (Oxford University Press, 2004); and Frank Michelman, "What (If Anything) Is Progressive-Liberal Democratic Constitutionalism?" *Widener Law Symposium,* 4 (1999), 181. See also Mark Tushnet, *Taking the Constitution Away from the Courts* (Princeton University Press, 2000).

3. SEPARATION OF POWERS AND THE RULE OF LAW

1. I discuss Montesquieu's formulations extensively in Section 6.

2. Eric Posner and Adrian Vermeule, in *The Executive Unbound: After the Madisonian Republic* (Oxford University Press, 2011), p. 208, speak of the separation of powers as "suffering through an enfeebled old age."

3. John Manning, "Separation of Powers as Ordinary Interpretation," *Harvard Law Review,* 124 (2011), 1939, at pp. 1944–45.

4. Ibid., p. 1944.

5. For example, Constitution of Indiana, Article II.1, and Constitution of Virginia, Article I.5. I say "at least textually" because, as one scholar has observed, recognition of separation of powers in the early state constitutions "'was verbal merely,' and that in practice it meant little more than a prohibition on plurality of office." See M. J. C. Vile, *Constitutionalism and the Separation of Powers* (Liberty Fund, 1998), p. 147, quoting Edward S. Corwin, "The Progress of Constitutional Theory between the Declaration of Independence and the Meeting of the Philadelphia Convention," *American Historical Review*, 30 (1925), 511, at p. 514.

6. I mean something along the lines of the analysis in Chapters 7 and 10 of Ronald Dworkin, *Law's Empire* (Harvard University Press, 1986), arguing that something is a legal principle if it figures in or follows from "the best constructive interpretation of a community's legal practice."

7. Manning, "Separation of Powers as Ordinary Interpretation," pp. 1950–58.

8. In Chapter 2, I discussed the many meanings of "constitutionalism."

9. And although Dicey argued that the rule of law stood alongside parliamentary sovereignty as one of two dominant features of English constitutionalism, he described it mostly as a "characteristic" of the constitution or "a special attribute of English institutions" rather than as one of its legal principles. A. V. Dicey, *Introduction to the Study of the Law of the Constitution* (Liberty Classics, 1982), pp. 107, 110, and 115. But compare ibid., p. 120, where Dicey *does* describe the rule of law as "a fundamental principle of the constitution."

10. Alexander Hamilton, James Madison, and John Jay, *The Federalist Papers,* ed. George W. Carey and James McClellan (Liberty Fund, 2001), pp. 249–50 (Number 47: Madison).

11. Ibid., p. 250.

12. See Madison's first "Helvidius" letter in Alexander Hamilton and James Madison, *The Pacificus-Helvidius Debates of 1793–1794* (Liberty Fund, 2006), p. 58.

13. It is possible that we should say about some instances of Principle 3 what I said about Principle 2: to identify, say, the Senate's role in ratifying treaties as a matter of checks and balances is to subscribe to a particular theory about why the Senate was given that power, and that theory may or may not be correct. For example, it may not be thought correct by one who believed—as Madison asserts in *The Pacificus-Helvidius Debates,* p. 59—that the Senate has this role simply because treaty-making is a form of lawmaking.

14. Vile, *Constitutionalism and the Separation of Powers*, p. 2.

15. Daryl Levinson and Richard Pildes, "Separation of Parties not Powers," *Harvard Law Review,* 119 (2006), 2311, at p. 2316.

16. Ibid., p. 2312.

17. Cf. Hannah Arendt, *On Revolution* (Viking Books, 1973), p. 152: "[T]he great and, in the long run, perhaps the greatest American innovation in politics as such was the consistent abolition of sovereignty within the body politic of the republic."

18. Vile, *Constitutionalism and the Separation of Powers,* pp. 68–69; cf. John Locke, *Two Treatises of Government,* ed. Peter Laslett (Cambridge University Press, 1988), pp. 366–67 (II, §§149–50).

19. Donald Elliott, "Why Our Separation of Powers Jurisprudence Is so Abysmal," *George Washington Law Review,* 57 (1989), p. 511.

20. Adrian Vermeule, "Second Opinions and Institutional Design," *Virginia Law Review,* 97 (2011), p. 1435.

21. Ibid., p. 1440.

22. Vile, *Constitutionalism and the Separation of Powers,* p. 11.

23. Ibid., p. 14. But having made the distinction of a pure theory of separation of powers, Vile spoils things a bit by adding immediately: "In this way each of the branches will be a check to the others and no single group of people will be able to control the machinery of the State." This seems to reintroduce a blurring between Principles 1, 2, and 3, just when we thought we were getting clear about the distinction between them. It is important to note, however, that Vile has in mind here only *negative* checks associated with the pure doctrine: "The pure doctrine as we have described it embodies what might be called a 'negative' approach to the checking of the power of the agencies of government. The mere existence of several autonomous decision-taking bodies with specific functions is considered to be a sufficient brake upon the concentration of power. Nothing more is needed. They do not actively exercise checks upon each other, for to do so would be to 'interfere' in the functions of another branch."

24. Vile, *Constitutionalism and the Separation of Powers,* p. 125, quoting *The Works of Jeremy Bentham,* Vol. 1, ed. John Bowring (William Tait, 1843), p. 123.

25. See Lon L. Fuller, *The Morality of Law,* second edition (Yale University Press, 1969), p. 162; Joseph Raz, "The Rule of Law and Its Virtue," in *The Authority of Law: Essays on Law and Morality,* second edition (Oxford University Press, 2009), 210, at p. 221; and Jeremy Waldron, "The Concept and the Rule of Law," *Georgia Law Review,* 43 (2008), 1, at p. 28.

26. The argument I am about to expound is not the "efficiency" justification, which Vile asserts as Locke's contribution when he says, in *Constitutionalism and the Separation of Powers,* p. 67:

> Locke argued that the legislative and executive powers should be placed in separate hands for the sake of efficiency, on the grounds of the division of labour. Laws which take only a short time to pass need "perpetual execution," and therefore there must be an executive always in being. The representative nature of the legislature renders it too large, and therefore too slow, for the execution of the law.

It is more a matter of principle than that. But Vile does also mention the argument I want to highlight (ibid., p. 68), citing Locke, *Two Treatises,* p. 364 (II, §143):

> Locke had that distrust both of Kings and of legislatures which made him unwilling to see power concentrated in the hands of either of them. For this reason, as well as for reasons of efficiency and convenience, he concluded that the legislative and executive powers should be in separate hands. "It may be too great a temptation to humane frailty, apt to grasp at Power, for the same Persons who have the power of making Laws, to have also in their hands the power to execute them, whereby they may exempt themselves from Obedience to the Laws they make, and suit the Law, both in its making and execution, to their own private advantage."

There could hardly be a clearer statement than this of the essence of the doctrine of the separation of powers.

27. Locke, *Two Treatises,* pp. 329–30 (II, §94).

28. Ibid., p. 364 (II, §143).

29. See F. A. Hayek, *The Constitution of Liberty* (University of Chicago Press, 1960), pp. 170–71.

30. Locke, *Two Treatises,* p. 364 (II, §143).

31. Pildes and Levinson, "Separation of Parties not Powers," p. 2344.

32. Locke, *Two Treatises,* p. 365 (II, §146).

33. Ibid., p. 366 (II, §§147–48).

34. Ibid., p. 366 (II, §148).

35. Ibid.

36. Thomas Hobbes, *Leviathan,* ed. Richard Tuck (Cambridge University Press, 1996), p. 127–28 (ch. 18). See also ibid., p. 225 (Ch. 29), where Hobbes maintains that "Powers divided mutually destroy each other."

37. Thomas Hobbes, *De Cive: The English Version,* ed. Howard Warrender (Oxford University Press, 1983), pp. 74–75 (VI. 9):

> [S]ince it . . . much more conduceth to Peace to prevent brawles from arising, then to appease them being risen; and that all controversies are bred from hence, that the opinions of men differ concerning Meum & Tuum, just and unjust, . . . good and evill, . . . and the like, which every man esteems according to his own judgement; it belongs to the same chiefe power to make some common Rules for all men, and to declare them publiquely, by which every man may know what may be called his, what anothers, what just, what unjust, what honest, what dishonest, what good, what evill, that is summarily, what is to be done, what to be avoyded in our common course of life. But those Rules and measures are usually called the civill Lawes, or the Lawes of the City, as being the Commands of him who hath the supreme power in the City. And the Civill Lawes (that we may define them) are nothing else but the commands of him who hath the chiefe authority in the City, for direction of the future actions of his Citizens.

38. Ibid., p. 74 (ch. VI.8).
39. Hobbes, *Leviathan,* p. 184 (ch. 26).
40. Compare also Jeremy Bentham, *Of Laws in General,* ed. H. L. A. Hart (Athlone Press, 1970), p. 153: "A Cadi comes by a baker's shop, and finds the bread short of weight: the baker is hanged in consequence. This, if it be part of the design that other bakers should take notice of it, is a sort of law forbidding the selling of bread short of weight under the pain of hanging." (It is left to Edmund Burke to argue, in the second day of his speech in opening the trial of Warren Hastings, that all this discourse rests on misapprehensions about the despotic and lawless character of Asian regimes: see Edmund Burke, "Speech in Opening" (Impeachment of Warren Hastings), in *The Works of Edmund Burke* (Little, Brown, 1866), Vol. 9, pp. 462ff., and "Speech in Reply," ibid., Vol. 11, pp. 204ff.
41. Montesquieu, *The Spirit of the Laws,* ed. Ann Cohler, Basia C. Miller, and Harold S. Stone (Cambridge University Press, 1989), p. 157 (Bk. XI, ch. 6).
42. Ibid., p. 74 (Bk. VI, ch. 2).
43. Cf. Max Weber's account of the futile call for straightforward social or ethical judging, as a protest against esoteric legalist technicality, in modern Europe: Max Weber, *Economy and Society,* ed. Guether Roth and Claus Wittich (University of California Press, 1978), pp. 882ff.
44. Vile, *Constitutionalism and the Separation of Powers,* pp. 89–90, notes the importance of the rule of law in Montesquieu's account of monarchy: "The idea of a separation of agencies and functions, in part at least, is implicit and explicit in his treatment of monarchy. The judges must be the depository of the laws; the monarch must never himself be a judge, for in this way the 'dependent intermediate powers' would be annihilated. The king's ministers ought not to sit as judges, because they would lack the necessary detachment and coolness requisite to a judge. There must

be many 'formalities' in the legal process in a monarchy in order to leave the defendant all possible means of making his defence, and the judges must conform to the law."

45. Montesquieu, *The Spirit of the Laws*, p. 75 (Bk. VI, ch. 2).

46. Vile, *Constitutionalism and the Separation of Powers*, p. 94.

47. Montesquieu, *The Spirit of the Laws*, p. 157 (Bk. XI, ch. 6).

48. In one other part of the book, ibid., p. 63 (Bk. V, ch. 14), Montesquieu alludes to the idea of checks and balances: "[O]ne must give one power a ballast, so to speak, to put it in a position to resist another."

49. Ibid., p. 157 (Bk. XI, ch. 6).

50. Ibid., p. 161 (Bk. XI, ch. 6).

51. See, e.g., Voltaire, *The ABC* (1768), in *Voltaire: Political Writings*, ed. David Williams (Cambridge University Press, 1994), p. 96: "I looked for a guide on a difficult road. I found a travelling companion who was hardly any better informed than I was. I found the spirit of the author, who has plenty, and rarely the spirit of the laws. He hops rather than walks."

52. Hamilton, Jay, and Madison, *The Federalist Papers*, ed. Carey and McClellan, pp. 251–52 (Number 47: Madison).

53. Ibid., p. 251 (Number 47: Madison).

54. Dicey, *Introduction to the Study of the Law of the Constitution*, p. 112.

55. See the discussion of "limited" government in Chapter 2.

56. Recall that Dicey used Voltaire's case to illustrate the first of his three principles of the rule of law (Dicey, *Introduction to the Study of the Law of the Constitution*, p. 110: "[N]o man is punishable or can be lawfully made to suffer in body or goods except for a distinct breach of law established in the ordinary manner before the ordinary Courts of the land").

57. Or, the general outlines of a normative strategy may be communicated to an agency that in turn develops rules that are communicated both to those who will be subject to them and to those charged with their administration. This does not make a difference to the general process of articulating an exercise of power into several stages, though it may make it much more difficult to map it onto the separate functions of government represented in the principle we are considering.

58. Ibid., p. 110.

59. See Lance Banning, *The Sacred Fire of Liberty: James Madison and the Founding of the Federal Republic* (Cornell University Press, 1995), p. 78; and James Liebman and Brandon Garrett, "Madisonian Equal Protection," *Columbia Law Review*, 104 (2004), 837, at p. 843: "[Madison's] overarching concern—what he called the most 'dreadful class of evils' besetting the new nation under the Articles of Confederation, . . . was the factious spirit in the states which chronically drove stable and interested majorities to enact unjust measures benefiting themselves while systematically neglecting or harming weaker groups and the public good."

60. See Section 6.

61. See, e.g., Jeffrey Kahn, "The Search for the Rule of Law in Russia," *Georgetown Journal of International Law*, 37 (2006), 353, at p. 385, citing, among others, Alexander Solzhenitsyn, *The Gulag Archipelago*, Vol. 3 (Harper and Row, 1974), p. 521: "In his mind's eye the judge can always see the shiny black visage of truth—the telephone in his chambers. This oracle will never fail you, as long as you do what it says."

62. *Liversidge v. Anderson*, [1942] AC 206, 244.

63. *Teague v. Lane*, 489 U.S. 288 (1989).

64. Lon Fuller, *The Morality of Law*, revised edition (Yale University Press, 1964), p. 176: "If these portents of what lies ahead can be trusted, then it is plain that we shall be faced with problems of institutional design unprecedented in scope and importance. It is inevitable that the legal profession will play a large role in solving these problems. The great danger is that we will unthinkingly carry over to new conditions traditional institutions and procedures that have already demonstrated their faults of design. As lawyers we have a natural inclination to 'judicialize' every function of government. Adjudication is a process with which we are familiar and which enables us to show to advantage our special talents. Yet we must face the plain truth that adjudication is an ineffective instrument for economic management and for governmental participation in the allocation of economic resources."

65. So this really illustrates an advantage of Manning's account in "Separation of Powers as Ordinary Interpretation." Once we see that separation of powers cannot be understood as a free-standing legal doctrine, we are free to explore its implications unentangled with other constitutional doctrines such as nondelegation. Whether Manning agrees with that is another matter. He is more interested, I think, in the *particular* separations that the constitution provides for (once the general principle is abandoned) rather than in ways in which the general principle can be conceived as an evaluative principle of political theory.

66. See Jeremy Waldron, *The Dignity of Legislation* (Cambridge University Press, 1999).

67. Posner and Vermeule, *The Executive Unbound*, p. 208.

68. Ibid., p. 19.

69. Ibid., p. 5.

4. BICAMERALISM AND THE SEPARATION OF POWERS

1. House of Lords Act (1999), section 1: "No-one shall be a member of the House of Lords by virtue of a hereditary peerage."

2. Constitutional Reform Act (2005).

3. Section 5 of the Bishoprics Act (1878) fixes the number of "Lords Spiritual" at twenty-six.

4. Life Peerages Act (1958), section 1: "(1) . . . Her Majesty shall have power by letters patent to confer on any person a peerage carrying right for life . . . (2) A peerage conferred under this section shall, during the of life of the person on whom it is conferred, entitle him (a) to rank as a baron under such style as may be appointed by the letters patent; and (b) . . . to receive writs of summons to attend the House of Lords and sit and vote therein accordingly—and shall expire on his death."

5. *Jeremy Bentham to his Fellow-Citizens of France, on Houses of Peers and Senates* (1830), XII §1 and XIII §8, available at http://oll.libertyfund.org/?option=com_staticxt&staticfile=show.php%3Ftitle=1925&chapter=116768&layout=html&Itemid=27.

6. Cf. Herman Bakvis, "Prime Minister and Cabinet in Canada: An Autocracy in Need of Reform?" *Journal of Canadian Studies,* 35 (2001), 60; and Paul Thomas, "An Upper House with Snow on the Roof and Frozen in Time: The Case of the Canadian Senate," in *Restraining Elective Dictatorship: The Upper House Solution,* ed. Nicholas Aroney, Scott Prasser, and J. R. Nethercote (University of Western Australia Press, 2008), p. 130.

7. For a good discussion, see Stephen Macedo, "Toward a More Democratic Congress? Our Imperfect Democratic Constitution: The Critics Examined," *Boston University Law Review,* 89 (2009), 609.

8. For a discussion, see Jeremy Waldron, *Parliamentary Recklessness: Why We Need to Legislate More Carefully* (Maxim Institute, New Zealand, 2008), available at http://www.maxim.org.nz/site/DefaultSite/filesystem/documents/Monograph%20web.pdf

9. Saul Levmore, "Bicameralism: When Are Two Decisions Better Than One?" *International Review of Law and Economics,* 12 (1992), 145, at p. 155, considers "the question of why, in the American Constitutional Convention and elsewhere, bicameralism was preferred over supermajoritarianism when either would seem to stop or stall legislation."

10. U.S. Constitution, Article II, §2. For a broad taxonomy of second-opinion mechanisms, see Adrian Vermeule, "Second Opinions and Institutional Design," *Virginia Law Review,* 97 (2011), p. 1435.

11. Bentham, *Houses of Peers and Senates,* III, §8.

12. Lewis Rockow, "Bentham on the Theory of Second Chambers," *American Political Science Review,* 22 (1928), 576, at p. 577.

13. Bentham himself observed at one stage that "I am straying into the path of garrulity—a tempting and seducing path to old age." See Bentham, *Houses of Peers and Senates,* XI, §5.

14. For an example, see ibid., III, §4: "Antecedently to all development in detail, one plain reason against [a second chamber] presents itself to a first glance. Of a chamber of deputies, in the character of a first chamber—that is to say, first in the order of importance—of a legislative body—principally, where not exclusively acting

as such—the utility, nay, the indispensable necessity, is recognised on all sides: the existence of this necessity therefore may be—it must be—taken for a postulate. But, that from the force and efficiency of this body, the existence of any other body—before which must be carried, ere the force of law be given to it, every proposed law—should not make deduction more or less considerable, is not possible: the time during which the measure continues in the second chamber before it is otherwise disposed of, is so much delay; and, even supposing adoption and consummation to be the ultimate result, in so much that an ultimate negative is not applied to it,—still delay, so long as it lasts, is a temporary negative: and, if the measure has any net benefit for its result, the value of the loss by the delay is in the exact proportion of the length of it."

15. Ibid., V, §§9 and 15; VI, §§7 and 32; and VII, §7.

16. Ibid., II, §5; and XI, §3.

17. As with these reflections on the late King George (I think he means the fourth of that name): "By cramming them with money, kings are . . . made fit for reigning. . . . By cramming, fowls are fitted for the table: true. . . . By that same process, when then will kings be fitted for this same seat? To the process of cramming, in the case of fowls, nature sets bounds. But, in the case of a king of England, or any of his creatures, where are the limits set by anything or anybody?" (ibid., V, §29).

18. Ibid., XII, §25.

19. Ibid. Apparently, "anility" means (according to the OED) "The state of being an old woman; old-womanishness; dotage, foolishness."

20. Ibid., VI, §36. See also ibid., VI, §26: "Of the matter of corruption in this shape (need it be said?) is composed, the motive, by which men are induced to do their utmost for the upholding of a form, system, and practice of government, on which the appellation of matchless constitution, in the endeavour of covering its deformity by a veil of unmerited laudation, is with such unblushing perseverance bestowed; the possessors and cravers of the matter of corruption in this shape, all the while bestowing upon themselves, and one another, the praise of disinterestedness, and so forth."

21. Ibid., XIII, §8.

22. Cf. David Lieberman, *The Province of Legislation Determined: Legal Theory in Eighteenth-Century Britain* (Cambridge University Press, 1989), pp. 217ff.

23. Bentham, *Houses of Peers and Senates,* III, §24.

24. The Sieyès pronouncement is cited by Nicholas Aroney, "Four Reasons for an Upper House: Representative Democracy, Public Deliberation, Legislative Outputs and Executive Accountability," *Adelaide Law Review,* 29 (2008), 205, at p. 213. But, in a footnote, Aroney adds: "Despite the fact that this line of reasoning is often attributed to Sieyès, there is reason to doubt whether he actually ever said (or even thought) anything like this."

25. Bentham, *Houses of Peers and Senates,* III, §6.

26. Ibid., III, §7.

27. Vermeule, "Second Opinions and Institutional Design," p. 1450.

28. Laurence Sterne, *The Life and Opinions of Tristram Shandy, Gentleman* (Wordsworth Editions, 1996), Vol. 6, ch. 17.

29. Sterne's narrator reports that Tristram Shandy's father was very much impressed by this and sought to emulate it in his own decision-making. The trouble was that Mr. Shandy Sr. was a teetotaler. We are told that:

> It was not till the seventh year of his marriage . . . that he hit upon an expedient which answered the purpose;—and that was, when any difficult and momentous point was to be settled in the family, which required great sobriety, and great spirit too, in its determination,—he fixed and set apart the first Sunday night in the month, and the Saturday night which immediately preceded it, to argue it over, in bed with my mother.

The narrator passes over in silence the exact difference in spirit of these two nights in what his father called "his beds of justice." But if you consider what used to be the rules upheld by the church for the conduct of married life on various days of the week, you will understand that he had found a method for successive and varied modes of deliberation so that, as Shandy puts it, "from the two different counsels taken in these two different humours, a middle [course] was generally found out which touched the point of wisdom as well, as if he had got drunk and sober a hundred times" (ibid., p. 292).

30. Publius Cornelius Tacitus, *Agricola and Germany,* trans. A. R. Birley (Oxford University Press, 1999), p. 49, quoted by Vermeule, "Second Opinions and Institutional Design," at p. 1451.

31. Walter Bagehot, *The English Constitution,* ed. Paul Smith (Cambridge University Press, 2001), p. 80.

32. See the discussion in Jeremy Waldron, "Democracy," in *Oxford Handbook of Political Philosophy*, ed. David Estlund (Oxford University Press, 2012), 187, at pp. 188–91.

33. Aroney, "Four Reasons for an Upper House," at p. 218.

34. Ibid., pp. 219–20: "Rather than giving us reasons to reject upper houses and bicameralism, the many 'peoples' with which we identify ourselves suggests that single houses of Parliament are going to struggle to represent us in our pluralities and diversities. Proportional voting systems can certainly go a long way towards remedying this problem, at least to the extent that they reproduce more accurately the many varied shades of opinion and commitment within our electorates. However, consolidating representation into one house within which majority rule prevails means that even in complicated proportional and mixed electoral systems, there is an assumption that there remains a unitary 'will of the people' which it is the task of the electoral and parliamentary system to consolidate and express."

35. Meg Russell, "Reform of the House of Lords: Lessons for Bicameralism," in *Restraining Elective Dictatorship,* ed. Aroney et al., 119, at p. 127.

36. Vernon Bogdanor, *The New British Constitution* (Hart Publishing, 2009), p. 160.

37. Ibid., p. 166.

38. Consider this observation by Chief Justice Earl Warren in the American case of *Reynolds v. Sims,* 377 U.S. 533, 576–77 (1964) about cases where, as he puts it, "the predominant basis of representation in the two . . . legislative bodies is required to be the same—population."

> Simply because the controlling criterion for apportioning representation is required to be the same in both houses does not mean that there will be no differences in the composition and complexion of the two bodies. . . . One body could be composed of single-member districts while the other could have at least some multimember districts. The length of terms of the legislators in the separate bodies could differ. The numerical size of the two bodies could be made to differ . . . and the geographical size of districts from which legislators are elected could also be made to differ. . . . [A]pportionment in one house could be arranged so as to balance off minor inequities in the representation of certain areas in the other house. . . . [T]hese and other factors could be, and are presently in many States, utilized to engender differing complexions and collective attitudes in the two bodies of a state legislature, although both are apportioned substantially on a population basis.

39. Bagehot, *The English Constitution,* p. 81. Bagehot adds, "it is not one house, so to say, but a set of houses" (ibid.).

40. John Stuart Mill, *Considerations on Representative Government* (Prometheus Books, 1991), p. 250.

41. Ibid., p. 385.

42. Ibid.

43. John Locke, *Two Treatises of Government,* ed. Peter Laslett (Cambridge University Press, 1988), pp. 365–66 (II, §§145–48).

44. For Madison on "the celebrated Montesquieu" and his view of the British constitution, see Alexander Hamilton, John Jay, and James Madison, *The Federalist Papers,* ed. George W. Carey and James McClellan (Liberty Fund, 2001), p. 250 (Number 47: Madison). For Madison on the requirements for separation of powers, see also ibid., pp. 267–69 (Number 51: Madison). For Montesquieu's own views on the constitution of England, see Montesquieu, *The Spirit of the Laws,* ed. Anne Cohler et al. (Cambridge University Press, 1989), pp. 156–66 (Bk. XI, ch. 6).

45. Hamilton, Jay, and Madison, *The Federalist Papers,* ed. Carey and McClellan, p. 251 (Number 47: Madison).

46. Bagehot, *The English Constitution,* p. 8, cited by Aroney, "Four Reasons for an Upper House," pp. 220–21.

47. Vernon Bogdanor, *Politics and the Constitution: Essays on British Government* (Dartmouth Publishing, 1996), p. 258.

48. For a proposal radically opposed to this, see Jeremy Mitchell and Ann Davies, *Reforming the Lords* (IPPR, 1993), p. 53, arguing that each department should have a minister from each house.

49. Hamilton, Madison, and Jay, *The Federalist Papers,* ed. Carey and McClellan, p. 321 (Number 62: Madison).

50. Bagehot, *The English Constitution,* pp. 80–81.

51. See Aroney, "Four Reasons for an Upper House."

52. Anthony King, *The British Constitution* (Oxford University Press, 2007), p. 310.

53. Some will say that, inasmuch as we can distinguish the House of Commons from the cabinet that dominates it, the function of the Commons, too, is primarily a matter of scrutiny. [See Adam Tomkins, "What Is Parliament for?" in *Public Law in a Multi-Layered Constitution,* ed. Nicholas Bamforth and Peter Leyland (Hart Publishing, 2003) p. 53.] My point, however, is that scrutiny under the whip hand of the government and in the occasional interstices of its dominance is different from scrutiny in a chamber whose members are genuinely independent of the executive.

54. John Locke, *A Letter Concerning Toleration,* ed. Patrick Romanell (Prentice-Hall, 1950), p. 50.

55. The Appellate Jurisdiction Act (1876) provided that a minimum of three Law Lords must be present to hear any appeal to "her Majesty the Queen in her Court of Parliament" but did not appear to prohibit Lords who were not Law Lords from participating.

56. Bentham, *On Houses of Peers and Senates,* X, §7.

57. See Chapter 9.

58. Jeremy Waldron, "Compared to What? Judicial Activism and New Zealand's Parliament," *New Zealand Law Journal,* December 2005, p. 442.

59. Aisling Reidy and Meg Russell, *Second Chambers as Constitutional Guardians and Protectors of Human Rights* (UCL Constitution Unit, 1999), p. 5 and passim.

60. Dawn Oliver, *Constitutional Reform in the United Kingdom* (Oxford University Press, 2003), p. 201.

61. Bogdanor, *Politics and the Constitution,* p. 247.

62. Consider the relevant section of the 2012 draft bill: "Clause 2: (1) Nothing in the provisions of this Act about the membership of the House of Lords, or in any other provision of this Act . . . (b) affects the primacy of the House of Commons. . . ."

63. Anthony King, *The British Constitution* (Oxford University Press, 2007), p. 2.

64. Parliament Act (1911), Preamble.

65. Bogdanor, *The New British Constitution,* pp. 154–55.

66. Dawn Oliver, "Reforming the United Kingdom Parliament," in *The Changing Constitution*, seventh edition, ed. Jeffrey Jowell and Dawn Oliver (Oxford University Press, 2011), pp. 169–70. Consider also D. Shell, "The Future of the Second Chamber," *Parliamentary Affairs*, 57 (2004), 852, at p. 865: "To go on talking about the need to maintain the supremacy of the Commons . . . is a mistake. It is naïve to go on arguing that British democracy depends on some form of unambiguous accountability, whereby the electorate know exactly which set of politicians to hold accountable for what, because only a single party wields power through a House of Commons that wields untrammelled supremacy. Doing so might flatter MPs; . . . but it is no longer in accord with reality. British democracy is more complicated in both its form and expression."

67. Montesquieu, *The Spirit of the Laws*, p. 161 (Bk. 11, ch. 6).

68. James Harrington, *The Commonwealth of Oceana and A System of Politics*, ed. J. G. A. Pocock (Cambridge University Press, 1992), p. 22.

69. Ibid., p. 24.

70. Ibid.

71. Ibid., p. 22.

72. David Hume, "Idea of a Perfect Commonwealth," in *Essays: Moral, Political, and Literary* (Liberty Classics, 1985), pp. 519–20 (Pt II, essay xvi).

73. As Anthony King remarks in *The British Constitution*, p. 311, "[T]hey would say that, wouldn't they?"

74. Considering the possibility of a chamber largely appointed on a party basis (i.e., on the nomination of parties), Dawn Oliver observes in *Constitutional Reform in the United Kingdom*, p. 200, that this would give "immense patronage and power to the parties, which could be open to abuse, for instance in rewarding party donors."

75. Harrington, *Oceana*, p. 23: "Twenty men, if they be not all idiots . . . can never come so together, but there will be such difference in them that about a third will be wiser, or at least less foolish, than all the rest. These upon acquaintance, though it be but small, will be discovered and . . . lead the herd; for while the six, discoursing and arguing one with another, show the eminence of their parts, the fourteen discover things that they never thought on, or are cleared in divers truths which had formerly perplexed them; wherefore in matter of common concernment, difficulty or danger, they hang upon their lips as children upon their fathers. . . . Wherefore this can be no other than a natural aristocracy diffused by God throughout the whole body of mankind to this end and purpose."

76. Or consider the suggestion of F. A. Hayek in *Law, Legislation and Liberty*, Vol. III: *The Political Order of a Free People* (University of Chicago Press, 1979), p. 113, that one might change the character of one representative chamber by restricting both its membership and its electorate to persons over forty-five years of age, while the other chamber was organized in a way that would be representative of all adults.

77. I use this phrase in a way that is slightly different from Kenneth Shepsle, "Congress Is a 'They,' not an 'It': Legislative Intent as Oxymoron," *International Review of Law and Economics*, 12 (1992), 239. In that article, Shepsle is interested mainly in the plurality of legislators; I am interested in the plurality of chambers.

78. I think this is a major function of John Locke's work in the second half of his *Second Treatise*—to disaggregate and analyze the different powers traditionally assigned to the Crown, to identify the limits on each one, and to make sure that the Crown does not escape these limits by blurring the public's understanding of its various functions. See Locke, *Two Treatises,* pp. 350–428 (II, §§123–243).

79. Alexander Hamilton and James Madison, *The Pacificus-Helvidius Debates of 1793–1794: Toward the Completion of the American Founding,* ed. Morton Frisch (Liberty Fund, 2007).

5. THE PRINCIPLE OF LOYAL OPPOSITION

1. Joseph Schumpeter, *Capitalism, Socialism, and Democracy* (George Allen & Unwin, 1976), p. 269.

2. Hannah Arendt, *On Revolution* (Penguin Books, 1973), p. 175.

3. John Rawls, *Political Liberalism* (Columbia University Press, 1996), p. 58.

4. See, e.g., Jeremy Waldron, *Law and Disagreement* (Oxford University Press, 1999).

5. Nancy Rosenblum, *On the Side of the Angels: An Appreciation of Parties and Partisanship* (Princeton University Press, 2008), p. 363, notes that "the system of regulated rivalry . . . means that unlike minorities in other arenas of majority decision making, partisans do not see minority status as irreversible. In other social and political contexts, the term of power is not periodic and fixed by rules; the conflict is not iterative; the future may disappear from view." But, she goes on, in ordinary politics, "[p]artisans do not secede or revolt, go underground or withdraw in defeat. 'Elections are not followed by waves of suicide'" (quoting E. E. Schattschneider).

6. Jean-Jacques Rousseau, *Social Contract,* trans. Maurice Cranston (Penguin Books, 1968), p. 141 (Bk. III, ch. 15). Consider also the following comment on American democracy in Walter Bagehot, *The English Constitution,* ed. Paul Smith (Cambridge University Press, 2001), p. 15: "[U]nder a presidential government a nation has, except at the electing moment, no influence; it has not the ballot box before it; its virtue is gone, and it must wait till its instant of despotism again returns."

7. Alexis de Tocqueville, *Democracy in America* (Alfred A. Knopf, 1994), p. 247 (Vol. I, ch. 14).

8. Aristotle, *The Politics,* trans. T. A. Sinclair (Penguin Books, 1962), p. 131 (Bk. III, ch. 13).

9. Ibid., p. 115 (Bk. III, ch. 6).

10. Ibid., pp. 109 and 134 (Bk. III, chs. 4 and 14).

11. Edmund Burke, *Letter to the Sheriffs of Bristol,* as quoted by George Anastaplo, "Loyal Opposition in a Modern Democracy," 35 *Loyola U Chicago Law Journal* 1009 (2004), at p. 1014. Anastaplo added: "It does take experience and discipline on the part of a people not to regard conscientious criticism as really subversive (ibid., p. 1015).

12. And actually the same is true of voting: we reduce our concern about wasted votes by coordinating our voting behavior with that of large numbers of like-minded people. For a helpful discussion, see Richard Tuck, *Free Riding* (Harvard University Press, 2008), pp. 30ff.

13. Rosenblum, *On the Side of the Angels,* p. 11: "From the standpoint of what I call 'holism,' all social and political groups threaten the unity and integrity of political order."

14. Ibid., p. 105.

15. Ibid., p. 38.

16. Ibid., p. 121.

17. Nevil Johnson, "Opposition in British Political System," *Government & Opposition,* 32 (1997), 487.

18. For a survey, see Dean E. McHenry, "Formal Recognition of the Leader of the Opposition in Parliaments of the British Commonwealth," *Political Science Quarterly,* 69 (1954), 438.

19. Ministers of the Crown Act (1937).

20. When it was instituted, the salary amount was the same as that for the minister of pensions, "much less than those of ministers usually of Cabinet rank, but more than those of junior ministers." (See McHenry, "Formal Recognition of the Leader of the Opposition," p. 440.)

21. One MP said, for example, that "[t]he function of an Opposition is to gain recognition from the electors of the country and to force it from the Government, not to receive it from the Government as a gift"—Sir Archibald Sinclair (Liberal) in the House of Commons, debating the 1937 measure (quoted from *Hansard* by McHenry, "Formal Recognition of the Leader of the Opposition," p. 441).

22. Viscount Hailsham in the House of Lords, debating the 1937 measure, quoted from *Hansard* by McHenry, "Formal Recognition of the Leader of the Opposition," p. 440.

23. Ivor Jennings, *Parliament,* second edition (Cambridge University Press, 1957), p. 82.

24. McHenry, "Formal Recognition of the Leader of the Opposition," p. 443. This was followed by a similar decision in Australia in 1920, which also included the Senate opposition leader in the stipendiary arrangement and (since 1947) some payment to the leadership of smaller parties (ibid., p. 448). There was no payment for the Leader of Opposition in New Zealand until 1951.

25. Johnson, "Opposition in the British Political System," p. 487, citing A. L. Lowell, *The Government of England* (Macmillan, 1924), Vol. 1, p. 451.

26. See Allen Potter, "Great Britain: Opposition with a Capital O," in *Political Oppositions in Western Democracies*, ed. Robert Dahl (Yale University Press, 1966), 3, at pp. 13–14.

27. There is a good account in Johnson, "Opposition in the British Political System."

28. This was formalized in the United Kingdom around 1955. R. M. Punnett, *Front-Bench Opposition: The Role of the Leader of the Opposition, the Shadow Cabinet and the Shadow Government in British Politics* (St. Martin's Press, 1973), as quoted in a review by Dell G. Hitchner in *Journal of Politics*, 37 (1975), 611, observes that as late as the close of the nineteenth century, the function was still left informally and primarily "to the tendency of many ex-Ministers when in opposition to concern themselves particularly with the affairs of their old departments to which they hoped to be appointed in the future." See also Jorgen S. Rasmussen's review of Punnett, *Front-Bench Opposition*, in *American Political Science Review*, 69 (1975), 1499.

29. Rasmussen's review of Punnett, *Front-Bench Opposition*. Also, those who attain cabinet office in a government will usually have had this as part of their training. As Ivor Jennings points out in *Cabinet Government*, third edition (Cambridge University Press, 1959), pp. 213–14: "The Cabinet consists of party leaders with parliamentary experience. For the most part, they will have borne the burden of opposition, itself a training for government."

30. Bagehot, *The English Constitution*, p. 125; and Jennings, *Cabinet Government*, p. 439. See also Jennings's comment in *Cabinet Government*, p. 16: "The Opposition is at once the alternative to the Government and a focus for the discontent of the people. Its function is almost as important as that of the Government. If there be no Opposition there is no democracy. 'Her Majesty's Opposition' is no idle phrase. Her Majesty needs an Opposition as well as a Government."

31. See the striking observation by Nancy Rosenblum, *On the Side of the Angels*, p. 132, on the lack of party organization and opposition parties in the Confederate legislature in the 1860s, making that a quite dysfunctional body. Rosenblum, *On the Side of the Angels*, p. 132, also quotes G. W. F. Hegel as follows: "Whoever has reflected a little on the nature of an Assembly of Estates . . . cannot fail to see that without an opposition such an assembly is without outer and inner life. It is precisely this antagonism within it that forms its essence and justification, and it is only when it has engendered an opposition within itself that it is properly constituted."

32. Cf. Jennings, *Cabinet Government*, p. 464: "The apparent absurdity that the Opposition asks for parliamentary time to be set aside by the Government in order that the Opposition may censure the Government, or that the Government is asked to move a vote of supplies for the Ministry of Labour in order that the Opposition

may attack the Minister of Labour is not an absurdity at all. It is the recognition by both sides of the House that the Government governs openly and honestly and that it is prepared to meet criticism not by secret police and concentration camps but by rational argument."

33. As quoted in Potter, "Great Britain: Opposition with a Capital O," pp. 14–15. See also Jennings, *Parliament,* pp. 83–84: "The Leader of the Opposition . . . watches for encroachments on the rights of minorities. . . . He must be familiar with all the tricks of skilled parliamentarians and all the opportunities of the rules of the House."

34. This language is taken from a Web page of the Parliamentary education service that appears no longer exists.

35. Jennings, *Parliament,* p. 83.

36. Daniel Defoe, as quoted by Rosenblum, *On the Side of the Angels,* p. 13: "The Parties who are Out, are always a Curb, and a Bridle to those which are In."

37. McHenry, "Formal Recognition of the Leader of the Opposition," p. 439.

38. Johnson, "Opposition in the British Political System," pp. 509–10.

39. See Potter, "Great Britain: Opposition with a Capital O," p. 6: "The development of opposition in Parliament was essentially from an opposition to particular men or measures to an opposition offering an alternative government."

40. Jennings, *Parliament,* p. 83.

41. Ibid., p. 79. Potter, "Great Britain: Opposition with a Capital O," p. 14, puts it this way: "More and more, the Leader of the Opposition is treated in effect as Her Majesty's alternative prime minister, in public ceremonies and in private conversations with the Prime Minister on confidential matters."

42. Anastaplo, "Loyal Opposition in a Modern Democracy," p. 1013.

43. Margaret Canovan, *The Political Thought of Hannah Arendt* (Methuen, 1977), p. 35.

44. Campion, as quoted in Potter, "Great Britain: Opposition with a Capital O," p. 16. Rosenblum, *On the Side of the Angels,* p. 227, observes that members of opposition parties "are less anxious to overthrow their rivals than to preserve the system which, in due course, and by the connivance of those rivals, will bring to them also the opportunities and emoluments of office."

45. Jennings, *Parliament,* p. 170. See also Bagehot, *The English Constitution,* p. 126: "An Opposition, on coming into power, is often like a speculative merchant whose bills become due."

46. Jennings, *Parliament,* p. 83.

47. Ibid.

48. Rosenblum, *On the Side of the Angels,* p. 12.

49. *The London Standard,* December 20, 1897, available at http://query.nytimes.com/gst/abstract.html?res=F10E16FE3B5416738DDDA90A94DA415B8785F0D3 (last accessed April 4, 2014).

50. Johnson, "Opposition in the British Political System," pp. 509–10.

51. See http://www.colbertnation.com/the-colbert-report-videos/218486/february-10–2009/the-word—-loyal-opposition (last accessed April 4, 2014).

52. Anastaplo, "Loyal Opposition in a Modern Democracy," p. 1014.

53. Edmund Burke, "Letter to the Sheriffs of Bristol," in Edmund Burke, *On Empire, Liberty, and Reform: Speeches and Letters,* ed. David Bromwich (Yale University Press, 2000), 135, at p. 180.

54. See, e.g., Ann Coulter, *Demonic: How the Liberal Mob is Endangering America* (Crown Forum, 2011).

55. For further discussion, see Jeremy Waldron, "Civility and Formality," in *Civility, Legality, and Justice in America,* ed. Austin Sarat (Cambridge University Press, 2014), 46.

56. Russell Muirhead and Nancy Rosenblum, "Political Liberalism vs. the Great Game of Politics: The Politics of Political Liberalism," *Perspectives on Politics,* 4 (2006), 99, speak of "the view that opponents are reasonable rivals not enemies to be destroyed."

57. Rosenblum, *On the Side of the Angels,* p. 121.

58. Albert Venn Dicey, *Introduction to the Study of the Law of the Constitution* (Liberty Classics, 1982), p. 107.

59. Vernon Bogdanor, *The New British Constitution* (Hart Publishing, 2009).

60. Ludger Helms, "Five Ways of Institutionalizing Political Opposition: Lessons from the Advanced Democracies," *Government and Opposition,* 39 (2004), 22.

61. Potter, "Great Britain: Opposition with a Capital O," p. 3.

62. Jennings, *Cabinet Government,* p. 16: "If there be no Opposition there is no democracy."

63. Ian Shapiro, "Review: Democratic Innovation: South Africa in Comparative Context," *World Politics,* 46 (1993), 121, considers "that unlike democratic systems that evolved gradually out of semiconstitutional monarchies, in transitions from authoritarianism there is no opportunity for counterélites, the seeds of a loyal opposition, to emerge during the predemocratic order."

64. Adam Przeworski, "Minimalist Conception of Democracy: A Defense," in *The Democracy Sourcebook,* ed. Robert Dahl et al. (MIT Press, 2003), 12, at p. 15.

65. David J. Siemers, *Ratifying the Republic: Antifederalists and Federalists in Constitutional Time* (Stanford University Press, 2004), pp. 219–22.

66. Anastaplo, "Loyal Opposition in a Modern Democracy," p. 1010: "Although they may have been excluded from the national executive up to that point, they may themselves have been in control of the national legislature or in control of one or more branches of State governments—with loyal oppositions of their own to deal with."

67. Nelson Polsby, "Political Opposition in the United States," *Government and Opposition,* 32 (1997), 511.

68. Ibid., p. 517.

69. See Daryl Levinson and Richard Pildes, "Separation of Parties, Not Powers," *Harvard Law Review,* 119 (2006), 2312.

70. Polsby, "Political Opposition in the United States," p. 513.

71. Of course, many judges would be horrified by the suggestion that they are simply the creatures of party, or that their oppositional role, such as it is, is defined by their party status compared with that of the occupiers of some other center of power. They may be part of the loyal opposition nonetheless, involving not only minority dissenting opposition to a perceived political majority on the court but also institutional opposition such as between the Court and the Congress or the presidency.

72. Polsby, "Political Opposition in the United States," p. 513. Actually, Polsby's complete phrase is: "forms of opposition . . . embedded in the routines of American government as a *natural* consequence of the constitutional necessity for checks and balances that require of actors who come to office by uncoordinated means coordination with one another in the conduct of ordinary business."

73. See also the discussion in Chapter 3.

74. For an excellent discussion, see David Fontana, "Government in Opposition," *Yale Law Journal,* 119 (2009), 548.

75. See Ronald Dworkin, *Law's Empire* (Harvard University Press, 1986), pp. 208–15 and 266–75; and Waldron, *Law and Disagreement,* pp. 188–89.

76. See Potter, "Great Britain: Opposition with a Capital O," p. 15.

77. Lord Chalfont in the House of Lords, *Hansard,* December 18, 1953.

78. Sir Arthur Baxter, Prolongation of Parliament Bill, House of Commons, *Hansard,* October 26, 1943.

79. Anastaplo, "Loyal Opposition in a Modern Democracy," p. 1020.

80. For example, the Liberal Democratic Party of Germany in the German Democratic Republic from 1946 to 1990 and the United People's Party in Poland from1948 to 1989.

81. *The London Standard,* December 20, 1897.

82. Johnson, "Opposition in the British Political System," p. 488.

83. Lord Bruce, House of Lords, Address in Reply, *Hansard,* May 16, 1979.

84. Bagehot, *The English Constitution,* p. 25. Indeed, Bagehot describes ways in which government and opposition sometimes work together to suppress such criticism by radical members.

85. Jennings, *Cabinet Government,* p. 465.

86. Cf. Edmund Burke, "Observations on the Conduct of the Minority," in *The Works of the Right Honourable Edmund Burke,* Vol. 4 (John West and Q. C. Greenleaf, 1804), p. 144: "The legitimate and sure mode of communication between this nation and foreign powers is rendered uncertain, precarious, and treacherous, by being divided into two channels,—one with the government, one with

the head of a party in opposition to that government; by which means the foreign powers can never be assured of the real authority or validity of any public transaction whatsoever."

87. Potter, "Great Britain: Opposition with a Capital O," pp. 14–15.

88. Ibid., p. 15.

89. This suggestion is made in Anastaplo, "Loyal Opposition in a Modern Democracy," p. 1013: "Their opposition is not to the Monarch, but rather to the Government. "

90. Jennings, *Cabinet Government,* pp. 363–64. See also Potter, "Great Britain: Opposition with a Capital O," p. 7.

91. Jennings, *Cabinet Government,* p. 354.

92. Fontana, "Government in Opposition," p. 599.

93. Ibid., p. 600.

94. This may be postulated also for the United Kingdom. Potter, "Great Britain: Opposition with a Capital O," p. 16, says that the Opposition must behave "so as not to call into question the structure of constitutional conventions and understandings regulating their relationship."

95. For example, William Lloyd Garrison, Letter to Rev. Samuel J. May, July 17, 1845, in Walter M. Merrill (ed.), *The Letters of William Lloyd Garrison,* Vol. 3 (Harvard University Press, 1973), p. 303.

96. Rosenblum, *On the Side of the Angels,* p. 125.

97. Rawls, *Political Liberalism,* pp. 227–30.

98. John Rawls, *Justice as Fairness: A Briefer Restatement* (Harvard University Press, 2001), p. 49.

99. Rawls, *Political Liberalism,* pp. 227–28.

100. Ibid., p. 214: "[T]he limits imposed by public reason do not apply to all political questions but only to those involving what we may call 'constitutional essentials.'"

101. Rawls, *Political Liberalism,* p. xlix.

102. In other words, Rawls seems to think that constitutional elements are not up for grabs: "[I]t is vital that the structure of government be changed only as experience shows it to be required by political justice or the general good, and not as prompted by the political advantage of one party or group that may at the moment have the upper hand. Frequent controversy over the structure of government, . . . when the changes proposed tend to favor some parties over others, raises the stakes of politics and may lead to distrust and turmoil that undermines constitutional government" (ibid., p. 228).

103. For a philosopher's view of constitutional consensus, see Kurt Baier, "Justice and the Aims of Political Philosophy," *Ethics,* 99 (1987), 771.

104. See Rawls, *Political Liberalism,* pp. 54–58; and Waldron, *Law and Disagreement,* pp. 151–52. See also the text accompanying notes 3 and 4 in this chapter.

105. Rawls, *Political Liberalism,* p. 407: "I would have . . . objections deriving (in my case) from the two principles of justice to our present constitution and society's basic structure as a system of social cooperation. To mention three: the present system woefully fails in public financing for political elections, leading to a grave imbalance in fair political liberties; it allows a widely disparate distribution of income and wealth that seriously undermines fair opportunities in education and employment, all of which undermine economic and social equality; and absent also are provisions for important constitutional essentials such as health care for many who are uninsured."

106. Rawls has acknowledged that, as things stand, the United States cannot be regarded as a well-ordered society. See John Rawls, "Kantian Constructivism in Moral Theory," in John Rawls, *Collected Papers,* ed. Samuel Freeman (Harvard University Press, 1999), p. 355.

107. Fontana, "Government in Opposition," p. 598.

108. As quoted in Potter, "Great Britain: Opposition with a Capital O," p. 16.

109. *Bush v. Gore,* 531 U.S. 98 (2000).

110. See Bruce Ackerman, *We the People,* Vol. 1: *Foundations* (Harvard University Press, 1993); and Bruce Ackerman, *We the People,* Vol. 2: *Transformations* (Harvard University Press, 2000).

111. See Harriet Sherwood, "Israel Proposes Jewish State Loyalty Oath for New Citizens," *The Guardian,* October 10, 2010.

112. Earl of Lauderdale, House of Lords, *Hansard,* January 14, 1976.

113. Otto Kirchheimer, "Germany: The Vanishing Opposition," in Dahl, *Political Opposition,* p. 237.

114. Similarly, Fontana, "Government in Opposition," p. 598, discusses what he calls "the Weimar Problem": "Hitler's Nazi Party, when still a minority party (but a part of the majority coalition), used the powers granted to several ministries to eliminate opposition and eventually repeal the entire Weimar Constitution itself. We might worry less about these destabilizing parties and this 'Weimar Problem' in stable democracies. . . . In stable democracies, we can talk about the 'loyal' opposition. . . . Parties that might be seen as ideologically extreme are still sympathetic enough to the basic goals of democratic systems that they can be incorporated into governing coalitions. . . . This, therefore, is more a concern about fragile democracies, and whether government in opposition rules undermine the core stability of these new democracies."

115. Kirchheimer, "Germany: The Vanishing Opposition," pp. 238–39.

116. Thus, I follow Giovanni Satori in thinking that the conditions for responsible political competition are more likely to be fostered by this openness than by insistence on an *ex ante* loyalty test. Sartori writes in *Parties and Party System: A Framework for Analysis* (Cambridge University Press, 1976), p. 192: "It should not be taken for granted . . . that twopartyism presupposes a set of favorable conditions—cultural homogeneity, consensus on fundamentals, and the like. If one reviews the

development of the two party countries historically, it appears that twopartyism has largely nurtured and molded such favorable conditions."

117. Otto Kirchheimer, "The Waning of Opposition in Parliamentary Regimes," in his collection *Politics, Law, and Social Change: Selected Essays,* ed. Frederic Burin and Kurt Schell (Columbia University Press, 1969), p. 292: "Political opposition is an eternal paradox. It postulates the principle that impediments to political action may be wholesome and are therefore to be protected."

118. Helms, "Five Ways of Institutionalizing Political Opposition," p. 22.

119. George Kateb, *The Inner Ocean: Individualism and Democratic Culture* (Cornell University Press, 1992), p. 37 (cited in Rosenblum, *On the Side of the Angels,* p. 539).

120. Rosenblum, *On the Side of the Angels,* p. 363.

6. REPRESENTATIVE LAWMAKING

1. See Chapter 9.

2. John Austin, *Lectures on Jurisprudence,* fifth edition, ed. R. Campbell (John Murray, 1885), pp. 266–67 and 315.

3. As I said in Jeremy Waldron, *Law and Disagreement* (Oxford University Press, 1999), pp. 28–29: "Political scientists remind us, correctly, that law-making is just one of the functions performed by the institutions we call legislatures, and, from the point of view of political power, not necessarily the most important. A political scientist's analysis of law-making behavior in legislatures is likely to be continuous with his analysis of other functions performed by these bodies—functions such as the mobilization of support for the executive (in the U.K. the actual election of the executive), the venting of grievances, the discussion of national policy, the processes of budgetary negotiation, the ratification of appointments, and so on. From an empirical point of view, it may be impossible to predict how a given set of legislators will behave in sessions devoted specifically to law-making without understanding what is going on between them (and between them and their constituents and various interest groups) in other 'legislative' contexts that really have nothing to do with that task. (Legislator A may promise to support B's bill, but only in return, say, for B's support in blocking a judicial appointment.) This is bound to contrast with the jurisprudential point of view, which regards law-making as an activity whose character and significance are *sui generis.*"

4. Perhaps I should qualify that. We vote for legislators for all sorts of reasons, not necessarily for their lawmaking role. British voters, for example, vote for legislators of one party rather than another because, in a Westminster-style system, that is the only way they can affect the choice of the executive (of the prime minister and his or her cabinet).

5. See Chapter 8.

6. Rawls, *Political Liberalism* (Columbia University Press, 1993), pp. 66ff.

7. What follows is adapted from Jeremy Waldron, "Legislation by Assembly," in *Judicial Power, Democracy, and Legal Positivism,* ed. Tom Campbell and Jeff Goldsworthy (Ashgate, 2001), 25.

8. But see Andrew Burrows, "Numbers Sitting in the Supreme Court," *Law Quarterly Review,* 129 (2013), 305.

9. For this distinction, see Walter Bagehot, *The English Constitution,* ed. Paul Smith (Cambridge University Press, 2001), pp. 5 and 94.

10. The Chinese legislature (the National People's Congress) has almost 3,000 members, but I doubt that real legislative power is distributed equally in that assembly.

11. This was the title of one of the panels at the conference at Boston University Law School at which this chapter was originally presented.

12. Niccolò Machiavelli, *Discourses on Livy,* ed. Nathan Tarcov and Harvey Mansfield (University of Chicago Press, 1996), p. 16 (Bk. I, ch. iv).

13. Marquis de Condorcet, "Essay on the Application of Mathematics to the Theory of Decision-Making," in *Condorcet: Selected Writings,* ed. Keith Michael Baker (Bobbs-Merrill, 1976), 33, at pp. 48–56.

14. Ibid., 49.

15. See also the discussion of the Condorcet effect in Chapter 10.

16. Aristotle, *The Politics,* in *Aristotle: The Politics and the Constitution of Athens,* ed. Stephen Everson (Cambridge University Press, 1996), p. 76 (Bk. III, ch. 11, 1281a43–69).

17. Jean-Jacques Rousseau, *The Social Contract,* trans. Maurice Cranston (Penguin Books, 1968), p. 141 (Bk. III, ch. 15): "Sovereignty cannot be represented; . . . its essence is the general will, and will cannot be represented. . . . Any law which the people have not ratified in person is void; it is not law at all." But many of Rousseau's near-contemporaries in the French radical position did not accept this; see, for example, Emmanuel Joseph Sieyès, "What Is the Third Estate?" in *Sieyès: Political Writings,* ed. Michael Sonenscher (Hackett Publishing, 2003), p. 139.

18. See Chapter 10.

19. Nadia Urbinati, "Representation as Advocacy: A Study of Democratic Deliberation," *Political Theory,* 28 (2000), 758, at p. 786; and Nadia Urbinati, *Representative Democracy: Principles and Genealogy* (University of Chicago Press, 2006).

20. Rousseau, *Social Contract,* p. 81 (Bk. II, ch. 6): "When I say that the object of laws is always general, I mean that law considers subjects en masse and actions in the abstract, and never a particular person or action. . . . [N]o function which has a particular object belongs to the legislative power."

21. See, e.g., the characterization of "generality" as an important element of "the inner morality of law" in Lon Fuller, *The Morality of Law,* revised edition (Yale University Press, 1969), pp. 46–49.

22. Rousseau, *Social Contract*, p. 81 (Bk. II, ch. 6).

23. Ibid., p. 82 (Bk. II, ch. 6).

24. Ibid., p. 141 (Bk. III, ch. 15).

25. See also the discussion of different uses of consent in political theory in Jeremy Waldron, "Theoretical Foundations of Liberalism," *Philosophical Quarterly*, 37 (1987), 127, at pp. 135–39.

26. For a similar view, see Alexander Hamilton, John Jay, and James Madison, *The Federalist Papers*, ed. George W. Carey and James McClellan (Liberty Fund, 2001), p. 279 (Number 53: Madison):

> How can foreign trade be properly regulated by uniform laws, without some acquaintance with the commerce, the ports, the usages, and the regulations of the different States? How can the trade between the different States be duly regulated, without some knowledge of their relative situations in these and other points? How can taxes be judiciously imposed and effectually collected if they be not accommodated to the different laws and local circumstances relating to these objects in the different States? How can uniform regulations for the militia be duly provided without a similar knowledge of some internal circumstances by which the States are distinguished from each other? These are the principal objects of federal legislation and suggest most forcibly the extensive information which the representatives ought to acquire.

27. Urbinati, "Representation as Advocacy," p. 760.

28. Ibid., p. 769.

29. See the discussion in R. M. Hare, *Freedom and Reason* (Oxford University Press, 1963), for the contrast of universal vs. particular on the one hand and general vs. specific on the other. (Hare uses "universal" in the sense that I am using "general.")

30. For discussion of the relationship between equitable decision-making and the generality required by the rule of law, see Lawrence Solum, "Equity and the Rule of Law"; and Stephen Burton, "Particularism, Discretion and Rule of Law," in *Nomos XXXVI: The Rule of Law*, ed. Ian Shapiro (New York University Press, 1994), pp. 120 and 190.

31. For a description, see the official New Zealand government account at Elections New Zealand, "Māori Electoral Option—FAQ," at http://www.elections.org.nz/voting-system/maori-representation (last visited August 13, 2014).

32. See Urbinati, *Representative Democracy*, p. 183.

33. Urbinati, "Representation as Advocacy," p. 768.

34. Ibid., p. 760.

35. Hannah Arendt, *On Revolution* (Penguin Books, 1977), p. 227. There she also observes that "limitation to a small and chosen body of citizens was to serve as the great purifier of both interests and opinion, to guard 'against the confusion of a multitude.'" It is not clear whether this is Arendt's own view or that of the American

Framers she is discussing. Arendt is no doubt drawing on the view expressed in *The Federalist* Number 10 about the importance of "refin[ing] and enlarg[ing] the public views by passing them through the medium of a chosen body of citizens, whose wisdom may best discern the true interest of their country and whose patriotism and love of justice will be least likely to sacrifice it to temporary or partial considerations." Hamilton, Jay, and Madison, *The Federalist Papers* (Number 10: Madison). See also the discussion in Chapter 12 of the present volume.

36. See Hannah Arendt, *The Origins of Totalitarianism,* new edition (Harcourt, Brace, Jovanovich, 1973), pp. 115 and 250–66.

37. Arendt, *On Revolution,* p. 228.

38. See Margaret Canovan, *Hannah Arendt: A Reinterpretation of Her Political Thought* (Cambridge University Press, 1992), p. 35.

39. Urbinati, *Representative Democracy,* p. 184.

40. Ibid., p. 149: "Through the arithmetical unit of the vote, the electors who vote for a candidate enter simultaneously into a pluriverse relation of reflection—to their representatives, to the members of their constituency, to all the electors in the nation, and to the legislative body."

7. PRINCIPLES OF LEGISLATION

1. *The Book of Common Prayer* (Cambridge University Press, 1928), p. 391.

2. Jeremy Bentham, *The Theory of Legislation* (Kegan Paul, Trench, Trubner & Co., 1931). This work was published originally in French as part of a larger work, *Traités de Legislation.*

3. Bentham, *Theory of Legislation,* p. 1.

4. Ibid., p. 32.

5. Ibid., pp. 66ff.

6. Ibid., pp. 77–78.

7. See also David Lieberman, *The Province of Legislation Determined: Legal Theory in Eighteenth Century Britain* (Cambridge University Press, 1989), Parts III and IV.

8. Cf. John Rawls, *A Theory of Justice* (Harvard University Press, 1971), p. 27.

9. Ibid., p. 302: "Social and economic inequalities are to be arranged so that they are both: (a) to the greatest benefit of the least advantaged, consistent with the just savings principle, and (b) attached to offices and positions open to all under conditions of fair equality of opportunity.... The second principle of justice is lexically prior to the principle of efficiency and to that of maximizing the sum of advantages."

10. Ibid., p. 199.

11. John Rawls, *Political Liberalism* (Columbia University Press, 1993), p. 35.

12. E.g., Louis Kaplow and Steven Shavell, *Fairness versus Welfare* (Harvard University Press, 2002).

13. See, e.g., Robert Nozick, *Anarchy, State and Utopia* (Basil Blackwell, 1974); Bruce Ackerman, *Social Justice in the Liberal State* (Yale University Press, 1980); and Ronald Dworkin, *Sovereign Virtue: The Theory and Practice of Equality* (Harvard University Press, 2000).

14. Jeremy Waldron, *The Dignity of Legislation* (Cambridge: Cambridge University Press, 1999); and Jeremy Waldron, *Law and Disagreement* (Oxford University Press, 1999), pp. 1–10 and 105–6.

15. Lon L. Fuller, *The Morality of Law,* revised edition (Yale University Press, 1969), pp. 33–38.

16. Ibid., pp. 96–97.

17. For criticism of the preoccupation of rule-of-law theorists with formal matters to the exclusion of procedural due process, see Jeremy Waldron, "The Rule of Law and the Importance of Procedure," in *Nomos 50: Getting to the Rule of Law,* ed. James Fleming (New York University Press, 2011), 3.

18. John Locke, *Two Treatises of Government,* ed. Peter Laslett (Cambridge University Press, 1988), p. 324 (II, §87).

19. Edward Rubin, "Law and Legislation in the Administrative State," *Columbia Law Review,* 89 (1989), 369, at pp. 370–71.

20. Ibid., p. 377 n25.

21. Much of Rubin's critique (ibid., pp. 397ff.) is directed at Fuller's "internal morality of law."

22. H. L. A. Hart, *The Concept of Law,* third edition (Oxford University Press, 1994), p. 21: "[N]o society could support the number of officials necessary to secure that every member of the society was officially and separately informed of every act which he was required to do."

23. See also Jeremy Waldron, "Does Law Promise Justice?" *Georgia State University Law Review,* 17 (2001), 759.

24. Hart, *Concept of Law,* pp. 157–67.

25. Ronald Dworkin, *Law's Empire* (Harvard University Press, 1986), ch. 6.

26. F. A. Hayek, *Law, Legislation and Liberty,* Vol. 1: *Rules and Order* (University of Chicago Press, 1983).

27. John Austin, *Lectures on Jurisprudence,* fifth edition, ed. R. Campbell (John Murray, 1885), pp. 266–67 and 315.

28. Rawls, *Political Liberalism,* pp. 66ff.

29. This idea has deep roots in Rousseau's political theory and in Kant's ethics. See Jean-Jacques Rousseau, *The Social Contract,* trans. Maurice Cranston (Penguin Books, 1968), Bk. II; and Immanuel Kant, *Groundwork of the Metaphysics of Morals,* ed. Mary Gregor (Cambridge University Press, 1997).

30. See Chapter 6.

31. See John Stuart Mill, *Considerations on Representative Government* (Prometheus Books, 1991), p. 109. See also Rawls, *Theory of Justice,* pp. 7–11, on the

importance of considering, from the point of view of justice, the basic structure of society as a whole.

32. See the discussion of bicameralism in Chapter 3.

33. See Waldron, *Law and Disagreement,* ch. 3, esp. pp. 56–67.

34. See Chapter 6.

35. Marquis de Condorcet, "Essay on the Application of Mathematics to the Theory of Decision-Making," in *Condorcet: Selected Writings*, ed. Keith Michel Baker (Bobbs-Merrill, 1976), 33, at pp. 48–49. I discuss and criticize theorists' recourse to Condorcet's theorem in Chapter 10.

36. Rawls, *Political Liberalism,* p. 56.

37. Ibid., p. 58.

38. See Waldron, *Law and Disagreement,* pp. 151–53.

39. Lon Fuller, "Forms and Limits of Adjudication," *Harvard Law Review,* 92 (1978), 353, at p. 366.

40. Cf. Cass R. Sunstein, "Beyond the Republican Revival," *Yale Law Journal,* 97 (1988), 1539, at pp. 1548–51.

41. Edmund Burke, "Speech to the Electors of Bristol" (Nov. 3, 1774), in *The Works of the Right Honourable Edmund Burke* (Little Brown, 1865), Vol. 2, 95–96.

42. I have discussed this in detail in Waldron, *Law and Disagreement,* ch. 4.

43. See Waldron, *Law and Disagreement,* pp. 69–87.

44. See the account of this practice in Antonin Scalia, *A Matter of Interpretation: Federal Courts and the Law* (Princeton University Press, 1997), p. 34.

45. See the discussion in Jeremy Waldron, "Deliberation, Disagreement and Voting," in *Deliberative Democracy and Human Rights*, ed. Harold Koh and Ron Slye (Yale University Press, 1999), 210, at pp. 211–14.

46. The matter is complicated in the American system by bicameralism and by certain supermajority requirements for terminating debate or moving from one legislative stage to another.

47. See, e.g., Matthias Risse, "Arguing for Majority Rule," *Journal of Political Philosophy,* 12 (2004), 41.

48. For the theorem (in social choice theory) that majority decision alone satisfies elementary conditions of fairness and rationality, see Kenneth May, "A Set of Independent Necessary and Sufficient Conditions for Simple Majority Decision," *Econometrica,* 20 (1952), 680.

49. See Jeremy Waldron, "Legislating with Integrity," *Fordham Law Review,* 72 (2003), 373.

50. See also Ronald Dworkin, "Principle, Policy, Procedure," in his collection *A Matter of Principle* (Harvard University Press, 1985), 72; and Jeremy Waldron, "How Law Protects Dignity," *Cambridge Law Journal,* 71 (2012), 200.

8. ACCOUNTABILITY AND INSOLENCE

1. See, e.g., Russell Hardin, "Democratic Epistemology and Accountability," in *Democracy*, ed. Ellen Frankel Paul, Fred Miller, and Jeffrey Paul (Cambridge University Press, 2000), 110, at p. 113.

2. For the complaint about simplistic identification with elections, see Edward Rubin, in "The Myth of Accountability and the Anti-Administrative Impulse," *Michigan Law Review*, 103 (2005), 2073, at p. 2091. Rubin worries that "accountability" is just "a fashionable term that judges and scholars are invoking whenever they have a position which favors elected officials in some way." For the identification of accountability with "catching people out," see Robert Behn, *Rethinking Democratic Accountability* (Brookings Institution, 2001), pp. 3–6.

3. Economists also talk about agency theory and something called "the problem of agency." See, e.g., Kathleen Eisenhardt, "Agency Theory: An Assessment and Review," *Academy of Management Review*, 14 (1989), 57. My view does not draw particularly on that literature. For a misleading suggestion that an agency conception of accountability necessarily implicates the economists' account, see Mark Philp, *Political Conduct* (Harvard University Press, 2007), pp. 221–22.

4. I follow James Fearon in thinking that agency is the key. See James Fearon, "Electoral Accountability and the Control of Politicians: Selecting Good Types versus Sanctioning Poor Performance," in *Democracy, Accountability, and Representation*, ed. Adam Przeworski, Susan Stokes, and Bernard Manin (Cambridge University Press, 1999), p. 55.

5. Judith Shklar, "The Liberalism of Fear," in her collection *Political Thought and Political Thinkers*, ed. Stanley Hoffman (University of Chicago Press, 1998), 3.

6. John Dunn, "Situating Democratic Political Accountability," in *Democracy, Accountability, and Representation*, ed. Przeworski, Stokes, and Manin, 329, at p. 330.

7. Cf. Christopher Hood, "The 'New Public Management' in the 1980s: Variations on a Theme," *Accounting, Organizations, and Society*, 20 (1995), 93, at p. 94.

8. Cf. Hardin, "Democratic Epistemology and Accountability," p. 114.

9. This is assumed, for example, in Bernard Manin, Adam Przeworski, and Susan Stokes, "Elections and Representation," in *Democracy, Accountability, and Representation*, ed. Przeworski, Stokes, and Manin, at p. 40.

10. Here I agree with Mark Philp, *Political Conduct*, p. 223, and I part company with James Fearon, who thinks that talk of accountability in the absence of sanctions "blurs accountability with moral responsibility and does not square with ordinary usage." See Fearon, "Electoral Accountability and the Control of Politicians," p. 55n. Behn, *Rethinking Democratic Accountability*, p. 4, complains that dictionary definitions of the term, by emphasizing "the responsibility to answer, to explain, and to justify specific actions (or inactions) . . . have not caught up with the vernacular. When the people seek to hold someone accountable, they are usually planning some

kind of punishment." I think he is quite wrong to want to dumb down our understanding of accountability in that way.

11. Dunn, "Situating Democratic Political Accountability," p. 335, sees this when he says that accountability means that rulers are "compelled to describe what they are doing as they govern us."

12. Rubin, "The Myth of Accountability," p. 2079.

13. I return to this point in Section 5, where I discuss at some length Edmund Burke's theory of the relation between instructions and electoral representation.

14. Psalm 51:4.

15. Quoted by Geoffrey Robertson, *The Tyrannicide Brief: The Story of the Man Who Sent Charles I to the Scaffold* (Pantheon Books, 2005), p. 199.

16. For some reason, modern political theorists who call themselves republicans veer away from this understanding to a much narrower one: Philip Pettit says that republicans believe freedom is nondomination (see Philip Pettit, *On the People's Terms: A Republican Theory and Model of Democracy* (Cambridge University Press, 2014), p. 1. And Cass Sunstein says that republicanism is the view that preferences should be open to change through deliberation. See Cass Sunstein, "Beyond the Republican Revival," *Yale Law Journal,* 97 (1988), p. 1539. It puzzles me that these theorists neglect the broader and more fundamental conception of republicanism mentioned in the text.

17. In Section 6, I will talk about *mediated* accountability, whereby in a parliamentary democracy, for example, ministers of state are accountable to committees of Parliament, and the members of parliamentary committees are accountable ultimately to the people who elect them. The system I am imagining is like an attenuated form of this, but one that does not mediate any ultimate accountability to the people.

18. Cf. the discussion of the difference between agency and trust in Section 2 and the discussion of the difference in their political applications at the end of this section.

19. See the excellent discussion by Edward Muir, "Was There Republicanism in the Renaissance Republics? Venice after Agnadello," in *Venice Reconsidered: The History and Civilization of an Italian City-State, 1297–1797,* ed. John Jeffries Martin and Dennis Romano (Johns Hopkins University Press, 2000), 137.

20. Cf. Vittorio Conti, "The Mechanisation of Virtue: Republican Rituals in Italian Political Thought in the Sixteenth and Seventeenth Centuries," in *Republicanism: A Shared European Heritage,* Vol. 2, ed. Martin van Gelderen and Quentin Skinner (Cambridge University Press, 2002), 73, at pp. 74–80, drawing on the work of Gaspari Contarini.

21. Alexander Hamilton, John Jay, and James Madison, *The Federalist Papers,* ed. George W. Carey and James McClellan (Liberty Fund, 2001), pp. 46–49 (Number 10: Madison).

22. It was criticized in the late eighteenth century by Emmanuel Sieyès (in his controversy with Thomas Paine over monarchy), and it should *not* be accepted now as canonical. See "The Debate between Sieyes and Tom Paine," in *Sieyès: Political Writings,* ed. Michael Sonenscher (Hackett Publishing, 2003), 163, at pp. 167–68.

23. Hamilton, Jay, and Madison, *The Federalist Papers,* ed. Carey and McClellan, pp. 42, 63, 194, and 271 (Number 10: Madison, Number 14: Madison, Number 39: Madison, and Number 51: Madison).

24. Ibid., pp. 295–6 (Number 57: Madison).

25. Ibid., p. 297 (Number 57: Madison).

26. John Locke, *Two Treatises of Government,* ed. Peter Laslett (Cambridge University Press, 1988), pp. 367, 371, 405, 412, and 426 (II, §§149, 156, 210, 221, and 240); and Emmanuel Sieyès, "What Is the Third Estate?" in *Sieyès: Political Writings,* ed. Sonenscher, 92, at 120n.

27. Locke, *Two Treatises,* p. 412 (II, §221).

28. See also Laslett's introductory remarks in his edition of Locke, *Two Treatises,* at p. 114.

29. John Dunn, "Situating Democratic Political Accountability," p. 341, talks of "the treacheries and seductions of trust." See also John Ferejohn's emphasis on "the agency model" in his paper "Accountability and Authority: Toward a Theory of Political Accountability," in *Democracy, Accountability, and Representation,* ed. Przeworski, Stokes, and Manin, 131, at p. 133.

30. Jean-Jacques Rousseau, *The Social Contract,* trans. Maurice Cranston (Penguin Books, 2004), p. 82 (Bk. III, ch. 5).

31. Ibid., p. 65 (Bk. III, ch. 1)

32. More or less directly, on account of the electoral college formalities for presidential elections. See U.S. Constitution, Article II, 1.

33. See the helpful discussion in Christopher Hood, "Blame Avoidance and Accountability," in *Accountable Governance: Problems and Promises,* ed. Melvin Dubnick and George Frederickson (M. E. Sharpe, 2011), 167; and Christopher Hood, *The Blame Game: Spin, Bureaucracy, and Self-Preservation in Government* (Princeton University Press, 2010).

34. I am grateful to Barry Friedman for this point.

35. See Fearon, "Electoral Accountability and the Control of Politicians," p. 56: "[I]n the case of electoral accountability, additional problems arise from the presence of multiple principals (voters . . .) rather than a single principal or a collective body that can act as a single principal. For instance with multiple principals, the question of saying what the principals would want can be difficult, even theoretically as Arrow's theorem suggests."

36. Thomas Hobbes, *Leviathan,* ed. Richard Tuck (Cambridge University Press, 1991), pp. 114 and 123 (chs. 16 and 18).

37. Ibid., pp. 151–53 (ch. 21). See also Bernard Williams, "Realism and Moralism in Political Theory," in his collection *In the Beginning Was the Deed,* ed. Geoffrey Hawthorn (Princeton University Press, 2005), 1, at pp. 3–6.

38. John Rawls, *A Theory of Justice,* revised edition (Harvard University Press, 1999), pp. 10–30.

39. Ferejohn, "Accountability and Authority," p. 132.

40. This was the gist of Kant's criticism of Hobbes in Immanuel Kant, "On the Common Saying: That May Be Correct in Theory, but It Is of No Use in Practice," in Immanuel Kant, *Practical Philosophy,* ed. Mary Gregor (Cambridge University Press, 1996), 277, at p. 302 (8: 303–4).

41. In modern democracies, politicians are often obliged to explain themselves to the people via the news media, and an unsatisfactory account, an account that the people or a majority of them are likely to judge harshly, can redound to the detriment of a politician's career. On some accounts, this informal accountability is becoming much more important in modern democracies than formal electoral accountability. One theorist has coined a whole new term to describe it, "monitory democracy"; see John Keane, *The Life and Death of Democracy* (W. W. Norton, 2009).

42. See Bernard Manin, *Principles of Representative Government* (Cambridge University Press, 1997), pp. 11–13; and Jon Elster, "Accountability in Athenian Politics," in *Democracy, Accountability, and Representation,* ed. Przeworski, Stokes, and Manin, 253.

43. Moreover, some political offices are elective but not representative. The presidency in the United States is an example, and so are elective judgeships in those states that have them.

44. See Edmund Burke, "Speech to the Electors of Bristol," in *Edmund Burke: Speeches and Letters on American Affairs,* ed. P. McKevitt (J. M. Dent and Sons, 1908), 68, at pp. 72–74.

45. Cf. Alexander Aleinikoff and Samuel Issacharoff, "Race and Redistricting: Drawing Constitutional Lines after *Shaw v. Reno,*" *Michigan Law Review,* 92 (1993), 588, at p. 632n.

46. See Edmund Burke, "A Letter to John Farr and John Harris (Sheriffs of the City of Bristol) on the Affairs of America," in *Edmund Burke,* ed. McKevitt, 188.

47. So I find it difficult to understand the claim by Hardin, "Democratic Epistemology and Accountability," p. 121, that he cannot imagine what it means to hold a Burkeian representative accountable.

48. Elective monarchy was practiced in Poland for five hundred years ending in 1791; the electors were nobles, but they constituted a very large electorate, perhaps as many as 100,000 potential voters.

49. See Fearon, "Electoral Accountability and the Control of Politicians," pp. 63–67, on "last period" effects.

50. Ibid.

51. As Dunn points out, in "Situating Democratic Political Accountability," p. 332, any system of punishment has a forward-looking aspect.

52. There is a toggle here between two senses of authority: the principal has given the agent authority to bind the principal in the deals the agent transacts on the principal's behalf, and the principal has the authority to control the agent.

53. Dunn, "Situating Democratic Political Accountability," p. 331.

54. Apart from anything else, a clear theoretical understanding of political obligation involves people being obligated to one another rather than to their rulers.

55. The two issues are separated nicely in Kant's dictum "Argue as much as you will and about what you will; only obey!" Immanuel Kant, "An Answer to the Question: What Is Enlightenment?" in Kant, *Practical Philosophy,* ed. Gregor, p. 22 (8: 41); and Jeremy Bentham's catechism: "[W]hat is the motto of a good citizen? To obey punctually; to censure freely"—Jeremy Bentham, *A Fragment on Government* (Cambridge University Press, 1988), p. 10.

56. But not all internal management techniques within administrations can be equated with mediated democratic accountability, even when the language of accountability is used. See Hood, "The 'New Public Management'"; and Rubin, "The Myth of Accountability," pp. 2119–20 and 2075.

57. John Dunn puts this grudgingly but correctly when he says, in "Situating Democratic Political Accountability," pp. 335–36, that "since in any modern state most citizens cannot really have the foggiest conception of most of what is politically going on," accountability has to be "very elaborately mediated."

58. John Ferejohn, "Incumbent Performance and Electoral Control," *Public Choice,* 50 (1986), does an excellent job in figuring out the rational choice basis on which the development of such an ethos might be predicated.

59. See Dunn, "Situating Democratic Political Accountability," p. 336, for a fine example of such condemnation.

60. The use of something like consumer accountability in internal management deserves much greater discussion than I can give it. See Hood, "The New Public Management"; and Christopher Hood, *The Art of the State: Culture, Rhetoric, and Public Management* (Oxford University Press, 1998), pp. 49ff.

61. See also the observations in Hood, *The Art of the State,* pp. 223–24, on our need to understand why "management-speak words like 'accountability' and 'empowerment' have the rhetorical power that they do."

62. Notice that this is quite a different point from the requirement that judges give an account of their decisions in their judicial opinions. That may enable us to hold the judges accountable. But it is not the same as judicial review being a form of democratic accountability.

63. Dunn, "Situating Democratic Political Accountability," pp. 331 and 333.

64. Ibid., p. 335.

9. THE CORE OF THE CASE AGAINST JUDICIAL REVIEW

1. *Goodridge v. Department of Public Health*, 798 N.E.2d. 941 (Mass. 2003). Twelve years later the U.S. Supreme Court made a similar ruling in *Obergefell v. Hodges*, 135 S.Ct.1039 (2015) that covers the whole country.

2. This adapts a phrase from Ronald Dworkin, "Political Judges and the Rule of Law," in his collection *A Matter of Principle* (Harvard University Press, 1985), 9, at p. 32.

3. *Lochner v. New York*, 198 U.S. 45 (1905). The calculation of the overall number of cases in which state or federal statutes on labor relations and labor conditions were struck down in the period 1880–1935 is based on lists given in appendices in William Forbath, *Law and the Shaping of the American Labor Movement* (Harvard University Press, 1991), pp. 177–92 and 199–203.

4. *Lawrence v. Texas*, 539 U.S. 558 (2003); *Roe v. Wade*, 410 U.S. 113 (1973); *Brown v. Board of Education*, 347 U.S. 483 (1954).

5. The locus classicus for the idea of legislative supremacy is John Locke, *Two Treatises of Government,* ed. Peter Laslett (Cambridge University Press, 1988), pp. 366–67 (§§149–50).

6. Alexander Bickel, *The Least Dangerous Branch: The Supreme Court at the Bar of Politics,* second edition (Yale University Press, 1986), pp. 16–17.

7. Ibid., pp. 17–18.

8. Medical Termination of Pregnancy Act of 1966 (United Kingdom); Sexual Offences Act, 1967 (United Kingdom); Murder Act, 1965 (United Kingdom).

9. Dworkin, *Freedom's Law*, p. 74.

10. See Larry D. Kramer, *The People Themselves: Popular Constitutionalism and Judicial Review* (Oxford University Press, 2004) and Mark Tushnet, *Taking the Constitution Away from the Courts* (Princeton University Press, 1999).

11. See, e.g., *United States v. Morrison*, 529 U.S. 598 (2000) (striking down part of the Violence against Women Act) and *United States v. Lopez*, 514 U.S. 549 (1995) (holding that Congress has no authority to legislate a prohibition on the possession of guns within a certain distance from a school).

12. See, e.g., Dworkin, *Freedom's Law*; Christopher Eisgruber, *Constitutional Self-Government* (Harvard University Press, 2000); and Lawrence Sager, *Justice in Plainclothes: A Theory of American Constitutional Practice* (Yale University Press, 2006).

13. See, e.g., Jeremy Waldron, "Judicial Review of Legislation," in *The Routledge Companion to Philosophy of Law*, ed. Andrei Marmor (Routledge, 2012); Jeremy Waldron, *Law and Disagreement* (Oxford University Press, 1999), pp. 10–17, 211–312; Jeremy Waldron, "Deliberation, Disagreement, and Voting," in *Deliberative Democracy and Human Rights*, ed. Harold Koh and Ron Slye (Yale University Press, 1999), 210; Jeremy Waldron, "Judicial Power and Popular Sovereignty," in *Marbury*

Versus Madison: Documents and Commentary, ed. Mark Graber and Michael Perhac (CQ Press, 2002), 181; and Jeremy Waldron, "A Right-Based Critique of Constitutional Rights," *Oxford Journal of Legal Studies,* 13 (1993), 18.

14. See Kramer, *The People Themselves*; and Tushnet, *Taking the Constitution Away from the Courts.*

15. Charles L. Black, *A New Birth of Freedom: Human Rights, Named and Unnamed* (Yale University Press, 1997), p. 109.

16. I asked whether the very idea of individual rights commits us to judicial review in Waldron, "A Right-Based Critique of Constitutional Rights." I considered its relation to civic republican ideas in Jeremy Waldron, "Judicial Review and Republican Government," in *That Eminent Tribunal: Judicial Supremacy and the Constitution,* ed. Christopher Wolfe (Princeton University Press, 2004), 159; its relation to the difference between Benthamite and Rousseauian conceptions of democracy in Jeremy Waldron, "Rights and Majorities: Rousseau Revisited," in *Nomos 32: Majorities and Minorities,* ed. John Chapman and Alan Wertheimer (New York University Press, 1990), 44; and its relation to revolutionary theories of popular sovereignty in Waldron, "Judicial Power and Popular Sovereignty." I considered the relation of the judicial review controversy to debates in meta-ethics about the objectivity of values in Jeremy Waldron, "The Irrelevance of Moral Objectivity," in *Natural Law Theory: Contemporary Essays,* ed. Robert P. George (Oxford University Press, 1992), 158 and Jeremy Waldron, "Moral Truth and Judicial Review," *American Journal of Jurisprudence,* 43 (1998), 75. I responded to various defenses of judicial review, ranging from the precommitment case, in Jeremy Waldron, "Precommitment and Disagreement," in *Constitutionalism: Philosophical Foundations,* ed. Larry Alexander (Cambridge University Press, 1998), 271, to the particular argument that Ronald Dworkin made in *Freedom's Law* about its ultimate compatibility with democracy, in Jeremy Waldron, "Judicial Review and the Conditions of Democracy," *Journal of Political Philosophy,* 6 (1998), 335.

17. I should also mention the powerful argument put forward in Richard Fallon, "The Core of an Uneasy Case *for* Judicial Review," *Harvard Law Review,* 121 (2008), 1693. I will refer to Fallon's argument at various points throughout this chapter.

18. Much of what is done by the European Court of Human Rights is judicial review of executive action. Some of it is judicial review of legislative action, and actually some of it is also judicial review of judicial action. See Seth Kreimer, "Exploring the Dark Matter of Judicial Review: A Constitutional Census of the 1990s," *William and Mary Bill of Rights Journal,* 5 (1997), 427, for the claim that the majority of constitutional decisions by lower federal courts in the United States concern challenges to the actions of low-level bureaucrats rather than those of legislatures.

19. The distinction between strong and weak judicial review is separate from the question of judicial supremacy. Judicial supremacy refers to a situation in which

(1) the courts settle important issues for the whole political system, (2) those settlements are treated as absolutely binding on all other actors in the political system, and (3) the courts do not defer to the positions taken on these matters in other branches (not even to the extent to which they defer to their own past decisions under a limited principle of stare decisis). See Barry Friedman, "The History of the Countermajoritarian Difficulty, Part One: The Road to Judicial Supremacy," *N.Y.U. Law Review,* 73 (1998), 333; and Waldron, "Judicial Power and Popular Sovereignty," pp. 191–98.

20. See Mauro Cappelletti and John Clarke Adams, "Judicial Review of Legislation: European Antecedents and Adaptations," *Harvard Law Review,* 79 (1966), 1207, at p. 1222.

21. A contrary impression may appear from *McCorvey v. Hill,* 385 F.3d 846, 849 (5th Cir. 2004), in which the Fifth Circuit held that the Texas abortion statute at issue in *Roe v. Wade,* 410 U.S. 113 (1973), must be deemed to have been repealed by implication. A close reading of that case, however, shows that the implicit repeal was held to have been effected by the Texas statutes regulating abortion after *Roe,* not by the decision in *Roe v. Wade* itself. (I am grateful to Carol Sanger for this reference.)

22. See Richard H. Fallon, Jr., "As-Applied and Facial Challenges and Third-Party Standing," *Harvard Law Review,* 113 (2000), 1321, at p. 1339.

23. See Stephen Gardbaum, *The New Commonwealth Model of Constitutionalism: Theory and Practice* (Cambridge University Press, 2013).

24. Human Rights Act, 1998 (UK), section 4 (2) and (6).

25. Ibid., section 10.

26. New Zealand Bill of Rights Act (1990), section 4: "No court shall, in relation to any enactment (whether passed or made before or after the commencement of this Bill of Rights), . . . [h]old any provision of the enactment to be impliedly repealed or revoked, or to be in any way invalid or ineffective; or . . . [d]ecline to apply any provision of the enactment—by reason only that the provision is inconsistent with any provision of this Bill of Rights." However, section 6 requires that "[w]herever an enactment can be given a meaning that is consistent with the rights and freedoms contained in this Bill of Rights, that meaning shall be preferred to any other meaning."

27. See *Moonen v. Film & Literature Bd. of Review,* [2000] 2 N.Z.L.R. 9, at pp. 22–23 (Court of Appeal). There are good discussions in Tom Hickman, "The New Zealand Bill of Rights Act: Going Beyond Declarations," Policy Quarterly, 10 (2014), 39 and Claudia Geiringer, "On a Road to Nowhere: Implied Declarations of Inconsistency and the New Zealand Bill of Rights Act," *Victoria University of Wellington Law Review,* 40 (2009), 613. In a very recent case, *Taylor v. Attorney General* [2015] NZHC 1706, a High Court judge took it upon himself to make a formal declaration of the incompatibility with the New Zealand Bill of Rights Act of a legislative provision restricting prisoner voting.

28. Canadian Charter of Rights and Freedoms, section 33(1). The full text of the provision reads: "(1) Parliament or the legislature of a province may expressly declare in an Act of Parliament or of the legislature, as the case may be, that the Act or a provision thereof shall operate notwithstanding a provision included in section 2 or sections 7 to 15 of this Charter. (2) An Act or a provision of an Act in respect of which a declaration made under this section is in effect shall have such operation as it would have but for the provision of this Charter referred to in the declaration."

29. When it has been invoked, it has mostly been in the context of Québécois politics. See Tsvi Kahana, "The Notwithstanding Mechanism and Public Discussion: Lessons from the Ignored Practice of Section 33 of the Charter," *Journal of the Institute of Public Administration in Canada,* 44 (2001), 255.

30. Jeffrey Goldsworthy has suggested that the notwithstanding provision provides a sufficient answer to those of us who worry, on democratic grounds, about the practice of strong judicial review. See Jeffrey Goldsworthy, "Judicial Review, Legislative Override, and Democracy," *Wake Forest Law Review,* 38 (2003), 451, at pp. 454–59. It matters not, he says, that the provision is rarely used:

> [S]urely that is the electorate's democratic prerogative, which Waldron would be bound to respect. It would not be open to him to object that an ingenuous electorate is likely to be deceived by the specious objectivity of constitutionalised rights, or dazzled by the mystique of the judiciary—by a naive faith in judges' expert legal skills, superior wisdom, and impartiality. That objection would reflect precisely the same lack of faith in the electorate's capacity for enlightened self-government that motivates proponents of constitutionally entrenched rights.

I believe that the real problem is that section 33 requires the legislature to misrepresent its position on rights. To legislate notwithstanding the Charter is a way of saying that you do not think Charter rights have the importance that the Charter says they have. But the characteristic standoff between courts and legislatures does not involve one group of people (judges) who think Charter rights are important and another group of people (legislators) who do not. What it usually involves is groups of people (legislative majorities and minorities, and judicial majorities and minorities) all of whom think Charter rights are important, though they disagree about how the relevant rights are to be understood. Goldsworthy acknowledges this (ibid., pp. 467–68):

> When the judiciary . . . is expected to disagree with the legislature as to the "true" meaning and effect of Charter provisions, the legislature cannot ensure that its view will prevail without appearing to override the Charter itself. And that is vulnerable to the politically lethal objection that the legislature is openly and self-confessedly subverting constitutional rights.

Perhaps there is no form of words that can avoid this difficulty. As a matter of practical politics, the legislature is always somewhat at the mercy of the courts' public declarations about the meaning of the society's Bill or Charter of Rights.

31. The most famous judicial defense of judicial review, *Marbury v. Madison*, 5 U.S. (1 Cranch) 137 (1803), had nothing to do with individual rights. It was about Congress's power to appoint and remove justices of the peace.

32. See Dworkin, *A Matter of Principle,* pp. 11–18; Andrei Marmor, *Interpretation and Legal Theory,* second edition (Oxford University Press, 2005), pp. 156–57.

33. See, e.g., the cases cited in note 11.

34. Some systems of the first kind make provision for ex ante advisory opinions in limited circumstances. For example, in Massachusetts, "[e]ach branch of the legislature . . . [has] authority to require the opinions of the justices of the supreme judicial court, upon important questions of law" or when "having some action in view, [it] has serious doubts as to [its] power and authority to take such action, under the Constitution." *Answer of the Justices,* 364 Mass. 838, 844, 302 N.E.2d 565 (1973). This procedure was used in the months following the *Goodridge* decision, discussed at the beginning of this chapter. In *Opinions of the Justices to the Senate,* 802 N.E.2d 565 (Mass. 2004), the Supreme Judicial Court of Massachusetts held that a legislative provision for civil unions for same-sex couples that also prohibited discrimination against civilly joined spouses would not be sufficient to avoid the constitutional objection to the ban on same-sex marriages noted in *Goodridge.*

35. See Jeremy Waldron, "Eisgruber's House of Lords," *University of San Francisco Law Review,* 37 (2002), 89. See also the discussion of the relation between bicameralism and judicial review in Chapter 4.

36. There is a good discussion in Cappelletti and Adams, "Judicial Review of Legislation: European Antecedents and Adaptations."

37. These are adapted from assumptions set out in Jeremy Waldron, "Some Models of Dialogue between Judges and Legislators," *Supreme Court Law Review* (Canada), 2nd series, 23 (2004), 7, at pp. 9–21.

38. For a general critique of the "bottom-line" mentality in political philosophy, see Jeremy Waldron, "What Plato Would Allow," in *Nomos 37: Theory and Practice,* ed. Ian Shapiro and Judith Wagner DeCew (NYU Press, 1995), 138.

39. It is sometimes said that elective institutions are incapable of reforming themselves because legislators have an entrenched interest in the status quo. This may be true of some of the pathological electoral and legislative arrangements in the United States. (But the issues for which this is most true in the United States are those on which the courts have scarcely dared to intervene—consider the disgraceful condition of American redistricting arrangements, for example.) It is patently false elsewhere. In New Zealand, for example, in 1993 the legislature enacted statutes changing the system of parliamentary representation from a first-past-the-post system to a system of proportional representation, in a way that unsettled existing patterns of incumbency.

40. Fallon, "The Core of an Uneasy Case," p. 1699, argues that "some rights deserve to be protected by multiple safeguards or veto powers." To answer that argument, I have to show that some veto powers are unfair to those whose decisions are rightly privileged in a democratic system. I attempt an answer in note 90.

41. See, e.g., Henry Hart and Albert Sacks, *The Legal Process: Basic Problems in the Making and Application of Law,* ed. William Eskridge and Philip Frickey (Foundation Press, 1994), pp. 640–47; and Lon Fuller, "Forms and Limits of Adjudication," *Harvard Law Review,* 92 (1978), 353.

42. See Jesse Choper, *Judicial Review and the National Political Process: A Functional Reconsideration of the Role of the Supreme Court* (University of Chicago Press, 1980). See also *Planned Parenthood of Southeastern Pennsylvania. v. Casey,* 505 U.S. 833 (1992), at pp. 864–69.

43. See Waldron, "A Right-Based Critique of Constitutional Rights," pp. 28–31 and 34–36.

44. My approach here is similar to that of John Rawls. I am using this device of the core case to define something like a well-ordered society with a publicly accepted theory of justice. See, e.g., John Rawls, *Political Liberalism* (Columbia University Press, 1993), pp. 35–36. Rawls seems to assume that judicial review of legislation is appropriate for even a well-ordered society. See ibid., pp. 165–66 and 233–40; and also John Rawls, *A Theory of Justice,* revised edition (Harvard University Press, 1999), pp. 200–3. One of my aims is to show that he is wrong about that.

45. See Waldron, "Judicial Power and Popular Sovereignty," p. 198.

46. For a discussion of the distinction between the concept of a right and various conceptions of it, see Ronald Dworkin, *Taking Rights Seriously* (Harvard University Press, 1977), pp. 134–36.

47. See Rawls, *Political Liberalism,* pp. 55–60. Rawls argues that "many of our most important judgments are made under conditions where it is not to be expected that conscientious persons with full powers of reason, even after free discussion, will arrive at the same conclusion." For an argument applying this to the right as well as the good, see Waldron, *Law and Disagreement,* ch. 7.

48. Rawls, *Political Liberalism,* p. 58.

49. See Waldron, "Irrelevance of Moral Objectivity," p. 182.

50. See Thomas Christiano, "Waldron on Law and Disagreement," *Law and Philosophy,* 19 (2000), 537.

51. Cf. Jon Stewart et al., *America (The Book): A Citizen's Guide to Democracy in Action* (Allen Lane, 2004), p. 90, discussing *Roe v. Wade,* 410 U.S. 113 (1973), and noting: "The [Supreme] Court rules that the right to privacy protects a woman's decision to have an abortion and the fetus is not a person with constitutional rights, thus ending all debate on this once-controversial issue."

52. Cf. New Zealand Bill of Rights Act (1990), section 7: "Where any Bill is introduced into the House of Representatives, the Attorney-General shall . . . as

soon as practicable after the introduction of the Bill—bring to the attention of the House of Representatives any provision in the Bill that appears to be inconsistent with any of the rights and freedoms contained in this Bill of Rights." For a controversial example of the exercise of this power, see Grant Huscroft, "Is the Defeat of Health Warnings a Victory for Human Rights? The Attorney-General and Pre-legislative Scrutiny for Consistency with the New Zealand Bill of Rights," *Public Law Review,* 14 (2003), 109.

53. Cf. Thomas Hobbes, *Leviathan,* ed. Richard Tuck (Cambridge University Press, 1996), p. 123.

54. Christiano, "Waldron on Law and Disagreement," p. 521, phrases the point in terms of a regress of procedures: "We can expect disagreement at every stage, if Waldron is right; so if we must have recourse to a higher order procedure to resolve each dispute as it arises, then we will be unable to stop the regress of procedures." But he makes no attempt to show that this is a vicious regress. For a discussion of the regress, see Waldron, *Law and Disagreement,* pp. 298–301.

55. I have heard people say that the errors are always likely to be worse on the legislative side. The legislature may actually violate rights, whereas the worst that the courts can do is fail to interfere to protect them. This is a mistake. Courts exercising the power of judicial review may sometimes violate rights by striking down a statute that aims to protect them. I will discuss this further at the end of Section 4.

56. Richard Wollheim, "A Paradox in the Theory of Democracy," in *Philosophy, Politics and Society,* second series, ed. Peter Laslett and W. G. Runciman (Basil Blackwell, 1969), 71.

57. Aileen Kavanagh, "Participation and Judicial Review: A Reply to Jeremy Waldron," *Law and Philosophy,* 22 (2003), 451, at p. 466.

58. Joseph Raz, "Disagreement in Politics," *American Journal of Jurisprudence,* 43 (1998), 25, at pp. 45–46. See also Rawls, *A Theory of Justice,* p. 230: "The fundamental criterion for judging any procedure is the justice of its likely results"; and Fallon, "The Core of an Uneasy Case," p. 1717: "It is almost too plain for argument that the fairness of procedures depends on the nature of the substantive ends that the procedures are designed to promote."

59. See, e.g., Louis Henkin, "That 'S' Word: Sovereignty, and Globalization, and Human Rights, Et Cetera," *Fordham Law Review,* 68 (1999), 1.

60. For the idea of various waves of duty being generated by a particular right, see Jeremy Waldron, "Rights in Conflict," *Ethics,* 99 (1989), 503, at pp. 509–12.

61. Ronald Dworkin, *Sovereign Virtue: The Theory and Practice of Equality* (Harvard University Press, 2000), p. 187.

62. These summary formulations of Dworkin's view are adapted from Kavanagh, "Participation and Judicial Review," pp. 458–59.

63. This is how the question is stated in Frank Michelman, *Brennan and Democracy* (Princeton University Press, 1999), pp. 59–60.

64. Raz, "Disagreement in Politics," p. 45.
65. See Hart and Sacks, *The Legal Process,* pp. 640–47.
66. Fuller, "Forms and Limits of Adjudication," pp. 368–70.
67. Raz, "Disagreement in Politics," p. 46.
68. *Korematsu v. United States,* 323 U.S. 214 (1944) (refusing to protect citizens of Japanese descent from internment during the Second World War); *Schenck v. United States,* 249 U.S. 47 (1919) (holding that criticizing conscription during the First World War was like shouting fire in a crowded theater); *Dred Scott v. Sanford,* 60 U.S. (19 How.) 393, 493 (1857) (Campbell, J., concurring) (refusing to recognize that a person of African descent could be a citizen of Missouri); *Prigg v. Pennsylvania,* 41 U.S. (16 Pet.) 539, 612 (1842) (striking down state legislation that sought to protect African Americans from slave-catchers).
69. Laurence Tribe, "Trial by Fury: Why Congress Must Curb Bush's Military Courts," *The New Republic,* December 10, 2001, p. 18. See also Ronald Dworkin, "The Threat to Patriotism," *New York Review of Books,* February 28, 2002, p. 44.
70. Raz, "Disagreement in Politics," p. 46.
71. See Rawls, *A Theory of Justice,* pp. 73–78. (We speak of pure procedural justice when we want to indicate that there is nothing more to the justice of the outcome than the fact that it was arrived at by scrupulously following a just procedure. We speak of imperfect procedural justice when we want to convey the point that a given outcome must be judged on its merits as well as on the basis of the procedure that yielded it.)
72. For a general critique of arguments that associate judicial review with careful moral deliberation among, for example, justices on the U.S. Supreme Court, see Kramer, *The People Themselves,* p. 240. Kramer gives a fine description of the way in which justices' political agendas, and the phalanxes of ideologically motivated clerks in the various chambers, interfere with anything that could be recognized as meaningful collegial deliberation among the justices.
73. See Jeremy Waldron, *The Dignity of Legislation* (Cambridge University Press, 1999), p. 2.
74. Michael Moore, "Law as a Functional Kind," in *Natural Law Theory,* ed. George, pp. 188 and 230. For a response, see Waldron, "Moral Truth and Judicial Review," pp. 83–88.
75. See Sarah Weddington, "Roe v. Wade: Past and Future," *Suffolk University Law Review,* 24 (1990), 601, at pp. 602–3.
76. Megan's Law (about creating a register of sex offenders) was enacted in New Jersey in 1995 after Megan Nicole Kanka was raped and murdered by a convicted sex offender. There is also now a Federal Megan's Law: 42 U.S.C. §14071 (2000). For a description of the enactment of this legislation, see Daniel M. Filler, "Making the Case for Megan's Law: A Study in Legislative Rhetoric," *Indiana Law Journal,* 76 (2001), 315.

77. See also Eisgruber, *Constitutional Self-Government*, p. 173: "Judges take up constitutional issues in the course of deciding controversies between particular parties. As a result, those issues come to them in a way that is incomplete. . . . Not all interested parties will have standing to appear before the court. Judges receive evidence and hear arguments from only a limited number of parties. . . . As a result, judges may not have the information necessary to gain a comprehensive perspective on the fairness of an entire social, political, or economic system." Eisgruber concludes from this that it is probably unwise for judges to attempt to address issues that turn on what he calls "comprehensive" moral principles.

78. See also Tushnet, *Taking the Constitution Away from the Courts*, p. 60: "Courts may design some doctrines to reflect their sense of their own limited abilities, not to reflect directly substantive constitutional values."

79. See *Jackson v. City of Joliet*, 715 F.2d 1200, 1203–04 (7th Cir. 1983), where Judge Posner observed that the American constitutional scheme "is a charter of negative rather than positive liberties." Cf. Mark Tushnet, "An Essay on Rights," *Texas Law Review*, 62 (1984), 1363, at pp. 1393–94: "We could of course have a different Constitution. . . . One can argue that the party of humanity ought to struggle to reformulate the rhetoric of rights so that Judge Posner's description would no longer seem natural and perhaps would even seem strained."

80. See, e.g., Henry Monaghan, "Stare Decisis and Constitutional Adjudication," *Columbia Law Review*, 88 (1988), 723.

81. See, e.g., *Planned Parenthood of Southeastern Pennsylvania v. Casey*, 505 U.S. 833 (1992), at pp. 854–69.

82. There is a tremendous amount of legal and social history in the opinion, but only a few pages address the actual moral issues at stake. See *Roe v. Wade*, 410 U.S. 113 (1973), at pp. 153–55 and 159–60.

83. Eisgruber, *Constitutional Self-Government*, p. 70, seems to concede this, acknowledging that "[t]oo often judges attempt to justify controversial rulings by citing ambiguous precedents, and . . . veil their true reasons behind unilluminating formulae and quotations borrowed from previous cases." See also ibid., p. 135: "[J]udges . . . often . . . pretend that they are not making political judgments themselves, and that their decisions were forced upon them by textual details or historical facts."

84. As Tushnet points out in *Taking the Constitution Away from the Courts*, pp. 63–65, we should not be criticizing legislators for failing to reason as judges do, for that may not be a good way to address the issues at stake.

85. Parliamentary Debates (*Hansard*), 5th series, 732 (1966), pp. 1067–1166.

86. See, ibid., p. 1152. Norman St. John-Stevas, a Catholic MP who voted against the bill, began his argument by noting, "We all agree that this has been a vitally important debate, conducted on a level which is worthy of the highest traditions of the House."

87. When I mention this example, my American friends tell me that the British legislature is organized to make forms of debate possible that are not possible in the United States. This is simply false. The debate I have just referred to worked because the House of Commons suspended one of its usual distinguishing features—strong party discipline—for the purpose of this issue of rights. MPs actually debated the matter much more in the style of their American counterparts, not necessarily toeing a party line but stating their own opinions clearly and forcefully.

88. Dworkin, "Political Judges and the Rule of Law," at pp. 33 and 69–71.

89. See Editorial, "Half-Measures on British Freedoms," *New York Times,* November 17, 1997, at p. A22.

90. In his response to the outcome-related part of my argument, Richard Fallon (in "An Uneasy Case," pp. 1704ff.) denied that we should view the issue in terms of either judicial supremacy or legislative supremacy. Where fundamental rights are involved, it is good to have *multiple* safeguards, giving various institutions vetoes that may be brought to bear on political decision-making. But this assumes, as he acknowledges (ibid., pp. 1699 and 1709), that "errors of under-protection . . . are more morally serious than errors of over-protection." It also assumes that there is no particular legitimacy problem with any of the veto-bearers. Both assumptions are questionable. The first assumes that little damage is done to rights when courts exercise a veto against democratic legislation, but there are many cases, imaginable and remembered, where strong judicial review has been used to strike down legislation that actually asserted rights of various kinds. The second assumption is also weak. One could multiply possible veto points by empowering an unelected monarch or a synod of bishops. If two vetoes are better than one, then three or four may be better than two. Or perhaps we could use the queen or the bishops simply as a second veto instead of the courts. Eventually we have to question whether a given person or institution is an appropriate veto-bearer in light of our underlying theory of political legitimacy. We would, I think, deny that to the queen or the bishops, and I believe we should also deny it to the courts, on exactly the same grounds.

91. For the theorem (in social choice theory) that MD alone satisfies elementary conditions of fairness, equality, and rationality, see Kenneth May, "A Set of Independent Necessary and Sufficient Conditions for Simple Majority Decision," *Econometrica,* 20 (1952), 680; and Amartya Sen, *Collective Choice and Social Welfare* (Holden Day, 1970), pp. 71–74. There are also useful discussions in Charles Beitz, *Political Equality* (Princeton University Press, 1989), pp. 58–67; and Robert A. Dahl, *Democracy and Its Critics* (Yale University Press, 1989), pp. 139–41.

92. Ronald Dworkin has convinced me that MD is not an appropriate principle to use in regard to first-order issues of justice among individuals. If we were in an overcrowded lifeboat and somebody had to go overboard, it would not be appropriate to use MD to decide who that should be. It is an appropriate principle, however, for choosing among general rules. If someone in the lifeboat proposes that we

should draw straws and someone else suggests that the oldest person should be required to leave the lifeboat, then MD seems a fair basis for choosing among these rules. See Jeremy Waldron, "A Majority in the Lifeboat," *Boston University Law Review*, 90 (2010), 1043; and Ronald Dworkin, *Justice for Hedgehogs* (Harvard University Press, 2012), pp. 483–85.

93. See also Michelman, *Brennan and Democracy,* pp. 57–59.

94. Richard Fallon ("An Uneasy Case," pp. 1715ff.) thinks it is a mistake to focus too much on questions about the democratic credentials of courts. He believes that a full theory of legitimacy must also take into account what courts can offer for the protection of rights. I worry, however, that in the grip of this view Fallon gives *no attention at all* to the democratic legitimacy of courts. Having insisted that it is not the be-all and end-all, he pays no further attention to democratic legitimacy as such. But as I argued in note 90, eventually one has to confront the issue of procedural legitimacy for the various institutions that one proposes to endow with a veto. For some possible candidates, it would be entirely inappropriate to endow them with a veto, even if they had a positive contribution to make to the protection of rights; I mentioned a synod of bishops or a constitutional monarch as possible examples. If the issue of procedural legitimacy has to be confronted in those instances, it also has to be confronted in the instance of the judiciary. And that is what I am doing in this section.

95. *Planned Parenthood of Southeastern Pennsylvania v. Casey,* 505 U.S. 833 (1992), at pp. 999–1000 (Scalia, J., dissenting).

96. Ibid., pp. 1000–1.

97. See Jon Elster, *Ulysses Unbound* (Cambridge University Press, 2000), pp. 88–96, casting doubt on arguments made in Jon Elster, *Ulysses and the Sirens: Studies in Rationality and Irrationality* (Cambridge University Press, 1984), p. 93. See also Waldron, *Law and Disagreement,* pp. 255–81.

98. See Waldron, *Law and Disagreement,* pp. 266–70.

99. See Eisgruber, *Constitutional Self-Government,* p. 4: "Though the justices are not chosen by direct election, they are nevertheless selected through a process that is both political and democratic. . . . [T]hey are chosen by elected officials: they are nominated by the president and confirmed by the Senate. . . . The justices have . . . a democratic pedigree: they owe their appointments to their political views and their political connections as much as . . . to their legal skills."

100. Cf. John Hart Ely, *Democracy and Distrust: A Theory of Judicial Review* (Harvard University Press, 1980).

101. Mill's one criticism of Tocqueville's *Democracy in America* was that the likely political effect of his popularizing the phrase "the tyranny of the majority" would be to give conservative forces additional rhetoric with which to oppose progressive legislation. See John Stuart Mill, "M. de Tocqueville on Democracy in America," in his collection *Dissertations and Discussions: Political, Philosophical, and Historical,* Vol. 2 (J. W. Parker, 1882), 79, at p. 81.

102. I am not referring to their sins of omission (failing to protect us against certain legislative rights abuses). I am referring here to their sins of commission. Sometimes the power of judicial review is exercised tyrannically to prevent legislatures from according people (what are in fact) their rights. A good example is *Prigg v. Pennsylvania*, 41 U.S. (16 Pet.) 539, 612 (1842), in which the U.S. Supreme Court struck down legislation in a free state that sought to protect African Americans from slave-catchers.

103. "Topical" because their rights and interests are the topic of the decision. The term "topical minority" is a loose one, and there is always likely to be dispute about whom it comprises (and the same is true of "topical majority"). But the looseness is not a problem. Even loosely defined, the distinction between topical and decisional minorities enables us to see that not everyone who votes for the losing side in an issue about rights should be regarded as a member of the group whose rights have been adversely affected by the decision. See Waldron, *Law and Disagreement*, pp. 13–14.

104. Rawls, *Political Liberalism*, pp. 54–58.

105. Dworkin, *Freedom's Law*, p. 25.

106. Dworkin is careful to say (ibid., p. 7) that it is not an argument for judicial review: "Democracy does not insist on judges having the last word, but it does not insist that they must not have it."

107. Ibid., pp. 32–33. Dworkin adds that, of course, "if we assume that the court's decision was wrong, then none of this is true. Certainly it impairs democracy when an authoritative court makes the wrong decision about what the democratic conditions require—but no more than it does when a majoritarian legislature makes a wrong constitutional decision that is allowed to stand. The possibility of error is symmetrical."

108. For a full response, see Waldron, *Law and Disagreement*, ch. 13.

109. See also the discussion in Jeremy Waldron, "Legislatures Judging in Their Own Cause," *Legisprudence*, 3 (2009), 125.

110. *United States v. Carolene Products Co.*, 304 U.S. 144 (1938), at p. 152n4. See also Keith E. Whittington, "An Indispensable Feature? Constitutionalism and Judicial Review," *N.Y.U. Journal of Legislation and Public Policy*, 6 (2002–2003), 21, at p. 31, stating that my neglect of this idea in *Law and Disagreement* is "striking from the perspective of American constitutional theory."

111. Ely, *Democracy and Distrust*, pp. 135–79.

112. Tushnet, *Taking the Constitution Away from the Courts*, p. 159: "Every law overrides the views of the minority that loses. . . . We have to distinguish between mere losers and minorities that lose because they cannot protect themselves in politics."

113. It is important also to distinguish between prejudices and views held strongly on religious or ethical grounds. We should not regard the views of pro-life advocates as prejudices simply because we do not share the religious convictions that

support them. Almost all views about rights—including pro-choice views—are deeply felt and rest in the final analysis on firm and deep-seated convictions of values.

114. See Tushnet, *Taking the Constitution Away from the Courts*, p. 218.

10. FIVE TO FOUR

1. Guha Krishnamurthi, Jon Reidy, Michael Stephan, and Shane Pennington, "An Elementary Defense of Judicial Majoritarianism," *Texas Law Review*, 88 (2009), 33, at pp. 33–34.

2. See, e.g., Barry Friedman, "Dialogue and Judicial Review," *Michigan Law Review*, 91 (1993), 577, at p. 600; and Richard H. Pildes, "Is the Supreme Court a 'Majoritarian' Institution?" *Supreme Court Review* (2010), 103.

3. *Citizens United v. Federal Election Commission*, 558 U.S. 310 (2010).

4. I follow Hannah Arendt in distinguishing "majority decision" from "majority rule." See Hannah Arendt, *On Revolution* (Penguin, 1973), p. 164: "Only where the majority, after the decision has been taken, proceeds to liquidate politically, and in extreme cases physically, the opposing minority, does the technical device of majority decision degenerate into majority rule."

5. By way of definition, I will say that MD is a decision procedure that determines the outcome of a binary choice—yes or no, petitioner versus respondent—by designating a set of individual voters and choosing the option favored by a majority of those voters, even if it is only a bare majority (such as 50 percent plus one). Note that MD so defined differs slightly from the method used for elections in a "first past the post" electoral system. That method selects the candidate who secures more votes than any other candidate, whether he receives more than 50 percent or not. But MD is more or less exactly the method used in most parliaments and congresses to make legislative decisions.

6. See, e.g., David Estlund, *Democratic Authority: A Philosophical Framework* (Princeton University Press, 2008), p. 98: "Democratic legitimacy requires that the procedure can be held, in terms acceptable to all qualified points of view, to be epistemically the best (or close to it) among those that are better than random."

7. See Thomas Christiano, *The Constitution of Equality: Democratic Authority and Its Limits* (Oxford University Press, 2008), p. 2: "[D]emocracy realizes public equality in collective decision-making."

8. For a discussion of the supposedly low costs of MD, see Adam Samaha, "Undue Process," *Stanford Law Review*, 59 (2006), 601, at pp. 618–20.

9. See, e.g., Christian List, "The Logical Space of Democracy," *Philosophy and Public Affairs*, 39 (2011), 262.

10. Daniel Farber and Philip Frickey, *Law and Public Choice* (University of Chicago Press, 1991), p. 55. See also Frank H. Easterbrook, "Ways of Criticizing the

Court," *Harvard Law Review,* 95 (1982), 802, at pp. 811–31, for a fine discussion of the application of Arrow's paradox and other decision-theory difficulties to judicial decision-making.

11. Of course, some decisions on the Supreme Court, like the decision to hear a case at all, are made on the basis of something less than a majority: four votes are sufficient to grant certiorari. For a discussion of this, see Richard Revesz and Pamela Karlan, "Nonmajority Rules and the Supreme Court," *University of Pennsylvania Law Review,* 136 (1988), 1067; Revesz and Karlan discuss the relation between "the Rule of Four" and the Court's use of MD to decide the merits of a case, but they refrain from any focus on the judicial use of MD itself.

12. Constitution of Nebraska, Article V, §2. The supermajority requirement was enacted in 1920. See also the discussion in *Mehrens v. Greenleaf,* 227 N.W. 325, 328 (Neb. 1929), where the court stated that "a legislative act is always presumed to be within constitutional limitations unless the contrary is clearly apparent—a rule consistently followed by this court. However, the people, ever alert, and jealous of their vested rights, in 1920 adopted as an amendment to the Constitution of our state, as an additional safeguard, the following provision (art. 5, §2): 'No legislative act shall be held unconstitutional except by the concurrence of five judges'—five-sevenths of the membership of the court as then and now composed."

13. Constitution of North Dakota, Article VI, §4.

14. See also text accompanying notes 72–76.

15. For an account of possible strategies that might be used to install a supermajority requirement, see Jed Shugerman, "A Six–Three Rule: Reviving Consensus and Deference on the Supreme Court," *Georgia Law Review,* 37 (2003), 893. However, translating the Nebraska rule to the federal context would be difficult. In Nebraska, all challenges to legislation are heard by the state's Supreme Court, so the default position (in the absence of a supermajority) is that the legislation stands. In a system that allowed challenges up through a hierarchy of courts, the use of a supermajoritarian decision procedure would be more complicated. If a federal district court struck down the statute, would a supermajority be needed in the appellate court above it to uphold that decision or to overturn it? What would the default position be?

16. See Michael Kirby, "Judicial Dissent: Common Law and Civil Law Traditions," *Law Quarterly Review,* 123 (2007), 379.

17. I am grateful to Pasquale Pasquino for letting me see his unpublished and untitled paper presented at the *Collège de France* in June 2010 that deals with this issue. See also Montesquieu, *The Spirit of the Laws,* ed. Anne Cohler et al. (Cambridge University Press, 1989), p. 76 (Bk. VI, ch. 4): "In monarchies the judges assume the manner of arbiters; they deliberate together, they share their thoughts, they come to an agreement; one modifies his opinion to make it like another's; opinions with the least support are incorporated into the two most widely held."

18. Consider the anguished closing lines of Justice Blackmun's concurrence in *Planned Parenthood of Southeast Pennsylvania v. Casey*, 505 U.S. 833 (1992), at p. 943: "I am 83 years old. I cannot remain on this Court forever."

19. *Roe v. Wade*, 410 U.S. 113 (1973).

20. Most discussions assume that there will be something like MD and focus instead on how to modify it. See, e.g., David Post and Steven Salop, "Rowing against the Tidewater: A Theory of Voting by Multi-judge Panels," *Georgia Law Journal*, 80 (1992), 743.

21. See, e.g., Jeffrey Rosen, *The Supreme Court: The Personalities and Rivalries that Defined America* (St. Martin's Griffin, 2006), pp. 177–82, for the claim that judges ought to be willing to vote strategically. For some criticism of this view, see Jeremy Waldron, "Temperamental Justice," *New York Review of Books*, May 10, 2007.

22. See H. Ron Davidson, "The Mechanics of Judicial Vote Switching," *Suffolk University Law Review*, 38 (2004), 17, addressing the way in which vote-switching practices emerged on the Supreme Court.

23. See, e.g., Andrew Burrows, "Numbers Sitting in the Supreme Court," *Law Quarterly Review*, 129 (2013), 305; and Jonathan Remy Nash, "The Majority that Wasn't: Stare Decisis, Majority Rule, and the Mischief of Quorum Requirements," *Emory Law Journal*, 58 (2009), 831.

24. See, e.g., Lewis Kornhauser and Lawrence Sager, "The One and the Many: Adjudication in Collegial Courts," *California Law Review*, 81 (1993), 1.

25. Shugerman, "A Six–Three Rule," comes closest, but even his long article is mainly an argument that we should insist on a 6–3 supermajority, not really an elaboration of the reasons for our present bare-majority rule.

26. Jeremy Waldron, "The Core of the Case against Judicial Review," *Yale Law Journal*, 115 (2006), 1346, at p. 1392n119.

27. Jeremy Waldron, "A Majority in the Lifeboat," *Boston University Law Review*, 90 (2010), 1043, at p. 1044.

28. Krishnamurthi et al., "An Elementary Defense of Judicial Majoritarianism," p. 33. Krishnamurthi and his coauthors go on to say: "In light of this, we aim to answer Waldron's challenge. Specifically, we will demonstrate that Waldron's challenge exposes no new problem regarding judicial review."

29. Particularly, Krishnamurthi et al. (ibid., pp. 33–34) wanted to rebut two points they thought I was making: "Waldron's challenge to provide an elementary defense of judicial majoritarianism may proceed from one of two distinct claims. First, Waldron may be simply suggesting that judicial majoritarianism effectively makes courts functionally equivalent to legislatures—thereby undermining the need for judicial review. Alternatively, Waldron may be suggesting that majoritarian decisionmaking . . . is inconsistent with prevailing justifications of judicial review."

30. Ronald Dworkin, "Response," *Boston University Law Review*, 90 (2010), 1059, at p. 1086.

31. Akhil Reed Amar, *America's Unwritten Constitution: The Precedents and Principles We Live By* (Basic Books, 2012), pp. 357–61.

32. Shugerman, "A Six–Three Rule."

33. Roderick Hills, "Are Judges Really More Principled than Voters?" *University of San Francisco Law Review*, 37 (2002), 37, at pp. 58–59.

34. Amar, *America's Unwritten Constitution*, p. 360.

35. Ibid., p. 358. There is a brief discussion of the "naturalness" view in Section 2.

36. Amar, *America's Unwritten Constitution*, pp. 358–59.

37. Shugerman, "A Six–Three Rule," p. 932.

38. Hills, "Are Judges Really More Principled than Voters?" discussing Christopher Eisgruber, *Constitutional Self-Government* (Harvard University Press, 2001). In his response, Eisgruber does not really engage with the argument about MD. See Christopher Eisgruber, "Constitutional Self-Government and Judicial Review: A Reply to Five Critics," *University of San Francisco Law Review*, 37 (2002), 115, at pp. 124–28.

39. Hills, "Are Judges Really More Principled than Voters?" p. 58.

40. Ibid., pp. 58–59.

41. Arendt, *On Revolution*, p. 163.

42. See Jeremy Waldron, *Law and Disagreement* (Oxford University Press, 1999), pp. 105–13.

43. Amar, *America's Unwritten Constitution*, p. 358, quoting John Locke, *Two Treatises of Government*, ed. Peter Laslett (Cambridge University Press, 1988), p. 350 (II, §96).

44. Ibid.

45. I used to have a more sympathetic view of Locke's account—see Jeremy Waldron, *The Dignity of Legislation* (Cambridge University Press, 1999), pp. 130–50-but I accept the critique of Thomas Nagel, "Waldron on Law and Politics," in his collection *Concealment and Exposure and Other Essays* (Oxford University Press, 2002), 141, at pp. 144–45.

46. See, e.g., Ronald Dworkin, *Freedom's Law: The Moral Reading of the Constitution* (Harvard University Press, 1996), pp. 15–19.

47. See, e.g., Arend Lijphart, *Thinking About Democracy: Power Sharing and Majority Rule in Theory and Practice* (Routledge, 2008); John W. Chapman and Alan Wertheimer (eds.), *Majorities and Minorities* (New York University Press, 1990); and Ian Shapiro, "Three Fallacies Concerning Minorities, Majorities, and Democratic Politics," in his collection *Democracy's Place* (Cornell University Press, 1996), 16.

48. Adam Przeworski, "Minimalist Conception of Democracy: A Defense," in *The Democracy Sourcebook*, ed. Robert A. Dahl et al. (MIT Press, 2003), 12, at p. 15.

49. Ibid.

50. Przeworski acknowledges this in a reference to professional armies: "Clearly, once physical force diverges from sheer numbers, when the ability to wage war becomes professionalized and technical, voting no longer provides a reading of chances in a violent conflict" (ibid.).

51. Cf. James Mill, "The Ballot," *Westminster Review,* July 1830, reprinted in *James Mill: Political Writings,* ed. Terence Ball (Cambridge University Press, 1992), 225, at pp. 266–67.

52. The alleged equivalence between MD and the principle of utility is even rougher than I have indicated, for even if voters know their self-interest and vote for it, it is not clear how a single vote, equal to all others, can convey intensity of preference. A majority of mild preferences might defeat a minority of very intense ones in a way that the Benthamite principle of utility would frown on.

53. Maybe they vote their *political* preferences, but the utilitarian argument for MD is not plausible if it is supposed to range over political, as opposed to personal, preferences.

54. The utilitarian argument for MD may work for legislators. In a properly apportioned polity, the vote of each legislator reflects a prospect for happiness aggregated over an equal number of constituents. But even in jurisdictions where judges are elected, we have no theory of representation that allows judges' votes to reflect the utility prospects of those who elected them.

55. Compare the argument in Thomas Hobbes, *De Cive*, ed. Howard Warrender (Oxford University Press, 1983), pp. 137–38, to the effect that in large assemblies,

> where the Votes are not so unequall, but that the conquered have hopes by the accession of some few of their own opinion at another sitting to make the stronger Party. . . . [They try therefore to see] that the same businesse may again be brought to agitation, that so what was confirmed before by the number of their then present adversaries, the same may now in some measure become of no effect. . . . It follows hence, that when the legislative power resides in such convents as these, the Laws must needs be inconstant, and change, not according to the alteration of the states of affaires, nor according to the changeablenesse of mens mindes, but as the major part, now of this, then of that faction, do convene; insomuch as the Laws do flote here, and there, as it were upon the waters.

56. See the discussion of "the principle of institutional settlement" in Henry Hart and Albert Sacks, *The Legal Process: Basic Problems in the Making and Application of Law,* ed. William Eskridge and Philip Frickey (Foundation Press, 1994), pp. 1–6.

57. I am most grateful to Jeanne Fromer, Erin Murphy, Rachel Shalev, and Kenji Yoshino for pressing points along these lines.

58. Hills, "Are Judges Really More Principled than Voters?" p. 59. See also Krishnamurthi et al., "An Elementary Defense of Judicial Majoritarianism," p. 34: "[T]o maximize the chances of getting the right answer . . . seems to be the dominant reason why the judiciary utilizes majority voting."

59. See John Gilbert Heinberg, "Theories of Majority Rule," *American Political Science Review*, 26 (1932), 452, at p. 453, observes that in canon law, "there was introduced the doctrine of the *maior et sanior pars* whereby the 'majority' was both counted and weighed. Thus it might be possible for a minority composed of *pars sanior* to prevail over a numerical majority. In time, however, the simple numerical count came to prevail, and a preponderance in number was taken as evidence of a preponderance in *sanitas*."

60. On the other hand, who among us is not curious about what the fifth dentist knows that the four others are not saying?

61. Cf. Shugerman, "A Six–Three Rule," p. 934: "A bare majority of experts is not at all convincing. If four out of five experts agree that Brand X is the best toothpaste, this consensus establishes a degree of reliability. But if five out of nine experts agree that Law X is unconstitutional, one cannot conclude that the experts have spoken one way or the other. With five–four decisions, there is some sense of randomness that the decision came out one way and not the other."

62. A pure expertise argument would also have to take account of the fact that experts in the courts below it have also had their say. Barry Friedman, in his article "The History of the Countermajoritarian Difficulty, Part Three: The Lesson of *Lochner*," *New York University Law Review*, 76 (2001), 1383, at p. 1451n337, cites this quotation from Melvin Urofsky, "State Courts and Protective Legislation During the Progressive Era: A Reevaluation," *Journal of American History*, 72 (1985), 63, at p. 79: "Of the twenty-two judges who participated in the four [*Lochner*] decisions, twelve thought it constitutional, but because five of the ten who disagreed sat on the United States Supreme Court, the law went down."

63. See Adam Samaha, "Randomization in Adjudication," *William and Mary Law Review*, 51 (2009), 1, for a discussion of areas where we are comfortable with randomization in judicial processes (like the assignment of judges or selection of jurors) and cases where we are not comfortable (like judicial decision-making itself).

64. Marquis de Condorcet, "Essay on the Application of Mathematics to the Theory of Decision-Making," in *Condorcet: Selected Writings*, ed. Keith Michael Baker (Bobbs Merrill, 1976), 33.

65. Ibid., pp. 48–49.

66. Suppose there are three voters—V, W, and X—voting independently, each with a 0.6 chance of being right. When V casts his vote, there is a 0.6 chance he's right and a 0.4 chance he's wrong. When W casts his vote, there is a $0.6 \times 0.6 = 0.36$ chance that a majority comprising at least W and V will be right, a $0.6 \times 0.4 = 0.24$

chance that V will be right and W wrong, and a $0.4 \times 0.6 = 0.24$ chance that V will be wrong and W right. Now X casts his vote. If V got it right and W wrong, there is a $0.24 \times 0.6 = 0.144$ chance that a majority comprising only V and X will be right. And if V got it wrong and W right, there is the same chance (0.144) that a majority comprising only W and X will be right. The overall probability that a majority will be right then is [0.36 (VWX or VW) + 0.144 (VX) + 0.144 (WX)] = 0.648, which is somewhat higher than the 0.6 individual competence we began with. For a sense of the difference that an increase in group size can make, consider that if we add to the group two additional voters of the same individual competence (0.6), we get a competence of 0.68256 for the five members deciding by a majority. To get a group competence of higher than 0.9, we need only add an additional thirty-seven members with individual competencies of 0.6. See Bernard Grofman and Scott L. Feld, "Rousseau's General Will: A Condorcetian Perspective," *American Political Science Review*, 82 (1988), 567, at p. 571.

67. Should we worry that deliberation among judges might spoil the Condorcet result? I think not. The theorem's assumptions do require that the individual votes be independent of one another but, in my reading, it is a mistake to think that this precludes prior deliberation. Provided the competence of the individual voters—the judges—is measured after the deliberation takes place, the Condorcet result will accrue irrespective of how each individual's competence came to be at the level it is at. We have to remember that the Jury Theorem is a purely arithmetical result; it has no epistemic substance that could be affected by facts about how the voters came to have a given level of epistemic competence. See Jeremy Waldron, "Democratic Theory and the Public Interest: Condorcet and Rousseau Revisited," *American Political Science Review*, 83 (1989), 1322, at pp. 1322–28.

68. Some might say that if the Condorcet theorem justifies the use of MD on judicial panels, then it surely justifies even more strongly the use of MD in legislatures where the numbers are one or two orders of magnitude higher. But Condorcet argued, in his "Essay on the Application of Mathematics to the Theory of Decision-Making," p. 49, that there is no guarantee that electable representatives individually have a greater than 0.5 chance of coming up with the right result: "A very numerous assembly cannot be composed of very enlightened men. It is even probable that those comprising this assembly will on many matters combine great ignorance with many prejudices. Thus there will be a great number of questions on which the probability of the truth of each voter will be below ½." If average individual competence falls below 0.5, the Condorcet effect goes into reverse. "It follows," said Condorcet, "that the more numerous the assembly, the more it will be exposed to the risk of making false decisions" (ibid.).

69. *Planned Parenthood of Southeastern Pennsylvania v. Casey*, 505 U.S. 833 (1992), at p. 1001, Scalia, J., dissenting: "The people know that their value judg-

ments are quite as good as those taught in any law school—maybe better. If, indeed, the 'liberties' protected by the Constitution are, as the Court says, undefined and unbounded, then the people should demonstrate, to protest that we do not implement their values instead of ours. . . . Value judgments, after all, should be voted on, not dictated."

70. Alexis de Tocqueville, *Democracy in America,* ed. Isaac Kramnick (Penguin, 2003), p. 281.

71. See Kenneth O. May, "A Set of Independent Necessary and Sufficient Conditions for Simple Majority Decisions," *Econometrica,* 20 (1952), 680. See also Charles Beitz, *Political Equality* (Princeton University Press, 1989), pp. 58–67; Robert A. Dahl, *Democracy and Its Critics* (Yale University Press, 1989), pp. 139–41; and Amartya Sen, *Collective Choice and Social Welfare* (Holden Day, 1970), pp. 71–74. Some have said that a lottery might also satisfy these conditions; see, e.g., Ben Saunders, "Democracy, Political Equality, and Majority Rule," *Ethics,* 121 (2010), 148, at p. 151: "In lottery voting, each person casts a vote for their favored option but, rather than the option with most votes automatically winning, a single vote is randomly selected and that one determines the outcome. This procedure is democratic, since all members of the community have a chance to influence outcomes, but is not majority rule, since the vote of someone in the minority may be picked. It is, as I describe it, egalitarian, since all have an equal chance of being picked. It gives each voter an equal chance of being decisive." See also Samaha, "Randomization in Adjudication." But MD assigns greater weight to each individual vote (in the direction in which it points) than lottery voting does.

72. Of course, fairness is partly dependent on context and partly a matter of who one is being fair to. In the context of a criminal trial, we use a method of unanimity for jury decision in order to be fair to the defendant. In other contexts, such as democratic decision, we use MD in order to be fair to the voters. These are different ideas, and it is unclear whether MD in court matches either of them.

73. See note 12. See also, in that same note, the quotation from *Mehrens v. Greenleaf,* 227 N.W. 325, 328 (Neb. 1929), elaborating the connection between the supermajority requirement and the presumption of constitutionality.

74. The classic statements are in *Ogden v. Saunders,* 25 U.S. 213 (1827), at p. 270: "It is but a decent respect due to the wisdom, the integrity, and the patriotism of the legislative body, by which any law is passed, to presume in favour of its validity, until its violation of the constitution is proved beyond all reasonable doubt," and in the *Sinking-Fund Cases,* 99 U.S. 700 (1878), at p. 718: "Every possible presumption is in favor of the validity of a statute, and this continues until the contrary is shown beyond a rational doubt."

75. Robert Eugene Cushman, "Constitutional Decisions by a Bare Majority of the Court," *Michigan Law Review,* 19 (1921), 771, at p. 772, quotes this statement

from *Watson on the Constitution,* II, p. 1190: "Can it be said that an act is a clear violation of the Constitution when five justices declare it to be so, and four declare with equal emphasis that it is clearly not so? All doubt must be resolved in favor of the constitutionality of the law, and it must be clear in the mind of the court that the law is unconstitutional. But can this condition exist when four of the justices are equally earnest, equally emphatic, equally persistent and equally contentious in their position that a law is clearly constitutional?" For a modern version of this view, see Shugerman, "A Six–Three Rule," p. 895: "Just as the criminal jury's unanimity voting rule supplements the individualized 'reasonable doubt' determination, a six–three voting rule would appropriately supplement the Justices' individualized determination of deference to Congress."

76. Justice Washington, writing for the Court in *Ogden v. Saunders,* 25 U.S. 213 (1827), which upheld the constitutionality of a bankruptcy statute, acknowledged generously that the presumption of constitutionality doctrine was held also by those dissenting justices who found the statute unconstitutional. He wrote (ibid., p. 270): "I am perfectly satisfied that it is entertained by those of them from whom it is the misfortune of the majority of the Court to differ on the present occasion, and that they feel no reasonable doubt of the correctness of the conclusion to which their best judgment has conducted them."

77. For some history of political arguments that the justices should follow a supermajority rule, see Evan Caminker, "Thayerian Deference to Congress and Supreme Court Supermajority Rule: Lessons from the Past," *Indiana Law Journal,* 78 (2003) 73, at p. 87.

78. Hills, "Are Judges Really More Principled than Voters?" p. 59.

79. Dworkin, "Response," p. 1086. (See the discussion in Section 2.)

80. Rank and seniority do matter in some contexts: the chief justice assigns the writing of the opinion of the Court, unless he is in the minority, in which case the senior justice in the majority does.

81. See also Dennis Baker and Rainer Knopf, "Minority Retort: A Parliamentary Power to Resolve Judicial Disagreement in Close Cases," *Windsor Year Book of Access to Justice,* 21 (2002), 347, at p. 356.

82. See Jeremy Waldron, "Deliberation, Disagreement and Voting," in *Deliberative Democracy and Human Rights*, ed. Harold Koh and Ronald Slye (Yale University Press, 1999), 210, pp. 223–24.

83. John Stuart Mill, *Considerations on Representative Government* (Prometheus Books, 1991), pp. 179–80: "[T]hough every one ought to have a voice . . . that every one should have an equal voice is a totally different proposition. . . . If, with equal virtue, one is superior to [another] in knowledge and intelligence—or if with equal intelligence, one excels the other in virtue—the opinion, the judgment of the higher moral or intellectual being is worth more than that of the inferior; and if the institutions of the country virtually assert that they are of the same value, they assert a thing which is not."

84. For a discussion, see James Buchanan and Gordon Tullock, *The Calculus of Consent: Logical Foundations of Constitutional Democracy* (Liberty Fund, 2004), pp. 233–48.

85. Shugerman, "A Six–Three Rule," p. 935, puts it this way: "Each Justice represents a snapshot of political consensus by the President and the Senate at the time of his or her confirmation."

86. It is quite remarkable that people put up with this—for example, that supporters of Vice-President Gore were willing to accept the bare-majority decision in *Bush v. Gore*, 531 U.S. 98 (2000). Would the supporters of Governor Bush have accepted a contrary result? No one knows. Remember the "Brooks Brothers Riot"? See Tim Padgett, "Mob Scene in Miami," *Time Magazine*, November 26, 2000.

87. Neal Riemer, "The Case for Bare Majority Rule," *Ethics*, 62 (1951), 16, at p. 17.

88. Hills, "Are Judges Really More Principled than Voters?" p. 59.

89. Pasquale Pasquino has suggested to me that it would be much easier to sustain the formal (Montesquieuian) view of the judge as just a "mouthpiece of the law" (respected on the same basis and to the same extent as every other judicial mouthpiece on the same panel) when individual judges are not celebrities and where there is no tradition of public dissent or of each judge's sustaining a consistent political line from individual opinion to opinion. (For Montesquieu's bon mot, see Montesquieu, *The Spirit of the Laws*, at p. 163 (Book XI, ch. 6): "[T]he judges of the nation are . . . only the mouth that pronounces the words of the law, inanimate beings who can moderate neither its force nor its rigor.")

90. Dworkin, *Freedom's Law*, p. 365.

91. Again, the phrase is Dworkin's, from *A Matter of Principle* (Harvard University Press, 1985), p. 33.

92. The obvious retort is that judges' votes are complemented by the reasons they give, which means that it is never just a matter of counting noses on a court as it is in the legislature. But legislators give reasons, too. I argued in Chapter 9 that a comparison between the reasons given for abortion law reform in a judicial context, say in *Roe v. Wade*, 410 U.S. 113 (1973), and in a legislative context, such as in the UK House of Commons second reading debate on the Medical Termination of Pregnancy Bill (1966), does not flatter the judicial reasoning.

93. Alexander Bickel, *The Least Dangerous Branch: The Supreme Court at the Bar of Politics* (Yale University Press, 1962), p. 16.

94. Baker and Knopf, "Minority Retort: A Parliamentary Power to Resolve Judicial Disagreement in Close Cases," p. 356.

95. See Thomas Nagel's acknowledgment in "Waldron on Law and Politics," pp. 141–42, concerning the U.S. Supreme Court's decision-making on basic principles of right and justice: "Since that Court also operates by voting and often decides cases by a five-to-four majority, the issue is not whether majorities should be permitted

to decide fundamental disputes of justice and rights but who it should be a majority of, how the members of the group should be selected, and what kind of debate should lead to the vote."

96. *Dred Scott v. Sandford*, 60 U.S. 393 (1856).

97. *Dickerson v. United States*, 530 U.S. 428 (2000) (striking down a federal statute that rendered admissible the voluntary statements made by suspects who had not received Miranda warnings).

98. *Planned Parenthood of Southeastern Pennsylvania v. Casey*, 505 U.S. 833 (1992).

99. For the distinction between (i) decisional majority and minority and (ii) topical majority and minority, see Chapter 9, Section 6.

100. See, e.g., Joshua Cohen, "Deliberation and Democratic Legitimacy," in *Deliberative Democracy: Essays on Reason and Politics*, ed. James Bohman and William Rehg (MIT Press, 1997), p. 67; and John Ferejohn, "Instituting Deliberative Democracy," in *Nomos XLII: Designing Democratic Institutions*, ed. Ian Shapiro and Stephen Macedo (New York University Press, 2000), p. 75.

101. See Jack Knight and James Johnson, "Aggregation and Deliberation: On the Possibility of Democratic Legitimacy," *Political Theory*, 22 (1994), 277.

102. See, e.g., Samuel Freeman, "Deliberative Democracy: A Sympathetic Comment," *Philosophy and Public Affairs*, 29 (2000), 371, at p. 372.

103. Shugerman, "A Six–Three Rule," p. 895.

11. ISAIAH BERLIN'S NEGLECT OF ENLIGHTENMENT CONSTITUTIONALISM

1. One might also invoke side contributions from David Hume in his essays on government, William Blackstone in his *Commentaries*, and Jeremy Bentham in *A Fragment on Government*.

2. Gordon Wood, "The American Enlightenment," in *America and Enlightenment Constitutionalism*, ed. Gary L. McDowell and Johnathan O'Neill (Palgrave Macmillan, 2006), 159, at p. 160.

3. Peter Gay, *The Enlightenment: An Interpretation*, Vol. 2: *The Science of Freedom* (W.W. Norton, 1969), p. 560: "Even George Washington, though less of an intellectual than his colleagues . . . almost automatically adopted . . . their enlightened philosophy. When he addressed the governors of the American states in June 1783, shortly after victory, his circular letter breathed pride in his philosophical century: 'The foundation of our Empire,' he said, 'was not laid in the gloomy age of Ignorance and Superstition, but at an Epocha when the rights of mankind were better understood and more clearly defined, than at any former period; the researches of the human mind after social happiness, have been carried to a great extent, the treasures of knowledge, acquired by the labours of Philosophers, Sages, and Legislators, through a long succession of years, are laid open for our use, and their collected

wisdom may be happily applied in the Establishment of our forms of Government.'" Gay's source for this quotation is cited as Douglass Adair, "'That Politics May Be Reduced to a Science': David Hume, James Madison, and the Tenth Federalist," *Huntington Library Quarterly*, 20 (1957), 343.

4. See Michael Kammen's observations on the influence of American constitution-making in France in *A Machine that Would Go of Itself: The Constitution in American Culture* (Transaction Publishers, 2006), p. 65. See also Gay, *The Enlightenment*, pp. 556–57: "America, wrote Turgot in that year, was bound to prosper, for the American people were 'the hope of the human race; they may well become its model.'" And Gay himself closes his book with the following observation: "[T]here was a time when tough-minded men looked to the young republic in America, saw there with delight the program of the philosophes in practice, and found themselves convinced that the Enlightenment had been a success" (ibid., p. 568).

5. Sieyès appears in one or two of Berlin's lists of Enlightenment *philosophes*, but beyond that I think there is nothing but a reference to his being the first to use the phrase "social science" (or its French equivalent) in *What Is the Third Estate?*

6. There is a one-line reference to Madison in Isaiah Berlin and Beata Planowska-Sygulska, *Unfinished Dialogue* (Prometheus Books, 2006), p. 210.

7. See Isaiah Berlin, "Montesquieu," in his collection *Against the Current: Essays in the History of Ideas* (Princeton University Press, 2001), 130.

8. Montesquieu, *The Spirit of the Laws*, ed. Anne Cohler, Basia Carolyn Miller, and Harold Samuel Stone (Cambridge University Press, 1989), p. 63 (Bk. V, ch.14).

9. Berlin, *Against the Current*, pp. 164–65. See also his letter to Morton White, July 19, 1957, in Isaiah Berlin, *Enlightening: Letters 1946–1960* (Chatto and Windus, 2009) (Kindle loc. 16883) p. 589, which repeated, without elaboration, the jibe at the United States.

10. Berlin, *Against the Current*, pp. 194–95. He also attacked Montesquieu's dutiful observations on natural law at the very beginning of *The Spirit of the Laws*, banal observations that in fact play virtually no role at all in his constitutionalist theory (Berlin, *Against the Current*, pp. 195–96). Cf. Montesquieu, *The Spirit of the Laws*, pp. 3–5 (Bk. I, ch. 1).

11. Cf. Montesquieu, *The Spirit of the Laws*, pp. 17–19 (Bk. II, ch. 4), 28–29 (Bk. III, ch. 9), and 72–75 (Bk. VI, chs. 1–2).

12. Berlin, *Against the Current*, p. 187.

13. Letter to Andrzej Walicki, March 25, 1970, in Isaiah Berlin, *Building: Letters 1960–1975* (Random House, 2013) p. 421.

14. The closest he gets to Montesquieu's views on legal and constitutional structure is in his portrayal of Montesquieu as cautious about change, in Isaiah Berlin, *Three Critics of the Enlightenment* (Princeton University Press, 2000), pp. 432–33, and the aspersions he casts on Montesquieu's conception of liberty, in Isaiah Berlin, "Two Concepts of Liberty," in *Four Essays on Liberty* (Oxford, 1990), 118. Montesquieu had

written in *The Spirit of the Laws,* p. 155 (Bk. XI, ch. 3), that "political liberty does not consist in an unlimited freedom. In . . . societies directed by laws, liberty can consist only in the power of doing what we ought to will, and in not being constrained to do what we ought not to will."

15. Alexander Hamilton, John Jay, and James Madison, *The Federalist Papers,* ed. George W. Carey and James McClellan (Liberty Fund, 2001), p. 67 (Number 14: Madison).

16. Emmanuel Sieyès, *Political Writings: Including the Debate between Sieyès and Tom Paine in 1791,* ed. Michael Sonenscher (Hackett, 2003), 92, at p. 133.

17. Ibid., p. 81.

18. Ibid., p. 143.

19. John Locke, *Two Treatises of Government,* ed. Peter Laslett (Cambridge University Press, 1988), pp. 323–30 (II, §§87–94), 364–66 (II, §§143–48), and 374–80 (II, §§159–68).

20. Isaiah Berlin, *The Crooked Timber of Humanity: Chapters in the History Of Ideas,* ed. Henry Hardy (Princeton University Press, 2013).

21. Immanuel Kant, "Idea for a Universal History," in *Toward Perpetual Peace and Other Writings on Politics, Peace and History,* ed. Pauline Kleingeld (Yale University Press, 2006), 3, at p. 9 (8: 24).

22. Immanuel Kant, "Towards Perpetual Peace," in *Kant: Practical Philosophy,* ed. Mary Gregor (Cambridge University Press, 1999), 311, at p. 335 (8: 366).

23. Ibid.

24. Berlin, *The Crooked Timber of Humanity,* pp. 19–20.

25. Kant, "Idea for a Universal History," pp. 8–9: "The greatest problem for the human species to which nature compels it to seek a solution is the achievement of a civil society which administers right universally. . . . Thus a society in which freedom under external laws is connected to the highest possible degree with irresistible power, that is, a perfectly just civil constitution, must be the highest goal of nature for the human species. . . . This problem is both the most difficult and also the last to be solved by the human species. . . . [I]ndeed, its perfect solution is impossible: nothing entirely straight can be fashioned from the crooked wood of which humankind is made. Nature has charged us only with approximating this idea. That this task is also the last to be carried out also follows from the fact that such a constitution requires the right conception of its nature, a great store of experience practiced in many affairs of the world, and, above all of this, a good will that is prepared to accept such a constitution" (8: 22–23).

26. Hamilton, Jay, and Madison, *The Federalist Papers,* ed. Carey and McClellan, p. 268 (Number 51: Madison).

27. Voltaire, "Thoughts on Public Administration" (1752), in *Voltaire: Political Writings,* ed. David Williams (Cambridge University Press, 1994), 212, at p. 222 (§ xxxviii).

28. Hamilton, Jay, and Madison, *The Federalist Papers,* ed. Carey and McClellan, pp. 269 (Number 51: Madison).

29. David Hume, "That Politics May Be Reduced to a Science," in David Hume, *Essays: Moral, Political, Literary,* ed. Eugene F. Miller (Liberty Classics, 1985), p. 14.

30. David Hume, "On the Independence of Parliament," in Hume, *Essays,* p. 42.

31. Adam Smith, *An Inquiry into the Nature and Causes of the Wealth of Nations,* ed. Edwin Cannan (University of Chicago Press, 1977), pp. 474–95 (Bk. IV, ch. 2).

32. Berlin, *Three Critics of the Enlightenment,* p. 119.

33. Berlin mentions Vico's admiration of England's oligarchy in *Three Critics of Enlightenment,* p. 493.

34. Sieyès, "What Is the Third Estate?" p. 131.

35. See Montesquieu, *The Spirit of the Laws,* pp. 156ff. (Bk. XI, ch. 6); and Voltaire, "Republican Ideas," in *Voltaire: Political Writings,* ed. Williams, 195, at pp. 202–4. See also Voltaire in *Letters on England,* ed. Leonard Tancock (Penguin Books, 2000), p. 45: "The English are the only people upon earth who have been able to prescribe limits to the power of kings by resisting them; and who, by a series of struggles, have at last established that wise Government where the Prince is all powerful to do good, and, at the same time, is restrained from committing evil; where the nobles are great without insolence, though there are no vassals; and where the people share in the Government without confusion."

36. Sieyès made the rather grudging acknowledgment in "What Is the Third Estate?" p. 131, that "I do not deny that the English Constitution was an astonishing piece of work at the time when it was established," adding that "what the English people have is a constitution, however incomplete it may be, while we have none" (ibid., p. 132). But he asked nevertheless: "Even if it is good in itself, is it likely to be good for France?" (ibid., p. 130).

37. Immanuel Kant, "On the Common Saying 'That May Be Correct in Theory but It Is of No Use in Practice,'" in Kant, *Practical Philosophy,* ed. Gregor, 273, at p. 301 (8: 303). See also Immanuel Kant, *The Conflict of the Faculties,* ed. Mary Gregor (University of Nebraska Press, 1992), p. 163 (7: 88).

38. Kammen, *A Machine that Would Go of Itself,* p. 65.

39. Hamilton, Jay, and Madison, *The Federalist Papers,* ed. Carey and McClellan, p. 1 (Number 1: Hamilton).

40. I should acknowledge some remarks in Berlin and Planowska-Sygulska, *Unfinished Dialogue,* p. 210, that do seem to be more hospitable to the design perspective in political theory. Responding to his interlocutor's question about whether political theory can ever construct anything enduring, Berlin said:

> American democracy had theory behind it. Jefferson and Madison and all these people were brought up on classical theory. America is a country built entirely upon

theory.... It is the first State created by metaphysics and sheer theorising. America is not perfect, but nevertheless the theory by which Americans live, the famous American way of life, the democracy in which they believe, is a force for good and not for evil.

41. Henry Hardy, "A Personal Impression of Isaiah Berlin," in *Isaiah Berlin, Flourishing: Letters 1928–1946*, ed. Henry Hardy (Chatto and Windus, 2004), p. xliii.

42. Ibid., p. xlii.

43. Gay, *The Enlightenment*, Vol. 2, p. 566.

44. Berlin, *The Crooked Timber of Humanity*, p. 250. See also Ira Katznelson, "Isaiah Berlin's Modernity," *Social Research*, 66 (1999), 1079, at p. 1100.

45. But see also the remarks attributed to Berlin in note 40.

46. Pauline Maier, *Ratification: The People Debate the Constitution, 1787–1788* (Simon and Schuster, 2010), pp. 36, 48, and 51.

47. Voltaire, "Republican Ideas," p. 198 (§xliii).

48. Hardy, "A Personal Impression of Isaiah Berlin," p. xliii.

49. George Crowder, *Isaiah Berlin: Liberty, Pluralism and Liberalism* (Polity Press, 2004), p. 146.

50. William Galston, "Constitutional Pluralism," *Social Philosophy and Policy*, 28 (2011), 228, actually puts Berlin's ethical pluralism to work in thinking about constitutional structure.

51. Isaiah Berlin, "Five Essays on Liberty: Introduction," in Isaiah Berlin, *Liberty*, ed. Henry Hardy (Oxford University Press, 2002), p. 48.

52. Isaiah Berlin, "Two Concepts of Liberty," in Berlin, *Liberty*, ed. Hardy, p. 169.

53. Ibid., p. 210.

54. Hamilton, Jay, and Madison, *The Federalist Papers*, ed. Carey and McClellan, p. 256 (Number 48: Madison).

55. Ramin Jahanbegloo, *Conversations with Isaiah Berlin*, second edition (Charles Scribner's Sons, 1991), pp. 113–14.

56. Sieyès, "What Is the Third Estate?" pp. 152–53 (my emphasis).

57. Berlin, "Political Ideas in the Twentieth Century," in Berlin, *Liberty*, ed. Hardy, p. 78. Berlin seemed to think that political freedom in the participatory sense was better associated with a positive conception of liberty ("Two Concepts of Liberty," in Berlin, *Liberty*, ed. Hardy, p. 176): "The desire to be governed by myself, or at any rate to participate in the process by which my life is to be controlled, may be as deep a wish as that for a free area for action, and perhaps historically older. But it is not a desire for the same thing."

58. Bernard Crick, "Politics as Freedom," in *Philosophy, Politics and Society*, third series, ed. Peter Laslett and W. G. Runciman (Basil Blackwell, 1976), p. 199: "What is missing in Berlin's analysis ... is any analysis of the link between freedom

and political action—a typically liberal lack, if a socialist may say so. . . . Freedom is being left alone from politics—is it?" See also Robert A. Kocis, "Reason, Development, and the Conflicts of Human Ends: Sir Isaiah Berlin's Vision of Politics," *American Political Science Review*, 74 (1980), 38. Berlin replied to Crick in a letter dated March 29, 1966, reprinted in Berlin, *Building,* ed. Hardy, p. 271.

59. Berlin, "Two Concepts of Liberty," p. 211.

60. See the discussion of this in Graeme Duncan and Steven Lukes, "The New Democracy," *Political Studies,* 11 (1963), 156, at p. 176; and the letter from Berlin to Lukes dated April 4, 1963, in Berlin, *Building*, ed. Hardy, p. 150.

61. Ibid., p. 177.

62. Berlin, "Two Concepts of Liberty," p. 208: "Democracy may disarm a given oligarchy, a given privileged individual, but it can still crush individuals as mercilessly as any previous ruler."

63. Ibid., p. 176 and note. In correspondence with a Polish philosopher, in Berlin and Planowska-Sygulska, *Unfinished Dialogue,* p. 88, Berlin also cited Joseph II, Holy Roman Emperor in the late eighteenth century, as an enlightened despot.

64. Immanuel Kant spoke of "a mode of government conforming to the spirit of a representative system," in *Toward Perpetual Peace* in Kant, *Practical Philosophy,* pp. 324–25 (8: 352–53). See also the discussion in Immanuel Kant, *The Conflict of the Faculties,* ed. Mary Gregor (University of Nebraska Press, 1979), pp. 159 and 163.

65. Montesquieu, *The Spirit of the Laws,* pp. 17–19 (Bk. II, ch. 4), 28–30 (Bk. III, chs. 9–10), and 59–65 (Bk. V, chs. 14–15).

66. Diderot, *"Observations sur le Nakaz,"* §VII, in Diderot, *Political Writings,* ed. John Hope Mason and Robert Wokler (Cambridge University Press, 1992), pp. 88–89.

67. See Berlin, *Liberty,* p. 380, for the index reference. (Henry Hardy acknowledges in conversation that this is a mistake.)

68. Berlin had no interest in Locke's speculation about the combination of representation, the rule of law, and the separation of powers as a partial security against oppression. I mean Locke's argument for investing legislative power in a large representative assembly. See Locke, *Two Treatises,* pp. 329–30 (II, §94). Legislative authority should be placed in a large assembly, says Locke, insisting also that the laws made in that assembly should be general in form and that the enforcement of the law should be separated from institutions devoted to their enactment. See also Locke, *Two Treatises*, p. 364 (II, §143). That way, legislators would be given pause by the thought that they and their families would have to bear the burden of any oppressive laws they enacted. (See also the discussion in Chapter 3.)

69. If it were, we would have to consider the rough, crude, and almost telegraphic notes that Berlin used for his lecture "Democracy, Communism and the

Individual" (1949), available in the Isaiah Berlin Virtual Library, at http://berlin.wolf.ox.ac.uk/lists/nachlass/demcomind.pdf (last visited October 22, 2014).

70. E.g., in Jahanbegloo, *Conversations with Isaiah Berlin*, p. 82: "I do not greatly respect the lady's ideas, I admit. Many distinguished persons used to admire her work. I cannot."

71. Berlin, "Felix Frankfurter at Oxford," in his collection *Personal Impressions*, ed. Henry Hardy (Princeton University Press, 2001), p. 112. In conversation, George Kateb has suggested to me that Berlin (like Frankfurter) was "horrified by the way the US Supreme Court, in the name of Enlightenment constitutionalism, had stymied FDR's New Deal." This, Kateb says, combined with the fact that, in other contexts, constitutionalism did not seem capable of blocking the descent into despotism, may have led him to the belief that its reputation is overrated. I suspect this is true, although Berlin's published writings do not directly disclose these as concerns about constitutionalism as such.

72. Isaiah Berlin, "The Great Amateur," *New York Review of Books*, March 14, 1968.

73. Isaiah Berlin, Letter to Chaim Weizmann, September 16, 1948, in *Enlightening*, ed. Hardy, p. 54. See also Berlin's observation in a letter to Rowland Burdon-Muller, September 11, 1974, in *Building*, ed. Hardy, p. 575, about the United States in the wake of the Watergate scandal: "[R]everence for law, constitution, justice is bound to be overwhelming in a nation whose bonds are not cultural or racial or religious or even linguistic or dynastic etc. but founded on a set of written principles which are evidently being flouted."

74. Jahanbegloo, *Conversations with Isaiah Berlin*, p. 46. Berlin went on: "The business of political philosophy is to examine the validity of various claims made for various social goals, and the justification of the methods of specifying and attaining these. . . . It sets itself to evaluate the arguments for and against various ends pursued by human beings. . . . This is the business of political philosophy and has always been such. No true political philosopher has omitted to do this." Later in the same set of interviews, Berlin reiterated the point: "[P]olitical theory is about the ends of life, about values, about the goals of social existence, about what men in society live by and should live by, about good and evil, right and wrong" (ibid., pp. 57–58).

75. Ibid., p. 46.

76. Ibid.

12. THE CONSTITUTIONAL POLITICS OF HANNAH ARENDT

1. Aristotle, *The Politics* (Cambridge University Press, 1988), p. 3 (1253a).

2. For doubts about Arendt's reading of Aristotle, see Bernard Yack, *The Problems of a Political Animal* (University of California Press, 1993), pp. 9–13.

3. Hannah Arendt, *On Revolution* (Penguin Books, 1973), p. 131.

4. See Bonnie Honig, *Political Theory and the Displacement of Politics* (Cornell University Press, 1993), pp. 76ff.

5. Hannah Arendt, *The Human Condition* (University of Chicago Press, 1958), p. 41.

6. See George Kateb, *Hannah Arendt: Politics, Conscience, Evil* (Rowman and Allenheld, 1984), 20ff., drawing on Hannah Arendt, "Civil Disobedience," in *Crises of the Republic* (Harcourt, Brace, Jovanovich, 1972), esp. pp. 96–102; and Arendt, *On Revolution*, ch. 5.

7. Honig, *Political Theory*, pp. 96–109.

8 Arendt, *On Revolution*, p. 232.

9. See, e.g., Hannah Arendt, *The Origins of Totalitarianism*, new edition (Harcourt, Brace, Jovanovich, 1973), pp. 115–16 and 251ff. I accept Margaret Canovan's suggestion in *Hannah Arendt: A Reinterpretation of Her Political Thought* (Cambridge University Press, 1992), p. 63, that *Origins of Totalitarianism* should be given more prominence in discussions of Arendt's philosophy.

10. See Hannah Arendt, "Civil Disobedience," in *Crises of the Republic*, p. 89.

11. Arendt, *The Human Condition*, p. 194.

12. Ibid. Compare the figure of the lawgiver in Jean-Jacques Rousseau, *The Social Contract*, ed. Maurice Cranston (Penguin Books, 1968), pp. 84ff. (Bk. II, ch. 7). See also Arendt's observations on the craftsman-like work of Plato's philosopher-king in *The Human Condition*, pp. 226–27.

13. See Arendt, *On Revolution*, p. 208; and Arendt, *The Human Condition*, p. 188.

14. Arendt, *The Human Condition*, p. 198. See also Hannah Arendt, "What Is Freedom?" in her collection *Between Past and Future* (Penguin Books, 1977), pp. 153–54.

15. Arendt, *On Revolution*, p. 175.

16. See also Stephen Holmes, *Passions and Constraint: On the Theory of Liberal Democracy* (University of Chicago Press, 1995), p. 163.

17. Cf. Arendt, *The Human Condition*, p. 52.

18. Hannah Arendt, *Eichmann in Jerusalem* (Penguin Books, 1977), pp. 262–63.

19. Arendt, *On Revolution*, p. 164.

20. Ibid., p. 157. And she emphasized more generally the importance of positive law as a tangible social reality, compared with the merely notional existence of the *ius naturale*. See Arendt, *Origins of Totalitarianism*, p. 464.

21. Arendt, *On Revolution*, pp. 125–26 and 145–46.

22. Cited in Arendt, *On Revolution*, p. 146.

23. Arendt, *On Revolution*, p. 126. See also Arendt, *The Human Condition*, p. 191, where Arendt talks of "the various limitations and boundaries we find in every body politic."

24. Arendt, *Eichmann in Jerusalem*, p. 264. See also her discussion of the plight of the stateless in a comprehensive system of states in *Origins of Totalitarianism*, pp. 293–94.

25. The identity she has in mind "relates not so much . . . to a piece of land as to the space between individuals in a group whose members are bound to, and at the same time separated and protected from, each other by all kinds of relationships, based on a common language, religion, a common history, customs, and laws. Such relationships become spatially manifest insofar as they themselves constitute the space wherein the different members of a group relate to and have intercourse with each other" (Arendt, *Eichmann in Jerusalem*, pp. 262–63). See also Arendt, *The Human Condition*, p. 19, where Arendt talks of "the territorial boundaries which protect and make possible the physical identity of a people." For her hesitations about national identity, see Arendt, *Origins of Totalitarianism*, pp. 230–31.

26. Arendt, *On Revolution*, p. 126.

27. Rousseau, *The Social Contract*, p. 90 (Bk. II, chs. 8–9).

28. Arendt, *On Revolution*, p. 275.

29. See Arendt, *Origins of Totalitarianism*, pp. 297–302.

30. In *The Human Condition*, p. 32, Arendt suggested that equality "presupposed . . . the existence of unequals." See also Kateb, *Hannah Arendt*, pp. 152–53.

31. See Arendt, *The Human Condition*, pp. 2, 28–37, and 244.

32. For an intriguing discussion, see Hanna Fenichel Pitkin, *The Attack of the Blob: Hannah Arendt's Concept of the Social* (University of Chicago Press, 1998).

33. Arendt, *Origins of Totalitarianism*, pp. 465–67.

34. Ibid.

35. See the account of the Mayflower compact in Arendt, *On Revolution*, p. 167.

36. Compare the remarks on Hobbesian philosophy in Arendt, *Origins of Totalitarianism*, pp. 139–47.

37. Arendt, *On Revolution*, pp. 141–54 and 218.

38. Ibid., pp. 59ff. But see Hannah Arendt, "Thoughts on Politics and Revolution," in *Crises of the Republic*, pp. 212–14, for the significance of legal obstacles to "expropriation," and Arendt, *The Human Condition*, pp. 70–73, for an account of the importance to individuals of the "darker ground" of privacy.

39. Arendt, *On Revolution*, p. 33. Compare Arendt's more ambivalent comment in "On Violence," in *Crises of the Republic*, p. 178: "The dissenters and resisters in the East demand free speech and thought as the preliminary conditions for political action; the rebels in the West live under conditions where these preliminaries no longer open the channels . . . for the meaningful exercise of freedom."

40. See Arendt, *Origins of Totalitarianism*, p. 460.

41. Ibid., p. 465.

42. See the discussion of Arendt regarding the debilitating hysteria of the McCarthy period in Pitkin, *Attack of the Blob*, pp. 102–4.

43. Arendt, *Origins of Totalitarianism*, pp. 290–302. I do not mean that Arendt rejects the international dimension altogether. See, e.g., her remarks on "consensus juris" in Arendt, *Origins of Totalitarianism*, p. 462, and on Adolf Eichmann as *hostis generis humani* in *Eichmann in Jerusalem*, pp. 260ff.

44. Arendt, *On Revolution*, pp. 148 and 154.

45. Cf. Honig, *Political Theory*, p. 76.

46. Arendt, *On Revolution*, p. 174.

47. Quoted in ibid., p. 173.

48. See Arendt, *The Human Condition*, p. 197.

49. Ibid., p. 189.

50. See Arendt, *Eichmann in Jerusalem*, p. 289. See also Arendt, "On Violence," p. 137.

51. Arendt, *The Human Condition*, p. 95.

52. Arendt, *On Revolution*, p. 220.

53. Arendt, *The Human Condition*, pp. 95 and 183. See also Seyla Benhabib, *The Reluctant Modernism of Hannah Arendt*, revised edition (Rowman and Littlefield, 2003), p. 125.

54. Kateb, *Hannah Arendt*, p. 158. See also Dana Villa, "Hannah Arendt: Modernity, Alienation and Critique," in *Hannah Arendt and the Meaning of Politics*, ed. Craig Calhoun and John McGowan (University of Minnesota Press, 1997), pp. 186–87.

55. Arendt, "Truth and Politics," in *Between Past and Future*, pp. 256–57.

56. Arendt, *On Revolution*, p. 93.

57. Ibid., pp. 30–31.

58. See the reflections on the wording of the Declaration of Independence in Arendt, "Truth and Politics," pp. 246–47. For further reflections on Arendt's view of equality, see Jeremy Waldron, "Arendt on the Foundations of Equality," in *Politics in Dark Times: Encounters with Hannah Arendt*, ed. Seyla Benhabib (Cambridge University Press, 2010), 17.

59. Arendt, *On Revolution*, p. 278: "Their title rested on nothing but the confidence of their equals, and this equality was not natural but political, it was nothing they had been born with; it was the equality of those who had committed themselves to, and now were engaged in, a joint enterprise."

60. Ibid., pp. 106–8.

61. Ibid., p. 71.

62. See the discussion of connections between "human nature" theories and "race" theories in Arendt, *Origins of Totalitarianism*, pp. 234–35.

63. Arendt accepts the view of James Madison that "[w]hen men exercise their reason coolly and freely on a variety of distinct questions, they inevitably fall into different opinions on some of them. When they are governed by a common passion, their opinions, if they are so to be called, will be the same." See Alexander Hamilton,

John Jay, and James Madison, *The Federalist Papers*, ed. George W. Carey and James McClellan (Liberty Fund, 2001), p. 266 (Number 50: Madison), quoted in Arendt, *On Revolution*, p. 225.

64. Arendt, "Truth and Politics," p. 241.

65. Arendt's most thoughtful discussions of this process are in her *Lectures on Kant's Political Philosophy*, ed. Ronald Beiner (University of Chicago Press, 1982), pp. 70ff. See also the discussion in Jeremy Waldron, "Kant's Legal Positivism," *Harvard Law Review*, 109 (1996), pp. 1559–60.

66. Arendt, *On Revolution*, p. 225.

67. Ibid., pp. 86–87. Compare Max Weber, "Politics as a Vocation," in *From Max Weber: Essays in Sociology*, ed. H. H. Gerth and C. Wright Mills (Routledge & Kegan Paul, 1970), p. 128: "Politics is a strong and slow boring of hard boards" and also Montesquieu, *The Spirit of the Laws*, ed. Anne Cohler, Basia Miller and Harold Stone (Cambridge University Press, 1989), p. 243 (Bk. 14, ch. 13): "Politics is a dull rasp which by slowly grinding away gains its end."

68. See Jeremy Waldron, *Law and Disagreement* (Oxford University Press, 1999), pp. 73–82.

69. Consider also her discussion of statelessness in Arendt, *Origins of Totalitarianism*, p. 296, as "the deprivation of a place in the world which makes opinions significant and actions effective."

70. Arendt, "Thoughts on Politics and Revolution," in *Crises of the Republic*, p. 232.

71. See Arendt, *On Revolution*, pp. 143 and 269. See also Kateb, *Hannah Arendt*, p. 118.

72. Arendt, *On Revolution*, p. 253.

73. See, e.g., Arendt, "Thoughts on Politics and Revolution," p. 253.

74. Arendt, *On Revolution*, p. 164.

75. Ibid.

76. Ibid., p. 236, quoting *The Table Talk of John Selden* (Reeves and Turner, 1890), p. 35.

77. Ibid., p. 279. Cf. Arendt's comments on "elitism" at ibid., pp. 275–80.

78. Ibid., p. 278.

79. Ibid., p. 227. There she also observes that "limitation to a small and chosen body of citizens was to serve as the great purifier of both interests and opinion, to guard 'against the confusion of a multitude.'" It is not clear from the context whether this is Arendt's own view or that of the American framers she is discussing.

80. See Arendt, *Origins of Totalitarianism*, pp. 115 and 250–66.

81. Arendt, *On Revolution*, p. 228.

82. See Canovan, *Hannah Arendt*, p. 35.

83. Arendt draws on Nietzsche's argument in *On the Genealogy of Morals*, ed. Keith Ansell-Pearson and Carol Diethe (Cambridge University Press, 1994), p. 35:

"To breed an animal which is able to make promises—is that not precisely the paradoxical task which nature has set herself with regard to humankind?"

84. Arendt, *On Revolution,* p. 167. She continues (ibid., p. 173): "No theory, theological or political or philosophical, but their own decision to leave the Old World behind and to venture forth into an enterprise entirely of their own led into a sequence of acts and occurrences in which they would have perished, had they not turned their minds to the matter long and intensely enough to discover, almost by inadvertence, the elementary grammar of political action."

85. Ibid., p. 206: "It is in the very nature of a beginning to carry with itself a measure of complete arbitrariness."

86. Ibid., pp. 201ff. Cf. Thomas Jefferson's proposal to provide in the Constitution itself "for its revision at stated periods," cited in Arendt, *On Revolution,* p. 234.

87. Hence Arendt's insistence in *On Revolution,* p. 182: "Neither compact nor promise . . . are sufficient to assure perpetuity, that is, to bestow upon the affairs of men that measure of stability without which they would be unable to build a world for their posterity, destined and designed to outlast their own mortal lives." See also Arendt, *The Human Condition,* p. 55: "If the world is to contain a public space, it cannot be erected for one generation and planned for them only; it must transcend the life-span of mortal man."

88. Arendt, "On Violence," p. 193 (appendix xi). See also Hannah Arendt, *The Life of the Mind—Two: Willing* (Harcourt, Brace, Jovanovich, 1978), p. 201.

89. I could have mentioned also her views on open government (Arendt, *On Revolution,* p. 253), institutional transparency (Arendt, *Origins of Totalitarianism,* p. 403), the rule of law (Arendt, *Origins of Totalitarianism,* pp. 243–44), procedural guarantees (Arendt, *Eichmann in Jerusalem,* p. 260), bicameralism (Arendt, *On Revolution,* p. 226), and judicial review of legislation (*On Revolution,* pp. 200 and 226–31).

90. Arendt, *On Revolution,* pp. 232ff.

91. See Arendt, "On Violence," p. 178.

92. Arendt, *On Revolution,* p. 239.

93. Christian Meier, *Caesar,* trans. David McLintock (Basic Books, 1995), pp. 358–59.

94. Kateb, *Hannah Arendt,* p. 31.

95. Honig, *Political Theory,* p. 80.

96. Arendt, "What Is Freedom?" p. 153.

97. Especially Arendt, *The Human Condition,* pp. 205–6.

98. Meier's own judgment is complicated by his understanding that other participants in Roman politics failed to grasp that the institutions needed to be "seen" in a way that permitted the question of their restructuring to be raised. See Meier, *Caesar,* pp. 360–63.

99. Arendt, *The Human Condition,* p. 53, regarding the contempt for institutions in modern mass society.

100. Cf. the discussion in Kateb, *Hannah Arendt,* pp. 36–38.

101. Arendt, *The Life of the Mind—One: Thinking* (Harcourt, Brace, Jovanovich, 1978), p. 179.

INDEX

abortion, 29, 196, 198, 210, 224–225, 234, 249, 257, 263–264, 270, 371
absolute prohibitions, 31
absolutism, 25, 57, 315
abstraction, 136, 198–199, 209, 284, 305
accountability, 18, 78, 101, 125, 167–194; agent-accountability, 168–169, 169–174, 176, 191–193; consumer, 191–192; democratic, 181–183, 194; electoral, 177, 183–188, 189–190; forensic, 167–169, 178, 191–192; informal, 348; and judicial review, 191–192; meanings of, 186–187, 191, 345–346; mediated, 168–169, 173, 179, 193, 346; and power, 188–189
accuracy, 10
Acemoğlu, Daron, 7, 311
Ackerman, Bruce, 120, 338, 343
action-in-concert, 298, 300
Act of Union (UK), 27
Adair, Douglass, 373
Adams, John, 108, 276, 290, 294–295
Adams, John Clarke, 352, 354
adjudicative functions, 45, 51. *See also* courts; judiciary
administration, public, 68–69

administrative agencies, 35, 52, 63–64; quasi-judicial functions of, 52; rule-making by, 69
adversarial process, 206, 217–218
affirmative action, 29, 196, 210, 270
Afghanistan, 7
agenda-setting, 67, 101–102
agents and principals, 168, 169–184, 189. *See also* accountability: agent-accountability
age-restrictions, 330
aggregation of preferences, 250
agonism, 187, 292, 297–298
Aleinikoff, Alexander, 348
Alexander, Larry, x, 40, 318
All Souls College, Oxford, xi, 287
Amar, Akhil, 24, 253, 255–256, 314, 364
American Civil War, 257
American Revolution, 283
Anastaplo, George, 103, 108, 114, 332, 334–337
ancestor worship, 29, 39–40
angels, 2, 281
Anti-Federalists. *See* Federalists and anti-Federalists
antiquity, politics of, 292
apathy, 285

Appellate Jurisdiction Act UK, 329
arbitrary government, 60
archives, 299
Arendt, Hannah, ix, 14, 28, 50, 93, 124, 274, 287, 290–307, 312, 313, 316, 320, 331, 341–342, 378–384; on constitution-framing, 13, 294; on importance of institutional housing for politics, 13, 15, 36, 293–295; on majority-decision, 255, 362; on representation, 142
argument, legal and constitutional, 10, 28
aristocracy, 39, 75, 89–91
Aristotle, ix, 20, 90, 96, 123, 132, 290, 315, 331, 340, 378
armed forces, 35
Aroney, Nicholas, 78, 84, 326–327, 329
Arrow, Kenneth, 248, 362–363
articulated governance, 46, 51, 57–58, 62–65, 70–71
association, freedom of, 97–99
assurance, mutual, 296
Athens, 90, 135, 177, 183–184
Atkin, James (Lord Atkin), 67
Atlee, Clement, 101, 115
attorney-general, duties of, 213, 355–356
Austen-Smith, David, 311
Austin, John, 127, 154, 339, 343
Australia, 25, 100, 104, 196, 332
authority, 34, 158, 189, 304
autocracy, 286
autonomy, 38, 154

back-room deals, 128
Bagehot, Walter, 77, 79, 84, 101, 105, 115, 130, 327–329, 331, 333, 336, 340
Baier, Kurt, 337
Baker, Dennis, 269, 370–371
Bakvis, Herman, 325
Banks, Jeffrey, 311
Banning, Lance, 322
Barber, Sotirios, 34, 317
battlefield, 68
Baxter, Arthur, 113, 336

Behn, Robert, 345–346
Beitz, Charles, 19, 314, 359, 369
Bell, Stringer, 14, 301
Bentham, Jeremy, 17, 28, 53–54, 58–59, 85, 148, 282, 320, 329, 349, 372; on bicameralism, 73, 74–79, 82, 84, 313, 325–326; on principles of legislation, 145–146, 156, 342; on unwritten law, 316, 322; writing style, 74
Berlin, Isaiah, ix, 4–5, 12, 274–289, 310, 314, 373–374, 376–378; contempt for Hannah Arendt, 13, 287, 290; on liberty, 284–286, 376; neglect of constitutional structure, 20, 375–377
bicameralism, ix, 6, 16, 35–36, 49, 73–92, 109, 156–157, 219, 278, 328; relation to judicial review, 73, 354. *See also* second chambers
Bickel, Alexander, 196, 350, 371
big government, anxiety about, 32
Bill of Rights (England), 27
Bill of Rights (in US Constitution), 34, 208
bills of attainder, 66, 136, 138
bills of rights, 201, 208, 211, 221–223, 232, 240; as parchment barriers, 285; bearing upon disagreements, 211–212, 221–222; bland formulations of, 211, 221; interpretation of, 211–212; provision for amendment of, 232; text of, 221
biography, 2
bishops, 72, 324, 359–360
Black, Charles, 198, 351
Blackmun, Harry, 364
Blackstone, William, 74, 326, 372
Bogdanor, Vernon, 78, 82, 87, 105, 328–329, 335
Bolingbroke, Henry St John, 29
Bonhoeffer, Dietrich, 115
Book of Common Prayer, 145, 342
Bosniak, Linda, 317
Boston University Law School, 340
bottom-line mentality, 203, 354
boundaries, 293, 295–296, 379–380

INDEX 387

Bristol (UK), 184–186
Brooks Brothers Riot, 371
Brown, Gordon, 83
Brown, John, 117
Brown v. Board of Education, 195, 197, 198, 244, 350
Buchanan, James, 371
budgetary priorities, 9
burdens of judgment, 94, 210
Burdon-Muller, Rowland, 378
bureaucracy, 130, 149, 298, 305
Burke, Edmund, 13, 97, 101, 102, 104, 312, 322, 332, 335, 336–337, 348; theory of representation, 161–162, 185–186, 344, 346
Burrows, Andrew, 340, 364
Burton, Stephen, 341
Bush, George W., 104, 120, 371
Bush v. Gore, 120, 338, 371
business, 191

cabinet, 17–18, 81, 83–84, 89, 130, 329
cadi justice, 58–59
Caesar, Julius, 14–15, 306
California, 135, 270
Caminker, Evan, 370
campaign finance, 29, 210, 212, 234, 246, 270
Campion, Gilbert, 102, 119–120
Canada, 24, 25, 104, 196; Charter of Rights and Freedoms, 200–201, 208–209, 353–354; unelected senate of, 73, 89, 100, 126, 325
Canovan, Margaret, 342, 382
capital punishment, 196, 270
Cappelletti, Mauro, 352, 354
care, duty of, 149, 155–157
Carrington, Peter, 83
ceremony, 13
Cerutti, Joseph Antoine, 282
Chalfont, Alun, 336
chancellor of the exchequer, 83
Charles I (of England), 175, 346

checks and balances, 6, 21, 26, 30, 45, 49, 52, 62, 65, 70, 73, 108, 110, 156–157
Chichele Chair in Social and Political Theory, xi, 8, 15
children, 219
China, 115, 340
Choper, Jesse, 355
Christiano, Thomas, 18, 313, 355–356, 362
Christian virtues, 3
church, 104. *See also* separation of church and state
circumstances of politics, 255
citizens, 54, 300
Citizens United v. Federal Election Commission, 246, 362
civil disobedience, 121, 292
civility, 270, 335
civil law systems, 249
civil liberties, 297, 305
Civil Rights Act (US), 244
civil service, 179; neutrality of, 6, 97
clarity, 148
class conflict, 93
clergy, 126
Clinton, Bill, 266
coalition, 114, 242
coercion, 62
Cohen, G.A., 3, 15, 310
Cohen, Joshua, 372
coin-tossing, 258–259
Coke, Sir Edward, 28
Colbert, Stephen, 103
collectivities, 181–182
colonialism, 204
Colorado, 12
committee system, 130, 156, 190, 204
common good, 13, 275
common law, 153, 249
common people, enfranchisement of, 37
Communist party, 121
community, 4, 12; basis of, 296; political, 180, 303

competition, political, 93–94, 142; analogy with military conflict, 107; between centers of power, 50–51; regulated, 102
compromise, 80
concentration camps, 297
concept and conception, 355
Condorcet, Marie Jean Antoine Nicolas de Caritat, 136, 263–264, 276, 289, 340; jury theorem of, 131–132, 157, 261–263, 268, 340, 344, 367–368
Confederate States of America, 333
conferences, 7
confidence, vote of, 101
Congress, United States, 69, 130
Congressional Record, 223
conscription, 138–139
consensus, political, 119, 271, 300, 301
consent, 295, 304–305
consequentialism, 8–9, 133, 146–147
Conservative Party (UK), 103
conservativism, 197
consistency, 148
Constant, Benjamin, 276
constituency, 161–162
constitutional adjudication, 24
constitutional change, 42, 118, 120, 232, 312
constitutional courts, 202
constitutional design, 26–27, 277, 278–279, 282–284
constitutional disagreement, 118–120
constitutional essentials, 118–119, 337
constitutional interpretation. *See* interpretation
constitutionalism, ix, 16, 22, 23–44, 70, 92, 287, 305; American, 24, 47, 292 (*see also* United States: constitutionalism in); comparative, 24; democratic, 43; and emnity towards democracy, 38, 42–43; laissez-faire constitutionalism, 32; and limited government, 23, 35; meanings of, 23–29, 314, 315; neutrality of, 32; popular, 43–44, 319, 350; positive, 317; and separation of powers, 45. *See also* Enlightenment: constitutionalism in
constitutional principles, 24–25
constitutional reform, 8, 13
Constitutional Reform Act (UK), 324
constitutional rights, 28, 31, 118, 124, 195, 208–212, 221, 270
constitutional structure, 1–2, 20–21, 25, 275, 285
constitutions, 1–2, 153, 305; affirmative tasks of, 34–36; as higher law, 27–28; as "parchment barriers," 28; codified and uncodified, 27; constraining power of, 25, 29–34, 284; in democratic and non-democratic societies, 37; democratic view of, 43, 284; design of, 2, 26–27, 282–284; endurance of, 303–304, 383; framing of, 293, 304; functions of, 295–297; interpretation of, 42; "living constitution," 24; respect for, 41; structures of, 6, 201, 297–298; study of, 24; task of constituting institutions of government, 34–36; texts of, 28; of US states, 117, 314; written and unwritten, 24, 27–29, 294. *See also* constitutional adjudication; constitutional change; constitutional courts; constitutional design; constitutional disagreement; constitutional essentials; constitutional principles; constitutional reform; constitutional structure; interpretation; United States Constitution
constraint, distinguished from control, 29–30
constructivism, 295
consumers, 191–192
Conti, Vittorio, 346
contractarianism, 180–181
contracts, 32, 180–181, 298
conventions (assemblies for framing or changing a constitution), 42
conventions of the constitution, 26, 28
cooperation, conditions of, 5, 298

cooption, 114–115
corporations, 104, 181
corruption, 3, 9, 171, 287
costs, 9
Coulter, Ann, 335
councils, 292
counter-majoritarian difficulty, 18, 196, 269. *See also* judicial review of legislation
courts, 6, 16, 19, 35, 41, 57, 205–207; appellate, 206, 220, 246; as law-makers, 126–129; deal-making in, 250, 364; legitimacy of decision-making by, 126; log-rolling in, 250; majority-voting in, 207, 246–273; multi-member, 206–207; orientation to particular cases, 220–221, 358; in private law cases, 247; procedures of, 10, 217–218; reason-giving by, 206, 250; role of, 67–68; use of foreign law, 24
Crick, Bernard, 285, 376–377
criminal procedure, 165–166, 210
crooked timber of humanity, 280–281
Crowder, George, 376
Crown, in United Kingdom, 73, 81
cultural rights, 210
Cushman, Robert, 369–370
customs, 26

Dahl, Robert, 359, 369
David, king of Israel, 174–175
Davidson, H. Ron, 364
Davies, Ann, 329
debate, parliamentary, 9, 14, 17, 160. *See also* deliberation
decision-procedures, 213–217, 247; costs of, 258–260; disagreement concerning, 213
declaration of incompatibility, 200, 352
Declaration of Independence, 292, 381
defeat, political, 95–99
Defoe, Daniel, 334
degradation, 12
delegation, 69
deliberation, 13–14, 21–22, 69, 133, 139, 141, 204, 223, 299; need for focus, 28, 300; principled, 250; relation to majority decision, 164, 250, 301; responsive, 160–162; structuring of, 14, 36, 300; and voting, 271–272, 301–302
democracy, 3, 6, 18, 36–39, 47, 93, 106, 125–126, 157; basic rules of, 119–120; conditions of, 237; constitution of, 36–37; and control of the state, 30–31; deliberative, 69, 160, 271–272; direct versus representative, 20, 78, 134–135, 142–143, 286, 302; distinguished from republics, 177, 347; empowerment of ordinary people, 36–37; institutions of, 5, 204; making the case for, 150; participatory, 9; philosophical foundations of, 16; points of access in, 36; prerequisites of, 106; redefinition of, 38; relation to liberty, 285–286; representative, 134, 275; role of opposition in, 106–107; true nature of, 18; utilitarian argument for, 257
democratic culture, 204–205
democratic process, 195, 204
democratic theory, 167–168
Democrats and Republicans, 103, 110, 120
deontic logic, 33
deontology, 12, 216
design perspective on society, 274–275, 283, 286
despair, 305–306
despotism, 21, 58–59; possibility of liberal or enlightened, 286
devils, constitution-building for a race of, 280, 309
devolution, 6, 8
dialogue between courts and legislatures, 354
Dicey, A.V., 36, 47, 63, 65, 105, 315, 317, 319, 323, 335
Dickerson v. United States, 271, 372
dictatorship, 26
Diderot, Denis, 276, 286, 377
Difference Principle, 147, 342

dignity, 9–12, 54, 64
Diplock courts, 57
disagreement, 5–7, 14, 77, 93–94, 147, 149, 158–160, 197, 270; about justice, 159; about rights, 235; among judges, 255; among principals (in agency relationship), 171–172; ethical, 158; framing of, 6, 14; and need for a decision-procedure, 239; pervasiveness of, 213; reasonable, 210–211; resolution of, 5–6
dissensus, 271
dissent, 96–97, 105, 380; in court, 249, 271
diversity, value of, 132–134, 157–158, 162–163
"divide and choose," 88
dogmatism, 280
Douglas-Home, Alec, 83
Dr. Bonham's Case, 28, 315
Dred Scott case. See *Scott v. Sandford*
drunkenness, 76
due process, 7, 63, 65, 67; substantive, 29
Duncan, Graeme, 377
Dunn, John, 170, 188, 193, 345–346, 347, 349
Dworkin, Ronald, x, 3, 47, 197, 225, 265, 269, 310, 313, 318, 336, 344, 350, 354, 355, 357, 359–360, 371; defense of judicial review, 38–39, 237–238, 350–351, 361; defense of majority-decision in courts, 251–252, 365, 370; on equality, 343, 356; on law as integrity, 112, 153, 319; on value of participation, 216–217

economy, 3
Edinburgh, 13
education, 219; vouchers for, 196
efficiency, 9, 155, 258–260
egalitarianism, ix; luck-egalitarianism, 20
Eichmann, Adolf, 295, 381
Eisenhardt, Kathleen, 345
Eisgruber, Christopher, 253, 350, 354, 358, 360

elections, 19, 29, 36, 65, 77, 90, 94, 106, 167, 177–178, 187–188, 301–302; accountability through, 184–188; alleged aristocratic character of, 90–91; as aggregation of preferences, 257; as proxies for combat, 256–257; debates during, 219; integrity of, 36; schedule of, 79, 94, 112
Electoral College (US), 347
electoral system, 162, 228–229, 354
Elliot, Donald, 62, 320
Elster, Jon, 318, 348, 360
Ely, John Hart, 241, 360–361
emergencies, 34, 302
empirical study of politics, 8, 15. See also political science
empowerment, 34, 37
ends of life, 4; Isaiah Berlin on, 4, 288; ends of political life, 7
enfranchisement, 37
English constitution (in Enlightenment theory), 81, 277, 282, 328, 375
Enlightenment, 275–276; in America, 276, 372–373; constitutionalism in, 274–286
equal, treatment as an, 38
equality, ix, 3, 6, 8, 16, 267, 295, 299–300, 381; of concern and respect, 38; natural, 299, 381; of opportunity, 147. See also political equality
equilibrium, as constitutional ideal, 283
equity, 140, 341
Eskridge, William, 314
Estlund, David, 18, 313, 362
ethics, 19, 288–289
European Convention on Human Rights, 200, 208
European Court of Human Rights, 8, 16, 351
European Union, 8, 27
euthynai, 183–184
executive, 45, 56, 68–69, 130, 279; agenda of, 17; as a committee of the legislature, 67; ascendancy in parliamentary system,

17, 86–87; authority of, 46; consent to legislation, 35; decisiveness of, 68; domestic enforcement of laws by, 56, 60; domination of, as an ideal, 22; external aspect of, 279; judges' sympathy for, 67; in relation to bicameralism, 81–85; rule-making, 126; separation from legislature, 55; unified, 51
exemptions, 54–55
extrapolitical action, 292

factions, 181
fairness, 155, 164–165
Fallon, Richard, xi, 351–352, 355–356, 359
Farber, Daniel, 248, 362–363
fear, 170, 193
Fearon, James, 187, 345, 347–348
federalism, 6, 25, 49, 78, 109, 201–202, 279, 302
Federalist Papers, 2, 20, 26, 48, 61, 177–178, 282, 309, 315, 318–319, 323, 328, 341, 346–347, 374–376, 381–382
Federalists and anti-Federalists, 29, 48
federative power, 56, 81, 279
Feld, Scott, 368
felon disenfranchisement. *See* prisoner voting
Ferejohn, John, ix, 19, 181, 313, 347–349
fighting, 6, 107
Filler, Daniel, 357
Finer, S.E., 6, 311
Fleming, James, 314
Fontana, David, 117, 336, 338
Forbath, William, 12, 312, 350
foreign policy, 112
formal aspects of law, 29, 147–149
formalism, 222
formality, 162–163, 291–292
founding moments, 292
framer, 294. *See also* constitutions: framing of; United States Constitution: Framers of
France, 59, 74, 92, 135–136, 274, 294

Frankfurter, Felix, 287, 378
Franklin, Benjamin, 253, 276
Frederick the Great, 286
freedom, 4, 297, 302. *See also* liberty
Freeman, Samuel, 372
free speech. *See* speech, freedom of
French Revolution (of 1789), 274, 282
Frickey, Philip, 248, 362–363
Friedman, Barry, xi, 246, 347, 352, 362, 367
Friedrich, Carl, 316
Fromer, Jeanne, 366
Fugitive Slave Acts, 271
Fuller, Lon, 54, 136, 160, 217–218, 311, 357; on inner morality of law, 7, 147–149, 316, 321, 340, 342; on institutional competence, 69, 324
functional understanding of institutions, 46, 49, 52–53, 62, 68
furniture of politics, 13–14, 36
future generations, 13

Galston, William, 376
Gardbaum, Stephen, 352
Garrett, Brandon, 323
Garrison, William, 337
Gaskell, Elizabeth, 10, 312
Gay, Peter, 283, 372–373, 376
Geiringer, Claudia, 352
general good, 145–146, 186
generality, 136, 148
general will, 137, 180
Germany, 76, 297, 336
Geuss, Raymond, 311
Ginsburg, Ruth Bader, 266
God, 11, 174–175
Goldsworthy, Jeffrey, 353–354
good, competing conceptions of, 94
Goodridge v. Department of Public Health, 195, 350, 354
Gordon, Scott, 30, 316
Gore, Al, 371
Goths, 74

government, 182; determining the quality of, 1–2; limited, 23, 31–34
Government of the Republic of South Africa v Grootboom, 33, 317
Greece, Ancient, 293
Grofman, Bernard, 368

Hailsham. *See* Hogg, Quintin
Hamilton, Alexander, 26, 28, 92, 276, 282, 309, 315–316, 374
Hamilton, Walton, 28, 315
Hansard, 223, 224, 358
Hardin, Russell, 345, 348
Hardy, Henry, 283, 284, 286, 376
Hare, R.M., 341
Harrington, James, 88–89, 90–91, 330
Hart, Henry, 355, 357, 366
Hart, H.L.A., 153, 311, 343
Harvard University, 7
Hastings, Warren, 322
hate speech, 196, 210
Hayek, F.A., 55, 153, 321, 330, 343
health system, 191–192
Hegel, G.W.F., 333
Heinberg, John, 367
Helms, Ludger, 123, 335, 339
Helvetius, Claude, 282
Henkin, Louis, 356
Henry VIII, 106
hereditary office, 17, 72, 126, 130, 324
Herodotus, 74
Herzen, Alexander, 287
Hickman, Tom, 352
higher law, 27–28
Hills, Rick, ix, 253–254, 260, 265, 267–269, 365, 367, 370–371
Hirst v. United Kingdom, 313
historic preservation, 212
history, 13; legal, 12; political, 2
history of ideas, 20
Hobbes, Thomas, ix, 20, 57–58, 179–180, 213, 318, 321, 347–348, 356; doctrine of indivisibility of powers, 57, 321; instability of decision by voting, 366; on the need for legislation, 57; on the sovereign, 57–58, 62, 180
Hobhouse, Cam, 103, 115
Hogg, Quintin, 322
Holmes, Stephen, 19, 30, 34, 313–314, 317, 379
homosexual law reform, 196
Honig, Bonnie, 379, 381, 383
honor, 12
honors, 72–74
Hood, Christopher, xi, 345, 347, 349
House of Commons (UK), 17–18, 72, 77, 196, 224–225, 240, 329, 371; abortion debates in, 224–225, 371; ascendancy of, 87, 329–330; opposition party in, 100–103
House of Lords, 8, 9, 17, 72–73, 87, 89, 130; hereditary element in, 130; judges and bishops in, 17, 85–87; non-elective character of, 126; reform of, 72–73, 87, 91–92, 311
House of Lords Act (UK), 324
House of Representatives (US), 69, 104, 109, 130, 269
housing for politics, 13–14, 36, 292–295
human rights, 3, 31, 296–297; social and economic rights, 33
Human Rights Act (UK), 16, 27, 86, 200–201, 208, 352
Hume, David, 1–3, 6, 21, 89, 281, 309, 310, 314, 330, 372, 375
humiliation, 10–12
humility, 245, 283–284
Huscroft, Grant, 356

ideals, political, 3, 5
identity, 295, 380
impartiality, 153
imperfection, human, 274–275, 280
inclusion, 7
incommensurability. *See* values: incommensurability of

INDEX 393

individualism, 4, 180–181
information, 172–173
initiatives, legislative, 135, 270
insolence, 190–191
institutional choices, 8, 12
institutional competence, 206, 355
institutional design, 1–2, 41
institutional settlement. *See* settlement, need for
institutions, ix, 3, 5–10, 284; alienation from, 292; complexity of, 21; costs of, 9
instructions, to representatives, 173–174, 185–186
insult, 10, 12
intelligence, 112
integrity, in law, 112, 153
interests, 132–133, 143–144, 158, 161, 171, 235–236. *See also* self-interest
internalization of norms, 64
international institutions, 8
international law, 8, 216
International Monetary Fund, 33
international relations, 4
interpretation, 29, 42, 67, 163, 211, 223; theories of, 29, 222
investment protection, 33
Iraq, 7
isonomy, 299. *See also* political equality
Israel, 26, 121, 288, 338
Issacharoff, Sam, xi, 19, 39, 317, 348

Jackson, William Keith, 311
Jackson v. City of Joliet, 317, 358
Jahanbegloo, Ramin, 310, 312, 376, 378
Jay, John, 309, 315, 374
Jefferson, Thomas, 108, 253, 276, 290, 383
Jennings, Ivor, 100–103, 105, 116, 332–335
Johnson, James, 372
Johnson, Nevil, 100, 103, 115, 332–336
Joseph II, 377
judges, 23, 57, 85, 160; appointment of, 206, 360; deliberation among, 357; elected, 125, 206, 348; equal respect for, 268; errors of, 219, 222–223, 356, 359, 361; expertise of, 257–258; high status of, 206; law-making by, 42, 67, 125, 126–129, 154; life tenure of, 112; majority decisions by, 197; opinion-writing by, 252; presence in House of Lords, 17, 72, 85; reason-giving by, 129, 223–226, 258, 349; seniority among, 252, 265–266; sympathy for the executive, 67; training of, 206–207
judgment. *See* will (versus judgment)
judicial process, 206
judicial review of executive action, 199, 351
judicial review of legislation, 12, 18, 25, 39, 41–43, 49, 86–87, 109–110, 125, 135, 195–245; and accountability, 192–193; as mode of citizen access to government, 233; as upholding constitution, 41; attacks upon, 197–198; challenge to democracy, 16, 41–42; conditional nature of the case against, 203; counter-majoritarian aspect of, 18; debate about, 16, 197–198; defenses of, 197; defined, 199–202; ex ante review, 202; legitimacy of, 199; relation to bicameralism, 73, 86; rights-based, 170, 201; strong versus weak, 199–200, 351–352; on watershed issues, 42
judicial supremacy, 351–352
judiciary, 12, 40, 85–87, 205–207; activism of, 16; anxieties of, 224; federal (in US), 179; independence of, 6, 70, 105, 205; legitimacy of, 154
Judiciary Act 1789 (US), 254
jurisprudence, 7
jury, 248
justice, ix, 3–6, 7, 8, 16, 153; global, 16, 20; industry of studying, 3; of outcomes, 8–9; political, 12, 19; primacy of, 4

Kahana, Tsvi, 353
Kahn, Jeffrey, 324
Kammen, Michael, 282, 373, 375

Kant, Immanuel, 2, 10, 282, 289, 312, 343, 348–349, 375, 382; crooked timber of mankind, 278, 280–281, 374; on problem of constitutional design, 280, 309, 374; republicanism of, 276, 286, 377
Kaplow, Louis, 342
Karlan, Pamela, 363
Kateb, George, xi, 124, 299, 339, 378, 379–384
Kavanagh, Aileen, xi, 215, 356
Kay, Richard, 315, 317
Keane, John, 348
King, Anthony, 84, 87, 329–330
Kirby, Michael, 363
Kirchheimer, Otto, 121–122, 338–339
Knight, Jack, 372
Knopf, Rainer, 269, 370–371
Kocis, Robert, 377
Korematsu v. United States, 219, 367
Kornhauser, Lewis, 364
Kramer, Larry, 197–198, 319, 350–351, 357
Kramer, Matthew, 311
Kreimer, Seth, 351
Krishnamurthi, Guha, 251, 362, 364, 367

labor, organized, 12, 195
Labour Party, 103
Lafayette, Marquis de, 74
laissez-faire, 32
language, for politics, 294
Laslett, Peter, 347
law, concept of, 150–151, 321; desanctification of, 152
Lawrence v. Texas, 195, 350
laws, 2, 12, 152–153, 296; accumulation of, 112; addressees of, 152; administration of, 7; and decrees, 125; federative power not governed by, 56; generality of, 55, 136; inner morality of, 7, 55, 147–149; international (*see* international law); justice and injustice of, 12, 153; making of, 125–129, 152; standing of, in the community, 150–153; study of, 12, 15–16; technicality of, 59
lawyers, 29, 211
Leader of the Opposition, 100–103, 160; absence of office in United States, 108
leadership, 21
legacy, 184, 187
legalism, 59, 225–226
legal process, 16, 206, 355. *See also* due process
Legal Process School, 217–218, 366
legal scholarship, 15–16, 19
legislation, 28, 45, 65–66, 125, 145–166; different roles in, 88; dignity of, 46, 70, 84–85; formality of, 162; function of, performed by other institutions, 67–68, 69–70; generality of, 136–137, 151; presumption of constitutionality, 265, 369–370; reckless, 155; science of, 146; unconstitutional, 39; very idea of, 128, 153–155
legislative drafting, 133, 157
legislative due process, 72, 141, 162–163
legislative history, 163
legislative supremacy, 20, 51, 196, 214
legislators, 9, 184; accountability of, 231; bound by the laws they enact, 54–55; collegiality of, 162; election of, 339; from labor movement, 12; and threat of tyranny of the majority, 234
legislatures, 34, 125–126, 204; agenda-setting in, 81, 89, 101–102; as large assembly, 54; authority of, 31, 34; complexity of, 91–92; debates in, 219; design of chambers, 294, 295; elective character of, 125–126, 227; idealization of, 143, 220; independence of, 17; pathologies of, 198; processes of, 35–36, 141, 162–163; representative character of, 54, 141–142, 155; size of, 130–134; transparent dedication to law-making by, 126–129, 149; tumultuous character of, 131; of US states, 126

legitimacy, 5, 34, 78, 91, 149, 159, 160, 166, 224, 240, 255, 362; democratic, 65, 125, 129, 135, 164; in the face of disagreement, 213–215, 226–231; of judicial review, 27–28, 40, 197, 199, 203–204, 222, 226–231, 236–237; of organized opposition, 105, 123
Leibniz, Gottfried, 80
Levinson, Daryl, 50, 55, 309, 320–321, 336
Levinson, Sanford, xi, 19, 314
Levmore, Saul, 325
Liberal Democrats, 114
liberalism, 24; of fear, 30, 170–171, 193
liberals, 197, 296
liberal society, 4–5
liberty, ix, 3, 6, 16, 64, 284–287; as value protected by separation of powers, 53–54; importance of institutions for, 285; negative versus positive, 284–285, 296–297; not necessarily secured by democracy, 285–286; political, 285, 296; threats to, 50
Lieberman, Avigdor, 121
Lieberman, David, 326, 342
Liebman, James, 323
life peerage, 72–73, 325, 330
life-process, 291, 296
Lijphart, Arend, 365
limited government, 23, 30, 31–32, 63
List, Christian, 362
litigation, 206
Liversidge v. Anderson, 67, 324
local politics, 181, 184
Lochner v. New York, 195, 350, 367
Locke, John, ix, 20, 29, 48, 85, 150, 153, 276, 289, 318, 328, 331, 343, 347; on consent, 256; on federative power, 56, 68, 81; on legislative supremacy, 51, 350; on majority-decision, 253, 256, 365; on monarchy, 279; on separation of powers, 54–56, 62, 320–321, 374, 377; on toleration, 329; on trust, 169, 178
lot, choice by. *See* sortition

loyal opposition, ix, 6, 93–124, 149, 159–160; Her Majesty's, 99–103, 116–117
loyalty, 12, 114–123
Lukes, Steven, 377

Macedo, Stephen, 325
Machiavelli, Niccolò, ix, 3, 131, 310, 340
machine, analogy of constitution to, 278–279
Madison, James, ix, 2–3, 6, 20, 28, 48, 62, 84, 277, 278, 285, 289, 309, 315–316, 323, 328, 341, 373–374, 381; as Helvidius, 48, 92, 320; on checks and balances, 70; on Montesquieu, 48, 61–62, 81, 328; on republics and democracies, 177–178, 347; on separation of powers, 48, 53, 61–62, 81–82, 281, 318, 328
Magnarella, Paul, 315
Maier, Pauline, 376
majoritarianism, 38, 269–273; judicial, 246, 269
majority, 80, 164–165, 180; on constitutional issues, 40; power of past over future, 40; topical versus decisional, 235–236, 361, 372; tyranny of, 5, 36, 38, 195, 233–239, 271, 360
majority-decision, 227–229, 301–302; appropriate contexts for, 359–360; as proxy for combat, 256–257, 366; canon law conceptions of, 357; conditions for legitimacy of, 237; connection with equality, 227–228, 253–254; in courts, 246–273; definition of, 362; disparaged by defenders of judicial review, 247–248; distinguished from majority rule, 302, 362; efficiency of, 258–260; epistemic defenses of, 247, 260–264; fairness of, 247, 264–267, 359, 369; on issues of principle, 270; justification of, 247; natural character of, 247, 255–256; obvious appeal of, 255, 301–302; relation to principle of utility, 257–258, 366; responsiveness of, 258–259
managerialism, 68

Mandelson, Peter, 83
Manin, Bernard, 90, 318, 345, 348
mankind, depravity of, 21
Manning, John, xi, 46–48, 69, 319, 324
Maori people, 140, 341
Marbury v. Madison, 27, 39, 197, 315, 318, 354
markets, 32, 210
Marmor, Andrei, 354
marriage, 145, 195, 212
Marshall, John, 27
Mary Barton. See Gaskell, Elizabeth
Massachusetts, 195, 202, 354
mass society, 13, 15, 142, 302
May, Kenneth, 264, 344. 359, 369
Mayflower compact, 298, 303, 383
McCarthy, Joseph, 380
McCorvey v. Hill, 352
McGinnis, John, 314
McHenry, Dean, 100, 332, 334
McIlwain, C.H., 30, 316
Megan's Law, 221, 357
Mehrens v. Greenleaf, 363, 369
Meier, Christian, 14–15, 306, 313, 383
members of parliament, 83, 95, 101, 160–162, 184–186
Michelman, Frank, 198, 319, 356, 360
military, 107; civilian control of, 6
Mill, James, 366
Mill, John Stuart, ix, 9–10, 13–14, 17, 20, 23, 311, 312, 314, 318, 343, 360; on bicameralism, 79–80, 82, 313, 328; plural voting, 266, 370
ministerial office, 83, 90
Ministers of the Crown Act (UK), 332
minorities, 181–182, 196; discrete and insular, 241–242; topical and decisional, 235–236, 361, 372
Mitchell, Jeremy, 329
mixed regime, 89
Monaghan, Henry, 358
monarchy, 105, 116–117, 174–175, 204, 279, 331, 359-160; constitutional, 275, 286, 363; elective, 186, 348

Montesquieu, Baron de, 20–21, 45, 48, 58–62, 88–89, 276–278, 289, 310, 314, 322–323, 330, 363, 373, 382; absence of arguments in, 60; on constitutional structure, 277; on despotism, 277, 286; on English constitution, 81, 277, 282; on judges as mouth-pieces of the law, 371; jurisprudence, 278, 287; Madison's criticisms of, 48; on moderate government, 277; on separation of powers, 45, 48, 53, 81, 277–278; tautologies of, in defense of separation of powers, 60–61; on "Turkish justice," 58–59, 322
Moonen v. Film and Literature Board of Review, 352
Moore, Michael, 220, 357
moral, priority over the political, 5
moralism, political, 5
moral philosophy, 288–289; applied, 4
Muir, Edward, 346
Muirhead, Russell, 104, 335
Murphy, Erin, 366
Murphy, Walter, 315

Nagel, Thomas, 365, 371–372
narcotics, 152, 234
narratives, 298
Nash, Jonathan, 364
nation, as focus of loyalty, 120–121
nationalism, 4
Nazi Germany, 115, 297
Nazi party, 121, 338
Nebraska, 109, 248–249, 260, 265, 363
nemo iudex in sua causa, 238–239, 361
neutrality, 164–165, 264
Newman, Sandra, 318
news media, 348
New York Review of Books, 287
New Zealand, 9, 196, 332; abolition of Legislative Council, 9, 73; constitution, nature of, 26; House of Representatives, 9; judicial review in, 86; Maori representation in, 140, 341; newspapers, 17; New

INDEX 397

Zealand Bill of Rights Act, 200, 208, 232, 352, 355–356; New Zealand Constitution Act, 27; proportional representation in, 140; unicameralism in, 73, 86; weak judicial review in, 200
Nietzsche, Friedrich, 382–383
nobility, 88
non-democratic societies, 37, 39
North Dakota, 248, 363
Northern Ireland, 57
"notwithstanding clause," 200–201
Nozick, Robert, 3, 7, 310, 343

Obama, Barack, 103, 109
Obergefell v. Hodges, 350
objectivity, 94, 211, 351, 355
officials, 182–184
Ogden v. Saunders, 369–370
Oliver, Dawn, 87–88, 329
ontology, 13
openness, 7
opinions, 36, 160–161, 302; formation of, 300; versus preferences, 257
opportunism, political, 155
opposition, 96–107; demonization of, 104; empowerment of, 106; legitimation of, 104; of principle, 121–122; responsible, 102–103, 142. *See also* loyal opposition
oppression, 38, 54–55
order, 5
originalism, 24, 170
ostracism, 96
others' points of view, 300
"ought implies can," 71
outcome-related considerations, 214–216, 217–226, 231, 356
Oxford University, 289; teaching of political theory at, ix, xi, 15–18

Pacificus-Helvidius debates, 48, 92, 320, 331
Paine, Thomas, 276
Paris peace talks, 13, 295
parliament, 8, 161–162, 184

Parliament Acts (UK), 27, 87, 329
parliamentarism, 22, 302
parliamentary procedure, 9, 14
parliamentary sovereignty, 25, 26, 105
participation, 9, 135, 150, 285, 286, 302; joys of, 290–291, 302; judicial review as a form of, 233; moral basis of demand for, 10, 216–217
parties, 6, 8, 82, 98–99, 139, 159–160, 161, 204, 302, 305; fragmentation of, 302; neglect of, in political theory, 19, 98, 123, 311; small, 103
partisanship. 159
party vote system, 9
Pasquino, Pasquale, xi, 363, 371
Pateman, Carole, 9, 311
patrimonialism, 174–175
patronage, 330
pedantry, 49
peers, 74–75
Pennington, Shane, 251, 362
people, the, 31, 39, 40, 78, 180, 182, 186
peoples, diversity of, 295
perfectionism, 274–275, 286–287
Pericles, 156, 299
persons, 10, 146–147
petition, 11
Pettit, Philip, 346
philosophers, 7, 18, 49, 255
philosophy, 4, 12. *See also* moral philosophy; philosophers; political philosophy
Philosophy, Politics, and Economics (PPE), 15; for those who are not seeking academic positions, 16
Philp, Mark, 345
Pildes, Richard, xi, 19, 50, 55, 309, 320–321, 336, 362
Pitkin, Hanna, 380
Planned Parenthood v. Casey, 229–230, 263, 271, 355, 358, 360, 364, 368–369, 372
planning, social and economic, 286
Planowska-Sygulska, Beata, 375–377
pluralism, 5, 12, 98–99, 157

Poland, 186, 336, 348
political animals, 290–291, 306
political equality, 37, 38, 141, 149, 164–165, 204–205, 228, 266, 290–300, 362
political liberty. *See* liberty: political
political obligation, 16, 151, 189
political paralysis, 279
political philosophy, 4–5, 15, 134, 141, 147, 209, 278, 288, 311, 354, 378; contrasted with political theory, 18
political responsibility, 102–103, 142, 291
political science, 2, 8, 15–16, 19
political theory, ix, 2–3, 5, 8, 53, 274, 279, 288–289; American, 47–48, 311; British, 6, 15–18, 311; canon of, ix, 20–21; contrasted with political philosophy, 18; engagement with legal scholarship, 15–16, 19; engagement with political science, 8, 19; ethical conception of, 4, 288–289, 311, 378 ; normative, ix, 8; *political* political theory, 6, 18; positive, 8, 190; relation to constitutional theory, 311; teaching of, ix, 15–19, 22
politics, 170, 291; study of, 1; vocation for, 183, 313
Polsby, Nelson, 108–109, 110, 335–336
poor people, 10–11, 22, 37
Pope, Alexander, 1
popular government, 177, 275
popular sovereignty, 29, 39–41; courts' adoption of the mantle of, 42–43; thinness of constitutionalists' commitment to, 43; and undemocratic government, 39
popular will, 43
positivism, 126, 154
positivity, legal, 48
Posner, Eric, 18, 46, 70–71, 313, 314
Posner, Richard, 34
Post, David, 364
Potter, Allen, 115–116, 333–338
poverty, 10–11, 31–32
power, 18, 170; abuse of, 30; accumulation of, 48, 50; dilution of, 35–36; dispersal of, 30, 45, 49–51, 62, 71, 110; effects of concentration of, 30; for poor people, 37; social and economic, 37; struggle for, 93, 95
powerless, empowerment of the, 37
Praetorian guards, 106
pragmatic considerations, 8
precedent, 67, 223–224, 358
precommitment, 232, 360
preferences, 188, 366
prejudice, 241–242, 361–362
presence, political, 13
President of the United States, 6, 73, 96, 125, 179, 348; accountability of, 186–187; enforcement of law by, 56; and judicial nominations, 230, 233, 266; veto of, 49; war powers of, 52, 56
press, freedom of the, 190
Prigg v. Pennsylvania, 219, 357, 361
prime minister, 82, 89, 101–103; opposition leader as alternative, 102
principles, moral and political, 48, 69, 133, 143–144, 161
prisoner voting, 17, 313, 352
privacy, 296, 380
Privy Council, 111
procedure, 7, 21, 35, 148; in political culture, 301; rules of, 14, 300. *See also* parliamentary procedure
process-related considerations, 214–217, 226–233
prohibition, 117
promising, 303–304
property, 296, 380
prosecution, 55, 63–64, 168–169
prosperity, 3, 7, 8
proximity, 307
Przeworski, Adam, 107, 256–257, 335, 345, 366
publicity, principle of, 128, 148, 154
public law, study of, 12
public/private distinction, 296
public realm, 13, 305; versus private realm, 21
public reason, 118

Pulzer, Peter, xi, 310
Punnett, R.M., 333
pure procedural justice, 220
Putney debates, 22, 37, 318

Québec, 120, 353
Queen, 116–117
Queen-in-Parliament, 82
quod omnes tangit ab omnibus decidentur, 268
quorum, 9

race, 198, 235
Rainsborough, Thomas, 22, 37, 318
Rappaport, Michael, 314
Rasmussen, Jorgen, 333
rational choice theory, 257
rationalism, 275
Rawls, John, ix, 3–4, 7, 8–9, 12, 20, 128, 145, 148, 180, 220, 288, 310, 311, 331, 340, 342–344, 348, 355–356, 361; attitude to US Constitution, 119; on burdens of judgment, 94, 119, 158–159, 210, 355; on justice, 147, 155; on loyal opposition, 118–119, 337; on public reason, 118; on the United States, 338
Raz, Joseph, 54, 215–216, 218–219, 316, 321, 356–357
Reagan, Ronald, 266
realism, 5, 191
reason-giving, 206, 223–226, 349
recognition, 95
reconciliation, 255
recourse, centers of, 50
redistribution, 210
referendum, 8
Reform Acts (UK), 106
regions, 181
Rehnquist, William, 197
Reidy, Aisling, 86, 329
Reidy, Jon, 251, 362
Reimer, Neal, 371
relativism, 210–211
religious freedom, 31, 209

remembrance, 298–299
representation, ix, 6, 16, 36, 54, 66, 134–143, 149, 204, 219, 286, 302; and accountability, 184–188; as deputization, 302; as major theme of Enlightenment thought, 286; and bicameralism, 72, 76; Burkeian, 185–186; enrichment of, 78; ethnic, 140, 341; geographical, 133–134, 137, 138–140, 157; logics of, 78–79; matrix of, 157; perfect, 77; proportional, 77, 120, 140, 327; in republics, 177–178; systems of, 77; territorial, 77
Representation of the People Acts (UK), 27
representatives, 17; choice of, 90; equality of, 164–165
republicanism, 3, 175–177, 183, 346, 351; democratic, 177
Republican party. *See* Democrats and Republicans
republics, 20, 275, 286, 299; large, 278
resistance, 121
respect, 10–12, 46, 64, 158, 165–166
responsibility, ethic of, 1, 14, 303
responsiveness, 181–182
restraints on government, 31, 41, 42
retroactivity, 68
Revesz, Richard, 363
revolution, 305
Reynolds v. Sims (1964), 328
rights, 16, 31, 96, 195; abstract principles of, 209; as conditions of democratic legitimacy, 237–238; commitment to, 207–209; deference to majorities on, 38; disagreement about, 209–212; of man (*see* human rights); negative versus positive, 34; skepticism about, 208; social and economic, 209, 222; theories of, 207. *See also* constitutional rights; human rights
rigor, in philosophical argument, 13
Risse, Matthias, 344
Robertson, Geoffrey, 346
Robert's Rules of Order, 14, 300, 305
Robinson, James, 7, 311

Rockow, Lewis, 325
Roe v. Wade (1973), 195, 198, 224–225, 249, 350, 352, 355, 358, 364, 371
Roman republic, 14–15, 306; decrepit institutions of, 15
Rosen, Jeffrey, 364
Rosenblum, Nancy, xi, 6, 19, 98–99, 105, 118, 123–124, 311, 331–335, 337, 339
rotation in office, 96, 99, 107, 108
Rousseau, Jean-Jacques, ix, 20, 98, 136–137, 178, 276, 295, 340–341, 343, 347; on the lawgiver, 379; on representation, 95, 134–135, 137; on the size of the polity, 295, 380
royal prerogative, 81
Rubin, Edward, 151–152, 343, 345–346, 349
rule of law, 6, 7, 16, 29, 33, 47, 51, 54, 56, 63–65, 105, 199, 275; Hobbesian opposition to, 58; Lockean understanding of, 150, 153; and republicanism, 176–177; versus rule by law, 64–65
rules (versus standards), 165–166
rules of the game, 119–120
Russell, Meg, xi, 78, 86, 328–329

Sacks, Albert, 355, 357, 366
sacramental aspects of politics, 13
Sager, Lawrence, 350, 364
Sajó, András, 30, 32, 35, 316, 317
Salisbury Convention, 87
Salop, Steven, 364
Samaha, Adam, xi, 362, 367
same-sex marriage, 117, 195–196
sampling, 79
sanctions, 171, 182, 187
Sanger, Carol, xi, 352
Satori, Giovanni, 338–339
Saunders, Ben, 369
Scalia, Antonin, 229–230, 263, 266, 271, 343, 360, 368–369
Schapiro, Robert, 318
Schenck v. United States, 219, 357
Schmitt, Carl (Nazi theorist), 296

Schumpeter, Joseph, 93, 188, 331
science, 2, 279
Scotland, possible independence of, 8, 16, 121
Scott v. Sandford, 219, 271, 357, 372
Scruton, Roger, 25, 315
secession, 16, 120–121
second chambers, 72; elective, 75, 82; gravity of deliberation in, 75. *See also* bicameralism
Second World War, 113–114
secrecy, 99, 193–194
sectarian interests, 218
security, 5, 6, 7, 8, 28, 112, 297, 310
sedition, 99
Selden, John, 382
self-government, 196, 216
self-interest, 2, 171; balance of one person's against another's, 2
Sen, Amartya, 3, 310, 359, 369
Senate, US, 17, 73, 92, 109, 130; elections to, 79; peculiar procedures of, 73; representation in, 73; role of in judicial appointments, 73, 110, 230, 233; role of in ratifying treaties, 49, 73, 92, 320
senates, 176–177
separate concurrence, principle of, 80, 82, 84
separation of church and state, 6, 296
separation of powers, ix, 2, 6, 16, 17, 20, 35–36, 45–71, 82, 85, 110–111, 201, 278; as obsolete, 319; as preventing tyranny, 60–61; as protecting liberty, 53–54; and bicameralism, 72; confusion concerning, 49; distinguished from checks and balances, 49–53; free-standing principle of, 46–47; functional, 49, 52, 55, 65–70, 111; narrow sense of, 50, 52; qualitative, 45; and rule of law, 54; in thought, 55–58; Vile's "pure" definition of, 53, 320
September 11, 2001 (terrorist attacks of), 219
settlement, need for, 159, 172, 212, 260, 366
Shalev, Rachel, 366
Shapiro, Ian, 335, 365
Shavell, Steven, 342

Shell, Donald, 330
Shepsle, Kenneth, 331
Shklar, Judith, 30, 317, 345
shouting, 13
Shugerman, Jed, 253, 273, 363–365, 367, 369–370, 372
side-effects, 9
Siemers, David, 335
Sieyès, Emmanuel, 136, 178, 276, 279, 285, 289, 318, 373–374, 376; on bicameralism, 75, 78, 326; on the English constitution, 282, 375; on representation, 340
Sinclair, Archibald, 332
Sinking Fund cases, 369
Sinn Fein, 117, 120
size of institutions, 130–134
skepticism, moral, 7
slavery, 117, 243, 257, 361
Smith, Adam, 281
sobriety, 76
socialism, 24, 159, 208
Socrates, 5
Solomon, 59
Solon, 156
Solum, Lawrence, 341
Solzhenitsyn, Alexander, 324
sortition, 90, 255, 369
South Africa, 33, 106
sovereignty, 6, 16, 20, 216; of British parliament, 50; lack of in U.S. Constitution, 50. *See also* popular sovereignty
Soviet Union, 67, 115, 299; 1936 constitution of, 27
Spanish Civil War, 115
specificity (versus generality), 139
speech, freedom of, 97, 99, 105, 190, 209
spoils system, 111
spontaneity, 292, 301
stability, 148
standards. *See* rules (versus standards)
stare decisis. *See* precedent
state, 4, 174–175; as provider of goods and services, 32

statelessness, 380, 382
Stephan, Michael, 251, 362
Sterne, Laurence, 76, 327
Stewart, Jon, 355
St. John-Stevas, Norman, 358
Stokes, Susan, 345
Stone, Harlan, 241–242
strategies in politics, 122
street, politics of the, 36, 142
structure, political, ix, 7
Sturm, Douglas, 317
suicide, assisted, 152
suffrage, 150, 165
Sunstein, Cass, 30, 316, 343, 346
supermajority requirements, 73, 232, 248, 255, 272–273, 325, 363–364, 370
Supreme Court. *See* United States Supreme Court
survival, 180
symbolism, 50

Tacitus, 76, 327
taxpayers, 9
Taylor, Charles, 15
Taylor v. Attorney-General, 352
Teague v. Lane (1989), 68, 324
telephone justice, 67, 324
term limits, 186–187
terror, 21, 297
text: as focus for constitutional argument, 28; fetishism of, 28–29
text, legislative, 163
thinking, 307
Thomas, Paul, 325
Thompson, Dennis, xi, 19, 314
thought-experiments, 220, 273
Tierney, George, 115
Tocqueville, Alexis de, 95, 264, 331, 360, 369
toleration, 3, 210, 270
Tomkins, Adam, 329
Tories. *See* Whigs and Tories
torture, 31, 59, 96, 297

totalitarianism, 275, 297
traditional rules, 26
traditions, 299
transparency, 7, 14, 26, 127–129, 154, 173
treason, 97, 99
treaties, 92, 115, 153, 320
treating like cases alike, 153
trial, 10, 165–166
Tribe, Laurence, 219, 357
tribunals, 168–169
Tristram Shandy principle, 76–77, 327
Trotsky, Leon, 299
trust, 298
trusts, 5, 169–170, 178
truth, 12, 211, 271
Tuck, Richard, 332
Tullock, Gordon, 371
Turkey, 58–59
turn-taking in politics, 95–96, 98, 123. *See also* rotation in office
Tushnet, Mark, 197, 319, 350–351, 358, 361–362
tyranny, 38, 48, 60–61, 235, 297; avoidance of, 45, 279. *See also* majority: tyranny of

Ulysses, 232
unanimity requirement, 248, 255
unicameral legislatures, 6
United Kingdom, 8, 18, 72–73, 86, 92, 184–186; abortion law in, 196, 224–225, 240, 350, 358–359, 371; alleged constitutional backwardness of, 225; cabinet government in, 17; capital punishment in, 196, 350; constitution, nature of, 26–28, 47; constitutional reform, 16–17; homosexual law reform in, 196, 350; loyal opposition in, 100–103; National Government during wartime, 113–114; parliament of, 10–11, 184–186, 196, 359; party system of, 142, 302; poverty and starvation in, 10–11; Supreme Court of, 16, 130; weak judicial review in, 200, 212–213

United States, 12, 18, 74, 179; cabinet appointments in, 83; constitutionalism in, 24, 47, 222, 287, 292; democracy in, 196, 331; federalism in, 25, 109, 111; Founding Fathers, 29; judicial review in, 86, 197, 199; legislature of, 130, 343; love of democracy in, 230; organized opposition in, 103, 108–111; particular states, 6, 24, 47; reverence for legality in, 378; study of political theory in, 18–19; study of public law in, 16
United States Constitution, 2, 24, 33, 34, 39, 49, 108–111, 274, 283, 305; age of, 223; Article I of, 69, 317; Article II of, 56, 325, 347; Article III of, 127; Article V of, 120, 232; Article VI of, 92, 117; as focus of loyalty, 117–119; Eighteenth Amendment to, 117; Framers of, 39–40, 51, 142, 292; no specific principle of democracy in, 47; no specific principle of rule of law in, 47; no specific provision for opposition, 108–111; ratification of, 281, 283, 285; requiring concurrence of separate powers, 52; separation of powers in, 46–48; silence on judicial decision-procedures, 254; text of, 202; Twelfth Amendment to, 108; vague terms of, 110, 211. *See also* Bill of Rights (in US Constitution)
United States Senate. *See* Senate, US
United States Supreme Court, 120, 130, 201–202, 221, 229–230; as forum of principle, 225, 253, 269; decision-procedures of, 363; disgraceful record on slavery, 243; equality of justices on, 253–254; opposition to New Deal, 378; voting on, 246, 272
United States v. Carolene Products, 241–244, 361
United States v. Lopez, 350
United States v. Morrison, 350
universality, 137
unwritten norms, 24, 26

INDEX

Urbinati, Nadia, xi, 135–137, 139, 142, 340–342
Urovsky, Melvin, 367
urgency in parliamentary procedure, 9
utility: principle of, 53–54, 145–146, 208, 257; relation to majority-decision, 257–258, 366
utopianism, 274–275, 283

vagueness, in law, 40
validity, 300
values, 8; competing, 283; dignitarian (*see* dignity); incommensurability of, 283; philosophical understanding of, 12; reconciliation of all, 283
Venice, 176–177, 346
Vermeule, Adrian, xi, 18, 19, 46, 52, 70–71, 76, 313, 314, 319, 320, 324–326
Veto-points, 49, 109, 355, 359–360
Vickers, Sir John, xi
Vico, Giambattista, 282, 375
Vietnam war, 13, 295
Vile, M.J.C., 49, 51, 52, 53, 60, 320–321, 322–323
Villa, Dana, 381
virtue, 1, 3, 6, 281–282
Voltaire, 63, 276, 281, 293–294, 323, 374, 376
voluntarism, 141
voting, 219, 256, 301–302, 332; in legislature, 9, 204; qualifications for, 36, 219

Waldron, Jeremy, 4, 54, 198–199, 310, 316, 327, 335, 336–337, 339–341, 344, 352, 354, 357, 364, 368, 370, 382; on appropriate uses of majority-decision, 359–360, 364; on the dignity of legislation, 324; hesitation about Condorcet's jury theorem, 262–264, 368; on human dignity, 312; importance of disagreement, 311, 331, 343, 356; on New Zealand parliamentary procedure, 311–312, 325, 329; opposition to strong judicial review, 197, 251, 313, 318, 350–351, 355; response to Dworkin's defense of judicial review, 361; on the rule of law, 317, 321
Walicki, Andrzej, 373
Walzer, Michael, 3, 310
war powers, 56
Warren, Earl, 79, 328
Washington, George, 92, 372–373
watershed issues, 209
wealth, impact on politics, 3, 37
Weber, Max, 1, 14, 298, 309, 313, 322, 382
Weddington, Sarah, 357
Weimar Republic, 121, 338
Weizman, Chaim, 288, 378
well-ordered society, 119, 147, 338, 355
Westminster systems, 17, 67, 73, 81, 86, 89, 92, 160, 184
Whigs and Tories, 99, 103
whips, 9, 73, 81–82
Whittington, Keith, 361
will (versus judgment), 141, 161–162, 185–186
Williams, Bernard, 5, 310
Wilson, James, 276
Wingo, Ajume, 312
Wire, The (television series), 14, 301, 313
Wollheim, Richard, 214, 234, 356
Wood, Gordon, 276, 372
work, hours and conditions of, 12, 212
World Bank, 33

Yack, Bernard, 378
Yoshino, Kenji, 366

zeitgeist, 4
Zinoviev, Grigory, 299

www.ingramcontent.com/pod-product-compliance
Ingram Content Group UK Ltd.
Pitfield, Milton Keynes, MK11 3LW, UK
UKHW010824200725
460874UK00008B/13/J